Institute of Financial Accountants

S T U D Y   G U I D E

FINANCIAL ACCOUNTANT DIPLOMA

P1
Financial Accounting and IFRS for SMEs

Est. 1916

LEARNING MEDIA

First edition January 2010

ISBN 9780 7517 7565 5

British Library Cataloguing-in-Publication Data
A catalogue record for this book
is available from the British Library

Published by

BPP Learning Media Ltd
BPP House, Aldine Place
London W12 8AA

www.bpp.com/learningmedia

Printed in the United Kingdom by
Martins the Printers, Berwick upon Tweed

Your learning materials, published by BPP
Learning Media Ltd, are printed on paper
sourced from sustainable, managed forests.

We are grateful to the Institute of Financial
Accountants for permission to reproduce the
syllabus and learning outcomes and the
specimen paper, to all of which the Institute
owns the copyright.

BPP Learning Media and IFA would like to
thank Denise Gallagher and acknowledge her
assistance in the development of this module
and her contribution to the development of
the IFA qualifications.

Contents

Introduction

This is the first edition of the BPP Learning Media Study Guide for the Institute of Financial Accountant's Professional module **Financial Accounting and IFRS for SMEs.** It is part of an exciting new range of Study Guides published by BPP Learning Media for the IFA's Diploma and Professional qualifications.

The IFA's modules and qualifications aim to support small and medium enterprises, which are the life blood of a dynamic economy, and to provide training and qualifications for accountants and financial managers.

This module is part of the Professional Financial Accountant qualification which develops and tests a wide range of accountancy, finance and business skills and broadens business and management expertise, including strategic thinking. It also promotes positive attitudes and ethical behaviour. IFA qualifications open up a wide choice of possible career directions and expand your options.

One of the attractive features of the IFA qualifications is their flexibility, and consequently the different ways you can use this Study Guide:

- You can study this module as part of the Professional Financial Accountant qualification and become an Associate member of IFA and use the AFA designation after your name to demonstrate your professional status

- You can take this module independently and gain a stand-alone certificate from the IFA

- You can use this Study Guide as a reference guide for your day to day work.

Professional Financial Accountant Syllabi

Qualification structure: six modules to complete

P1. Financial Accounting and IFRS *for Small & Medium Size Enterprises (SMEs)*
P2. Financial Management
P3. Management and Control Systems
P4. Professional Skills for SMEs
P5. Business and Regulatory Environment
P6. The Ethical Professional

Purpose & target market

The Financial Accountant Professional qualification develops and tests a wide range of accountancy and finance skills for those who manage or seek to manage the day to day finances and financial needs of an SME. It develops understanding and awareness of technology, systems, legal and regulatory issues, business operations and management; improving skills and developing strategic awareness. The Qualification also promotes positive attitudes and ethical behaviour.

Having passed the Professional FA Qualification you will be entitled to become an Associate IFA member, use the AFA designation and describe yourself as a 'Financial Accountant'.

Level and access

Access to the Financial Accountant Professional is open to those who possess the FA Diploma. Otherwise entrants should ideally have:

- a related degree or HND qualification, or equivalent level 4 qualification
- at least two years' workplace experience in finance or accounting role.

In the interests of open access if entrants do not possess any of these qualifications they will be expected to sit and pass the 'Professional Challenge Module' first, which is P1 Financial Accounting and IFRS.

The Professional FA Qualification syllabus specifications are based upon UK 'Regulatory arrangements for the Qualification and Credit Framework' (QCA/Ofqual, August 2008) guidance. Students pursuing the Professional FA Qualification are tested at Level 5.

Learning commitment

All modules require the following approximate minimum learning commitment:

- At least 72 hours of dedicated learning time

- An additional minimum of 48 hours other set or directed work, such as homework, practise questions, group work, etc

- At least 20 hours revision which may be supported by a study provider but otherwise personal time

Suggested total learning time per module: 140 hours.

Professional Financial Accountant Syllabus

P1. Financial Accounting and International Financial Reporting Standards (IFRS) *for Small & Medium Size Enterprises (SMEs)*

Module aim

The aim of this module is to understand the conceptual and regulatory framework for accounting for Small and Medium-Sized Enterprises (SMEs). The concepts and pervasive principles in the International Financial Reporting Standard (IFRS) for SMEs will then be considered.

The module will continue by the consideration of the IFRS for SMEs both in the preparation of financial statements and their presentation. The analysis and interpretation of the business performance from the financial statements will follow concluding with the role of external audit and the associated audit reports.

Module learning outcomes and sub-set outcomes

Understand the conceptual and regulatory framework for financial reporting for SMEs   7%

- Understand the position of International Accounting Standards Board (IASB) and its standard setting process

- Understand who are the users of financial statements and their differing requirements

- Understand the need for an International Financial Reporting Standard for Small and Medium-Sized Entities and what constitute Small and Medium-Sized Entities

Understand concepts and pervasive principles in the IFRS for SMEs   8%

- Understand the objectives of compiling financial statements for SMEs

- Understand the qualities that make information contained in the financial statements useful to SME stakeholders

- Be aware of the concepts and basic principles underlying an SME's financial statements

Understand the presentation and content of financial statements for SMEs   10%

- Statement of financial position
- Statement of comprehensive income and income statement
- Statement of changes in equity and statement of income and retained earnings
- Notes to the accounts
- Statements of cash flows

Understand and apply the IFRs for SME in the preparation of financial statements identified above   60%

- Review the preparation of Statement of Comprehensive Income and Statement of Financial Position for limited companies

- Understand and apply the following components of the International Standard when preparing an SME's financial statements

    - Statement of cash flows
    - Consolidated and separate financial statements
    - Accounting policies, estimates and errors
    - Financial instruments
    - Inventories
    - Investments in Associates
    - Investments in Joint Ventures

- Investment property
- Property, plant and equipment
- Intangible assets other than goodwill
- Business combinations and goodwill
- Leases
- Provisions and contingencies
- Revenue
- Government grants
- Borrowing costs
- Share-based payments
- Impairment of assets
- Employee benefits
- Income tax
- Foreign currency translation
- Events after the end of the reporting period
- Related party disclosures

Analyse and interpret financial statements	**10%**
Understand statutory audit requirements	**5%**

Module requirements

Learning outcome	Detailed criteria	Chapter where covered
1. Understand the conceptual and regulatory framework for financial reporting for SMEs	1.1 Understand what IFRS are and the process by which they are set	1
	1.2 Understand the need for an IFRS for SMEs and understand the needs of users of those financial statements.	1
2. Understand concepts and pervasive principles in the IFRS for SMEs	2.1 Understand the objectives of financial statements for SMEs	2
	2.2 Understand the qualitative characteristics of information in financial statements • Understandability • Relevance • Materiality • Reliability • Substance over form • Prudence • Completeness • Comparability • Timeliness • Balance between benefit and cost	2
	2.3 Understand the significance of an SME's financial position as presented in the statement of financial position	3
	2.4 Understand the significance of an SME's performance in its statement of comprehensive income	3
	2.5 Understand how assets, liabilities, income and expenses are recognised and measured based on pervasive recognition and measurement principles derived from IASB Framework for the Preparation and Presentation of Financial Statements	2

	• Accruals basis • Recognition in financial statements • Initial recognition and subsequent measurement • Offsetting	
3. Financial statement presentation – the information that should be shown and how it should be presented in the following: • **Statement of financial position** • **Statement of comprehensive income and income statement** • **Statement of changes in equity and statement of income and retained earnings** • **Statement of cash flows** • **Notes to the financial statements**	3.1 Understand what fair presentation means	3
	3.2 Understand that an entity complying with IFRS for SME must state that it has complied with the standard	1
	3.3 Understand the requirements of the following • Going concern • Frequency of reporting • Consistency of presentation • Comparative information • Materiality and aggregation	3
	3.4 Understand the contents of a complete set of financial statements and the identification of each of the financial statements	3
	3.5 Understand the information to be presented in the statement of financial position and the information that can be presented either in the statement of financial position or in the notes	3
	3.6 Understand the difference between a current and non-current asset	3
	3.7 Understand the presentation of the total comprehensive income using single-statement and the two statement approach	3
	3.8 Understand that expenses can be analysed either by nature of expense or function of expense	3
	3.9 Understand the purpose of the statement of changes in equity and the information to be presented	3
	3.10 Understand the purpose of the statement of income and retained earnings and the information to be presented	3
	3.11 Understand the information to be presented in the statement of cash flows – operating activities, investing activities, financing activities	20
	3.12 Understand that there are two methods of reporting cash flows from operating activities – indirect and direct methods	20
	3.13 Understand and apply the treatment and presentation of foreign currency cash flows, interest and dividends, income tax and non-cash transactions in a statement of cash flows	20
	3.14 Understand the structure of the notes and the information that should be disclosed therein.	3

Learning outcome	Detailed criteria	Chapter where covered
4. Understand and apply IFRS for SMEs in the preparation of their financial statements	4.1 Revise the content of a statement of comprehensive income and statement of financial position to comply with the relevant IFRS	3
	4.2 Preparation of statements of cash flow using direct and indirect methods; also interpretation of these statements per section 7 of the IFRS for SMEs	20
	4.3 Preparation of consolidated and separate financial statements as per section 9 of the IFRS for SMEs	15, 16, 17
	4.4 Understand the use of accounting policies, estimates and treatment of errors as per section 10 of the IFRS for SMEs	4
	4.5 Understand and apply section 11 of IFRS for SMEs when an SME has basic financial instruments *(section 12 Other Financial Instruments Issues and Section 22, Liabilities and equity will not be examined)*	4, 12
	4.6 Understand and apply section 12 of IFRS for SMEs for recognising and measuring inventories	
	4.7 Understand and apply section 14 of IFRS for SMEs when an SME is required to account for an investment in associates.	18
	4.8 Understand and apply section 15 of IFRS for SMEs when an SME is required to account for an investment in joint ventures.	18
	4.9 Understand and apply section 16 of IFRS for SMEs when an SME is required to account for an investment that is defined as an investment property.	6
	4.10 Understand and apply section 17 of IFRS for SMEs when an SME accounts for property, plant and equipment both in its recognition and future measurement	6
	4.11 Understand and apply section 18 of IFRS for SMEs when an SME accounts for intangible assets other than goodwill	7
	4.12 Understand and apply section 19 of IFRS for SMEs when the SME carries a business combination and how to treat goodwill.	16, 17
	4.13 Understand and apply section 20 of IFRS for SMEs when an SME is required to account for leases	9
	4.14 Understand and apply section 21 of IFRS for SMEs when an SME has provisions and contingencies	10
	4.15 Understand and apply section 23 of IFRS for SMEs when an SME accounts for its revenue	4
	4.16 Understand and apply section 24 of IFRS for SMEs when an SME receives Government grants	6
	4.17 Understand and apply section 25 of IFRS for SMEs when an SME is required to account for borrowing costs	7

Learning outcome	Detailed criteria	Chapter where covered
	4.18 Obtain an understanding of share-based payments and employee benefits as contained in section 26 and 28 of the IFRS for SMEs	13
	4.19 Understand and apply section 14 of IFRS for SMEs when an SME needs to impair an asset	8
	4.20 Understand and apply section 29 of IFRS for SMEs to account for income tax payable by an SME	11
	4.21 Understand and apply section 30 of IFRS for SMEs when an SME is required to account for foreign currency. *Section 31 accounting for hyperinflation will not be examined*.	19
	4.22 Understand and apply section 32 of IFRS for SMEs when an SME accounts for events occurring after the end of the reporting period.	10
	4.23 Understand and apply section 33 of IFRS for SMEs for an SME which needs to consider related party disclosures.	14
5. Analyse and evaluate financial statements	5.1 Calculation of a range of ratios over time, between different businesses and against bench marks	21
	5.2 Be able to communicate the limitations of ratio analysis when writing a report to users	21
	5.3 Communicate findings and conclusions in a professional written manner.	21
6. Understand audit requirements for SMEs	6.1 Understand what an external audit involves and understand International Auditing and Assurance Standards	22
	6.32 Understand the audit thresholds relating to an SME	22
	6.4 Understand the appropriate audit report for an SME.	22

Study weightings

Against each learning outcome a percentage weighting is shown as a guide.

Instructions to candidates:

Time allowed 3 hours 10 minutes which includes 10 minutes' reading time.

Use of a silent non-programmable calculator which is NOT part of a mobile phone or any other device capable of communication is allowed.

This is a closed book examination.

The pass mark is 50%

The examination paper will consist of

Section A	three compulsory questions, each worth 10 marks	30
Section B	two compulsory questions, each worth 20 marks	40
Section C	one compulsory question, worth 30 marks	30
Total		100

Booklist

Recommended:

BPP Study Guide IFA Finance Accounting

Others:

At present there are no other textbooks dealing with IFRS for SMEs

Useful Websites

International Accounting Standards Board
http://www.iasb.org/IFRS+for+SMEs/IFRS+for+SMEs.htm

Deloitte
http://www.iasplus.com/standard/ifrsforsmes.htm

PWC
http://www.pwc.com.ar/en_GX/gx/ifrs-reporting/pdf/IFRSSME09.pdf

Unit features

Each chapter contains a number of helpful features to guide you through each topic.

Learning objectives   Show the referenced IFA learning outcomes.

Topic list   Tells you what you will be studying in this chapter.

Introduction   Puts the chapter content in the context of the syllabus as a whole.

Fast forward   This summarises the key content of the particular section that you are about to start.

Key terms   Definitions of important concepts. You really need to know and understand these before the exam.

Exam focus   These highlight points that are likely to be particularly important or relevant to the exam.

Eg   Worked examples to demonstrate techniques.

Activity (and answers)   This is a question that enables **you** to practise a technique or test your understanding. Solutions are provided.

Unit round-up   Reviews the key areas covered in the unit.

Case study   This is a practical example or illustration, usually involving a real world scenario.

Formula to learn   These are formulae or equations that you need to learn as you may need to apply then in the exam.

Quick quiz questions   A quick test of your knowledge of the main topics in this unit.

End of chapter question   Suggested questions of exam style and standard for you to try. A suggested time allocation is also given.

Part A

The conceptual and regulatory framework

The regulatory framework

Unit topic list

1   The International Accounting Standards Board (IASB)
2   Setting of International Financial Reporting Standards
3   International Financial Reporting Standard for Small and Medium-sized Entities
4   Users' and stakeholders' needs

Assessment criteria

1   **Understand the conceptual and regulatory framework for financial reporting for SMEs**

1.1   Understand what IFRS are and the process by which they are set

1.2   Understand the need for an IFRS for SMEs and understand the needs of users of those financial statements

3.2   Understand that an entity complying with IFRS for SMEs must state that it has complied with the standard

1 The International Accounting Standards Board (IASB)

Global international accounting is regulated by an overall international set of organisations.

The organisational structure consists of:

- The IASC Foundation
- The IASB
- The Standards Advisory Council (SAC)
- The International Financial Reporting Interpretations Committee (IFRIC)

1.1 Introduction

The International Accounting Standards Board is an independent, privately-funded accounting standard setter based in London.

In March 2001 the IASC Foundation was formed as a not-for-profit corporation incorporated in the USA. The IASC Foundation is the parent entity of the IASB.

From April 2001 the IASB assumed accounting standard setting responsibilities from its predecessor body, the International Accounting Standards Committee (IASC).

1.2 How the IASB is made up

The 15 members of the IASB come from nine countries and have a variety of backgrounds with a mix of auditors, preparers of financial statements, users of financial statements and an academic. The Board will be expanded to 16 members by 2012.

1.3 Objectives of the IASB

The formal objectives of the IASB, formulated in its mission statement are:

(a) To develop, in the public interest, a single set of high quality, understandable and enforceable global accounting standards that require high quality, transparent and comparable information in general purpose financial statements

(b) To provide the use and vigorous application of those standards

(c) To work actively with national accounting standard setters to bring about convergence of national accounting standards and IFRS to high quality solutions.

1.4 Structure of the IASB

The structure of the IASB has the following main features.

(a) The IASC Foundation is an independent corporation having two main bodies – the Trustees and the IASB. The IASC Foundation holds the copyright of IFRSs and all other IASB publications.

(b) The IASC Foundation trustees appoint the IASB members, exercise oversight and raise the funds needed.

(c) The IASB has sole responsibility for setting accounting standards.

(d) There are also two further bodies, the Standards Advisory Council and the International Financial Reporting Interpretations Committee (see below).

The structure can be illustrated as follows.

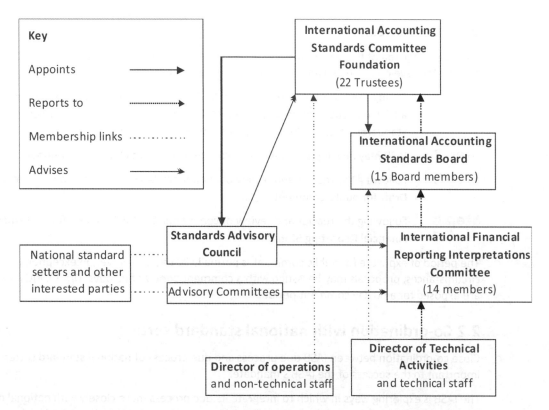

Trustees. The Trustees comprise a group of twenty two individuals, with diverse geographic and functional backgrounds. The Trustees appoint the Members of the Board, the International Financial Reporting Interpretations Committee and the Standards Advisory Council. In addition to monitoring IASC's effectiveness and raising its funds, the Trustees will approve IASC's budget and have responsibility for constitutional changes. Trustees were appointed so that initially there were six from North America, six from Europe, four from Asia Pacific, and three others from any area, as long as geographic balance is maintained.

(a) The International Federation of Accountants (IFAC) suggested candidates to fill five of the nineteen Trustee seats and international organisations of preparers, users and academics each suggested one candidate.

(b) The remaining eleven Trustees are 'at-large' in that they were not selected through the constituency nomination process.

Standards Advisory Council. The Standards Advisory Council provides a formal vehicle for further groups and individuals with diverse geographic and functional backgrounds to give advice to the Board and, at times, to advise the Trustees. It comprises about fifty members and meets at least three times a year. It is consulted by the IASB on all major projects and its meetings are open to the public. It advises the IASB on prioritisation of its work and on the implications of proposed standards for users and preparers of financial statements.

International Financial Reporting Interpretations Committee. The IFRIC provides timely guidance on the application and interpretation of International Financial Reporting Standards. It deals with newly identified financial reporting issues not specifically addressed in IFRSs, or issues where unsatisfactory or conflicting interpretations have developed, or seem likely to develop.

2 Setting of International Financial Reporting Standards

IFRSs are developed through a formal system of due process and broad international consultation involving accountants, financial analysts and other users and regulatory bodies from around the world.

2.1 Due process

The overall agenda of the IASB is initially set by discussion with the Standards Advisory Council. The process for developing an individual standard involves the following steps.

Step 1   During the early stages of a project, IASB may establish an **Advisory Committee** to give advice on issues arising in the project. Consultation with the Advisory Committee and the Standards Advisory Council occurs throughout the project.

Step 2   IASB may develop and publish **Discussion Documents** for public comment.

Step 3   Following the receipt and review of comments, IASB develops and publishes an **Exposure Draft** for public comment.

Step 4   Following the receipt and review of comments, the IASB issues a final **International Financial Reporting Standard**.

The period of exposure for public comment is normally 90 days. However, in exceptional circumstances, proposals may be issued with a comment period of 60 days. Draft IFRIC Interpretations are exposed for a 60 day comment period.

2.2 Co-ordination with national standard setters

Close co-ordination between IASB due process and due process of national standard setters is important to the success of the IASB's mandate.

The IASB is exploring ways in which to integrate its due process more closely with national due process. Such integration may grow as the relationship between IASB and national standard setters evolves. In particular, the IASB is exploring the following procedure for projects that have international implications.

(a)   IASB and national standard setters would co-ordinate their work plans so that when the IASB starts a project, national standard setters would also add it to their own work plans so that they can play a full part in developing international consensus. Similarly, where national standard setters start projects, the IASB would consider whether it needs to develop a new Standard or review its existing Standards. Over a reasonable period, the IASB and national standard setters should aim to review all standards where significant differences currently exist, giving priority to the areas where the differences are greatest.

(b)   National standards setters would not be required to vote for IASB's preferred solution in their national standards, since each country remains free to adopt IASB standards with amendments or to adopt other standards. However, the existence of an international consensus is clearly one factor that members of national standard setters would consider when they decide how to vote on national standards.

(c)   The IASB would continue to publish its own Exposure Drafts and other documents for public comment.

(d)   National standard setters would publish their own exposure document at approximately the same time as IASB Exposure Drafts and would seek specific comments on any significant divergences between the two exposure documents. In some instances, national standard setters may include in their exposure documents specific comments on issues of particular relevance to their country or include more detailed guidance than is included in the corresponding IASB document.

(e)   National standard setters would follow their own full due process, which they would ideally choose to integrate with the IASB's due process. This integration would avoid unnecessary delays in completing standards and would also minimise the likelihood of unnecessary differences between the standards that result.

2.3 Current IASs/IFRSs

The current list is as follows.

International Accounting Standards		Date of issue
IAS 1 (revised)	Presentation of financial statements	Sep 2007
IAS 2	Inventories	Dec 2003
IAS 7	Statement of cash flows	Dec 1992
IAS 8	Accounting policies, changes in accounting estimates and errors	Dec 2003
IAS 10	Events after the reporting period	Dec 2003
IAS 11	Construction contracts	Dec 1993
IAS 12	Income taxes	Nov 2000
IAS 16	Property, plant and equipment	Dec 2003
IAS 17	Leases	Dec 2003
IAS 18	Revenue	Dec 1993
IAS 19	Employee benefits	Dec 2004
IAS 20	Accounting for government grants and disclosure of government	Jan 1995
IAS 21	The effects of changes in foreign exchange rates	Dec 2003
IAS 23 (revised)	Borrowing costs	Jan 2008
IAS 24	Related party disclosures	Dec 2003
IAS 26	Accounting and reporting by retirement benefit plans	Jan 1995
IAS 27 (revised)	Consolidated and separate financial statements	Jan 2008
IAS 28	Investments in associates	Dec 2003
IAS 29	Financial reporting in hyperinflationary economies	Jan 1995
IAS 30	Disclosures in the financial statements of banks and similar financial institutions	Jan 1995
IAS 31	Interests in joint ventures	Dec 2003
IAS 32	Financial instruments: presentation	Dec 2003
IAS 33	Earnings per share	Dec 2003
IAS 34	Interim financial reporting	Feb 1998
IAS 36	Impairment of assets	Mar 2004
IAS 37	Provisions, contingent liabilities and contingent assets	Sept 1998
IAS 38	Intangible assets	Mar 2004
IAS 39	Financial instruments: recognition and measurement	Dec 2004
IAS 40	Investment property	Dec 2003
IAS 41	Agriculture	Feb 2001
IFRS 1	First time adoption of International Financial Reporting Standards	June 2003
IFRS 2	Share-based payment	Feb 2004
IFRS 3 (revised)	Business combinations	Jan 2008
IFRS 4	Insurance contracts	Mar 2004
IFRS 5	Non-current assets held for sale and discontinued operations	Mar 2004
IFRS 6	Exploration for and evaluation of mineral resources	Dec 2004
IFRS 7	Financial instruments: disclosures	Aug 2005
IFRS 8	Operating segments	Nov 2006
IFRS 9	Financial instruments	July 2009
IFRS for SMEs	IFRS for Small and Medium-sized Entities	July 2009

3 International Financial Reporting Standard for Small and Medium-sized entities

3.1 Introduction

It has long been considered that the volume of IASs and IFRSs listed above and their detailed content were excessive for smaller companies. Therefore in July 2009 the IASB issued the *IFRS for Small and Medium-sized Entities (IFRS for SMEs)*. This standard provides an alternative approach for eligible entities. Instead of applying all of the requirements in place in the full set of IFRSs in issue they can choose to apply the *IFRS for SMEs* which is considerably shorter than full IFRS and contains only about 10% of the disclosure requirements.

This text is based upon the requirements of the IFRS for SMEs.

3.2 What is the *IFRS for SMEs*?

The *IFRS for SMEs* is a completely self-contained standard which is based upon the same accounting principles as full IFRS and the principles set out in the IASB's *Framework for the preparation and presentation of financial statements*. However the *IFRS for SMEs* has been simplified compared to full IFRS in the following ways:

- some accounting treatments permitted by full IFRS have been removed
- some topics and disclosures that are not generally relevant to SMEs have been eliminated
- requirements for recognition and measurement have been simplified.

3.3 Eligibility for use of *IFRS for SMEs*

The eligibility criteria for use of the *IFRS for SMEs* are not actually based upon size. The definition of an SME for the purposes of the IFRS is an entity that:

- does not have public accountability; and
- publishes general purpose financial statements for external users.

An entity has public accountability if either:

- its debt or equity instruments are publicly traded; or
- it is a financial institution/other entity, that as part of its primary activities, holds and manages financial resources on behalf of its clients.

The final decision regarding eligibility may lie with the national regulatory authorities and standard-setters who may specify more detailed criteria based upon such factors as revenue, assets or number of employees. However if an entity prepares its financial statements according to the *IFRS for SMEs* in accordance with national requirements but is a listed company or financial institution then such financial statements cannot be described as conforming to the *IFRS for SMEs*.

If a **subsidiary** is part of a group that uses full IFRS then the subsidiary is allowed to follow *IFRS for SMEs* in its own financial statements provided that it meets the IASB criteria.

3.4 Auditors' report

Where the financial statements are prepared using the *IFRS for SMEs* then the basis of presentation note, and if applicable the auditors' report, should refer to compliance with the IFRS. It is thought that this may help many entities with their access to external capital.

3.5 Date of compliance with *IFRS for SMEs*

The IASB has not set an effective date for introduction of the *IFRS for SMEs* as this is a matter for each individual jurisdiction.

3.6 Why companies may wish to apply the IFRS for SMEs

Those companies which are eligible to use the IFRS for SMEs may find that its application is **allowed** in the jurisdiction in which they operate rather than **required**. They may choose to use the IFRS for SMEs rather than local GAAP in order to take advantage of the benefits of applying global financial reporting standards without the costs and complexity involved in the adoption of full IFRS.

The benefits of applying global financial reporting standards and preparing financial statements that are comparable in an international arena are as follows:

- Access to cross border bank financing

- An increased ability to trade overseas with partners who are better able to understand the financial health of the company

- The ability to achieve a cross border credit rating from an international agency

4 Users' and stakeholders' needs

4.1 The need for financial statements

There are various groups of people who need information about the activities of a business.

Why do businesses need to produce financial statements? If a business is being run efficiently, why should it have to go through all the bother of accounting procedures in order to produce financial information?

The International Accounting Standards Board states in Chapter 2 of the IFRS for SMEs *Concepts and Pervasive Principles* (which we will examine in detail later):

'The objective of financial statements of an SME is to provide information about the **financial position, performance** and **cash flows** of the entity that is useful for economic decision making by a broad range of users.'

In other words, a business should produce information about its activities because there are various groups of people who want or need to know that information. This sounds rather vague: to make it clearer, we will study the classes of people who need information about a business. We need also to think about what information in particular is of interest to the members of each class.

The IASB has stated in the *IFRS for SMEs* that the likely external users of these general purpose financial statements are owners who are not managers of the business, current and potential creditors and providers of loan finance.

We will now consider some of these potential users of financial statements and their information needs.

4.2 Users of financial statements and accounting information

The following people are likely to be interested in financial information about an SME.

(a) **Managers of the company** appointed by the company's owners to supervise the day-to-day activities of the company. They need information about the company's financial situation as it is currently and as it is expected to be in the future. This is to enable them to manage the business efficiently and to make effective decisions.

(b) **Shareholders of the company**, ie the company's owners, want to assess how well the management is performing. They want to know how profitable the company's operations are and how much profit they can afford to withdraw from the business for their own use.

(c) **Trade contacts** include suppliers who provide goods to the company on credit and customers who purchase the goods or services provided by the company. **Suppliers** want to know about the company's ability to pay its debts; **customers** need to know that the company is a secure source of supply and is in no danger of having to close down.

(d) **Providers of finance to the company** might include a bank which allows the company to operate an overdraft, or provides longer-term finance by granting a loan. The bank wants to ensure that the company is able to keep up interest payments, and eventually to repay the amounts advanced.

(e) **The taxation authorities** want to know about business profits in order to assess the tax payable by the company, including sales taxes.

(f) **Employees of the company** should have a right to information about the company's financial situation, because their future careers and the size of their wages and salaries depend on it.

Accounting information is summarised in financial statements to satisfy the **information needs** of these different groups. Not all will be equally satisfied.

4.3 Needs of different users

Managers of a business need the most information, to help them make their planning and control decisions. They obviously have 'special' access to information about the business, because they are able to demand whatever internally produced statements they require. When managers want a large amount of information about the costs and profitability of individual products, or different parts of their business, they can obtain it through a system of cost and management accounting.

Activity

Which of the following statements is particularly useful for managers?

A   Financial statements for the last financial year
B   Tax records for the past five years
C   Budgets for the coming financial year
D   Bank statements for the past year

Answer

The correct answer is C. Managers need to look forward and make plans to keep the business profitable. Therefore the most useful information for them would be the budgets for the coming financial year.

In addition to management information, financial statements are prepared (and perhaps published) for the benefit of other user groups, which may demand certain information.

(a)   The **national laws** of a country may provide for the provision of some accounting information for shareholders and the public.

(b)   **National taxation** authorities will receive the information they need to make tax assessments.

(c)   A **bank** might demand a forecast of a company's expected future cash flows as a pre-condition of granting an overdraft.

(d)   Some companies provide, voluntarily, specially prepared financial information for issue to their employees. These statements are known as '**employee reports**'.

Unit Roundup

- Global international accounting is regulated by an overall international set of organisations. The organisational structure consists of:

  - the IASC Foundation
  - the IASB
  - the Standards Advisory Council (SAC)
  - the International Financial Reporting Interpretations Committee (IFRIC)

- IFRSs are developed through a formal system of due process and broad international consultation involving accountants, financial analysts and other users and regulatory bodies from around the world.

- The *IFRS for SMEs* is a self-contained IFRS which provides an alternative framework for eligible entities from the use of full IFRS in issue.

- There are various different parties with an interest in the financial statements of an SME and each will have different information needs.

Quick Quiz

1   One objective of the IASB is to promote the preparation of financial statements using the euro.

    True ☐

    False ☐

2   How many IASs and IFRSs have been published?

3   When was the *IFRS for SMEs* published?

4   What are the size criteria for a small or medium-sized enterprise according to the IASB?

5   Identify six user groups who need accounting information.

Answers to Quick Quiz

1   False

2   41 IASs and 9 IFRSs, plus the IFRS for SMEs

3   July 2009

4   There are no size criteria. However the entity must have no public accountability but does publish general purpose financial statements.

5   See paragraph 4.2

Now try the question below

Information needs   18 mins

Discuss the information needs of the various users of financial information.   **(10 marks)**

Information needs

(a) **Investors** are the providers of risk capital

    (i)   Information is required to help make a decision about buying or selling shares, taking up a rights issue and voting.

    (ii)   Investors must have information about the level of dividend, past, present and future and any changes in share price.

    (iii) Investors will also need to know whether the management has been running the company efficiently.

    (iv) As well as the position indicated by the statement of comprehensive income, statement of financial position and earnings per share (EPS), investors will want to know about the liquidity position of the company, the company's future prospects, and how the company's shares compare with those of its competitors.

(b) **Employees** need information about the security of employment and future prospects for jobs in the company, and to help with collective pay bargaining.

(c) **Lenders** need information to help them decide whether to lend to a company. They will also need to check that the value of any security remains adequate, that the interest repayments are secure, that the cash is available for redemption at the appropriate time and that any financial restrictions (such as maximum debt/equity ratios) have not been breached.

(d) **Suppliers** need to know whether the company will be a good customer and pay its debts.

(e) **Customers** need to know whether the company will be able to continue producing and supplying goods.

(f) **Government's** interest in a company may be one of creditor or customer, as well as being specifically concerned with compliance with tax and company law, ability to pay tax and the general contribution of the company to the economy.

(g) The **public** at large would wish to have information for all the reasons mentioned above, but it could be suggested that it would be impossible to provide general purpose accounting information which was specifically designed for the needs of the public.

Accounting concepts and principles

2

Unit topic list

1   Concepts and Pervasive Principles
2   The objective of financial statements
3   Underlying assumptions
4   Qualitative characteristics of financial statements
5   Financial position
6   Performance
7   Recognition of assets, liabilities, income and expenses
8   Measurement of assets, liabilities, income and expenses

Assessment criteria

2   Understand concepts and pervasive principles in the IFRS for SMEs

2.1   Understand the objectives of financial statements for SMEs

2.2   Understand the qualitative characteristics of information in financial statements

2.5   Understand how assets, liabilities, income and expenses are recognised and measured based on pervasive recognition and measurement principles derived from *IASB Framework for the Preparation and Presentation of Financial Statements*

1 Concepts and Pervasive Principles

Chapter 2, Concepts and Pervasive Principles, of the IFRS for SMEs provides the conceptual framework for the development of accounting guidance within the standard.

In July 1989 the IASB (then IASC) produced a document, *Framework for the preparation and presentation of financial statements* (*'Framework'*). The *Framework* is, in effect, the **conceptual** framework upon which all IASs/IFRSs are based and hence which determines how financial statements are prepared and the information they contain. When the IASB developed the IFRS for SMEs, it used this *Framework* as the basis for Chapter 2 of the standard, *Concepts and Pervasive Principles.*

Concepts and Pervasive Principles includes a number of sections. These deal with:

- Objective of financial statements of small and medium sized entities
- Qualitative characteristics of information in financial statements
- Financial position
- Performance
- Recognition of assets, liabilities, income and expenses
- Measurement of assets, liabilities, income and expenses
- Accruals basis of accounting
- Offsetting

1.1 Preface

The fundamental reason why financial statements are produced worldwide is to **satisfy the requirements of external users**, but that practice varies due to the individual pressures in each country. These pressures may be social, political, economic or legal, but they result in variations in practice from country to country, including the form of statements, the definition of their component parts (assets, liabilities etc), the criteria for recognition of items and both the scope and disclosure of financial statements.

It is these differences which the IASB wishes to narrow by **harmonising** all aspects of financial statements.

Financial statements are used to make economic decisions and thus financial statements should be prepared to this end. The types of economic decisions for which financial statements are likely to be used include the following.

- Decisions to buy, hold or sell equity investments
- Assessment of management stewardship and accountability
- Assessment of the entity's ability to pay employees
- Assessment of the security of amounts lent to the entity
- Determination of taxation policies
- Determination of distributable profits and dividends
- Inclusion in national income statistics
- Regulations of the activities of entities

Any additional requirements imposed by **national governments** for their own purposes should not affect financial statements produced for the benefit of other users.

1.2 Introduction

As mentioned already, *Concepts and Pervasive Principles* within the IFRS for SMEs is based upon the *Framework*. The introduction to the *Framework* lays out the purpose of the document.

1.2.1 Purpose and status

The introduction gives a list of the purposes of the *Framework*.

(a) Assist the Board of the IASB in the **development of future IFRSs** and in its review of existing IFRSs.

(b) Assist the Board of the IASB in **promoting harmonisation** of regulations, accounting standards and procedures relating to the presentation of financial statements by providing a basis for reducing the number of alternative accounting treatments permitted by IFRSs.

(c) Assist **national standard-setting bodies** in developing national standards.

(d) Assist **preparers of financial statements** in applying IFRSs and in dealing with topics that have yet to form the subject of an IFRS.

(e) Assist **auditors** in forming an opinion as to whether financial statements conform with IFRSs.

(f) Assist **users of financial statements** in interpreting the information contained in financial statements prepared in conformity with IFRSs.

(g) Provide those who are interested in the work of IASB with **information** about its approach to the formulation of IFRSs.

The purpose of *Concepts and Pervasive Principles,* although not explicitly stated within the IFRS for SMEs, is to an extent similar: It will assist the IASB when it makes amendments to the IFRS for SMEs and may also help national standard setters to develop accounting standards relevant to private entities.

1.2.2 Scope

Concepts and Pervasive Principles deals with:

(a) The **objective** of financial statements

(b) The **qualities** that make the information in the financial statements of SMEs useful.

(c) The **concepts and basic principles** underlying the financial statements of SMEs

A complete set of financial statements includes:

(a) A statement of financial position

(b) A statement of comprehensive income

(c) A statement of changes in equity

(d) A statement of cash flows

(e) Notes, other statements and explanatory material

Supplementary information may be included, but some items are not included in the financial statements themselves, namely commentaries and reports by the directors, the chairman, management etc.

Key term

> A **reporting entity** is an entity for which there are users who rely on the financial statements as their major source of financial information about the entity.

2 The objective of financial statements

Concepts and Pervasive Principles states that:

'The objective of financial statements of an SME is to provide information about the financial position, performance and cash flows of an entity that is useful for economic decision-making by a broad range of users.'

The users of the financial statements of SMEs are described as 'being not in a position to demand reports tailored to meet their particular information needs'.

Such financial statements will meet the needs of most users. The information is, however, **restricted**.

(a) It is based on **past events** not expected future events.

(b) It does not necessarily contain **non-financial information**.

The statements also show the results of **management's stewardship**.

2.1 Financial position, performance and changes in financial position

It is important for users to assess the **ability of an entity to produce cash and cash equivalents** to pay employees, lenders etc.

The financial position of an entity is the relationship of its assets, liabilities and equity as of a specific date as presented in the statement of financial position. Information is affected by the following and information about each one can aid the user.

(a)   **Economic resources controlled ie assets**: to predict the ability to generate cash

(b)   **Financial structure**: to predict borrowing needs, the distribution of future profits/cash and likely success in raising new finance

(c)   **Liquidity and solvency**: to predict whether financial commitments will be met as they fall due (liquidity relates to short-term commitments, solvency is longer-term)

Key term

> **Liquidity**. The availability of sufficient funds to meet deposit withdrawals and other short-term financial commitments as they fall due.
>
> **Solvency**. The availability of cash over the longer term to meet financial commitments as they fall due.

In all these areas, the capacity to adapt to changes in the environment in which the entity operates is very important.

Financial performance (statement of comprehensive income) information, particularly profitability, is used to assess potential changes in the economic resources the entity is likely to control in future. Information about performance variability is therefore important.

Cash flow information is used to assess the entity's investing, financing and operating activities. It shows the entity's ability to produce cash and the needs which utilise those cash flows.

All parts of the financial statements are **interrelated**, reflecting different aspects of the same transactions or events. Each statement provides different information; none can provide all the information required by users.

3 Underlying assumptions

Accruals and **going concern** are the two underlying assumptions in preparing financial statements.

The accruals basis of accounting is specifically mentioned within *Concepts and Pervasive Principles* as the basis on which financial statements must be prepared. Although going concern is not specifically addressed in this part of the IFRS for SMEs, it is identified by the standard as an underlying assumption.

3.1 Accruals basis

Key term

> **Accruals basis**. The effects of transactions and other events are recognised when they occur (and not as cash or its equivalent is received or paid) and they are recorded in the accounting records and reported in the financial statements of the periods to which they relate.   *(IFRS for SMEs)*

Financial statements prepared under the accruals basis show users past transactions involving cash and also obligations to pay cash in the future and resources which represent cash to be received in the future.

3.2 Going concern

Key term

> **Going concern**. An entity is a going concern unless management either intends to liquidate the entity or to cease trading, or has no realistic alternative but to do so.   *(IFRS for SMEs)*

It is assumed that the entity has no intention to liquidate or curtail major operations. If it did, then the financial statements would be prepared on a **different (disclosed) basis**.

4 Qualitative characteristics of financial statements

Qualitative characteristics are the attributes that make the information provided in financial statements useful to users.

The four principal qualitative characteristics are understandability, relevance, reliability and comparability.

4.1 Understandability

Users must be able to understand financial statements. They are assumed to have some business, economic and accounting knowledge and to be able to apply themselves to study the information properly. However relevant information should not be omitted simply because it is too difficult for some users to understand.

4.2 Relevance

The **predictive and confirmatory roles** of information are interrelated.

Key term

> **Relevance** The quality of information that allows it to influence the economic decisions of users by helping them evaluate past, present or future events or confirming, or correcting, their past evaluations. *(IFRS for SMEs)*

Information on financial position and performance is often used to predict future position and performance and other things of interest to the user, eg likely dividend, wage rises. The **manner of showing information** will enhance the ability to make predictions, eg by highlighting unusual items.

4.2.1 Materiality

The relevance of information is affected by its **nature and materiality**.

Key term

> **Material**. Omissions or misstatements of items are material if they could, individually or collectively, influence the economic decisions of users taken on the basis of the financial statements.   *(IFRS for SMEs)*

Materiality depends on the size of the item or error judged in the particular circumstances of its omission or misstatement. However, it is inappropriate to make, or leave uncorrected, immaterial departures from the *IFRS for SMEs* to achieve a particular presentation of an entity's financial position, financial performance or cash flows.

4.3 Reliability

Information must also be reliable to be useful.

Key term

> **Reliability**. The quality of information that makes it free from material error and bias and represent faithfully that which it either purports to represent or could reasonably be expected to represent. *(IFRS for SMEs)*

Even if information is relevant, if it is very unreliable it may be **misleading to recognise it**, eg a disputed claim for damages in a legal action.

4.3.1 Substance over form

Faithful representation of a transaction is only possible if it is accounted for according to its **substance and economic reality**, not with its legal form.

Key term

> **Substance over form**. The principle that transactions and other events are accounted for and presented in accordance with their substance and economic reality and not merely their legal form.

For instance, one party may sell an asset to another party and the sales documentation may record that legal ownership has been transferred. However, if agreements exist whereby the party selling the asset continues to enjoy the future economic benefits arising from the asset, then in substance no sale has taken place.

4.3.2 Prudence

Uncertainties exist in the preparation of financial information, eg the collectability of doubtful receivables.

Prudence is the inclusion of a degree of caution in the exercise of the judgements needed in making the estimates required under conditions of uncertainty, such that assets or income are not overstated and liabilities or expenses are not understated.

These uncertainties are recognised through disclosure and through the application of prudence. Prudence does not, however, allow the creation of hidden reserves or excessive provisions, understatement of assets or income or overstatement of liabilities or expenses.

4.3.3 Completeness

Financial information must be complete, within the **restrictions of materiality and cost**, to be reliable. Omission may cause information to be misleading.

4.4 Comparability

Users must be able to compare an entity's financial statements:

(a)   **Through time** to identify trends

(b)   **With other entities' statements**, to evaluate their relative financial position, performance and cash flows

The consistency of treatment is therefore important across like items over time, within the entity and across all entities.

The **disclosure of accounting policies** is particularly important here. Users must be able to distinguish between different accounting policies in order to be able to make a valid comparison of similar items in the accounts of different entities.

Comparability is **not the same as uniformity**. Entities should change accounting policies if they become inappropriate.

Corresponding information for **preceding periods** should be shown to enable comparison over time.

4.5 Timeliness

Information may become irrelevant if there is a delay in reporting it. There is a **balance between timeliness and the provision of reliable information**. Information may be reported on a timely basis when not all aspects of the transaction are known, thus compromising reliability.

If every detail of a transaction is known, it may be too late to publish the information because it has become irrelevant. The overriding consideration is how best to satisfy the economic decision-making needs of the users.

4.6 Balance between benefits and cost

The benefits derived from information should exceed the cost of providing it. The evaluation of benefits and costs is substantially a judgemental process. Furthermore, the costs are not necessarily borne by those users who enjoy the benefits, and often the benefits of the information are enjoyed by a broad range of external users. Financial reporting information helps capital providers make better decisions, which results in more efficient functioning of capital markets and a lower cost of capital for the economy as a whole. Individual entities also enjoy benefits, including improved access to capital markets, favourable effect on public relations, and perhaps lower costs of capital. The benefits may also include better management decisions because financial information used internally is often based at least partly on information prepared for general purpose financial reporting purposes.

5 Financial position

> The financial position of an entity is the relationship of its assets, liabilities and equity as of a specific date.

Concepts and Pervasive Principles provides the following definitions in relation to financial position:

Key terms

> - **Asset**. A resource controlled by an entity as a result of past events and from which future economic benefits are expected to flow to the entity.
>
> - **Liability**. A present obligation of the entity arising from past events, the settlement of which is expected to result in an outflow from the entity of resources embodying economic benefits.
>
> - **Equity**. The residual interest in the assets of the entity after deducting all its liabilities.
>
> *(IFRS for SMEs)*

These definitions are important, but they do not cover the **criteria for recognition** of any of these items, which are discussed later in this unit. This means that the definitions may include items which would not actually be recognised in the statement of financial position because they fail to satisfy recognition criteria particularly, as we will see below, the **probable flow of any economic benefit** to or from the business.

Whether an item satisfies any of the definitions above will depend on the **substance and economic reality** of the transaction, not merely its legal form. For example, leases (see Unit 9).

5.1 Assets

We can look in more detail at the components of the definitions given above.

Key term

> **Future economic benefit**. The potential of an asset to contribute, directly or indirectly, to the flow of cash and cash equivalents to the entity. Those cash flows may come from using the asset or from disposing of it. *(IFRS for SMEs)*

Assets are usually employed to produce goods or services for customers; customers will then pay for these. **Cash itself** renders a service to the entity due to its command over other resources.

The existence of an asset, particularly in terms of **control**, is not reliant on:

(a)   **physical form** (hence patents and copyrights); *nor*
(b)   **legal rights** (hence leases).

Transactions or events **in the past** give rise to assets; those expected to occur in the future do not in themselves give rise to assets. For example, an intention to purchase a non-current asset does not, in itself, meet the definition of an asset.

5.2 Liabilities

Again we can look more closely at some aspects of the definition. An essential characteristic of a liability is that the entity has a **present obligation**.

Key term

> **Obligation**. A duty or responsibility to act or perform in a certain way. Obligations may be either a legal obligation or a constructive obligation. A legal obligation is legally enforceable as a consequence of a binding contract or statutory requirement. A constructive obligation is an obligation that derives from an entity's actions when by established pattern of past practice the entity has indicated that it will accept certain responsibilities and has created an expectation on other parties that it will discharge those responsibilities. *(IFRS for SMEs)*

It is important to distinguish between a present obligation and a **future commitment**. A management decision to purchase assets in the future does not, in itself, give rise to a present obligation.

Settlement of a present obligation will involve the entity giving up resources embodying economic benefits in order to satisfy the claim of the other party. This may be done in various ways, not just by payment of cash.

Liabilities must arise from **past transactions or events**. In the case of, say, recognition of future rebates to customers based on annual purchases, the sale of goods in the past is the transaction that gives rise to the liability.

5.2.1 Provisions

Is a provision a liability?

Key term

> **Provision**. A liability of uncertain timing or amount.
> *(IFRS for SMEs)*

Activity

Consider the following situations. In each case, do we have an asset or liability within the definitions given by the *Framework?* Give reasons for your answer.

(a)   Pat Co has purchased a patent for $20,000. The patent gives the company sole use of a particular manufacturing process which will save $3,000 a year for the next five years.

(b)   Baldwin Co paid Don Brennan $10,000 to set up a car repair shop, on condition that priority treatment is given to cars from the company's fleet.

(c)   Deals on Wheels Co provides a warranty with every car sold.

Answer

(a)   This is an asset, albeit an intangible one. There is a past event, control and future economic benefit (through cost savings).

(b)   This cannot be classified as an asset. Baldwin Co has no control over the car repair shop and it is difficult to argue that there are 'future economic benefits'.

(c)   The warranty claims in total constitute a liability; the business has taken on an obligation. It would be recognised when the warranty is issued rather than when a claim is made.

5.3 Equity

Equity is defined above as a **residual**, but it may be sub-classified in the statement of financial position. For example, subclassifications may include funds contributed by shareholders, retained earnings and gains or losses recognised directly in equity.

6 Performance

Performance is the relationship of the income and expenses of an entity during a reporting period.

Profit is used as a **measure of performance**, or as a basis for other measures (eg EPS). It depends directly on the measurement of income and expenses.

The elements of income and expense are therefore defined.

Key term

> •   **Income**. Increases in economic benefits during the reporting period in the form of inflows or enhancements of assets or decreases of liabilities that result in increases in equity, other than those relating to contributions from equity investors.

- **Expenses**. Decreases in economic benefits during the reporting period in the form of outflows or depletions of assets or incurrences of liabilities that result in decreases in equity, other than those relating to distributions to equity investors. *(IFRS for SMEs)*

Income and expenses can be **presented in different ways** in the statement of comprehensive income, to provide information relevant for economic decision-making. The *IFRS for SMEs* gives a choice about the presentation of income and expenses. It can be either in one single **statement of comprehensive income** or in two separate statements, **an income statement** and a statement of comprehensive income.

Items of income and expense can be **distinguished** from each other or **combined** with each other.

6.1 Income

Both **revenue** and **gains** are included in the definition of income. **Revenue** arises in the course of ordinary activities of an entity.

Key term

Gains. Increases in economic benefits that meet the definition of income but that are not revenue. *(IFRS for SMEs)*

Gains include those arising on the disposal of non-current assets. The definition of income also includes **unrealised gains**, eg on revaluation of marketable securities.

6.2 Expenses

As with income, the definition of expenses includes losses as well as those expenses that arise in the course of ordinary activities of an entity.

Key term

Losses. Other items that meet the definition of expenses and may arise in the course of the ordinary activities of the entity. *(IFRS for SMEs)*

Losses will include those arising on the disposal of non-current assets. The definition of expenses will also include **unrealised losses**, eg exchange rate effects on borrowings.

7 Recognition of assets, liabilities, income and expenses

Items which meet the definition of assets or liabilities may still not be recognised in financial statements because they must also meet certain **recognition criteria**.

Key term

Recognition. The process of incorporating in the financial statements an item that meets the definition of an asset, liability, income or expense and satisfies the following criteria:

(a) it is probable that any future economic benefit associated with the item will flow to or from the entity; and

(b) the item has a cost or value that can be measured reliably. *(IFRS for SMEs)*

Regard must be given to **materiality** (see Section 5 above).

7.1 Probability of future economic benefits

Probability here means the **degree of uncertainty** that the future economic benefits associated with an item will flow to or from the entity. This must be judged on the basis of the **characteristics of the entity's environment** and the **evidence available** when the financial statements are prepared.

7.2 Reliability of measurement

The cost or value of an item, in many cases, **must be estimated**. *Concepts and Pervasive Principles* states, however, that the use of reasonable estimates is an essential part of the preparation of financial statements and does not undermine their reliability. Where no reasonable estimate can be made, the item should not be recognised, although its existence should be disclosed in the notes, or other explanatory material.

Items may still qualify for recognition **at a later date** due to changes in circumstances or subsequent events.

7.3 Recognition of items

We can summarise the recognition criteria for assets, liabilities, income and expenses, based on the definition of recognition given above.

Item	Recognised in	When
Asset	The statement of financial position	It is probable that the future economic benefits will flow to the entity and the asset has a cost or value that can be measured reliably.
Liability	The statement of financial position	It is probable that an outflow of resources embodying economic benefits will result from the settlement of a present obligation and the amount at which the settlement will take place can be measured reliably.
Income	The statement of comprehensive income	An increase in future economic benefits related to an increase in an asset or a decrease of a liability has arisen that can be measured reliably.
Expenses	The statement of comprehensive income	A decrease in future economic benefits related to a decrease in an asset or an increase of a liability has arisen that can be measured reliably.

8 Measurement of assets, liabilities, income and expenses

A number of different measurement bases are used in financial statements. The *IFRS for SMEs* states that there are two commonly used measurement bases:

– Historical cost
– Fair value

Measurement is defined as follows.

Key term

Measurement. The process of determining the monetary amounts at which an entity measures assets, liabilities, income and expenses in its financial statements. *(IFRS for SMEs)*

This involves the selection of a particular **basis of measurement**.

Key terms

Historical cost. Assets are recorded at the amount of cash or cash equivalents paid or the fair value of the consideration given to acquire them at the time of their acquisition. Liabilities are recorded at the amount of proceeds received in exchange for the obligation, or in some circumstances (for example, income taxes), at the amounts of cash or cash equivalents expected to be paid to satisfy the liability in the normal course of business.

Fair value. The amount for which an asset could be exchanged, or a liability settled, between knowledgeable willing parties in an arm's length transaction.

(IFRS for SMEs)

Historical cost is the most commonly adopted measurement basis, but this is usually combined with other bases, eg inventory is carried at the lower of cost and net realisable value.

8.1 Offsetting

An entity shall not offset assets and liabilities, or income and expenses, unless specifically allowed by the *IFRS for SMEs.*

Unit roundup

- Chapter 2, *Concepts and Pervasive Principles,* of the IFRS for SMEs provides the conceptual framework for the accounting guidance within the standard.

- The objective of financial statements of an SME is to provide information about the financial position, performance and cash flows of an entity that is useful for economic decision-making by a broad range of users.

- **Accruals** and **going concern** are the two underlying assumptions in preparing financial statements.

- Qualitative characteristics are the attributes that make the information provided in financial statements useful to users.

- The financial position of an entity is the relationship of its assets, liabilities and equity as of a specific date.

- Performance is the relationship of the income and expenses of an entity during a reporting period.

- Items which meet the definition of assets or liabilities may still not be recognised in financial statements because they must also meet certain **recognition criteria**.

- A number of different measurement bases are used in financial statements. They include:

    − Historical cost
    − Fair value

Quick Quiz

1   Define 'relevance'.

2   In which two ways should users be able to compare an entity's financial statements?

3   A provision can be a liability. True or false?

4   Define 'recognition'.

5   The cost or value of items in the financial statements is never estimated. True or false?

6   What is the most common basis of measurement used in financial statements?

Answers to Quick Quiz

1   Information has relevance when it influences the economic decisions of users by helping them evaluate past, present or future events or confirming (or correcting) their past evaluations.

2   • Through time to identify trends
     • With other entities' statements

3   True. It satisfies the definition of a liability but the amount may need to be estimated.

4   See Key Term Section 7.

5   False. Monetary values are often estimated.

6   Historical cost.

Now try the question below

Relevance, reliability and comparability   27 mins

(a) The qualitative characteristics of relevance, reliability and comparability identified in the IFRS for SMEs are some of the attributes that make financial information useful to the various users of financial statements.

Explain what is meant by relevance, reliability and comparability and how they make financial information useful.   **(10 marks)**

(b) Of particular importance within the *IFRS for SMEs* are the definitions and recognition criteria for assets and liabilities.

Required

Define assets and liabilities and explain the important aspects of their definitions. Explain why these definitions are of particular importance to the preparation of an entity's statement of financial position and statement of comprehensive income.   **(5 marks)**

(Total = 15 marks)

Relevance, reliability and comparability

(a) **Relevance**

The relevance of information must be considered in terms of the decision-making needs of users. It is relevant when it can influence their economic decisions or allow them to reassess past decisions and evaluations. Economic decisions often have a predictive quality – users may make financial decisions on the basis of what they expect to happen in the future. To some degree past performance gives information on expected future performance and this is enhanced by the provision of comparatives, so that users can see the direction in which the company is moving.

One aspect of relevance is materiality. An item is material if its omission or misstatement could influence the economic decisions of users. Relevance would not be enhanced by the inclusion of immaterial items which may serve to obscure the important issues.

Reliability

Information can be considered to be reliable when it is free from error or bias and gives a true and fair view of what it is expected to represent. The statement of comprehensive income must be a reliable statement of the results of the entity for the period in question and the statement of financial position must fairly present its financial position at the end of the period. Financial statements in which provision had not been made for known liabilities or in which asset values had not been correctly stated could not be considered reliable. This also brings in the issue of substance over form. Transactions should be represented in accordance with their economic substance, rather than their legal form.

Comparability

Comparability operates in two ways. Users must be able to compare the financial statements of the entity with its own past performance and they must also be able to compare its results with those of other entities. This means that financial statements must be prepared on the same basis from one year to the next and that, where a change of accounting policy takes place, the results for the previous year must also be restated so that comparability is maintained. Comparability with other entities is made possible by use of appropriate accounting policies, disclosure of accounting policies and compliance with the *IFRS for SMEs*. The *IFRS for SMEs* has eliminated alternative treatments, so this has greatly enhanced comparability.

(b) *Assets* are defined as 'rights or access to future economic benefits controlled by an entity as a result of past transactions or events'. The use of 'controlled' means that where an entity does not legally 'own' an asset but has control of the rights to future economic benefits accruing from it, the asset should be recognised. The most obvious example of this is an asset held under a finance lease. This is not legally owned, but is shown in the statement of financial position as a non-current asset. The emphasis on 'past transactions or events' prevents the recognition of contingent assets.

Liabilities are defined as 'obligations of an entity to transfer economic benefits as a result of past transactions or events'. This obligation may be legal or it may be constructive. For instance, a company may have no legal obligation to fulfil certain environmental requirements, but it may have created, by its previous actions, the expectation that it will do so. This will be regarded as a constructive obligation and the cost of carrying it out will be provided for. Again, 'past transactions or events' prevents the use of liabilities for 'profit smoothing'. An entity cannot set up a provision for an obligation which has not yet been incurred, such as a restructuring which it intends to carry out in the following year.

The emphasis placed upon correctly defining and recognising assets and liabilities underlines the importance of the statement of financial position. The elements of financial statements identified in the *IFRS for SMEs*, other than assets and liabilities themselves, are measured in terms of changes in assets and liabilities. Equity is the excess of assets over liabilities and gains and losses are defined as increases or decreases in equity, aside from contributions from and distributions to owners. So correct identification and measurement of assets and liabilities is crucial to the preparation of financial statements which present a true and fair view.

Presentation and content of financial statements

3

Unit topic list

1 Financial statement presentation
2 Statement of financial position
3 The current/non-current distinction
4 Statement of comprehensive income
5 Income statement
6 Revision of basic accounts
7 Changes in equity

Assessment criteria

2   **Understand concepts and pervasive principles in the IFRS for SMEs**

2.3   Understand the significance of an SME's financial position as presented in the statement of financial position

2.4   Understand the significance of an SME's performance in its statement of comprehensive income

3   **Financial statement presentation – the information that should be shown and how it should be presented**

3.1   Understand what fair presentation means

3.3   Understand the requirements of the following:
- going concern
- frequency of reporting
- consistency of presentation
- comparative information
- materiality and aggregation

3.4 Understand the contents of a complete set of financial statements and the identification of each of the financial statements

3.5 Understand the information to be presented in the statement of financial position and the information that can be presented either in the statement of financial position or in the notes

3.6 Understand the difference between a current and non-current asset

3.7 Understand the presentation of the total comprehensive income using single-statement and the two statement approach

3.8 Understand that expenses can be analysed either by nature of expense or function of expense

3.9 Understand the purpose of the statement of changes in equity and the information to be presented

3.10 Understand the purpose of the statement of income and retained earnings and the information to be presented

3.14 Understand the structure of the notes and the information that should be disclosed therein

4 Understand and apply IFRS for SMEs in the preparation of their financial statements

4.1 Revise the content of a statement of comprehensive income and statement of financial position to comply with the relevant IFRS

1 Financial statement presentation

The *IFRS for SMEs* covers the form and content of financial statements for SMEs. The main components are:

– Statement of financial position
– Statement of comprehensive income
– Statement of changes in equity
– Statement of cash flows
– Notes to the financial statements

1.1 Content of financial statements

The *IFRS for SMEs* gives guidance on the figures that should appear in each of the key financial statements and also provides, in a separate document, illustrative financial statements and a presentation and disclosure checklist.

1.2 How items are disclosed

Disclosures of certain items are required in certain ways.

- Some items must appear on the face of the statement of financial position or statement of comprehensive income
- Other items can appear in a **note to the financial statements** instead

1.3 Identification of financial statements

It is most important that entities **distinguish the financial statements** very clearly from any other information published with them. This is because the *IFRS for SMEs* applies *only* to the financial statements (ie the main statements and related notes), so readers of the annual report must be able to differentiate between the parts of the report which are prepared under the IFRS, and other parts, such as a directors' report or business review, which are not.

The entity should **identify each** financial statement and the notes very clearly and it is also required that the disclosure of the following information is in a prominent position. If necessary it should be repeated wherever it is felt to be of use to the reader in his understanding of the information presented.

- **Name** of the reporting entity (or other means of identification)
- Whether the accounts cover the **single entity** only or a group of entities
- The **date of the end of the reporting period** or the period covered by the financial statements (as appropriate)
- The **presentation currency**

1.4 Reporting period and frequency of reporting

It is normal for entities to present financial statements **annually** and they should be prepared at least as often as this. If (unusually) the end of an entity's reporting period is changed, for whatever reason, the period for which the statements are presented will be less or more than one year. In such cases the entity should also disclose:

(a)   the **reason(s) why** a period other than one year is used; and

(b)   the fact that the comparative figures given **are not in fact comparable**.

1.5 Fair presentation

The financial statements are required to present fairly the financial position, financial performance and cash flows of the SME. The application of the *IFRS for SMEs*, with additional disclosure when necessary, is presumed to result in financial statements that achieve a fair presentation of the financial position, financial performance and cash flows of SMEs.

1.6 Going concern

When preparing financial statements in accordance with the IFRS for SMEs, management should assess the entity's ability to continue as a going concern. In assessing this, management should take into account all available information about the future which is at least 12 months from the reporting date.

Any material uncertainties which cast doubt on an entity's ability to continue as a going concern should be disclosed. Where financial statements are not prepared on the going concern basis, that fact should be disclosed together with the basis on which the financial statements were prepared and the reason why it is not considered to be a going concern.

1.7 Consistency of presentation

The presentation and classification of items in the financial statements should remain the same from one period to the next except where:

- A change in the nature of the business or a review of the financial statements indicates that another presentation or classification would be more appropriate
- The IFRS for SMEs requires a change in presentation.

Where the presentation or classification of items is changed, comparative amounts should be reclassified, unless this is impracticable, in which case that fact should be disclosed.

1.8 Comparative information

Unless the IFRS for SMES requires or permits otherwise, comparative information should be provided for all amounts presented in the financial statements.

1.9 Materiality and aggregation

Each material class of similar items should be presented separately within the financial statements. Dissimilar items should also be presented separately.

An item is material if an omission or misstatement of the item could influence the economic decisions of the users of the accounts. Items may be material due to their size or nature.

The financial statements presented later in this unit illustrate the separate presentation of different types of assets, liabilities, income and expenses.

1.10 Compliance with *IFRS for SMEs*

An entity which is complying with the *IFRS for SMEs* must make an explicit and unreserved statement in the notes to its financial statements of that compliance.

In extremely rare circumstances management of an entity may decide that compliance with some element of the IFRS would be so misleading that the financial statements would not comply with the objectives of financial statements and not provide a fair presentation. In these circumstances the entity can depart from that element of the IFRS but must disclose the following:

- that management have concluded that the financial statements present fairly the entity's financial position, financial performance and cash flows.

- that the entity has complied with the IFRS except for this particular matter.

- the nature of the departure including the treatment the IFRS would have required, the reason why that treatment would be so misleading and the treatment actually adopted.

2 Statement of financial position

The implementation guidance to the IFRS for SMEs suggests a format for the statement of financial position. The standard also specifies certain items for **disclosure on the face of the financial statements**.

The IFRS discusses the distinction between current and non-current items in some detail, as we shall see in the next section. First of all we can look at the **suggested format** of the statement of financial position and then look at further disclosures required. Although the term 'Statement of financial position' is used throughout the IFRS it is noted that other titles for this statement can be used the most common being a 'balance sheet'.

2.1 Statement of financial position example

XYZ GROUP – STATEMENT OF FINANCIAL POSITION AT 31 DECEMBER

	20X7	20X6
Assets	$	$
Current assets		
Cash and cash equivalents	312,400	322,900
Trade receivables	91,600	110,800
Inventories	135,230	132,500
Other current assets	25,650	12,540
	564,880	578,740
Non-current assets		
Property, plant and equipment	493,200	516,020
Goodwill	80,800	91,200
Other intangible assets	227,470	227,470
Investments in associates	100,150	110,770
	901,620	945,460
Total assets	1,466,500	1,524,200
Liabilities and equity		
Equity attributable to owners of the parent		
Current liabilities		
Trade and other payables	115,100	187,620
Short-term borrowings	150,000	200,000
Current portion of long-term borrowings	10,000	20,000
Current tax payable	35,000	42,000
Short-term provisions	5,000	4,800
Total current liabilities	315,100	454,420

Non-current liabilities		
Long-term borrowings	120,000	160,000
Deferred tax	28,800	26,040
Long-term provisions	28,850	52,240
Total non-current liabilities	177,650	238,280
Total liabilities	492,750	692,700
Equity		
Share capital	650,000	600,000
Retained earnings	243,500	161,700
Other components of equity	10,200	21,200
	903,700	782,900
Non-controlling interest	70,050	48,600
Total equity	973,750	831,500
Total equity and liabilities	1,466,500	1,524,200

As a minimum, the statement of financial position shall include line items that present the following amounts:

(a)   cash and cash equivalents

(b)   trade and other receivables

(c)   financial assets (excluding amounts shown under (a), (b), (j) and (k))

(d)   inventories

(e)   property, plant and equipment

(f)   investment property carried at fair value through profit or loss

(g)   intangible assets

(h)   biological assets carried at cost less accumulated depreciation and impairment

(i)   biological assets carried at fair value through profit or loss

(j)   investments in associates

(k)   investments in jointly controlled entities

(l)   trade and other payables

(m)   financial liabilities (excluding amounts shown under (l) and (p))

(n)   liabilities and assets for current tax

(o)   deferred tax liabilities and deferred tax assets (these shall always be classified as non-current)

(p)   provisions

(q)   non-controlling interest, presented within equity separately from the equity attributable to the owners of the parent

(r)   equity attributable to the owners of the parent

We will look at these items in subsequent units

An entity shall present additional line items, headings and subtotals in the statement of financial position when such presentation is relevant to an understanding of the entity's **financial position**.

2.2 Information presented either on the face of the statement of financial position or by note

An SME must disclose, either in the statement of financial position or in the notes, the following subclassifications of the line items presented:

(a)   property, plant and equipment in classifications appropriate to the entity

(b)   trade and other receivables showing separately amounts due from related parties, amounts due from other parties, and receivables arising from accrued income not yet billed

(c)   inventories, showing separately amounts of inventories:

   (i)   held for sale in the ordinary course of business

   (ii)   in the process of production for such sale

   (iii)   in the form of materials or supplies to be consumed in the production process or in the rendering of services

(d)   trade and other payables, showing separately amounts payable to trade suppliers, payable to related parties, deferred income and accruals

(e)   provisions for **employee benefits** and other provisions

(f)   classes of equity, such as paid-in capital, share premium, retained earnings and items of income and expense that, as required by this IFRS, are recognised in other comprehensive income and presented separately in equity

An entity with share capital shall disclose the following, either in the statement of financial position or in the notes:

(a)   for each class of share capital:

    (i)   the number of shares authorised

    (ii)   the number of shares issued and fully paid, and issued but not fully paid

    (iii)   par value per share, or that the shares have no par value

    (iv)   a reconciliation of the number of shares outstanding at the beginning and at the end of the period

    (v)   the rights, preferences and restrictions attaching to that class including restrictions on the distribution of dividends and the repayment of capital

    (vi)   shares in the entity held by the entity or by its subsidiaries or associates

    (vii)   shares reserved for issue under options and contracts for the sale of shares, including the terms and amounts

(b)   a description of each reserve within equity

2.3 Sequencing and format of items in the statement of financial position

The IFRS for SMEs does not prescribe the sequence or format in which items are to be presented in the statement of financial position. The illustrative format shown in section 2.1 is taken from the implementation guidance of the IFRS for SMEs. It is, however, different in terms of sequencing from the example statement of financial position which accompanies full IFRS, given in IAS 1 (revised). Companies applying the IFRS for SMES may choose to follow the IAS 1 (revised) sequencing (which lists non-current assets before current assets and equity before non-current liabilities before current liabilities), and you will see examples of this alternative format throughout this text.

3 The current/non-current distinction

You should appreciate the distinction between current and non-current assets and liabilities and their different treatments.

3.1 Introduction

An entity must present **current** and **non-current** assets as separate classifications on the face of the statement of financial position. A presentation based on liquidity should only be used where it provides more relevant and reliable information, in which case all assets and liabilities must be presented broadly **in order of liquidity**.

In either case, the entity should disclose any portion of an asset or liability which is expected to be recovered or settled **after more than twelve months**. For example, for an amount receivable which is due in instalments over 18 months, the portion due after more than twelve months must be disclosed.

This distinction between current and non-current assets/liabilities distinguishes them from those net assets used in the long-term operations of the entity. Assets that are expected to be realised and liabilities that are due for settlement within the operating cycle are therefore highlighted.

3.2 Current assets

An asset should be classified as a **current asset** when it:

- is expected to be realised in, or is held for sale or consumption in, the normal course of the entity's operating cycle; or
- is held primarily for trading purposes or for the short-term and expected to be realised within twelve months of the end of the reporting period; or
- is cash or a cash equivalent asset which is not restricted in its use.

All other assets should be classified as non-current assets.

Non-current assets includes tangible, intangible, operating and financial assets of a long-term nature. Other terms with the same meaning can be used (eg 'fixed', 'long-term').

Current assets therefore include inventories and trade receivables that are sold, consumed and realised as part of the normal operating cycle. **This is the case even where they are not expected to be realised within twelve months**.

Current assets will also include **marketable securities** if they are expected to be realised within twelve months after the reporting period. If expected to be realised later, they should be included in non-current assets.

3.3 Current liabilities

A liability should be classified as a **current liability** when it:

- Is expected to be settled in the normal course of the entity's operating cycle; or
- Is held primarily for the purpose of trading; or
- Is due to be settled within twelve months after the reporting period; or
- The entity does not have an unconditional right to defer settlement of the liability for at least twelve months after the reporting period.

All other liabilities should be classified as non-current liabilities.

The categorisation of current liabilities is very similar to that of current assets. Thus, some current liabilities are part of the **working capital** used in the normal operating cycle of the business (ie trade payables and accruals for employee and other operating costs). Such items will be classed as current liabilities **even where they are due to be settled more than twelve months after the end of the reporting period.**

There are also current liabilities which are not settled as part of the normal operating cycle, but which are due to be settled within twelve months of the end of the reporting period. These include bank overdrafts, income taxes, other non-trade payables and the current portion of interest-bearing liabilities. Any interest-bearing liabilities that are used to finance working capital on a long-term basis, and that are not due for settlement within twelve months, should be classed as **non-current liabilities**.

4 Statement of comprehensive income

The *IFRS for SMEs* requires all items of income and expense in a period to be shown in a **statement of comprehensive income**. This may be a single statement of comprehensive income or two separate statements: the income statement and the statement of comprehensive income.

4.1 Statement of comprehensive income – format

The IFRS allows income and expense items to be presented either:

(a)   in a single statement of comprehensive income; or

(b)   in two statements: a separate income statement and statement of other comprehensive income.

The format for a single statement of comprehensive income is shown as follows in the guidance to the standard. The section down to 'profit for the year' can be shown as a separate 'income statement' with an additional 'statement of other comprehensive income'.

XYZ GROUP – STATEMENT OF COMPREHENSIVE INCOME FOR THE YEAR ENDED 31 DECEMBER 20X7

	20X7	20X6
	$	$
Revenue	390,000	355,000
Cost of sales	(245,000)	(230,000)
Gross profit	145,000	125,000
Other income	20,667	11,300
Distribution costs	(9,000)	(8,700)
Administrative expenses	(20,000)	(21,000)
Other expenses	(2,100)	(1,200)
Finance costs	(8,000)	(7,500)
Share of profit of associates	35,100	30,100
Profit before tax	161,667	128,000
Income tax expense	(40,417)	(32,000)
Profit for the year	121,250	96,000
Other comprehensive income:		
Exchange differences on translating foreign operations	5,334	10,667
Share of other comprehensive income of associates	400	(700)
Income tax relating to components of other comprehensive income	4,667	(9,334)
Total comprehensive income for the year	131,651	96,633

Companies are given the option of presenting this information in two statements as follows:

XYZ GROUP – INCOME STATEMENT FOR THE YEAR ENDED 31 DECEMBER 20X7

	20X7	20X6
	$'000	$'000
Revenue	390,000	355,000
Cost of sales	(245,000)	(230,000)
Gross profit	145,000	125,000
Other income	20,667	11,300
Distribution costs	(9,000)	(8,700)
Administrative expenses	(20,000)	(21,000)
Other expenses	(2,100)	(1,200)
Finance costs	(8,000)	(7,500)
Share of profit of associates	35,100	30,100
Profit before tax	161,667	128,000
Income tax expense	(40,417)	(32,000)
Profit for the year	121,250	96,000

XYZ GROUP – STATEMENT OF COMPREHENSIVE INCOME FOR THE YEAR ENDED 31 DECEMBER 20X7

	20X7	20X6
	$	$
Profit for the year	121,250	96,000
Other comprehensive income:		
Exchange differences on translating foreign operations	5,334	10,667
Share of other comprehensive income of associates	400	(700)
Income tax relating to components of other comprehensive income	4,667	(9,334)
Total comprehensive income for the year	131,651	96,633

5 Income statement

The IFRS for SMEs offers two possible formats for the income statement section of the statement of comprehensive income or separate income statement - by function or by nature. Classification by function is more common.

5.1 Examples of separate income statements

XYZ GROUP
INCOME STATEMENT FOR THE YEAR ENDED 31 DECEMBER 20X8

Illustrating the classification of expenses by function

	20X8 $'000	20X7 $'000
Revenue	X	X
Cost of sales	(X)	(X)
Gross profit	X	X
Other income	X	X
Distribution costs	(X)	(X)
Administrative expenses	(X)	(X)
Other expenses	(X)	(X)
Finance costs	(X)	(X)
Share of profit of associates	X	X
Profit before tax	X	X
Income tax expense	(X)	(X)
Profit for the year	X	X
Attributable to:		
Owners of the parent	X	X
Non-controlling interest	X	X
	X	X

Illustrating the classification of expenses by nature

	20X8 $'000	20X7 $'000
Revenue	X	X
Other operating income	X	X
Changes in inventories of finished goods and work in progress	(X)	X
Work performed by the entity and capitalised	X	X
Raw material and consumables used	(X)	(X)
Employee benefits expense	(X)	(X)
Depreciation and amortisation expense	(X)	(X)
Impairment of property, plant and equipment	(X)	(X)
Other expenses	(X)	(X)
Finance costs	(X)	(X)
Share of profit of associates	X	X
Profit before tax	X	X
Income tax expense	(X)	(X)
Profit for the year	X	X
Attributable to:		
Owners of the parent	X	X
Non-controlling interest	X	X
	X	X

Note: The usual method of presentation is expenses by function and this is the format likely to appear in your exam.

5.2 Information presented in the statement of comprehensive income or separate income statement

The IFRS lists the following as the **minimum** to be disclosed on the face of the income statement.

(a) revenue

(b) finance costs

(c) share of the profit or loss of investments in associates and jointly controlled entities

(d) tax expense excluding tax allocated to items (e), (g) and (h) below

(e) a single amount comprising the total of

    (i) the post-tax profit or loss of a **discontinued operation**, and

    (ii) the post-tax gain or loss recognised on the measurement to fair value less costs to sell or on the disposal of the net assets constituting the discontinued operation

(f) profit or loss (if an entity has no items of other comprehensive income, this line need not be presented)

(g) each item of other comprehensive income classified by nature (excluding amounts in (h))

(h) share of the other comprehensive income of associates and jointly controlled entities accounted for by the equity method

(i) total comprehensive income (if an entity has no items of other comprehensive income, it may use another term for this line such as profit or loss)

The following items must be disclosed in the income statement as allocations of profit or loss for the period.

(a) Profit or loss attributable to non-controlling interest

(b) Profit or loss attributable to owners of the parent

The allocated amounts must not be presented as items of income or expense. (These relate to group accounts, covered later in this Study Guide.)

Income and expense items can only be **offset** when, and only when:

(a) It is permitted or required by an IFRS, or

(b) Gains, losses and related expenses arising from the same or similar transactions and events are immaterial, in which case they can be aggregated.

5.3 Information presented either in the statement or in the notes

An analysis of expenses must be shown either in the income statement section (as above, which is encouraged by the standard) or by note, using a classification based on *either* the nature of the expenses *or* their function. This **sub-classification of expenses** indicates a range of components of financial performance; these may differ in terms of stability, potential for gain or loss and predictability.

5.3.1 Nature of expense method

Expenses are not reallocated amongst various functions within the entity, but are aggregated in the income statement **according to their nature** (eg purchase of materials, depreciation, wages and salaries, transport costs). This is by far the easiest method, especially for smaller entities.

5.3.2 Function of expense/cost of sales method

You are likely to be more familiar with this method. Expenses are classified according to their function as part of cost of sales, distribution or administrative activities. This method often gives **more relevant information** for users, but the allocation of expenses by function requires the use of judgement and can be arbitrary. Consequently, perhaps, when this method is used, entities should disclose **additional information** on the nature of expenses, including staff costs, and depreciation and amortisation expense.

Which of the above methods is chosen by an entity will depend on **historical and industry factors**, and also the **nature of the organisation**. Under each method, there should be given an indication of costs which are likely to vary (directly or indirectly) with the level of sales or production. The choice of method should fairly reflect the main elements of the entity's performance. **This is the method you should expect to see in your exam.**

6 Revision of basic accounts

It would be useful at this point to refresh your memory of the basic accounting you have already studied and these questions will help you. Make sure that you understand everything before you go on.

Activity

A friend has bought some shares in a company and has received the latest accounts. There are some areas that he is having difficulty in understanding.

Briefly, but clearly, answer his questions.

(a)   What is a statement of financial position?
(b)   What is an asset?
(c)   What is a liability?
(d)   What is share capital?
(e)   What are reserves?
(f)   Why does the statement of financial position balance?
(g)   To what extent does the statement of financial position value my investment?

Answer

(a)   A **statement of financial position** is a statement of the assets, liabilities and capital of a business as at a stated date. It is laid out to show total assets as equivalent to total liabilities and capital.

(b)   An **asset** is a resource controlled by a business and is expected to be of some future benefit. Its value is determined as the historical cost of producing or obtaining it. Examples of assets are:

(i)   Plant, machinery, land and other **non-current assets**

(ii)   **Current** assets such as inventories, cash and debts owed to the business with reasonable assurance of recovery: these are assets which are not intended to be held on a continuing basis in the business

(c)   A **liability** is an amount owed by a business, other than the amount owed to its proprietors (capital). Examples of liabilities are:

(i)   Amounts owed to the government (sales or other taxes)
(ii)   Amounts owed to suppliers
(iii)   Bank overdraft
(iv)   Long-term loans from banks or investors

It is usual to differentiate between 'current' and 'long-term' liabilities. The former fall due within a year of the end of the reporting period.

(d)   **Share capital** is the permanent investment in a business by its owners. In the case of a limited company, this takes the form of *shares* for which investors subscribe on formation of the company. Each share has a **nominal** or **par** (ie face) **value** (say $1). In the statement of financial position, total issued share capital is shown at its par value.

(e)   If a company issues shares for more than their par value (at a **premium**) then (usually) by law this premium must be recorded separately from the par value in a 'share premium account'. This is an example of a reserve. It belongs to the shareholders but cannot be distributed to them, because it is a **capital reserve**.

Share capital and capital reserves are not distributable except on the winding up of the company, as a guarantee to the company's creditors that the company has enough assets to meet its debts. This is necessary because shareholders in limited liability companies have 'limited liability'; once they have paid the company for their shares they have no further liability to it if it becomes insolvent. The proprietors of other businesses are, by contrast, personally liable for business debts.

Retained earnings constitute accumulated profits (less losses) made by the company and can be distributed to shareholders as **dividends**. They too belong to the shareholders, and so are a claim on the resources of the company.

(f) Statements of financial position do not always balance on the first attempt, as all accountants know! However, once errors are corrected, all statements of financial position balance. This is because in **double entry bookkeeping** every transaction recorded has a dual effect. Assets are always equal to liabilities plus capital and so capital is always equal to assets less liabilities. This makes sense as the owners of the business are entitled to the net assets of the business as representing their capital plus accumulated surpluses (or less accumulated deficit).

(g) The statement of financial position is not intended as a statement of a business's worth at a given point in time. This is because, except where some attempt is made to adjust for the effects of rising prices, assets and liabilities are recorded at **historical cost** and on a prudent basis. For example, if there is any doubt about the recoverability of a debt, then the value in the accounts must be reduced to the likely recoverable amount. In addition, where non-current assets have a finite useful life, their cost is gradually written off to reflect the use being made of them.

The figure in the statement of financial position for capital and reserves therefore bears **no relationship** to the market value of shares. Market values are the product of a large number of factors, including general economic conditions, alternative investment returns (eg interest rates), likely future profits and dividends and, not least, market sentiment.

Activity

The accountant of Fiddles Co, a limited liability company, has begun preparing final accounts but the work is not yet complete. At this stage the items included in the list of account balances are as follows.

	$'000
Land	100
Buildings	120
Plant and machinery	170
Depreciation provision	120
Ordinary shares of $1	100
Retained earnings brought forward	380
Trade accounts receivable	200
Trade accounts payable	110
Inventory	190
Profit before tax	80
Allowance for receivables	3
Bank balance (asset)	12
Suspense	1

Notes (i) to (v) below are to be taken into account.

(i) The accounts receivable control account figure, which is used in the list of account balances, does not agree with the total of the sales ledger. A contra of $5,000 has been entered correctly in the individual ledger accounts but has been entered on the wrong side of both control accounts.

A batch total of sales of $12,345 had been entered in the double entry system as $13,345, although the individual ledger accounts entries for these sales were correct. The balance of

$4,000 on the sales returns account has inadvertently been omitted from the trial balance though correctly entered in the ledger records.

(ii) A standing order of receipt from a regular customer for $2,000, and bank charges of $1,000, have been completely omitted from the records.

(iii) A receivable for $1,000 is to be written off. The allowance for receivables balance is to be adjusted to 1% of receivables.

(iv) The opening inventory figure had been overstated by $1,000 and the closing inventory figure had been understated by $2,000.

(v) Any remaining balance on the suspense account should be treated as purchases if a debit balance and as sales if a credit balance.

Required

(a) Prepare journal entries to cover items in notes (i) to (v) above. You are not to open any new accounts and may use only those accounts included in the list of account balances as given.

(b) Prepare a statement of financial position in accordance with the IFRS for SMEs within the limits of the available information. For presentation purposes all the items arising from notes (i) to (v) above should be regarded as material.

 Answer

(a) JOURNAL ENTRIES FOR ADJUSTMENTS

		Debit $	Credit $
(i)	Trade accounts payable	10,000	
	Trade accounts receivable		10,000
	Profit before tax	1,000	
	Trade accounts receivable		1,000
	Profit before tax	4,000	
	Suspense		4,000
(ii)	Bank	2,000	
	Trade accounts receivable		2,000
	Profit before tax	1,000	
	Bank		1,000
(iii)	Profit before tax	1,000	
	Trade accounts receivable		1,000
	Allowance for receivables (W1)	1,140	
	Profit before tax		1,140
(iv)	Inventories	2,000	
	Profit before tax		2,000
	Retained earnings brought forward	1,000	
	Profit before tax		1,000
(v)	Suspense	3,000	
	Profit before tax		3,000

(b) FIDDLES CO
STATEMENT OF FINANCIAL POSITION

	$	$	$
Assets			
Current assets			
Inventories (190 + 2)		192,000	
Accounts receivable (W1)	186,000		
Less allowance	(1,860)		
		184,140	
Bank (12 + 2 – 1)		13,000	
		389,140	

Non-current assets		
Land and buildings	220,000	
Plant and machinery	170,000	
Depreciation	(120,000)	
		270,000
Total assets		659,140
Liabilities and equity		
Current liabilities		
Accounts payable (110 – 10)		100,000
Equity		
Share capital	100,000	
Retained earnings (W2)	459,140	
		559,140
Total equity and liabilities		659,140

Workings

1	*Accounts receivable*	$
	Per opening trial balance	200,000
	Contra	(10,000)
	Miscasting	(1,000)
	Standing order	(2,000)
	Written off	(1,000)
		186,000
	Allowance b/f	3,000
	Allowance required	1,860
	Journal	1,140

2		$
	Profit before tax (W3)	80,140
	Retained earnings brought forward ($380,000 – 1,000)	379,000
	Retained earnings carried forward	459,140

3	*Profit before tax*	$
	Per question	80,000
	Wrong batch total	(1,000)
	Returns	(4,000)
	Bank charges	(1,000)
	Irrecoverable debt	(1,000)
	Allowance for receivables	1,140
	Inventory (2,000 + 1,000)	3,000
	Suspense (sales)	3,000
		80,140

7 Changes in equity

The IFRS for SMEs requires a statement of changes in equity. This shows the movement in the equity section of the statement of financial position. A full set of financial statements includes a statement of changes in equity or in some circumstances a statement of income and retained earnings.

7.1 Format of statement of changes in equity

This is the format of the statement of changes in equity.

XYZ GROUP – STATEMENT OF CHANGES IN EQUITY FOR THE YEAR ENDED 31 DECEMBER 20X7

	Share capital $'000	Retained earnings $'000	Total $'000	Non-Controlling Interest $'000	Total equity $'000
Balance at 1 January 20X6	600,000	118,100	718,100	29,800	688,300
Changes in accounting policy	–	400	400	100	300
Restated balance	600,000	118,500	718,500	29,900	688,600
Changes in equity for 20X6					
Dividends	–	(10,000)	(10,000)	–	(10,000)
Total comprehensive income for year	–	53,200	53,200	18,700	34,500
Balance at 31 December 20X6	600,000	161,700	761,700	48,600	713,100
Changes in equity for 20X7					
Issue of share capital	50,000	–	50,000	–	50,000
Dividends	–	(15,000)	(15,000)	–	(15,000)
Total comprehensive income for the year	–	96,600	96,600	21,450	75,150
Balance at 31 December 20X7	650,000	243,300	893,300	70,050	823,250

Note that where there has been a change of accounting policy necessitating a retrospective restatement, the adjustment is disclosed for each period. So, rather than just showing an adjustment to the balance b/f on 1.1.X7, the balances for 20X6 are restated (see next unit for more details).

7.2 Statement of income and retained earnings

If the only changes to equity during the periods for which financial statements are presented arise from profit or loss, payment of dividends, corrections of prior period errors, and changes in accounting policy, the entity may present a single **statement of income and retained earnings** in place of the statement of comprehensive income and statement of changes in equity

In this statement of income and retained earnings the minimum requirements are:

(a)   retained earnings at the beginning of the reporting period
(b)   dividends declared and paid or payable during the period
(c)   restatements of retained earnings for corrections of prior period errors
(d)   restatements of retained earnings for changes in accounting policy
(e)   retained earnings at the end of the reporting period

Unit Roundup

- The *IFRS for SMEs* covers the **form and content** of financial statements. The main components are:
    - Statement of financial position
    - Statement of comprehensive income
    - Statement of changes in equity
    - Statement of cash flows (see Unit 20)
    - Notes to the financial statements

- Each component must be **identified clearly**.

- The Implementation guidance to the IFRS for SMEs suggests **formats** for the statement of financial position and statement of comprehensive income, but these are not rigid. Certain items are specified, however, for **disclosure on the face of the financial statements.**

- You should appreciate the distinction between **current and non-current** assets and liabilities and their different treatments.

- The IFRS for SMEs requires all items of income and expense in a period to be shown in a **statement of comprehensive income** or in certain circumstances a separate income statement and statement of other comprehensive income

- There are **two** possible formats for the income statement section of the statement of comprehensive income – by function or by nature. Classification by function is more common.

- The IFRS for SMEs requires a statement of changes in equity. This shows the movement in the equity section of the statement of financial position. A full set of financial statements includes a statement of changes in equity. However in certain circumstances only a statement of income and retained earnings is required.

Quick Quiz

1   Which of the following are examples of current assets?

(a)   Property, plant and equipment
(b)   Prepayments
(c)   Cash equivalents
(d)   Manufacturing licences
(e)   Retained earnings

2   Provisions must be disclosed in the statement of financial position.

True ☐

False ☐

3   Which of the following must be disclosed on the face of the income statement?

(a)   Tax expense
(b)   Analysis of expenses
(c)   Net profit or loss for the period.

4   What is the alternative to a statement of changes in equity for an SME and when can it be used in the financial statements?

1   (b) and (c) only

2   True

3   (a) and (c) only. (b) may be shown in the notes.

4   The alternative is a statement of income and retained earnings. This can be used when the only changes to equity during the periods for which financial statements are presented arise from profit or loss, payment of dividends, corrections of prior period errors, and changes in accounting policy.

Now try the question below

Wislon Co   45 mins

The accountant of Wislon Co has prepared the following list of account balances as at 31 December 20X7.

	$'000
50c ordinary shares (fully paid)	450
10% debentures (secured)	200
Retained earnings 1.1.X7	242
General reserve 1.1.X7	171
Land and buildings 1.1.X7 (cost)	430
Plant and machinery 1.1.X7 (cost)	830
Accumulated depreciation	
Buildings 1.1.X7	20
Plant and machinery 1.1.X7	222
Inventory 1.1.X7	190
Sales	2,695
Purchases	2,152
Ordinary dividend	15
Debenture interest	10
Wages and salaries	254
Light and heat	31
Sundry expenses	113
Suspense account	135
Trade accounts receivable	179
Trade accounts payable	195
Cash	126

Notes

(a)   Sundry expenses include $9,000 paid in respect of insurance for the year ending 1 September 20X8. Light and heat does not include an invoice of $3,000 for electricity for the three months ending 2 January 20X8, which was paid in February 20X8. Light and heat also includes $20,000 relating to salesmen's commission.

(b)   The suspense account is in respect of the following items.

	$'000
Proceeds from the issue of 100,000 ordinary shares	120
Proceeds from the sale of plant	300
	420
Less consideration for the purchase of land	285
	135

(c)   The plant which was sold had cost $350,000 and had a net book value of $274,000 as on 1.1.X7. $36,000 depreciation is to be charged on plant and machinery and $2,000 on buildings for 20X7.

(d)   The management wish to provide for:

     (i)   Debenture interest due

     (ii)   A transfer to general reserve of $16,000

     (iii)   Audit fees of $4,000

(e)   Inventory as at 31 December 20X7 was valued at $220,000 (cost).

(f)   Taxation is to be ignored.

Required

Prepare the financial statements of Wislon Co as at 31 December 20X7. You do not need to produce notes to the statements.

(25 marks)

Answer

Wislon Co

(a)   Normal adjustments are needed for accruals and prepayments (insurance, light and heat, debenture interest and audit fees). The debenture interest accrued is calculated as follows.

	$'000
Charge needed in income statement (10% × $200,000)	20
Amount paid so far, as shown in list of account balances	10
Accrual: presumably six months' interest now payable	10

The accrued expenses shown in the statement of financial position comprise:

	$'000
Debenture interest	10
Light and heat	3
Audit fee	4
	17

(b)   The misposting of $20,000 to light and heat is also adjusted, by reducing the light and heat expense, but charging $20,000 to salesmen's commission.

(c)   The carrying value of the land and buildings is calculated at the end of the year as:

	$000
Cost b/f	430
Additions	285
Depreciation b/f	(20)
Depreciation for year	(2)
	693

(d)   The profit on disposal of plant is calculated as proceeds $300,000 (per suspense account) less carrying value $274,000, ie $26,000. The cost of the remaining plant is calculated at $830,000 – $350,000 = $480,000. The depreciation provision at the year end is:

	$'000
Balance 1.1.X7	222
Charge for 20X7	36
Less depreciation on disposals (350 – 274)	(76)
	182

(e)   The other item in the suspense account is dealt with as follows.

	$'000
Proceeds of issue of 100,000 ordinary shares	120
Less nominal value 100,000 × 50c	50
Excess of consideration over par value (= share premium)	70

(f)   The transfer to general reserve increases it to $171,000 + $16,000 = $187,000.

    We can now prepare the financial statements.

WISLON CO
STATEMENT OF COMPREHENSIVE INCOME FOR THE YEAR ENDED 31 DECEMBER 20X7

	$'000
Revenue	2,695
Cost of sales (W1)	(2,122)
Gross profit	573
Other income (profit on disposal of plant)	26
Administrative expenses (W2)	(437)
Finance costs	(20)
Profit for the year	142

Note

There were no items of 'other comprehensive income' for the year therefore only an income statement was required.

Workings

1   *Cost of sales*

	$'000
Opening inventory	190
Purchases	2,152
Closing inventory	(220)
	2,156

2   *Administrative expenses*

	$'000
Wages, salaries and commission (254 + 20)	274
Sundry expenses (113 – 6)	107
Light and heat (31 – 20 + 3)	14
Depreciation: buildings	2
plant	36
Audit fees	4
	437

WISLON CO
STATEMENT OF FINANCIAL POSITION AS AT 31 DECEMBER 20X7

	$'000	$'000
Assets		
Current assets		
Cash		126
Trade accounts receivable		179
Prepayments		6
Inventory		220
		531
Non-current assets		
Property, plant and equipment		
Land and buildings		693
Plant: cost	480	
Accumulated depreciation	(182)	
		298
Total assets		1,522

	$'000	$'000
Liabilities and equity		
Current liabilities		
Trade accounts payable		195
Accrued expenses		17
		212
Non-current liabilities		
10% loan stock (secured)		200
Total liabilities		412
Equity		
50c ordinary shares	500	
Share premium	70	
General reserve	187	
Retained earnings	353	
		1,110
Total equity and liabilities		1,522

WISLON CO
STATEMENT OF CHANGES IN EQUITY
FOR THE YEAR ENDED 31 DECEMBER 20X7

	Share capital $'000	Share premium $'000	Retained earnings $'000	General reserve $'000	Total $'000
Balance at 1.1.X7	450	–	242	171	863
Issue of share capital	50	70			120
Dividends			(15)		(15)
Total comprehensive income for the year			142		142
Transfer to reserve			(16)	16	
Balance at 31.12.X7	500	70	353	187	1,110

Part B

Reporting financial
performance

Reporting financial performance

4

Unit topic list

1 Accounting policies
2 Changes in accounting policies
3 Errors
4 Revenue recognition
5 Examples of revenue recognition

Assessment criteria

4 Understand and apply IFRS for SMEs in the preparation of their financial statements

4.4 Understand the use of accounting policies, estimates and treatment of errors as per section 10 of the IFRS for SMEs

4.15 Understand and apply section 23 of IFRS for SMEs when an SME accounts for its revenue

1 Accounting policies

The *IFRS for SMEs* deals with the treatment of changes in accounting estimates, changes in accounting policies and errors.

1.1 Definitions

The following definitions are given in the standard. Apart from the definition of accounting policies, most of the definitions are either new or heavily amended.

- **Accounting policies** are the specific principles, bases, conventions, rules and practices applied by an entity in preparing and presenting financial statements.

- A **change in accounting estimate** is an adjustment of the carrying amount of an asset or a liability or the amount of the periodic consumption of an asset, that results from the assessment of the present status of, and expected future benefits and obligations associated with, assets and liabilities. Changes in accounting estimates result from new information or new developments and, accordingly, are not corrections of errors.

- **Prior period errors** are omissions from, and misstatements in, the entity's financial statements for one or more prior periods arising from a failure to use, or misuse of, reliable information that:
  - Was available when financial statements for those periods were authorised for issue, and
  - Could reasonably be expected to have been obtained and taken into account in the preparation and presentation of those financial statements.

  Such errors include the effects of mathematical mistakes, mistakes in applying accounting policies, oversights or misinterpretations of facts, and fraud.

1.2 Accounting policies

If the IFRS for SMEs specifically addresses a transaction, other event or condition, then this policy should be applied.

However if the IFRS does not specifically address a transaction, other event or condition, then management shall use its judgement in developing and applying an accounting policy that results in information that is:

(a) **relevant** to the economic decision-making needs of users, and
(b) **reliable**.

In making this judgement management shall refer to, and consider the applicability of, the following sources in descending order:

(a) the requirements and guidance in this IFRS dealing with similar and related issues, and
(b) the definitions, **recognition** criteria and **measurement** concepts for assets, liabilities, income and expenses and the pervasive principles outlined earlier.

Management may also consider the requirements and guidance in **full IFRSs** dealing with similar and related issues.

2 Changes in accounting policies

Changes in accounting policy are applied **retrospectively**.

2.1 Introduction

The same accounting policies are usually adopted from period to period, to allow users to analyse trends over time in profit, cash flows and financial position. **Changes in accounting policy will therefore be rare** and should be made only if:

(a)   Required by changes to the IFRS for SMEs

(b)   If the change will result in providing reliable and more relevant information about the effects of events or transactions in the financial statements of the entity

The standard highlights three types of event which do not constitute changes in accounting policy.

(a)   Adopting an accounting policy for a **new type of transaction** or event not dealt with previously by the entity.

(b)   Adopting a **new accounting policy** for a transaction or event which has not occurred in the past or which was not material.

(c)   A change to the cost model when a reliable measure of fair value is no longer available (or vice versa) for an asset that this IFRS would otherwise require or permit to be measured at fair value.

Changes in accounting policy should be accounted for as follows:

(a)   an entity shall account for a change in accounting policy resulting from a change in the requirements of this IFRS in accordance with the transitional provisions, if any, specified in that amendment;

(b)   when an entity has elected to follow IAS 39 *Financial Instruments: Recognition and Measurement* instead of following Section 11 *Basic Financial Instruments* and Section 12 *Other Financial Instruments Issues* as permitted by the IFRS, and the requirements of IAS 39 change, the entity shall account for that change in accounting policy in accordance with the transitional provisions, if any, specified in the revised IAS 39; and

(c)   an entity shall account for all other changes in accounting policy **retrospectively**

Retrospective application means that the new accounting policy is applied to transactions and events as if it had always been in use. In other words, at the earliest date such transactions or events occurred, the policy is applied from that date.

When it is **impracticable** to determine the individual-period effects of a change in accounting policy on comparative information for one or more prior periods presented, then the new accounting policy should be applied to the carrying amounts of assets and liabilities as at the beginning of the earliest period for which retrospective application is practicable.

2.2 Disclosure requirements

Certain **disclosures** are required when a change in accounting policy has a material effect on the current period or any prior period presented, or when it may have a material effect in subsequent periods.

(a)   Reasons for the change

(b)   Amount of the adjustment for the current period and for each period presented

(c)   Amount of the adjustment relating to periods prior to those included in the comparative information

(d)   The fact that comparative information has been restated or that it is impracticable to do so

2.3 Changes in accounting estimates

Changes in accounting estimate are **not** applied retrospectively.

Estimates arise in relation to business activities because of the **uncertainties inherent within them**. Judgements are made based on the most up to date information and the use of such estimates is a necessary part of the preparation of financial statements. It does not undermine their reliability. Here are some examples of accounting estimates.

(a)   A necessary **irrecoverable debt allowance**
(b)   **Useful lives** of depreciable assets
(c)   Provision for **obsolescence of inventory**

The rule here is that the **effect of a change in an accounting estimate** should be included in the determination of net profit or loss in one of:

(a)   The period of the change, if the change affects that period only
(b)   The period of the change and future periods, if the change affects both

Changes may occur in the circumstances which were in force at the time the estimate was calculated, or perhaps additional information or subsequent developments have come to light.

An example of a change in accounting estimate which affects only the **current period** is the irrecoverable debt estimate. However, a revision in the life over which an asset is depreciated would affect both the **current and future periods**, in the amount of the depreciation expense.

Reasonably enough, the effect of a change in an accounting estimate should be included in the **same expense classification** as was used previously for the estimate. This rule helps to ensure **consistency** between the financial statements of different periods.

The **materiality** of the change is also relevant. The nature and amount of a change in an accounting estimate that has a material effect in the current period (or which is expected to have a material effect in subsequent periods) should be disclosed. If it is not possible to quantify the amount, this impracticability should be disclosed.

3 Errors

Prior period errors must be corrected **retrospectively**.

3.1 Introduction

Errors discovered during a current period which **relate to a prior period** may arise through:

(a)   Mathematical mistakes
(b)   Mistakes in the application of accounting policies
(c)   Misinterpretation of facts
(d)   Oversights
(e)   Fraud

A more formal definition is given in the Key Terms in Paragraph 1.1.

Most of the time these errors can be **corrected through net profit or loss for the current period**. Where they are material prior period errors, however, this is not appropriate. The standard considers two possible treatments.

3.2 Accounting treatment

Where it is practicable a material prior period error should be corrected retrospectively in the first financial statements authorised for issue after its discovery by:

(a)   restating the comparative amounts for the prior period(s) presented in which the error occurred, or

(b)   if the error occurred before the earliest prior period presented, restating the opening balances of assets, liabilities and equity for the earliest prior period presented.

Where it is impracticable to determine the period-specific effects of an error on comparative information for one or more prior periods presented, then the opening balances of assets, liabilities and equity for the earliest period for which retrospective restatement is practicable (which may be the current period) should be restated.

Activity

During 20X7 Global discovered that certain items had been included in inventory at 31 December 20X6, valued at $4,200, which had in fact been sold before the year end. The following figures for 20X6 (as reported) and 20X7 (draft) are available.

	20X7 (draft) $	20X6 $
Sales	67,200	47,400
Cost of goods sold	(55,800)	(34,570)
Profit before taxation	11,400	12,830
Income taxes	(3,400)	(3,880)
Profit for the period	8,000	8,950

Retained earnings at 1 January 20X6 were $13,000. The cost of goods sold for 20X7 includes the $4,200 error in opening inventory. The income tax rate was 30% for 20X6 and 20X7. No dividends have been declared or paid.

Required

Show the statement of comprehensive income for 20X7, with the 20X6 comparative, and retained earnings.

Answer

STATEMENT OF COMPREHENSIVE INCOME

	20X7 $	20X6 $
Sales	67,200	47,400
Cost of goods sold (W1)	(51,600)	(38,770)
Profit before tax	15,600	8,630
Income tax (W2)	(4,660)	(2,620)
Profit for the year	10,940	6,010

RETAINED EARNINGS

	20X7 $	20X6 $
Opening retained earnings		
As previously reported	21,950	13,000
Correction of prior period error (4,200 – 1,260)	(2,940)	–
As restated	19,010	13,000
Profit for the year	10,940	6,010
Closing retained earnings	29,950	19,010

Workings

1 Cost of goods sold

	20X7 $	20X6 $
As stated in question	55,800	34,570
Inventory adjustment	(4,200)	4,200
	51,600	38,770

2 Income tax

	20X7 $	20X6 $
As stated in question	3,400	3,880
Inventory adjustment (4,200 × 30%)	1,260	(1,260)
	4,660	2,620

Activity

On 18 February 20X8 Random Co discovered that, as a result of a system error, depreciation expense for 20X7 is overstated by $15,000. The company's 31 December 20X7 financial statements were authorised for issue on 12 February 20X8. The entity must:

A   reissue its 31 December 20X7 financial statements with the correct depreciation expense.

B   reduce depreciation for the year ended 31 December 20X8 by $15,000

C   restate the depreciation expense reported for the year ended 31 December 20X7 in the comparative figures of its 20X8 financial statements

Answer

The correct answer is C.

Activity

Which of the following is a change in accounting policy?

A   A company changes the basis on which it measures an investment property from the fair value model to the cost model because fair value can no longer be measured reliably without undue cost or effort.

B   A company changes the method applied when costing inventory from the weighted average method to the first in first out method.

C   In the current reporting period a company changes the method on which it calculates depreciation of buildings, classified as property, plant and equipment, from the reducing balance method to the straight-line method.

Answer

The correct answer is B.

4 Revenue recognition

Revenue recognition is straightforward in most business transactions, but some situations are more complicated and some give opportunities for manipulation.

4.1 Introduction

Accruals accounting is based on the **matching of costs with the revenue they generate**. It is crucially important under this convention that we can establish the point at which revenue may be recognised so that the correct treatment can be applied to the related costs. For example, the costs of producing an item of finished goods should be carried as an asset in the statement of financial position until such time as it is sold; they should then be written off as a charge to the trading account. Which of these two treatments should be applied cannot be decided until it is clear at what moment the sale of the item takes place.

The decision has a **direct impact on profit** since under the prudence concept it would be unacceptable to recognise the profit on sale until a sale had taken place in accordance with the criteria of revenue recognition.

Revenue is generally recognised as **earned at the point of sale**, because at that point four criteria will generally have been met.

- The product or service has been **provided to the buyer**.
- The buyer has **recognised his liability** to pay for the goods or services provided. The converse of this is that the seller has recognised that ownership of goods has passed from himself to the buyer.
- The buyer has indicated his **willingness to hand over cash** or other assets in settlement of his liability.
- The **monetary value** of the goods or services has been established.

At earlier points in the business cycle there will not in general be **firm evidence** that the above criteria will be met. Until work on a product is complete, there is a risk that some flaw in the manufacturing process will necessitate its writing off; even when the product is complete there is no guarantee that it will find a buyer.

At later points in the business cycle, for example when cash is received for the sale, the recognition of revenue may occur in a period later than that in which the related costs were charged. Revenue recognition would then depend on fortuitous circumstances, such as the cash flow of a company's customers, and might fluctuate misleadingly from one period to another.

However, there are times when revenue is **recognised at other times than at the completion of a sale**. For example, in the recognition of profit on long-term construction contracts where contract revenue and contract costs associated with the construction contract should be recognised as revenue and expenses respectively by reference to the stage of completion of the contract activity at the end of the reporting period.

(a) Owing to the length of time taken to complete such contracts, to defer taking profit into account until completion may result in the statement of comprehensive income reflecting, not so much a fair view of the activity of the company during the year, but rather the results relating to contracts which have been completed by the year end.

(b) Revenue in this case is recognised when production on, say, a section of the total contract is complete, even though no sale can be made until the whole is complete.

4.2 Scope

The *IFRS for SMEs* covers the revenue from specific types of transaction or events.

- **Sale of goods** (manufactured products and items purchased for resale)
- **Rendering of services**
- **Construction contracts** (considered in detail in Unit 5)
- Use by others of entity assets yielding **interest, royalties and dividends**

Interest, royalties and dividends are included as income because they arise from the use of an entity's assets by other parties.

Key terms

Interest is the charge for the use of cash or cash equivalents or amounts due to the entity.

Royalties are charges for the use of non-current assets of the entity, eg patents, computer software and trademarks.

Dividends are distributions of profit to holders of equity investments, in proportion with their holdings, of each relevant class of capital.

4.3 Definitions

Revenue is the gross inflow of economic benefits during the period arising in the course of the ordinary activities of an entity when those inflows result in increases in equity, other than increases relating to contributions from equity participants.

Fair value is the amount for which an asset could be exchanged, or a liability settled, between knowledgeable, willing parties in an arm's length transaction. *(IFRS for SMEs)*

Revenue **does not include** sales taxes, value added taxes or goods and service taxes which are only collected for third parties, because these do not represent an economic benefit flowing to the entity. The same is true for revenues collected by an agent on behalf of a principal. Revenue for the agent is only the commission received for acting as agent.

4.4 Measurement of revenue

When a transaction takes place, the amount of revenue is usually decided by the **agreement of the buyer and seller**. The revenue is actually measured, however, as the **fair value of the consideration received**, which will take account of any trade discounts and volume rebates.

4.5 Identification of the transaction

Normally, each transaction can be looked at **as a whole**. Sometimes, however, transactions are more complicated, and it is necessary to break a transaction down into its **component parts**. For example, a sale may include the transfer of goods and the provision of future servicing, the revenue for which should be deferred over the period the service is performed.

At the other end of the scale, **seemingly separate transactions must be considered together** if apart they lose their commercial meaning. An example would be to sell an asset with an agreement to buy it back at a later date. The second transaction cancels the first and so both must be considered together. We looked at sale and repurchase in paragraph 4.2.

4.6 Sale of goods

Revenue from the sale of goods should only be recognised when *all* these conditions are satisfied.

(a)   The entity has transferred the **significant risks and rewards** of ownership of the goods to the buyer

(b)   The entity has **no continuing managerial involvement** to the degree usually associated with ownership, and no longer has effective control over the goods sold

(c)   The amount of revenue can be **measured reliably**

(d)   It is probable that the **economic benefits** associated with the transaction will flow to the entity

(e)   The **costs incurred** in respect of the transaction can be measured reliably

The transfer of risks and rewards can only be decided by examining each transaction. Mainly, the transfer occurs at the same time as either the **transfer of legal title**, or the **passing of possession** to the buyer – this is what happens when you buy something in a shop.

If **significant risks and rewards remain with the seller**, then the transaction is *not* a sale and revenue cannot be recognised, for example if the receipt of the revenue from a particular sale depends on the buyer receiving revenue from his own sale of the goods.

It is possible for the seller to retain only an **'insignificant' risk of ownership** and for the sale and revenue to be recognised. The main example here is where the seller retains title only to ensure collection of what is owed on the goods. This is a common commercial situation, and when it arises the revenue should be recognised on the date of sale.

The probability of the entity receiving the revenue arising from a transaction must be assessed. It may only become probable that the economic benefits will be received when an uncertainty is removed, for example government permission for funds to be received from another country. Only when the uncertainty is removed should the revenue be recognised. This is in contrast with the situation where revenue has already been recognised but where the **collectability of the cash** is brought into doubt. Where recovery has ceased to be probable, the amount should be recognised as an expense, *not* an adjustment of the revenue previously recognised. These points also refer to services and interest, royalties and dividends below.

Matching should take place, ie the revenue and expenses relating to the same transaction should be recognised at the same time. It is usually easy to estimate expenses at the date of sale (eg warranty costs, shipment costs, etc). Where they cannot be estimated reliably, then revenue cannot be recognised; any consideration which has already been received is treated as a liability.

4.7 Example

A washing machine sells for $500 with a one-year warranty. The dealer knows from experience that 15% of these machines develop a fault in the first year and that the average cost of repair is $100. He sells 200 machines. How does he account for this sale?

Solution

He will recognise revenue of $100,000 ($500 × 200) and an associated expense of $3,000 ($100 × 200 × 15%).

4.8 Servicing fees included in the price

The sales price of a product may include an identifiable amount for subsequent servicing. In this case, that amount is deferred and recognised as revenue over the period during which the service is performed. The amount deferred must cover the cost of those services together with a reasonable profit on those services.

4.9 Example

A computerised accountancy package is sold with one year's after sales support. The cost of providing support to one customer for one year is calculated to be $50. The company has a mark-up on cost of 15%. The product is sold for $350. How is this sale accounted for?

Solution

$57.50 (50 + (50 × 15%)) will be treated as deferred income and recognised over the course of the year.

The remaining $292.50 will be treated as revenue.

4.10 Rendering of services

When the outcome of a transaction involving the rendering of services can be estimated reliably, the associated revenue should be recognised by reference to the **stage of completion of the transaction** at the end of the reporting period. The outcome of a transaction can be estimated reliably when *all* these conditions are satisfied.

(a)   The amount of revenue can be **measured reliably**

(b)   It is probable that the **economic benefits** associated with the transaction will flow to the entity

(c)   The **stage of completion** of the transaction at the end of the reporting period can be measured reliably

(d)   The **costs incurred** for the transaction and the costs to complete the transaction can be measured reliably

The parties to the transaction will normally have to agree the following before an entity can make reliable estimates.

(a)   Each party's **enforceable rights** regarding the service to be provided and received by the parties

(b)   The **consideration** to be exchanged

(c)   The **manner and terms of settlement**

There are various methods of determining the stage of completion of a transaction, but for practical purposes, when services are performed by an indeterminate number of acts over a period of time, revenue should be recognised on a **straight line basis** over the period, unless there is evidence for the use of a more appropriate method. If one act is of more significance than the others, then the significant act should be carried out *before* revenue is recognised.

In uncertain situations, when the outcome of the transaction involving the rendering of services cannot be estimated reliably, the standard recommends a **no loss/no gain approach**. Revenue is recognised only to the extent of the expenses recognised that are recoverable.

This is particularly likely during the **early stages of a transaction**, but it is still probable that the entity will recover the costs incurred. So the revenue recognised in such a period will be equal to the expenses incurred, with no profit.

Obviously, if the costs are not likely to be reimbursed, then they must be recognised as an expense immediately. **When the uncertainties cease to exist**, revenue should be recognised as laid out in the first paragraph of this section.

4.11 Interest, royalties and dividends

When others use the entity's assets yielding interest, royalties and dividends, the revenue should be recognised on the bases set out below when:

(a)   it is probable that the **economic benefits** associated with the transaction will flow to the entity; and

(b)   the amount of the revenue can be **measured reliably**.

The revenue is recognised on the following bases.

(a)   **Interest** is recognised on a time proportion basis that takes into account the effective yield on the asset. This is known as the effective interest method.

(b)   **Royalties** are recognised on an accruals basis in accordance with the substance of the relevant agreement

(c)   **Dividends** are recognised when the shareholder's right to receive payment is established

It is unlikely that you would be asked about anything as complex as this in the exam, but you should be aware of the basic requirements of the standard. The **effective yield** on an asset mentioned above is the rate of interest required to discount the stream of future cash receipts expected over the life of the asset to equate to the initial carrying amount of the asset.

Royalties are usually recognised on the same basis that they accrue **under the relevant agreement**. Sometimes the true substance of the agreement may require some other systematic and rational method of recognition.

Once again, the points made above about **probability and collectability** on sale of goods also apply here.

4.12 Disclosure

The following items should be disclosed.

(a)   The **accounting policies** adopted for the recognition of revenue, including the methods used to determine the stage of completion of transactions involving the rendering of services

(b)   The amount of each **significant category of revenue** recognised during the period including revenue arising from:

(i)   The sale of goods
(ii)   The rendering of services
(iii)   Interest
(iv)   Royalties
(v)   Dividends
(vi)   Commissions
(vii)   Government grants
(viii) Any other significant types of revenue.

5 Examples of revenue recognition

The section of the IFRS for SMEs that deals with revenue recognition is followed by an appendix which provides examples of revenue recognition. This appendix is provided as revenue recognition is traditionally thought to be a 'grey area' of accounting, open to subjectivity. The provision of the appendix therefore reduces the scope for manipulation.

The following examples are drawn from the appendix:

 ## 5.1 Example

Alpha manufactures and installs mechanical ventilation systems. On 31 March 20X9, Alpha delivers a unit to a customer, Zeta Co. Alpha's engineer returns to the Zeta premises on 25 April 20X9 in order to undertake the specialised installation of the unit.

On which date should Alpha record the revenue resulting from the sale to Zeta?

Solution

Where installation of goods is a simple process which can be undertaken by the buyer, the seller recognises revenue upon delivery.

In this case, however, specialised installation is necessary and therefore Alpha does not recognise the revenue associated with the sale until that installation is complete on 25 April.

 ## 5.2 Example

Moorfield delivers goods to Westville on a consignment sales basis. That is, Westville undertakes to sell the goods on behalf of Moorfield. Any goods which remain unsold after a 3 month period are returned to Moorfield.

At what stage should Moorfield recognise revenue in respect of the consignment sales?

Solution

The risks and rewards of ownership are not transferred to Westville upon delivery of the goods and therefore no revenue should be recognised at this stage. In fact the risks and rewards of ownership are only transferred by Moorfield when Westville achieves a sale to a third party within the 3 month period. Therefore Moorfield should only recognise revenue when this takes place.

 ## 5.3 Example

Nande Cost is a magazine publisher. It enters into an agreement with a customer to supply a periodical on a monthly basis throughout 20X9. The customer is required to pay the full cost of the subscription in advance.

How should Nande Cost account for the revenue arising from the subscription agreement?

Solution

Revenue should be recognised by Nande Cost on a straight line basis over the period in which the periodicals are dispatched.

Unit Roundup

- The IFRS for SMEs deals with the treatment of changes in accounting estimates, changes in accounting policies and errors.

- Changes in accounting policy are applied retrospectively.

- Changes in accounting estimate are not applied retrospectively.

- Prior period errors must be corrected retrospectively.

- Revenue recognition is straightforward in most business transactions, but some situations are more complicated and give some opportunities for manipulation.

Quick Quiz

1   How should a prior period error be corrected?

2   Give two circumstances when a change in accounting policy might be required.

3   When should a transaction be recognised?

1   By adjusting the opening balance of retained earnings.

2   (a)   By a change in the *IFRS for SMEs*
     (b)   For a reliable and more relevant presentation of information

3   When it is probable that a future inflow or outflow of economic benefit to the entity will occur and the item can be measured in monetary terms with sufficient reliability.

Now try the question below

Prudence   18 mins

Given that prudence is the main consideration, discuss under what circumstances, if any, revenue might be recognised at the following stages of a sale.

(a)   Goods are acquired by the business which it confidently expects to resell very quickly.
(b)   A customer places a firm order for goods.
(c)   Goods are delivered to the customer.
(d)   The customer is invoiced for goods.
(e)   The customer pays for the goods.
(f)   The customer's cheque in payment for the goods has been cleared by the bank.

(10 marks)

Answer

Prudence

(a) A sale must never be recognised before the goods have even been ordered by a customer. There is no certainty about the value of the sale, nor when it will take place, even if it is virtually certain that goods will be sold.

(b) A sale must never be recognised when the customer places an order. Even though the order will be for a specific quantity of goods at a specific price, it is not yet certain that the sale transaction will go through. The customer may cancel the order, the supplier might be unable to deliver the goods as ordered or it may be decided that the customer is not a good credit risk.

(c) A sale will be recognised when delivery of the goods is made only when:

    (i)   the sale is for cash, and so the cash is received at the same time; or
    (ii)   the sale is on credit and the customer accepts delivery (eg by signing a delivery note).

(d) The critical event for a credit sale is usually the despatch of an invoice to the customer. There is then a legally enforceable debt, payable on specified terms, for a completed sale transaction.

(e) The critical event for a cash sale is when delivery takes place and when cash is received; both take place at the same time.

It would be too cautious or 'prudent' to await cash payment for a credit sale transaction before recognising the sale, unless the customer is a high credit risk and there is a serious doubt about his ability or intention to pay.

(f) It would again be over-cautious to wait for clearance of the customer's cheques before recognising sales revenue. Such a precaution would only be justified in cases where there is a very high risk of the bank refusing to honour the cheque.

Inventories and construction contracts

5

Unit topic list

1   Inventories and short term WIP
2   Construction contracts

Assessment criteria

4   Understand and apply IFRS for SMEs in the preparation of their financial statements

4.6   Understand and apply section 12 of IFRS for SMEs for recognising and measuring inventories

Understand and apply section 23 of IFRS for SMEs when an SME accounts for its revenue in relation to construction contracts

1 Inventories and short-term WIP

1.1 Introduction

In most businesses the value put on inventory is an important factor in the determination of profit. Inventory valuation is, however, a highly subjective exercise and consequently there is a wide variety of different methods used in practice.

1.2 Inventories

The *IFRS for SMEs* lays out the required accounting treatment for inventories (sometimes called stocks) under the historical cost system. The major area of contention is the cost **value of inventory** to be recorded. This is recognised as an asset of the entity until the related revenues are recognised (ie the item is sold) at which point the inventory is recognised as an expense (ie cost of sales). Part or all of the cost of inventories may also be expensed if a write-down to **net realisable value** is necessary. The IFRS also provides guidance on the cost formulas that are used to assign costs to inventories.

In other words, the fundamental accounting assumption of **accruals** requires costs to be matched with associated revenues. In order to achieve this, costs incurred for goods which remain unsold at the year end must be carried forward in the statement of financial position and matched against future revenues.

1.3 Definitions

The IFRS gives the following important definitions.

> - **Inventories** are assets:
>   - held for sale in the ordinary course of business;
>   - in the process of production for such sale; or
>   - in the form of materials or supplies to be consumed in the production process or in the rendering of services.
>
> - **Fair value** is the amount for which an asset could be exchanged or a liability settled between knowledgeable, willing parties in an arm's length transaction. *(IFRS for SMEs)*

Inventories can **include** any of the following.

- **Goods purchased and held for resale**, eg goods held for sale by a retailer, or land and buildings held for resale
- **Finished goods** produced
- **Work in progress** being produced
- Materials and supplies awaiting use in the production process (**raw materials**)

1.4 Measurement of inventories

The standard states that '**Inventories should be measured at the lower of cost and estimated selling price less costs to complete and sell**.' Estimated selling price less costs to complete and sell is often known as net realisable value (NRV).

> This is a very important rule and you will be expected to apply it in the exam.

1.5 Cost of inventories

The cost of inventories will consist of all costs of:

- **Purchase**
- **Costs of conversion**
- **Other costs** incurred in bringing the inventories to their **present location and condition**

1.5.1 Costs of purchase

The IFRS lists the following as comprising the costs of purchase of inventories:

- **Purchase price** *plus*
- **Import duties** and other taxes *plus*
- Transport, handling and any other cost **directly attributable** to the acquisition of finished goods, services and materials *less*
- **Trade discounts**, rebates and other similar amounts

1.5.2 Costs of conversion

Costs of conversion of inventories consist of two main parts.

(a) Costs **directly related** to the units of production, eg direct materials, direct labour

(b) Fixed and variable **production overheads** that are incurred in converting materials into finished goods, allocated on a systematic basis.

You may have come across the terms 'fixed production overheads' or 'variable production overheads' elsewhere in your studies. The IFRS defines them as follows.

Key terms

- **Fixed production overheads** are those indirect costs of production that remain relatively constant regardless of the volume of production, eg the cost of factory management and administration.

- **Variable production overheads** are those indirect costs of production that vary directly, or nearly directly, with the volume of production, eg indirect materials and labour.

The IFRS emphasises that fixed production overheads must be allocated to items of inventory on the basis of the **normal capacity of the production facilities**. This is an important point.

(a) **Normal capacity** is the expected achievable production based on the average over several periods/seasons, under normal circumstances.

(b) The above figure should take account of the capacity lost through **planned maintenance**.

(c) If it approximates to the normal level of activity then the **actual level of production** can be used.

(d) **Low production** or **idle plant** will *not* result in a higher fixed overhead allocation to each unit.

(e) **Unallocated overheads** must be recognised as an expense in the period in which they were incurred.

(f) When production is **abnormally high**, the fixed production overhead allocated to each unit will be reduced, so avoiding inventories being stated at more than cost.

(g) The allocation of variable production overheads to each unit is based on the **actual use** of production facilities.

1.5.3 Other costs

Any other costs should only be recognised if they are incurred in bringing the inventories to their **present location and condition**.

The IFRS lists types of cost which **would not be included** in cost of inventories. Instead, they should be recognised as an **expense** in the period they are incurred.

(a) **Abnormal amounts** of wasted materials, labour or other production costs

(b) **Storage costs** (except costs which are necessary in the production process before a further production stage)

(c) **Administrative overheads** not incurred to bring inventories to their present location and conditions

(d) **Selling costs**

1.5.4 Techniques for the measurement of cost

Two techniques are mentioned by the IFRS, both of which produce results which **approximate to cost**, and so both of which may be used for convenience.

(a) **Standard costs** are set up to take account of normal production values: amount of raw materials used, labour time etc. They are reviewed and revised on a regular basis.

(b) **Retail method**: this is often used in the retail industry where there is a large turnover of inventory items, which nevertheless have similar profit margins. The only practical method of inventory valuation may be to take the total selling price of inventories and deduct an overall average profit margin, thus reducing the value to an approximation of cost. The percentage will take account of reduced price lines. Sometimes different percentages are applied on a department basis.

1.6 Cost formulas

Cost of inventories should be assigned by **specific identification** of their individual costs for:

(a) Items that are **not ordinarily interchangeable**
(b) Goods or services produced and segregated for **specific projects**

Specific costs should be attributed to individual items of inventory when they are segregated for a specific project, but not where inventories consist of a large number of interchangeable (ie identical or very similar) items. In the latter case the rule is as specified below.

1.6.1 Interchangeable items

> **Rule to learn**
>
> The cost of inventories should be assigned by using the **first-in, first-out (FIFO)** or **weighted average** cost formulas, although only the first of these is examinable. The LIFO formula (last in, first out) is **not permitted** by the *IFRS for SMEs*.

1.7 FIFO (first in, first out)

FIFO assumes that materials are **issued out of inventory in the order in which they were delivered into inventory**, ie issues are priced at the cost of the earliest delivery remaining in inventory.

The cost of issues and closing inventory value in the example, using FIFO, would be as follows (note that OI stands for opening inventory).

Date of issue	Quantity Units	Value issued	Cost of issues $	$
4 May	200	100 OI at $2	200	
		100 at $2.10	210	
				410
11 May	400	300 at $2.10	630	
		100 at $2.12	212	
				842
20 May	100	100 at $2.12		212
				1,464
Closing inventory value	200	100 at $2.12	212	
		100 at $2.40	240	
				452
				1,916

Note that the cost of materials issued plus the value of closing inventory equals the cost of purchases plus the value of opening inventory ($1,916).

1.8 Estimated selling price less costs to complete and sell (NRV)

As a general rule assets should not be carried at amounts greater than those expected to be realised from their sale or use. In the case of inventories this amount could fall below cost when items are **damaged or become obsolete**, or where the **costs to completion have increased** in order to make the sale.

In fact we can identify the principal situations in which **NRV is likely to be less than cost**, ie where there has been:

(a)   An **increase in costs** or a **fall in selling price**

(b)   A **physical deterioration** in the condition of inventory

(c)   **Obsolescence** of products

(d)   A decision as part of the company's marketing strategy to manufacture and sell products at a **loss**

(e)   **Errors in production or purchasing**

A write down of inventories would normally take place on an item by item basis, but similar or related items may be **grouped together**. This grouping together is acceptable for, say, items in the same product line, but it is not acceptable to write down inventories based on a whole classification (eg finished goods) or a whole business.

The assessment of NRV should take place **at the same time** as estimates are made of selling price, using the most reliable information available. Fluctuations of price or cost should be taken into account if they relate directly to **events after the reporting period,** which confirm conditions existing at the end of the period.

The reasons why inventory is held must also be taken into account. Some inventory, for example, may be held to satisfy a firm contract and its NRV will therefore be the **contract price**. Any additional inventory of the same type held at the period end will, in contrast, be assessed according to general sales prices when NRV is estimated.

Net realisable value must be reassessed at the end of each period and compared again with cost. If the NRV has risen for inventories held over the end of more than one period, then the previous write down must be **reversed** to the extent that the inventory is then valued at the lower of cost and the new NRV. This may be possible when selling prices have fallen in the past and then risen again.

On occasion a write down to NRV may be of such size, incidence or nature that it must be **disclosed separately**.

1.9 Recognition as an expense

The following treatment is required **when inventories are sold**.

(a)   The **carrying amount** is recognised as an expense in the period in which the related revenue is recognised

(b)   The amount of any **write-down of inventories** to NRV and all losses of inventories are recognised as an expense in the period the write-down or loss occurs

(c)   The amount of any **reversal of any write-down of inventories**, arising from an increase in NRV, is recognised as a reduction in the amount of inventories recognised as an expense in the period in which the reversal occurs

Activity

You are the accountant at Water Pumps and you have been asked to calculate the valuation of the company's inventory at cost at its year end of 30 April 20X5.

Water Pumps manufactures a range of pumps. The pumps are assembled from components bought by Water Pumps (the company does not manufacture any parts).

The company does not use a standard costing system, and work in progress and finished goods are valued as follows.

(a) Material costs are determined from the product specification, which lists the components required to make a pump.

(b) The company produces a range of pumps. Employees record the hours spent on assembling each type of pump, this information is input into the payroll system which prints the total hours spent each week assembling each type of pump. All employees assembling pumps are paid at the same rate and there is no overtime.

(c) Overheads are added to the inventory value in accordance with the *IFRS for SMEs*. The financial accounting records are used to determine the overhead cost, and this is applied as a percentage based on the direct labour cost.

For direct labour costs, you have agreed that the labour expended for a unit in work in progress is half that of a completed unit.

The draft accounts show the following materials and direct labour costs in inventory.

	Raw materials	Work in progress	Finished goods
Materials ($)	74,786	85,692	152,693
Direct labour ($)		13,072	46,584

The costs incurred in April, as recorded in the financial accounting records, were as follows.

	$
Direct labour	61,320
Selling costs	43,550
Depreciation and finance costs of production machines	4,490
Distribution costs	6,570
Factory manager's wage	2,560
Other production overheads	24,820
Purchasing and accounting costs relating to production	5,450
Other accounting costs	7,130
Other administration overheads	24,770

For your calculations assume that all work in progress and finished goods were produced in April 20X5 and that the company was operating at a normal level of activity.

Required

Calculate the value of overheads which should be added to work in progress and finished goods in accordance with the *IFRS for SMEs*.

Note. You should include details and a description of your workings and all figures should be calculated to the nearest $.

Answer

Calculation of overheads for inventories

Production overheads are as follows.

	$
Depreciation/finance costs	4,490
Factory manager's wage	2,560
Other production overheads	24,820
Accounting/purchasing costs	5,450
	37,320

Direct labour = $61,320

$$\therefore \text{Production overhead rate} = \frac{37,320}{61,320} = 60.86\%$$

Inventory valuation

	Raw materials	WIP	Finished goods	Total
	$	$	$	$
Materials	74,786	85,692	152,693	313,171
Direct labour	–	13,072	46,584	59,656
Production overhead (at 60.86% of labour)	–	7,956	28,351	36,307
	74,786	106,720	227,628	409,134

2 Construction contracts

Sales revenue on a construction contract is normally based upon stage of completion.

2.1 Introduction

Imagine that you are the accountant at a construction company. Your company is building a large tower block that will house offices, under a contract with an investment company. It will take three years to build the block and over that time you will obviously have to pay for building materials, wages of workers on the building, architects' fees and so on. You will receive periodic payments from the investment company at various predetermined stages of the construction. How do you decide, in each of the three years, **what to include as income and expenditure** for the contract in the statement of comprehensive income?

2.2 Example: construction contract

A numerical example might help to illustrate the problem. Suppose that a contract is started on 1 January 20X5, with an estimated completion date of 31 December 20X6. The final contract price is $1,500,000. In the first year, to 31 December 20X5:

(a) Costs incurred amounted to $600,000.

(b) Half the work on the contract was completed.

(c) Certificates of work completed have been issued, to the value of $750,000. (*Note*. It is usual, in a construction contract, for a qualified person such as an architect or engineer to inspect the work completed, and if it is satisfactory, to issue certificates. This will then be the notification to the customer that progress payments are now due to the contractor. Progress payments are commonly the amount of valuation on the work certificates issued, minus a precautionary retention of 10%).

(d) It is estimated with reasonable certainty that further costs to completion in 20X6 will be $600,000.

What is the contract profit in 20X5, and what entries would be made for the contract at 31 December 20X5 if:

(a) Profits are deferred until the completion of the contract?

(b) A proportion of the estimated revenue and profit is credited to profit or loss in 20X5?

Solution

(a) If profits were deferred until the completion of the contract in 20X6, the revenue and profit recognised on the contract in 20X5 would be nil, and the value of work in progress on 31 December 20X5 would be $600,000. The view is that this policy is unreasonable, because in 20X6, the total profit of $300,000 would be recorded. Since the contract revenues are earned throughout 20X5 and 20X6, a profit of nil in 20X5 and $300,000 in 20X6 would be contrary to the accruals concept of accounting.

(b) **It is fairer to recognise revenue and profit throughout the duration of the contract.**

As at 31 December 20X5 revenue of $750,000 should be matched with cost of sales of $600,000 in the statement of comprehensive income, leaving an attributable profit for 20X5 of $150,000.

The only entry in the statement of financial position as at 31 December 20X5 is a receivable of $750,000 recognising that the company is owed this amount for work done to date. No balance remains for work in progress, the whole $600,000 having been recognised in cost of sales.

2.3 What is a construction contract?

A construction contract does not have to last for a period of more than one year. The main point is that the contract activity **starts in one financial period and ends in another**, thus creating the problem: to which of two or more periods should contract income and costs be allocated?

2.4 Combining and segmenting construction contracts

The IFRS lays out the factors which determine whether the construction of a **series of assets** under one contract should be treated as several contracts.

- **Separate proposals** are submitted for each asset

- **Separate negotiations** are undertaken for each asset; the customer can accept/reject each individually

- **Identifiable costs and revenues** can be separated for each asset

There are also circumstances where a **group of contracts** should be treated as **one single construction contract**.

- The group of contracts are negotiated as a **single package**
- Contracts are **closely interrelated**, with an overall profit margin
- The contracts are performed **concurrently** or **in a single sequence** on any particular contract

2.5 Recognition of contract revenue and expenses

Revenue and costs associated with a contract should be recognised according to the stage of completion of the contract at the end of the reporting period, but *only when* the **outcome of the activity can be estimated reliably**. If a loss is predicted on a contract, then it should be recognised immediately. This is often known as the **percentage of completion method**.

The **percentage of completion method** is an application of the accruals assumption. Contract revenue is matched to the contract costs incurred in reaching the stage of completion, so revenue, costs and profit are attributed to the proportion of work completed.

We can **summarise** the treatment as follows.

- Recognise **contract revenue** as revenue in the accounting periods in which the work is performed

- Recognise **contract costs** as an expense in the accounting period in which the work to which they relate is performed

- Any **expected excess** of total contract costs over total contract revenue should be recognised as an expense immediately

- Any costs incurred which relate to **future activity** should be recognised as an asset if it is probable that they will be recovered (often called contract work in progress, ie amounts due from the customer)

2.6 Determining the stage of completion

How should you decide on the stage of completion of any contract? The standard lists several methods.

- **Proportion of contract costs incurred** for work carried out to date
- **Surveys** of work carried out
- **Physical proportion** of the contract work completed

2.7 Outcome of the contract cannot be reliably estimated

When the contract's outcome cannot be reliably estimated the following treatment should be followed.

- Only recognise revenue to the extent of contract costs incurred which are expected to be **recoverable**
- Recognise contract costs as an **expense** in the period they are incurred

This **no profit/no loss approach** reflects the situation near the beginning of a contract, ie the outcome cannot be reliably estimated, but it is likely that costs will be recovered.

Contract costs which **cannot be recovered** should be recognised as an expense straight away.

2.8 Recognition of expected losses

Any loss on a contract should be **recognised as soon as it is foreseen**. The loss will be the amount by which total expected contract revenue is exceeded by total expected contract costs. The loss amount is not affected by whether work has started on the contract, the stage of completion of the work or profits on other contracts (unless they are related contracts treated as a single contract).

2.9 Section summary

In valuing long-term contracts and the other disclosures required under the *IFRS for SMEs*, an organised approach is essential. The following suggested method breaks the process down into five logical steps.

Step 1   **Compare the contract value** and the **total costs** expected to be incurred on the contract. If a loss is foreseen (that is, if the costs to date plus estimated costs to completion exceed the contract value) then it must be charged against profits. If a loss has already been charged in previous years, then only the difference between the loss as previously and currently estimated need be charged.

Step 2   Using the percentage completed to date (or other formula given in the question), calculate sales revenue **attributable** to the contract for the period (for example percentage complete × total contract value, less of course, revenue taken in previous periods).

Step 3   **Calculate the cost of sales** on the contract for the period.

	$
Total contract costs × percentage complete (or follow instructions in question)	X
Less any costs charged in previous periods	(X)
	X
Add foreseeable losses in full (not previously charged)	X
Cost of sales on contract for the period	X

Step 4   **Deduct the cost of sales** for the period as calculated above (including any foreseeable loss) from the sales revenue calculated at step 2 to give profit (loss) recognised for the period.

Step 5 **Calculate amounts due to/from** customers as below.

	$
Contract costs incurred to date	X
Recognised profits/(losses) to date	X
	X
Progress billings to date	(X)
Amounts due from/(to) customers	X

Note: This represents unbilled revenue. Unpaid billed revenue will be shown under trade receivables.

2.10 Summary of accounting treatment

The following summarises the accounting treatment for long-term contracts – **make sure that you understand it.**

2.10.1 Statement of comprehensive income (income statement)

(a) **Revenue and costs**

    (i) Sales revenue and associated costs should be recorded in the income statement section as the contract activity progresses.

    (ii) Include an appropriate proportion of total contract value as sales revenue in the income statement.

    (iii) The costs incurred in reaching that stage of completion are matched with this sales revenue, resulting in the reporting of results which can be attributed to the proportion of work completed.

    (iv) Sales revenue is the value of work carried out to date.

(b) **Profit recognised in the contract**

    (i) It must reflect the proportion of work carried out.

    (ii) It should take into account any known inequalities in profitability in the various stages of a contract.

2.10.2 Statement of financial position

(a) **Inventories**

	$
Costs to date	X
Plus recognised profits	X
	X
Less recognised losses	(X)
	X
Less progress billings	(X)
Amount due from customers	X

(b) **Receivables**

	$
Unpaid progress billings	X

(c) **Payables**. Where (a) gives a net 'amount due to customers' this amount should be included in payables under 'payments on account'.

 Activity

The main business of Santolina is construction contracts. At the end of September 20X3 there is an uncompleted contract on the books, details of which are as follows.

CONTRACT B

Date commenced	1.4.X1
Expected completion date	23.12.X3
	$
Final contract price	290,000
Costs to 30.9.X3	210,450
Value of work certified to 30.9.X3	230,000
Progress billings to 30.9.X3	210,000
Cash received to 30.9.X3	194,000
Estimated costs to completion at 30.9.X3	20,600

Required

Prepare calculations showing the amount to be included in the statement of financial position at 30 September 20X3 in respect of the above contract.

Answer

Contract B is a construction contract and will be included in the statement of financial position at cost plus attributable profit less progress billings.

The estimated final profit is:

	$
Final contract price	290,000
Less: costs to date	(210,450)
estimated future costs	(20,600)
Estimated final profit	58,950

The attributable profit is found as follows.

$$\text{Estimated final profit} \times \frac{\text{Work certified}}{\text{Total contract price}}$$

$$\$58,950 \times \frac{230,000}{290,000}$$

Attributable profit = $46,753

Long-term contract work in progress

CONTRACT B

	$
Costs to date	210,450
Attributable profit	46,753
	257,203
Progress billings	(210,000)
Amount due from customers	47,203
Trade receivables	16,000

Activity

Haggrun Co has two contracts in progress, the details of which are as follows.

	Happy (profitable) $'000	Grumpy (loss-making) $'000
Total contract price	300	300
Costs incurred to date	90	150
Estimated costs to completion	135	225
Progress payments invoiced and received	116	116

Required

Show extracts from the statement of comprehensive income and the statement of financial position for each contract, assuming they are both:

(a)   40% complete; and
(b)   36% complete.

 Answer

Happy contract

(a)   *40% complete*

	$'000
Statement of comprehensive income	
Revenue (300 × 40%)	120
Cost of sales ((90+ 135) × 40%)	(90)
Profit to date (W)	30

Working

Profit to date

	$'000
Total contract price	300
Costs to date	(90)
Cost to completion	(135)
Total expected profit	75
Profit to date (75 × 40%)	30

Statement of financial position

	$'000
Costs to date	90
Profit recognised to date	30
Progress billings	(116)
Amount due from customers	4

(b)   *36% complete*

	$'000
Statement of comprehensive income	
Revenue (300 × 36%)	108
Cost of sales (((90 + 135) × 36%))	(81)
Profit to date (75 × 36%)	27
Statement of financial position	
Costs to date	90
Profit recognised to date	27
Progress billings	(116)
Amount due from customers	1

Grumpy contract

(a)   *40% complete*

	$'000
Statement of comprehensive income	
Revenue (300 × 40%)	120
Cost of sales*	(195)
Foreseeable loss (W)	(75)

Working

	$'000
Total contract revenue	300
Costs to date	(150)
Costs to complete	(225)
Foreseeable loss	(75)

Statement of financial position

Costs to date	150
Foreseeable loss	(75)
Progress billings	(116)
Amounts due to customers	(41)

	$'000
* Costs to date (150 + 225) × 40%	150
Foreseeable loss (75) × 60%**	45
	195

** The other 40% is taken into account in costs to date. We make this adjustment to bring in the **whole** of the foreseeable loss.

(b) *36% complete*

	$'000
Statement of comprehensive income	
Revenue (300 × 36%)	108
Cost of sales*	(183)
Foreseeable loss	(75)

Statement of financial position

Costs to date	150
Foreseeable loss	(75)
Progress billings	(116)
Amount due to customers	(41)

	$'000
* Costs to date (150 + 225) × 36%	135
Foreseeable loss (75) × 64%**	48
	183

Unit roundup

- The *IFRS for SMEs* requires that the statement of financial position should show **inventories** classified in a manner appropriate to the entity. Common **classifications** are:

  Merchandise
  Production supplies
  Materials
  Work in progress
  Finished goods

- Inventory should be valued at the lower of cost and estimated selling price less costs to complete and sell, often known as net realisable value (NRV).

- The use of **LIFO** is **prohibited.** Only FIFO and average cost are generally used, although only FIFO is examinable.

- The rules for calculating accounting entries on **construction contracts** can be summarised as follows.
    - Sales revenue is based upon the stage of completion.
    - Calculate profit to date and cost of sales is a balancing figure.
    - Foreseeable losses are recognised immediately.
    - The financial position amount (amounts due from/(to) customers) is calculated as:

Costs to date	X
Profits (losses) to date	X
Progress billings	(X)
	X

Quick Quiz

1 Net realisable value = Selling price **less** .... **less** ....

2 Which inventory costing method is allowed under IFRS for SMEs?

  (a) FIFO
  (b) LIFO

3 Any expected loss on a construction contract must be recognised, in full, in the year it was identified.

  True ☐

  False ☐

4 List the five steps to be taken when valuing construction contracts.

5 Which items in the statement of comprehensive income and statement of financial position are potentially affected by construction contracts?

1   Net realisable value = selling price **less** costs to completion **less** costs necessary to make the sale.

2   (a)   FIFO. LIFO is not allowed.

3   True

4   See paragraph 2.9

5   Statement of comprehensive income: revenue and cost of sales.
       Statement of financial position: inventories, receivables, payables

Now try the question below

Sampi   18 mins

Sampi is a manufacturer of garden furniture. The company uses FIFO (first in, first out) in valuing inventory.

At 28 February 20X8 the company had an inventory of 4,000 standard plastic tables, and has computed its value as $16 per unit.

During March 20X8 the movements on the inventory of tables were as follows.

Received from factory:

	Number of units	Production cost per unit $
Date		
8 March	3,800	15
22 March	6,000	18

Sales:

	Number of units
Date	
12 March	5,000
18 March	2,000
24 March	3,000
28 March	2,000

Required

Compute what the value of the inventory at 31 March 20X8 is on the FIFO basis.

(In arriving at the total inventory values you should make calculations to two decimal places (where necessary) and deal with each inventory movement in date order.)

(10 marks)

Sampi

	Opening inventory	Transfer from factory 8 March	Transfer from factory 22 March
Cost per unit	$16	$15	$18
Number of units	4,000	3,800	6,000
Issues:			
12 March	(4,000)	(1,000)	
18 March	–	(2,000)	
24 March	–	(800)	(2,200)
28 March	–	–	(2,000)
Balance	–	–	1,800
Value			$32,400

Non-current assets

Unit topic list

1 Property, plant and equipment
2 Depreciation accounting
3 Government grants
4 Investment property
5 Borrowing costs

Assessment criteria

4   Understand and apply IFRS for SMEs in the preparation of their financial statements

4.9   Understand and apply section 16 of IFRS for SMEs when an SME is required to account for an investment which is defined as an investment property

4.10   Understand and apply section 17 of IFRS for SMEs when an SME accounts for property, plant and equipment both in its recognition and future measurement

4.16   Understand and apply section 24 of IFRS for SMEs when an SME receives Government grants

4.17   Understand and apply section 25 of IFRS for SMEs when an SME is required to account for borrowing costs

1 Property, plant and equipment

The IFRS for SMEs covers all aspects of accounting for property, plant and equipment. This represents the bulk of items which are 'tangible' non-current assets.

1.1 Definitions

We will start with some definitions.

Key terms

- **Property, plant and equipment** are tangible assets that:

    - are held for use in the production or supply of goods or services, for rental to others, or for administrative purposes; and
    - are expected to be used during more than one period.

- **Cost** is the amount of cash or cash equivalents paid or the fair value of the other consideration given to acquire an asset at the time of its acquisition or construction.

- **Residual value** is the estimated amount that an entity would currently obtain from disposal of an asset after deducting the expected costs of disposal if the asset were already of the age and in the condition expected at the end of its useful life.

- **Entity specific value** is the present value of the cash flows an entity expects to arise from the continuing use of an asset and from its disposal at the end of its useful life, or expects to incur when settling a liability.

- **Fair value** is the amount for which an asset could be exchanged between knowledgeable, willing parties in an arm's length transaction.

- **Carrying amount** is the amount at which an asset is recognised in the statement of financial position after deducting any accumulated depreciation and accumulated impairment losses.

- An **impairment loss** is the amount by which the carrying amount of an asset exceeds its recoverable amount.

1.2 Recognition

In this context, recognition simply means incorporation of the item in the business's accounts, in this case as a non-current asset. The recognition of property, plant and equipment depends on two criteria.

(a)   It is probable that **future economic benefits** associated with the asset will flow to the entity
(b)   The cost of the asset to the entity can be **measured reliably**

These recognition criteria apply to **subsequent expenditure** as well as costs incurred initially. There are no longer any separate criteria for recognising subsequent expenditure.

Property, plant and equipment can amount to **substantial amounts** in financial statements, affecting the presentation of the company's financial position and the profitability of the entity, through depreciation and also if an asset is wrongly classified as an expense and taken to profit or loss.

1.2.1 First criterion: future economic benefits

The **degree of certainty** attached to the flow of future economic benefits must be assessed. This should be based on the evidence available at the date of initial recognition (usually the date of purchase). The entity should thus be assured that it will receive the rewards attached to the asset and it will incur the associated risks, which will only generally be the case when the rewards and risks have actually passed to the entity. Until then, the asset should not be recognised.

1.2.2 Second criterion: cost measured reliably

It is generally easy to measure the cost of an asset as the **transfer amount on purchase**, ie what was paid for it. **Self-constructed assets** can also be measured easily by adding together the purchase price of all the constituent parts (labour, material etc) paid to external parties.

1.3 Separate items

Most of the time assets will be identified individually, but this will not be the case for **smaller items**, such as tools, dies and moulds, which are sometimes classified as inventory and written off as an expense.

Major components or spare parts, however, should be recognised as property, plant and equipment.

For very **large and specialised items**, an apparently single asset should be broken down into its composite parts. This occurs where the different parts have different useful lives and different depreciation rates are applied to each part, eg an aircraft, where the body and engines are separated as they have different useful lives.

1.4 Safety and environmental equipment

When such assets as these are acquired they will qualify for recognition where they enable the entity to **obtain future economic benefits** from related assets in excess of those it would obtain otherwise. The recognition will only be to the extent that the carrying amount of the asset and related assets does not exceed the total recoverable amount of these assets.

1.5 Initial measurement

Once an item of property, plant and equipment qualifies for recognition as an asset, it will initially be **measured at cost**.

1.5.1 Components of cost

The IFRS lists the components of the cost of an item of property, plant and equipment.

- **Purchase price**, less any trade discount or rebate
- **Import duties** and non-refundable purchase taxes
- **Directly attributable costs** of bringing the asset to working condition for its intended use, eg:
    - The cost of site preparation
    - Initial delivery and handling costs
    - Installation costs
    - Testing
    - Professional fees (architects, engineers)
- Initial estimate of the unavoidable cost of dismantling and removing the asset and restoring the site on which it is located

The following costs **will not be part of the cost** of property, plant or equipment unless they can be attributed directly to the asset's acquisition, or bringing it into its working condition.

- Administration and other general overhead costs
- Start-up and similar pre-production costs
- Initial operating losses before the asset reaches planned performance

All of these will be recognised as an **expense** rather than an asset.

1.5.2 Exchanges of assets

The exchange of items of property, plant and equipment, regardless of whether the assets are similar, are measured at **fair value**, **unless the exchange transaction lacks commercial substance** or the fair value of neither of the assets exchanged can be **measured reliably**. If the acquired item is not measured at fair value, its cost is measured at the carrying amount of the asset given up.

1.5.3 Replacement of components

Expenditure incurred in replacing or renewing a component of an item of property, plant and equipment must be **recognised in the carrying amount of the item**. The carrying amount of the replaced or renewed component must be derecognised. A similar approach is also applied when a separate component of an item of property, plant and equipment is identified in respect of a major inspection to enable the continued use of the item.

1.6 Measurement subsequent to initial recognition

All items of property, plant and equipment should be measured at cost less depreciation and any accumulated impairment loss.

1.7 Depreciation

The IFRS states:

- The **depreciable amount** of an item of property, plant and equipment should be allocated on a systematic basis over its useful life.
- The **depreciation method** used should reflect the pattern in which the asset's economic benefits are consumed by the entity.
- The **depreciation charge** for each period should be recognised as an expense unless it is included in the carrying amount of another asset.

Land and buildings are dealt with separately even when they are acquired together because land normally has an unlimited life and is therefore not depreciated. In contrast buildings do have a limited life and must be depreciated. Any increase in the value of land on which a building is standing will have no impact on the determination of the building's useful life.

Depreciation is usually treated as an **expense**, but not where it is absorbed by the entity in the process of producing other assets. For example, depreciation of plant and machinery can be incurred in the production of goods for sale (inventory items). In such circumstances, the depreciation is included in the cost of the new assets produced.

1.8 Review of useful life, residual value and depreciation method

The useful life, residual value and depreciation method for a non-current asset need only be reviewed if there are indications that it may have altered.

1.8.1 Example: review of useful life

B Co acquired a non-current asset on 1 January 20X2 for $80,000. It had no residual value and a useful life of 10 years.

On 1 January 20X5 it was decided that due to technological advancements the total useful life was reviewed and revised to 7 years.

What will be the depreciation charge for 20X5?

Solution

	$
Original cost	80,000
Depreciation 20X2 – 20X4 (80,000 × 3/10)	(24,000)
Carrying amount at 31 December 20X5	56,000
Remaining life (7 – 3) =	4 years
Depreciation charge years 20X5 – 20X8 (56,000/4)	14,000

1.9 Retirements and disposals

When an asset is permanently **withdrawn from use, or sold or scrapped**, and no future economic benefits are expected from its disposal, it should be withdrawn from the statement of financial position.

Gains or losses are the difference between the estimated net disposal proceeds and the carrying amount of the asset. They should be recognised as income or expense in profit or loss.

1.10 Derecognition

An entity is required to **derecognise the carrying amount** of an item of property, plant or equipment that it disposes of on the date the **criteria for the sale of goods** would be met. This also applies to parts of an asset.

An entity cannot classify as revenue a gain it realises on the disposal of an item of property, plant and equipment.

1.11 Disclosure

The standard has a long list of disclosure requirements, for each class of property, plant and equipment.

(a)   **Measurement bases** for determining the gross carrying amount

(b)   **Depreciation methods** used

(c)   **Useful lives** or depreciation rates used

(d)   **Gross carrying amount** and accumulated depreciation (aggregated with accumulated impairment losses) at the beginning and end of the period

(e)   **Reconciliation** of the carrying amount at the beginning and end of the period showing:

    (i)   Additions
    (ii)   Disposals
    (iii)   Acquisitions through business combinations (see Chapter 15)
    (iv)   Transfers to investment property if a reliable measure of fair value becomes available
    (v)   Impairment losses recognised in profit or loss
    (vi)   Impairment losses reversed in profit or loss
    (vii)   Depreciation
    (viii) Other changes

This reconciliation need not be prepared for prior periods.

The financial statements should also disclose the following.

(a)   Existence and amounts of **restrictions on title**, and items pledged as security for liabilities
(b)   Amount of commitments to **acquisitions**

	Total $	Land and buildings $	Plant and equipment $
Cost			
At 1 January 20X4	50,000	40,000	10,000
Additions in year	4,000	–	4,000
Disposals in year	(1,000)	–	(1,000)
At 31 December 20X4	53,000	40,000	13,000
Depreciation			
At 1 January 20X4	16,000	10,000	6,000
Charge for year	4,000	1,000	3,000
Eliminated on disposals	(500)	–	(500)
At 31 December 20X4	19,500	11,000	8,500
Carrying amount			
At 31 December 20X4	33,500	29,000	4,500
At 1 January 20X4	34,000	30,000	4,000

Activity

In a statement of financial position prepared in accordance with the *IFRS for SMEs*, what does the carrying value of a non-current asset represent?

Answer

In simple terms the carrying value of an asset is the cost of an asset less the 'accumulated depreciation', that is, all depreciation charged so far. It should be emphasised that the main purpose of charging depreciation is to ensure that profits are fairly reported. Thus depreciation is concerned with the statement of comprehensive income rather than the statement of financial position. In consequence the carrying value figure in the statement of financial position can be quite arbitrary. In particular, it does not necessarily bear any relation to the market value of an asset and is of little use for planning and decision making.

An obvious example of the disparity between carrying value and market value is found in the case of buildings, which may be worth much more than their carrying value.

2 Depreciation accounting

Where assets held by an entity have a **limited useful life** to that entity it is necessary to apportion the value of an asset over its useful life.

2.1 Non-current assets

If an asset's life extends over more than one accounting period, it earns profits over more than one period. It is a **non-current asset**.

With the exception of land held on freehold or very long leasehold, **every non-current asset eventually wears out over time**. Machines, cars and other vehicles, fixtures and fittings, and even buildings do not last for ever. When a business acquires a non-current asset, it will have some idea about how long its useful life will be, and it might decide what to do with it.

(a)   Keep on using the non-current asset until it becomes **completely worn out**, useless, and worthless.

(b)   **Sell off** the non-current asset at the end of its useful life, either by selling it as a second-hand item or as scrap.

Since a non-current asset has a cost, and a limited useful life, and its value eventually declines, it follows that a charge should be made in profit or loss to reflect the use that is made of the asset by the business. This charge is called **depreciation**.

Key terms

- **Depreciation** is the systematic allocation of the depreciable amount of an asset over its useful life.

- **Depreciable assets** are assets which:

    - Are expected to be used during more than one accounting period
    - Have a limited useful life
    - Are held by an entity for use in the production or supply of goods and services, for rental to others, or for administrative purposes

- **Useful life** is one of two things.

    - The period over which a depreciable asset is expected to be used by the entity, or
    - The number of production or similar units expected to be obtained from the asset by the entity.

> • **Depreciable amount** of a depreciable asset is the historical cost or other amount substituted for cost in the financial statements, less the estimated residual value.

2.2 Depreciation

The *IFRS for SMEs* requires the depreciable amount of a depreciable asset to be allocated on a **systematic basis** to each accounting period during the useful life of the asset. **Every part of an item of property, plant and equipment with a cost that is significant in relation to the total cost of the item must be depreciated separately**.

One way of defining depreciation is to describe it as a means of **spreading the cost** of a non-current asset over its useful life, and so matching the cost against the full period during which it earns profits for the business. Depreciation charges are an example of the application of the accrual assumption to calculate profits.

There are situations where, over a period, an asset has **increased in value**, ie its current value is greater than the carrying value in the financial statements. You might think that in such situations it would not be necessary to depreciate the asset. However, this is irrelevant, and depreciation should still be charged to each accounting period, based on the depreciable amount, irrespective of a rise in value due to the accruals concept of matching costs with revenue.

An entity is required to begin depreciating an item of property, plant and equipment when it is available for use and to continue depreciating it until it is derecognised even if it is idle during the period.

2.3 Useful life

The following factors should be considered when **estimating the useful life** of a depreciable asset.

- Expected **physical wear and tear**
- **Obsolescence**
- Legal or other **limits** on the use of the assets

The assessment of useful life requires **judgement** based on previous experience with similar assets or classes of asset. When a completely new type of asset is acquired (ie through technological advancement or through use in producing a brand new product or service) it is still necessary to estimate useful life, even though the exercise will be much more difficult. You also need to consider that the physical life of the asset might be longer than its useful life to the entity in question. One of the main factors to be taken into consideration is the **physical wear and tear** the asset is likely to endure. This will depend on various circumstances, including the number of shifts for which the asset will be used, the entity's repair and maintenance programme and so on. Other factors to be considered include obsolescence (due to technological advances/improvements in production/ reduction in demand for the product/service produced by the asset) and legal restrictions, eg length of a related lease.

2.4 Residual value

In most cases the residual value of an asset is **likely to be immaterial**. If it is likely to be of any significant value, that value must be estimated at the date of purchase. The amount of residual value should be estimated based on the current situation with other similar assets, used in the same way, which are now at the end of their useful lives. Any expected costs of disposal should be offset against the gross residual value.

2.5 Depreciation methods

Consistency is important. The depreciation method selected should be applied consistently from period to period unless altered circumstances justify a change. When the method *is* changed, the effect should be quantified and disclosed and the reason for the change should be stated. A change in depreciation method is treated as a change in accounting estimate.

Various methods of allocating depreciation to accounting periods are available, but whichever is chosen must be applied **consistently** to ensure comparability from period to period. Change of policy is not allowed simply because of the profitability situation of the entity.

You should be familiar with the various **accepted methods of allocating depreciation** and the relevant calculations and accounting treatments, which are revised in questions at the end of this section.

2.6 What is depreciation?

The need to depreciate non-current assets arises from the **accruals assumption**. If money is expended in purchasing an asset then the amount expended must at some time be charged against profits. If the asset is one which contributes to an entity's revenue over a number of accounting periods it would be inappropriate to charge any single period (eg the period in which the asset was acquired) with the whole of the expenditure. Instead, some method must be found of spreading the cost of the asset over its useful economic life.

This view of depreciation as a process of allocation of the cost of an asset over several accounting periods is the view adopted by the IFRS. It is worth mentioning here two **common misconceptions** about the purpose and effects of depreciation.

(a) It is sometimes thought that the carrying value of an asset is equal to its net realisable value and that the object of charging depreciation is to **reflect the fall in value of an asset over its life**. This misconception is the basis of a common, but incorrect, argument which says that freehold properties (say) need not be depreciated in times when property values are rising. It is true that historical cost statements of financial position often give a misleading impression when a property's carrying value is much below its market value.

(b) Another misconception is that depreciation is provided **so that an asset can be replaced at the end of its useful life**. This is not the case.

   (i) If there is no intention of replacing the asset, it could then be argued that there is no need to provide for any depreciation at all.

   (ii) If prices are rising, the replacement cost of the asset will exceed the amount of depreciation provided.

The following questions are for revision purposes only.

Activity

A lorry bought for a business cost $17,000. It is expected to last for five years and then be sold for scrap for $2,000. Usage over the five years is expected to be:

Year 1	200 days
Year 2	100 days
Year 3	100 days
Year 4	150 days
Year 5	40 days

Required

Work out the depreciation to be charged each year under:

(a) The straight line method
(b) The diminishing balance method (using a rate of 35%)
(c) The machine hour method
(d) The sum-of-the digits method

Answer

(a) Under the straight line method, depreciation for each of the five years is:

$$\text{Annual depreciation} = \frac{\$(17,000 - 2,000)}{5} = \$3,000$$

(b) Under the diminishing balance method, depreciation for each of the five years is:

Year	Depreciation		
1	35% × $17,000	=	$5,950
2	35% × ($17,000 – $5,950) = 35% × $11,050	=	$3,868
3	35% × ($11,050 – $3,868) = 35% × $7,182	=	$2,514
4	35% × ($7,182 – $2,514) = 35% × $4,668	=	$1,634
5	Balance to bring book value down to $2,000 = $4,668 – $1,634 – $2,000	=	$1,034

(c) Under the machine hour method, depreciation for each of the five years is calculated as follows.

Total usage (days) = 200 + 100 + 100 + 150 + 40 = 590 days

$$\text{Depreciation per day} = \frac{\$(17,000 - 2,000)}{590} = \$25.42$$

Year	Usage (days)	Depreciation ($) (days × $25.42)
1	200	5,084.00
2	100	2,542.00
3	100	2,542.00
4	150	3,813.00
5	40	1,016.80
		14,997.80

Note. The answer does not come to exactly $15,000 because of the rounding carried out at the 'depreciation per day' stage of the calculation.

(d) The sum-of-the digits method begins by adding up the years of expected life. In this case, 5 + 4 + 3 + 2 + 1 = 15.

The depreciable amount of $15,000 will then be allocated as follows:

Year		
1	15,000 × 5/15	= 5,000
2	15,000 × 4/15	= 4,000
3	15,000 × 3/15	= 3,000
4	15,000 × 2/15	= 2,000
5	15,000 × 1/15	= 1,000

Activity

(a) What are the purposes of providing for depreciation?

(b) In what circumstances is the diminishing balance method more appropriate than the straight-line method? Give reasons for your answer.

Answer

(a) The accounts of a business try to recognise that the cost of a non-current asset is gradually consumed as the asset wears out. This is done by gradually writing off the asset's cost to profit or loss over several accounting periods. This process is known as depreciation, and is an example of the accruals assumption. The *IFRS for SMEs* requires that depreciation should be allocated on a systematic basis to each accounting period during the useful life of the asset.

With regard to the accrual principle, it is fair that the profits should be reduced by the depreciation charge; this is not an arbitrary exercise. Depreciation is not, as is sometimes supposed, an attempt to set aside funds to purchase new non-current assets when required. Depreciation is not generally provided on freehold land because it does not 'wear out' (unless it is held for mining etc).

(b) The diminishing balance method of depreciation is used instead of the straight line method when it is considered fair to allocate a greater proportion of the total depreciable amount to the earlier years and a lower proportion to the later years on the assumption that the benefits obtained by the business from using the asset decline over time.

In favour of this method it may be argued that it links the depreciation charge to the costs of maintaining and running the asset. In the early years these costs are low and the depreciation charge is high, while in later years this is reversed.

Activity

A business purchased two rivet-making machines on 1 January 20X5 at a cost of $15,000 each. Each had an estimated life of five years and a nil residual value. The straight line method of depreciation is used.

Owing to an unforeseen slump in market demand for rivets, the business decided to reduce its output of rivets, and switch to making other products instead. On 31 March 20X7, one rivet-making machine was sold (on credit) to a buyer for $8,000.

Later in the year, however, it was decided to abandon production of rivets altogether, and the second machine was sold on 1 December 20X7 for $2,500 cash.

Prepare the machinery account, provision for depreciation of machinery account and disposal of machinery account for the accounting year to 31 December 20X7.

Answer

MACHINERY ACCOUNT

		$			$
20X7			*20X7*		
1 Jan	Balance b/f	30,000	31 Mar	Disposal of machinery account	15,000
			1 Dec	Disposal of machinery account	15,000
		30,000			30,000

ACCUMULATED DEPRECIATION OF MACHINERY

		$			$
20X7			*20X7*		
31 Mar	Disposal of machinery account*	6,750	1 Jan	Balance b/f	12,000
1 Dec	Disposal of machinery account**	8,750	31 Dec	Statement of comprehensive income***	3,500
		15,500			15,500

*   Depreciation at date of disposal = $6,000 + $750
**   Depreciation at date of disposal = $6,000 + $2,750
***   Depreciation charge for the year = $750 + $2,750

DISPOSAL OF MACHINERY

		$			$
20X7			*20X7*		
31 Mar	Machinery account	15,000	31 Mar	Account receivable (sale price)	8,000
			31 Mar	Provision for depreciation	6,750
1 Dec	Machinery	15,000	1 Dec	Cash (sale price)	2,500
			1 Dec	Provision for depreciation	8,750
			31 Dec	Statement of comprehensive income (loss on disposal)	4,000
		30,000			30,000

You should be able to calculate that there was a loss on the first disposal of $250, and on the second disposal of $3,750, giving a total loss of $4,000.

Workings

1   At 1 January 20X7, accumulated depreciation on the machines will be:

2 machines × 2 years × $\dfrac{\$15,000}{5}$ per machine pa = $12,000, or $6,000 per machine

2   Monthly depreciation is $\dfrac{\$3,000}{12}$ = $250 per machine per month

3   The machines are disposed of in 20X7.

(a)   On 31 March – after 3 months of the year. Depreciation for the year on the machine = 3 months × $250 = $750.

(b)   On 1 December – after 11 months of the year. Depreciation for the year on the machine = 11 months × $250 = $2,750

3 Government grants

It is common for entities to receive government grants for various purposes (grants may be called subsidies, premiums, etc). They may also receive other types of assistance which may be in many forms.

3.1 Definition

Key term

> **Government grants** Assistance by government in the form of transfers of resources to an entity in return for past or future compliance with certain conditions relating to the operating activities of the entity. They exclude those forms of government assistance which cannot reasonably have a value placed upon them and transactions with government which cannot be distinguished from the normal trading transactions of the entity.

3.2 Government grants

Government grants should be recognised as follows:

(a)   A grant that does not impose specified future performance conditions on the recipient is recognised in income when the grant proceeds are receivable.

(b)   A grant that imposes specified future performance conditions on the recipient is recognised in income only when the performance conditions are met.

(c)   Grants received before the revenue recognition criteria are satisfied are recognised as a liability.

All grants shall be measured at the fair value of the asset received or receivable.

3.3 Disclosure

Disclosure is required of the following.

- **Nature and extent** of government grants recognised and other forms of assistance received
- **Unfulfilled conditions and other contingencies** attached to recognised government assistance
- Other forms of Government assistance benefited from

4 Investment property

An entity may own land or a building **as an investment** rather than for use in the business. It may therefore generate cash flows largely independently of other assets which the entity holds.

4.1 Definition

Consider the following definition.

Key term

> **Investment property** is property (land or a building – or part of a building – or both) held (by the owner or by the lessee under a finance lease) to earn rentals or for capital appreciation or both, rather than for:
>
> (a) Use in the production or supply of goods or services or for administrative purposes, or
> (b) Sale in the ordinary course of business

Examples of investment property include:

(a) **Land held for long-term capital appreciation** rather than for short-term sale in the ordinary course of business

(b) A **building** owned by the reporting entity (or held by the entity under a finance lease) and **leased out under an operating lease**

 Activity

Rich Co owns a piece of land. The directors have not yet decided whether to build a factory on it for use in its business or to keep it and sell it when its value has risen.

Would this be classified as an investment property?

 Answer

Yes. If an entity has not determined that it will use the land either as an owner-occupied property or for short-term sale in the ordinary course of business, the land is considered to be held for capital appreciation.

4.2 Recognition

Investment property should be recognised as an asset when **two conditions** are met.

(a) It is **probable** that the **future economic benefits** that are associated with the investment property will **flow to the entity**.

(b) The **cost** of the investment property can be **measured reliably**.

4.3 Initial measurement

An investment property should be measured initially at its **cost,** including transaction costs.

A property interest held under a lease and classified as an investment property shall be accounted for **as if it were a finance lease**. The asset is recognised at the lower of the fair value of the property and the present value of the minimum lease payments. An equivalent amount is recognised as a liability.

4.4 Measurement subsequent to initial recognition

Investment property whose fair value can be measured reliably without undue cost or effort shall be measured at fair value at each reporting date with changes in fair value recognised in profit or loss. If a property interest held under a lease is classified as investment property, the item accounted for at fair value is that interest and not the underlying property.

An entity shall account for all other investment property as property, plant and equipment using the cost-depreciation-impairment model.

4.5 Transfers

If a reliable measure of fair value is no longer available without undue cost or effort for an item of investment property measured using the fair value model, then the property will be treated as an item as property, plant and equipment under the cost-depreciation-impairment model until a reliable measure of fair value becomes available. The carrying amount of the investment property on that date becomes its cost.

4.6 Disclosure requirements

These relate to:

- Assumptions in determining fair value
- Use of independent professional valuer (encouraged but not required)
- Rental income and expenses
- Any restrictions or obligations
- Reconciliation of carrying amount for investment properties at start and end of the period. This is only required for the current period.

5 Borrowing costs

The *IFRS for SMEs* looks at the treatment of **borrowing costs**, particularly where the related borrowings are applied to the construction of certain assets. These are what are usually called 'self-constructed assets', where an entity builds its own inventory or non-current assets over a substantial period of time.

5.1 What are borrowing costs?

Borrowing costs are interest and other costs that an entity incurs in connection with the borrowing of funds. Borrowing costs include:

(a) interest expense calculated using the effective interest method
(b) finance charges in respect of finance leases
(c) exchange differences arising from foreign currency borrowings to the extent that they are regarded as an adjustment to interest costs.

5.2 Recognition

All borrowing costs are to be treated as an expense in the statement of comprehensive income even if they are related to the acquisition, construction or production of non-current assets.

Unit Roundup

- The IFRS for SMEs covers all aspects of accounting for property, plant and equipment. This represents the bulk of items which are 'tangible' non-current assets.

- Where assets held by an entity have a limited useful life it is necessary to apportion the value of an asset over its useful life.

- It is common for entities to receive government grants for various purposes.

- An entity may own land or a building as an investment rather than for use in the business. It may therefore generate cash flows largely independently of other assets which the entity holds. Investment property is recognised at fair value through profit or loss but this will depend upon cost and effort. If fair value is not easily available then the property is treated as property, plant and equipment and accounted for in accordance with the cost – depreciation – impairment model.

- Borrowing costs are treated as an expense in the statement of comprehensive income.

Quick Quiz

1 Define depreciation.

2 Which of the following elements can be included in the production cost of a non-current asset?

    (i)   Purchase price of raw materials
    (ii)   Architect's fees
    (iii) Import duties
    (iv) Installation costs

3 Investment properties must always be shown at fair value.

    True ☐

    False ☐

4 What is the correct treatment of borrowing costs relating to the construction of a non-current asset?

Answers to Quick Quiz

1   See paragraph 2.1

2   All of them.

3   False. The cost model may be used if fair value cannot be determined easily bearing in mind cost and effort.

4   Treat as an expense in profit or loss.

Now try the question below

Burley Woodhead   36 mins

The broad principles of accounting for property, plant and equipment involve distinguishing between capital and revenue expenditure, measuring the cost of assets, determining how they should be depreciated and dealing with the problems of subsequent measurement and subsequent expenditure.

(a)   Explain:

    (i)   How the initial cost of property, plant and equipment should be measured

    (ii)   The circumstances in which subsequent expenditure on those assets should be capitalised

(b)   (i)   Burley Woodhead has recently purchased an item of plant from Menston, the details of this are:

	$	$
Basic list price of plant		240,000
Trade discount applicable to Burley Woodhead	12.5% on list price	
Ancillary costs:		
Shipping and handling costs		2,750
Estimated pre-production testing		12,500
Maintenance contract for three years		24,000
Site preparation costs:		
electrical cable installation	14,000	
concrete reinforcement	4,500	
own labour costs	7,500	
		26,000

Burley Woodhead paid for the plant (excluding the ancillary costs) within four weeks of order, thereby obtaining an early settlement discount of 3%.

The plant is expected to last for 10 years. At the end of this period there will be compulsory costs of $15,000 to dismantle the plant and $3,000 to restore the site to its original use condition.

Required

Calculate the amount at which the plant will be measured at recognition. (Ignore discounting.)

(20 marks)

Answer

Burley Woodhead

Measurement of non-current assets

(i) The IFRS for SMEs requires that property, plant and equipment is measured initially at cost, which may include:

- Purchase price including import duties (after trade discounts)

- Direct costs in bringing the asset to the location and condition necessary for normal operation, such as costs of site preparation, delivery costs, installation costs, assembly and testing costs

- An initial estimate of future dismantling costs where there is an obligation to dismantle the asset after use.

Administration and general overhead costs may not be capitalised as part of property, plant and equipment.

(ii) Subsequent expenditure on property, plant and equipment may only be capitalised where it meets the definition of an asset. In other words the expenditure enhances the economic benefits expected to flow from the asset. This may be the result of:

- An extension of useful life
- Increased quality of output
- Reduced operating costs

The IFRS also considers complex assets and major inspections:

Complex assets are those which are comprised of a number of different parts, each depreciated separately. Where one of the parts reaches the end of its useful life and is replaced, the replacement cost may be capitalised.

Certain assets, such as buses, require major inspections periodically. The IFRS for SMEs allows the cost of these to be capitalised and depreciated to the next inspection.

Measurement of plant

	$
List price	240,000
Trade discount (12.5% x 240,000)	(30,000)
	210,000
Shipping and handling costs	2,750
Estimated pre-production testing	12,500
Site preparation costs:	
Cabling	14,000
Concrete reinforcement	4,500
Own labour costs	7,500
Dismantling and restoration costs (15,000 + 3,000)	18,000
	269,250

7

Intangible assets

Unit topic list

1 Intangible assets
2 Recognition and measurement

Assessment criteria

4 **Understand and apply IFRS for SMEs in the preparation of their financial statements**

4.11 Understand and apply section 18 of IFRS for SMEs when an SME accounts for intangible assets other than goodwill

1 Intangible assets

Intangible assets are defined as non-monetary assets without physical substance.

1.1 Definition of an intangible asset

The definition of an intangible asset is a key aspect because the rules for deciding whether or not an intangible asset may be **recognised** in the accounts of an entity are based on the definition of what an intangible asset is.

Key term

> An **intangible asset** is an identifiable non-monetary asset without physical substance The asset must be:
>
> (a) controlled by the entity as a result of events in the past, and
> (b) something from which the entity expects future economic benefits to flow.

An asset is identifiable when:

(a) it is separable, ie capable of being separated or divided from the entity and sold, transferred, licensed, rented or exchanged, either individually or together with a related contract, asset or liability, or

(b) it arises from contractual or other legal rights, regardless of whether those rights are transferable or separable from the entity or from other rights and obligations.

Intangible assets do not include:

(a) financial assets, or

(b) mineral rights and mineral reserves, such as oil, natural gas and similar non-regenerative resources.

Examples of items that might be considered as intangible assets include computer software, patents, copyrights, motion picture films, customer lists, franchises and fishing rights. An item should not be recognised as an intangible asset, however, unless it **fully meets the definition** in the IFRS.

1.1.1 Intangible asset: must be identifiable

An intangible asset must be identifiable in order to distinguish it from goodwill. With non-physical items, there may be a problem with **'identifiability'**.

(a) If an intangible asset is **acquired separately through purchase**, there may be a transfer of a legal right that would help to make an asset identifiable.

(b) An intangible asset may be identifiable if it is **separable**, ie if it could be rented or sold separately. However, 'separability' is not an essential feature of an intangible asset.

1.1.2 Intangible asset: control by the entity

Another element of the definition of an intangible asset is that it must be under the control of the entity as a result of a past event. The entity must therefore be able to enjoy the future economic benefits from the asset, and prevent the access of others to those benefits. A **legally enforceable right** is evidence of such control, but is not always a *necessary* condition.

(a) Control over **technical knowledge or know-how** only exists if it is protected by a **legal right**.

(b) The skill of employees, arising out of the benefits of **training costs**, are most unlikely to be recognisable as an intangible asset, because an entity does not control the future actions of its staff.

(c) Similarly, **market share and customer loyalty** cannot normally be intangible assets, since an entity cannot control the actions of its customers.

1.2 Recognition of an intangible asset

The IFRS for SMEs requires that an intangible asset is recognised in the statement of financial position only if:

- It is probable that the expected future economic benefits that are attributable to the asset will flow to the entity;
- The cost or value of the asset can be measured reliably, and
- The asset does not result from expenditure incurred internally on an intangible item.

1.2.1 Intangible asset: expected future economic benefits

An item can only be recognised as an intangible asset if economic benefits are expected to flow in the future from ownership of the asset. Economic benefits may come from the **sale** of products or services, or from a **reduction in expenditures** (cost savings).

Management has to exercise its judgement in assessing the degree of certainty attached to the flow of economic benefits to the entity. External evidence is best.

1.2.2 Intangible asset: measured reliably

If an intangible asset is **acquired separately**, its cost can usually be measured reliably as its purchase price (including incidental costs of purchase such as legal fees, and any costs incurred in getting the asset ready for use).

When an intangible asset is acquired as **part of a business combination** (ie an acquisition or takeover), the cost of the intangible asset is its fair value at the date of the acquisition.

The IFRS explains that the fair value of intangible assets acquired in business combinations can normally be measured with sufficient reliability to be **recognised separately** from goodwill.

1.2.3 Exchanges of assets

If one intangible asset is exchanged for another, the cost of the intangible asset is measured at fair value unless:

(a) The exchange transaction lacks commercial substance, or
(b) The fair value of neither the asset received nor the asset given up can be measured reliably.

Otherwise, its cost is measured at the carrying amount of the asset given up.

1.3 Internally generated intangible assets

Rule to learn

An entity shall recognise expenditure incurred internally on an intangible item, including all expenditure for both research and development activities, as an expense when incurred, unless it forms part of the cost of another asset meeting the recognition criteria of the IFRS for SMES.

The IFRS lists items which may not be recognised as an internally generated intangible asset. They include:

(a) Internally generated brands, logos, publishing titles, customer lists and items similar in substance.

(b) Start-up activities (ie start-up costs), which include establishment costs such as legal and secretarial costs incurred in establishing a legal entity, expenditure to open a new facility or business (ie pre-opening costs) and expenditure for starting new operations or launching new products or processes (ie pre-operating costs).

(c) Training activities.

(d) Advertising and promotional activities.

(e) Relocating or reorganising part or all of an entity.

(f) Internally generated goodwill.

2 Recognition and measurement

2.1 Measurement of intangible assets subsequent to initial recognition

An intangible asset should be **carried at its cost**, less any accumulated amortisation and less any accumulated impairment losses.

2.2 Useful life

All intangible assets are assumed to have a finite useful life. If an entity is unable to make a reliable estimate of the useful life of an intangible asset, the life shall be presumed to be ten years.

2.3 Amortisation period and amortisation method

An intangible asset with a finite useful life should be amortised over its **expected useful life**.

(a)   Amortisation should start when the asset is **available for use**.

(b)   Amortisation should cease when the asset is **derecognised**.

(c)   The amortisation method used should reflect the **pattern in which the asset's future economic benefits are consumed**. If such a pattern cannot be predicted reliably, the straight-line method should be used.

(d)   The amortisation charge for each period should normally be recognised **in profit or loss**.

The **residual value** of an intangible asset with a finite useful life is **assumed to be zero** unless a third party is committed to buying the intangible asset at the end of its useful life or unless there is an active market for that type of asset (so that its expected residual value can be measured) and it is probable that there will be a market for the asset at the end of its useful life.

The amortisation period and the amortisation method used for an intangible asset with a finite useful life should be **reviewed** if there are any indicators that change may be needed.

Activity

It may be difficult to establish the useful life of an intangible asset, and judgement will be needed. Consider how to determine the useful life of a *purchased* brand name.

Answer

Factors to consider would include the following.

(a)   Legal protection of the brand name and the control of the entity over the (illegal) use by others of the brand name (ie control over pirating)

(b)   Age of the brand name

(c)   Status or position of the brand in its particular market

(d)   Ability of the management of the entity to manage the brand name and to measure activities that support the brand name (eg advertising and PR activities)

(e)   Stability and geographical spread of the market in which the branded products are sold

(f)   Pattern of benefits that the brand name is expected to generate over time

(g)   Intention of the entity to use and promote the brand name over time (as evidenced perhaps by a business plan in which there will be substantial expenditure to promote the brand name)

2.4 Disposals/retirements of intangible assets

An intangible asset should be eliminated from the statement of financial position when it is disposed of or when there is no further expected economic benefit from its future use. On disposal the gain or loss arising from the **difference between the net disposal proceeds and the carrying amount** of the asset should be taken to profit or loss as a gain or loss on disposal (ie treated as income or expense).

2.5 Section summary

- An intangible asset should be recognised if, and only if, it is probable that future economic benefits will flow to the entity and the cost of the asset can be measured reliably.
- An asset is initially recognised at cost.
- Costs that do not meet the recognition criteria should be expensed as incurred. This includes all research and development costs.
- All intangible assets are assumed to have a finite useful life and should be amortised over their useful life. If the useful life cannot be estimated then the asset should be amortised over a period of 10 years.

Unit Roundup

- **Intangible assets** are defined as non-monetary assets without physical substance. They must be:
    - **Identifiable**
    - **Controlled** as a result of a past event
    - Able to provide **future economic benefits**

- Intangible assets should initially be measured at cost.

- **Internally-generated assets** are normally written off to profit and loss immediately.

- All intangible assets are assumed to have a finite useful life and must be amortised over that useful life. However if the useful life cannot be estimated then a period of 10 years is used for amortisation.

Quick Quiz

1   Intangible assets can only be recognised in a company's accounts if:
    - It is probable that .... will flow to the entity
    - The cost can be ....

2   Start up costs must be expensed.

    True ☐

    False ☐

3   What is the treatment required for research and development costs?

4   If an intangible asset's useful life cannot be reliably estimated over what period should it be amortised?

Answers to Quick Quiz

1   Future economic benefits. Measured reliably.

2   True

3   They must be written off to profit and loss.

4   10 years.

Now try the question below

Intangible assets   18 mins

Discuss whether intangible assets should be recognised, and if so how they should be initially recorded and subsequently amortised in the following circumstances:

(i)   When they are purchased separately from other assets
(ii)   When they are obtained as part of acquiring the whole of a business
(iii)   When they are developed internally.

(10 marks)

Answer

Intangible assets

Intangibles can be recognised if they can be distinguished from goodwill; typically this means that they can be separated from the rest of the business, or that they arise from a legal or contractual right.

Intangibles acquired as part of a business combination are recognised at fair value provided that they can be valued separately from goodwill. The acquirer will recognise an intangible even if the asset had not been recognised previously. If an intangible cannot be valued, then it will be subsumed into goodwill.

Internally generated intangibles can be recognised if they are acquired as part of a business combination. For example, a brand name acquired in a business combination is capitalised whereas an internally generated brand isn't. Expenditure on research and development and other intangible assets cannot be capitalised.

Intangibles are amortised over their useful lives. If the useful life however is not clear then they are amortised over a period of 10 years. Intangibles are tested for impairment only if there is an indication that an impairment has taken place.

Impairment of assets

8

Unit topic list

1   Impairment of assets
2   Cash generating units
3   Goodwill and the impairment of assets
4   Accounting treatment of an impairment loss

Assessment criteria

4   Understand and apply IFRS for SMEs in the preparation of their financial statements

4.19   Understand and apply section 14 of IFRS for SMEs when an SME needs to impair an asset

1 Impairment of assets

> Impairment is determined by comparing the carrying amount of the asset with its recoverable amount. This is the higher of its **fair value less costs to sell** and its **value in use**.

There is an established principle that assets should not be carried at above their recoverable amount. An entity should write down the carrying value of an asset to its recoverable amount if the carrying value of an asset is not recoverable in full.

1.1 Definitions

Key terms

- **Impairment**: a fall in the value of an asset, so that its 'recoverable amount' is now less than its carrying value in the statement of financial position.
- **Carrying amount**: is the net value at which the asset is included in the statement of financial position (ie after deducting accumulated depreciation and any impairment losses).

The basic principle underlying impairment adjustments is relatively straightforward. If an asset's value in the accounts is higher than its realistic value, measured as its 'recoverable amount', the asset is judged to have suffered an impairment loss. It should therefore be reduced in value, by the amount of the **impairment loss**. The amount of the impairment loss should be **written off against profit** immediately.

The main accounting issues to consider are therefore as follows.

(a) How is it possible to **identify when** an impairment loss may have occurred?

(b) How should the **recoverable amount** of the asset be measured?

(c) How should an 'impairment loss' be **reported in the accounts**?

1.2 Identifying a potentially impaired asset

An entity should assess at the end of each reporting period whether there are any indications of impairment to any assets. The concept of **materiality** applies, and only material impairment needs to be identified.

If there are indications of possible impairment, the entity is required to make a formal estimate of the **recoverable amount** of the assets concerned.

The standard suggests how **indications of a possible impairment** of assets might be recognised. The suggestions are based largely on common sense.

(a) **External sources of information**

  (i) A fall in the asset's market value that is more significant than would normally be expected from passage of time over normal use.

  (ii) A significant change in the technological, market, legal or economic environment of the business in which the assets are employed.

  (iii) An increase in market interest rates or market rates of return on investments likely to affect the discount rate used in calculating value in use.

  (iv) The carrying amount of the entity's net assets being more than its market capitalisation.

(b) **Internal sources of information**: evidence of obsolescence or physical damage, adverse changes in the use to which the asset is put, or the asset's economic performance

1.3 Measuring the recoverable amount of the asset

1.3.1 What is an asset's recoverable amount?

Key term

> The **recoverable amount of an asset** should be measured as the *higher value* of:
>
> (a)   the asset's fair value less costs to sell; and
> (b)   its value in use.

An asset's fair value less costs to sell is the amount net of selling costs that could be obtained from the sale of the asset. Selling costs include sales transaction costs, such as legal expenses.

(a)   If there is **an active market** in the asset, the net selling price should be based on the **market value**, or on the price of recent transactions in similar assets.

(b)   If there is **no active market** in the assets it might be possible to **estimate** a net selling price using best estimates of what 'knowledgeable, willing parties' might pay in an arm's length transaction.

The concept of 'value in use' is very important.

Key term

> The **value in use** of an asset is measured as the present value of estimated future cash flows (inflows minus outflows) generated by the asset, including its estimated net disposal value (if any) at the end of its expected useful life.

1.4 Recognition and measurement of an impairment loss

The rule for assets at historical cost is:

Rule to learn

If the recoverable amount of an asset is lower than the carrying amount, the carrying amount should be reduced by the difference (ie the impairment loss) which should be charged as an expense in profit or loss.

2 Cash generating units

When it is not possible to calculate the recoverable amount of a single asset, then that of its **cash generating unit** should be measured instead.

2.1 Use of cash-generating unit

The IFRS goes into quite a large amount of detail about the important concept of cash generating units. As a basic rule, the recoverable amount of an asset should be calculated for the **asset individually**. However, there will be occasions when it is not possible to estimate such a value for an individual asset, particularly in the calculation of value in use. This is because cash inflows and outflows cannot be attributed to the individual asset. If it is not possible to calculate the recoverable amount for an individual asset, the recoverable amount of the asset's cash-generating unit should be measured instead.

Key term

> A **cash-generating unit** is the smallest identifiable group of assets for which independent cash flows can be identified and measured.

Activity

Can you think of some examples of how a cash-generating unit would be identified?

Answer

Here are two possibilities.

(a) A mining company owns a private railway that it uses to transport output from one of its mines. The railway now has no market value other than as scrap, and it is impossible to identify any separate cash inflows with the use of the railway itself. Consequently, if the mining company suspects an impairment in the value of the railway, it should treat the mine as a whole as a cash generating unit, and measure the recoverable amount of the mine as a whole.

(b) A bus company has an arrangement with a town's authorities to run a bus service on four routes in the town. Separately identifiable assets are allocated to each of the bus routes, and cash inflows and outflows can be attributed to each individual route. Three routes are running at a profit and one is running at a loss. The bus company suspects that there is an impairment of assets on the loss-making route. However, the company will be unable to close the loss-making route, because it is under an obligation to operate all four routes, as part of its contract with the local authority. Consequently, the company should treat all four bus routes together as a cash generating unit, and calculate the recoverable amount for the unit as a whole.

 Activity

Minimart belongs to a retail store chain Maximart. Minimart makes all its retail purchases through Maximart's purchasing centre. Pricing, marketing, advertising and human resources policies (except for hiring Minimart's cashiers and salesmen) are decided by Maximart. Maximart also owns 5 other stores in the same city as Minimart (although in different neighbourhoods) and 20 other stores in other cities. All stores are managed in the same way as Minimart. Minimart and 4 other stores were purchased 5 years ago and goodwill was recognised.

What is the cash-generating unit for Minimart?

 Answer

In identifying Minimart's cash-generating unit, an entity considers whether, for example:

(a) Internal management reporting is organised to measure performance on a store-by-store basis.
(b) The business is run on a store-by-store profit basis or on a region/city basis.

All Maximart's stores are in different neighbourhoods and probably have different customer bases. So, although Minimart is managed at a corporate level, Minimart generates cash inflows that are largely independent from those of Maximart's other stores. Therefore, it is likely that Minimart is a cash-generating unit.

If an active market exists for the output produced by the asset or a group of assets, this asset or group should be identified as a cash generating unit, even if some or all of the output is used internally.

Cash-generating units should be identified consistently from period to period for the same type of asset unless a change is justified.

The group of net assets less liabilities that are considered for impairment should be the same as those considered in the calculation of the recoverable amount. (For the treatment of goodwill and corporate assets see below.)

 ## 2.2 Example: Recoverable amount and carrying amount

Fourways Co is made up of four cash generating units. All four units are being tested for impairment.

(a) Property, plant and equipment and separate intangibles would be allocated to be cash-generating units as far as possible.

(b) Current assets such as inventories, receivables and prepayments would be allocated to the relevant cash-generating units.

(c) Liabilities (eg payables) would be deducted from the net assets of the relevant cash-generating units.

(d) The net figure for each cash-generating unit resulting from this exercise would be compared to the relevant recoverable amount, computed on the same basis.

3 Goodwill and the impairment of assets

3.1 Allocating goodwill to cash-generating units

Goodwill acquired in a business combination does not generate cash flows independently of other assets. It must be **allocated** to each of the acquirer's **cash-generating units** (or groups of cash-generating units) that are expected to benefit from the synergies of the combination.

3.2 Testing cash-generating units with goodwill for impairment

There are two situations to consider.

(a) Where goodwill has been allocated to a cash-generating unit

(b) Where it has not been possible to allocate goodwill to a specific cash-generating unit, but only to a group of units

A cash-generating unit to which goodwill has been allocated is tested for impairment annually. The **carrying amount** of the unit, including goodwill, is **compared with the recoverable amount**. If the carrying amount of the unit exceeds the recoverable amount, the entity must recognise an impairment loss.

Where goodwill relates to a cash-generating unit but has not been allocated to that unit, the unit is tested for impairment by **comparing its carrying amount** (excluding goodwill) **with its recoverable amount**. The entity must recognise an impairment loss if the carrying amount exceeds the recoverable amount.

4 Accounting treatment of an impairment loss

If, and only if, the recoverable amount of an asset is less than its carrying amount in the statement of financial position, an impairment loss has occurred. This loss should be **recognised immediately**.

(a) The asset's **carrying amount** should be reduced to its recoverable amount in the statement of financial position.

(b) The **impairment loss** should be recognised immediately in profit or loss

After reducing an asset to its recoverable amount, the **depreciation charge** on the asset should then be based on its new carrying amount, its estimated residual value (if any) and its estimated remaining useful life.

An impairment loss should be recognised for a **cash generating unit** if (and only if) the recoverable amount for the cash generating unit is less than the carrying amount in the statement of financial position for all the assets in the unit. When an impairment loss is recognised for a cash generating unit, the loss should be allocated between the assets in the unit in the following order.

(a) First, to any assets that are obviously damaged or destroyed

(b) Next, to the **goodwill** allocated to the cash generating unit

(c) Then to all other assets in the cash-generating unit, on a **pro rata basis**

In allocating an impairment loss, the carrying amount of an asset should not be reduced below the highest of:

(a) Its fair value less costs to sell

(b) Its value in use (if determinable)

(c) Zero

Any remaining amount of an impairment loss should be recognised to the other assets on a pro rata basis.

4.1 Example 1: impairment loss

A company that extracts natural gas and oil has a drilling platform in the Caspian Sea. It is required by legislation of the country concerned to remove and dismantle the platform at the end of its useful life. Accordingly, the company has included an amount in its accounts for removal and dismantling costs, and is depreciating this amount over the platform's expected life.

The company is carrying out an exercise to establish whether there has been an impairment of the platform.

(a)   Its carrying amount in the statement of financial position is $3m.

(b)   The company has received an offer of $2.8m for the platform from another oil company. The bidder would take over the responsibility (and costs) for dismantling and removing the platform at the end of its life.

(c)   The present value of the estimated cash flows from the platform's continued use is $3.3m (before adjusting for dismantling costs).

(d)   The carrying amount in the statement of financial position for the provision for dismantling and removal is currently $0.6m.

What should be the value of the drilling platform in the statement of financial position, and what, if anything, is the impairment loss?

Solution

Fair value less costs to sell	=	$2.8m
Value in use	=	PV of cash flows from use less the carrying amount of the provision/liability = $3.3m – $0.6m = $2.7m
Recoverable amount	=	Higher of these two amounts, ie $2.8m
Carrying value	=	$3m
Impairment loss	=	$0.2m

The carrying value should be reduced to $2.8m

4.2 Example 2: impairment loss

A company has acquired another business for $4.5m: tangible assets are valued at $4.0m and goodwill at $0.5m.

An asset with a carrying value of $1m is destroyed in a terrorist attack. The asset was not insured. The loss of the asset, without insurance, has prompted the company to assess whether there has been an impairment of assets in the acquired business and what the amount of any such loss is.

The recoverable amount of the business (a single cash generating unit) is measured as $3.1m.

Solution

There has been an impairment loss of $1.4m ($4.5m – $3.1m).

The impairment loss will be recognised in profit or loss. The loss will be allocated between the assets in the cash generating unit as follows.

(a)   A loss of $1m can be attributed directly to the uninsured asset that has been destroyed.

(b)   The remaining loss of $0.4m should be allocated to goodwill.

The carrying value of the assets will now be $3m for tangible assets and $0.1m for goodwill.

4.3 Reversal of an impairment loss

For all assets other than goodwill, there should be an assessment at each reporting date whether there is any indication that an impairment loss recognised in prior periods may no longer exist or may have decreased. If any such indication exists, then it will be necessary to determine whether all or part of the prior impairment loss should be reversed.

In some cases, the recoverable amount of an asset that has previously been impaired might turn out to be **higher** than the asset's current carrying value. In other words, there might have been a reversal of some of the previous impairment loss.

(a) The reversal of the impairment loss should be **recognised immediately** as income in profit or loss.

(b) The carrying amount of the asset should be increased to its **new recoverable amount**.

An exception to this rule is for **goodwill**. An impairment loss for goodwill should not be reversed in a subsequent period.

Activity

A cash generating unit comprising a factory, plant and equipment etc and associated purchased goodwill becomes impaired because the product it makes is overtaken by a technologically more advanced model produced by a competitor. The recoverable amount of the cash generating unit falls to $60m, resulting in an impairment loss of $80m, allocated as follows.

	Carrying amounts before impairment $m	Carrying amounts after impairment $m
Goodwill	40	–
Patent (with no market value)	20	–
Tangible non-current assets (market value $60m)	80	60
Total	140	60

After three years, the entity makes a technological breakthrough of its own, and the recoverable amount of the cash generating unit increases to $90m. The carrying amount of the tangible non-current assets had the impairment not occurred would have been $70m.

Required

Calculate the reversal of the impairment loss.

Answer

The reversal of the impairment loss is recognised to the extent that it increases the carrying amount of the tangible non-current assets to what it would have been had the impairment not taken place, ie a reversal of the impairment loss of $10m is recognised and the tangible non-current assets written back to $70m. Reversal of the impairment is not recognised in relation to the goodwill and patent because the effect of the external event that caused the original impairment has not reversed – the original product is still overtaken by a more advanced model.

Exam focus point An exam question may ask you to calculate and allocate an impairment loss. Make sure you know the order in which to allocate the loss.

4.4 Summary

The main aspects of the IFRS to consider are:

- **Indications** of impairment of assets
- **Measuring recoverable amount**, as net selling price or value in use
- **Measuring value in use**
- **Cash generating units**
- **Accounting treatment** of an impairment loss, for individual assets and cash generating units
- **Reversal** of an impairment loss

Unit Roundup

- Impairment is determined by comparing the carrying amount of the asset with its **recoverable amount**. This is the higher of its **fair value less costs to sell** and its **value in use**.

- When it is not possible to calculate the recoverable amount of a single asset, then that of its **cash generating unit** should be measured instead.

Quick Quiz

1   Define recoverable amount of an asset.

2   How is an impairment loss allocated to the assets in a cash-generating unit?

Answers to Quick Quiz

1   Higher of fair value less costs to sell and value in use.

2   In the following order:

   a) against any damaged or destroyed assets; then

   b) against goodwill; then

   c) against all other assets on a pro rata basis.

Now try the question below

Impairment   18 mins

(i)   Define an impairment loss explaining the relevance of fair value less costs to sell and value in use; and
      state how frequently assets should be tested for impairment;

      Note: your answer should NOT describe the possible indicators of an impairment.

(ii) Explain how an impairment loss is accounted for after it has been calculated.

                                                                 (10 marks)

Answer

Impairment

(i) **Define an impairment loss**

An impairment occurs when the carrying value of an asset exceeds its recoverable amount. Recoverable amount represents the amount of cash that an asset will generate either through use (value in use) or through disposal (fair value less costs to sell).

The value in use is the present value of all future cash flows derived from an asset, including any disposal proceeds at the end of the asset's life. The present value of future cash flows will be affected by the timing, volatility and uncertainty of the cash flows. This can be reflected in the forecasted cash flows or the discount rate used.

Very few business assets generate their own cash flows, and so assets are often grouped together into cash generating units for impairment purposes. A cash generating unit is the smallest group of assets generating independent cash flows

Fair value less costs to sell is the amount obtainable for an asset in an arm's length transaction between knowledgeable, willing parties, less the cost of disposal. The fair value of used assets with no active market will have to be estimated. Valuations are based on willing parties, and so a 'forced sale' value would not normally be used.

Impairment reviews should take place when there is an indication of impairment of an asset.

(ii) **Accounting for an impairment loss**

Impairment losses should be recognised immediately. They will be charged to profit or loss alongside depreciation. Future depreciation charges will be based on the impaired value and the remaining useful life at the date of the impairment.

Impairments of cash generating units must be apportioned to the individual assets within that unit. The impairment is firstly allocated to goodwill, and then it is apportioned to all other assets (both tangible and intangible) on a pro rata basis. However, individual assets are not impaired below their own realisable value; any unused impairment being re-apportioned to the other assets.

Leases

9

Unit topic list

1 Types of lease
2 Lessees

Assessment criteria

4 **Understand and apply IFRS for SMEs in the preparation of their financial statements**

4.13 Understand and apply section 20 of IFRS for SMEs when an SME is required to account for leases

1 Types of lease

A finance lease is a means of acquiring the long-term use of an asset whereas an operating lease is a short-term rental agreement. Substance over form is important in distinguishing between them.

1.1 What is a lease?

Where goods are acquired other than on immediate cash terms, arrangements have to be made in respect of the future payments on those goods. In the simplest case of **credit sales**, the purchaser is allowed a period of time (say one month) to settle the outstanding amount and the normal accounting procedure in respect of receivables/payables will be adopted. However, in recent years there has been considerable growth in leasing agreements (some types of lease are called **hire purchase agreements** in some countries).

In a leasing transaction there is a **contract** between the lessor and the lessee for the hire of an asset. The lessor retains legal ownership but conveys to the lessee the right to use the asset for an agreed period of time in return for specified rentals. The *IFRS for SMEs* defines a lease and recognises two types.

Key terms

> **Lease.** An agreement whereby the lessor conveys to the lessee in return for payments the right to use an asset for an agreed period of time.
>
> **Finance lease.** A lease that transfers substantially all the risks and rewards incident to ownership of an asset. Title may or may not eventually be transferred.
>
> **Operating lease.** An operating lease is a lease other than a finance lease.
>
> *(IFRS for SMEs)*

A **finance lease** may be a **hire purchase agreement**. (The difference is that under a hire purchase agreement the customer eventually, after paying an agreed number of instalments, becomes entitled to exercise an option to purchase the asset. Under other leasing agreements, ownership remains forever with the lessor.)

In this chapter the **user** of an asset will often be referred to simply as the **lessee**, and the **supplier** as the **lessor**. You should bear in mind that identical requirements apply in the case of hirers and vendors respectively under hire purchase agreements.

To expand on the definition above, a finance lease should be presumed if at the inception of a lease the **present value of the minimum lease payments** is approximately equal to the **fair value of the leased asset**.

The present value should be calculated by using the **interest rate implicit in the lease**.

Key terms

> * **Minimum lease payments**. The payments over the lease term that the lessee is or can be required to make.
>
> * **Interest rate implicit in the lease**.
>
>   The discount rate that, at the inception of the lease, causes the aggregate present value of
>
>   (a)   the minimum lease payments, and
>   (b)   the unguaranteed residual value
>
>   to be equal to the sum of
>
>   (a)   the fair value of the leased asset, and
>   (b)   any initial direct costs.
>
> * **Lease term**. The non-cancellable period for which the lessee has contracted to lease the asset together with any further terms for which the lessee has the option to continue to lease the asset, with or without further payment, when at the inception of the lease it is reasonably certain that the lessee will exercise the option.

Note that in an exam question you will be given the interest rate implicit in the lease.

1.2 Accounting for operating leases

Operating leases do not really pose an accounting problem. The lessee pays amounts periodically to the lessor and these are **charged to the statement of comprehensive income**.

Where the lessee is offered an incentive such as a **rent-free period** or **cashback incentive**, this is effectively a **discount**, which will be spread over the period of the operating lease in accordance with the accruals principle. For instance, if a company entered into a 4-year operating lease but was not required to make any payments until year 2, the total payments to be made over years 2-4 should be charged evenly over years 1-4.

Where a cashback incentive is received, the total amount payable over the lease term, less the cashback, should be charged evenly over the term of the lease. This can be done by crediting the cashback received to deferred income and releasing it to profit or loss over the lease term.

1.3 Accounting for finance leases

For assets held under **finance leases or hire purchase** this accounting treatment would not disclose the reality of the situation. If a **lessor** leases out an asset on a finance lease, the asset will probably never be seen on his premises or used in his business again. It would be inappropriate for a lessor to record such an asset as a non-current asset. In reality, what he owns is a **stream of cash flows receivable** from the lessee. **The asset is an amount receivable rather than a non-current asset.**

Similarly, a **lessee** may use a finance lease to fund the 'acquisition' of a major asset which he will then use in his business perhaps for many years. **The substance of the transaction is that he has acquired a non-current asset**, and this is reflected in the accounting treatment prescribed by the IFRS, even though in law the lessee never becomes the owner of the asset.

The following summary diagram should help you when deciding whether a lease is an operating lease or a finance lease.

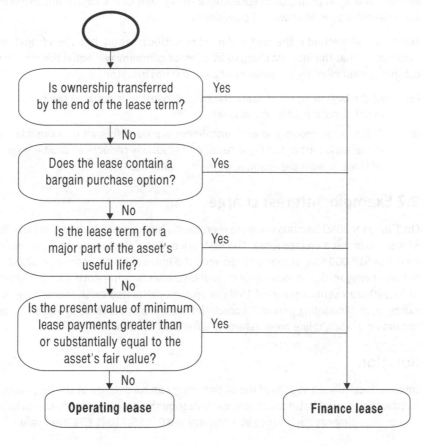

2 Lessees

You must learn the accounting and disclosure requirements for lessees under finance leases and operating leases.

2.1 Accounting treatment of finance leases

The IFRS requires that, when an asset changes hands under a **finance lease, lessor and lessee should account for the transaction as though it were a credit sale**. In the lessee's books therefore:

DEBIT   Asset account
CREDIT   Lessor (liability) account

The amount to be recorded in this way is the **lower of** the **fair value** and the **present value** of the **minimum lease payments**.

The asset should be **depreciated** as for property, plant and equipment (see unit 6) over the shorter of:

- The lease term
- The asset's useful life

2.1.1 Apportionment of rental payments

When the lessee makes a rental payment it will comprise two elements.

(a) An **interest charge** on the finance provided by the lessor. This proportion of each payment is interest payable in the statement of comprehensive income of the lessee.

(b) A repayment of part of the **capital cost** of the asset. In the lessee's books this proportion of each rental payment must be debited to the lessor's account to reduce the outstanding liability.

The accounting problem is to decide what proportion of each instalment paid by the lessee represents interest, and what proportion represents a repayment of the capital advanced by the lessor. The actuarial method is what we will consider here.

The **actuarial method** is the best and most scientific method. It derives from the common-sense assumption that the interest charged by a lessor company will equal the rate of return desired by the company, multiplied by the amount of capital it has invested.

(a) At the beginning of the lease the capital invested is equal to the fair value of the asset (less any initial deposit paid by the lessee).

(b) This amount reduces as each instalment is paid. It follows that the interest accruing is greatest in the early part of the lease term, and gradually reduces as capital is repaid. In this section, we will look at a simple example of the actuarial method.

2.2 Example: interest charge

On 1 January 20X0 Bacchus Co, wine merchants, buys a small bottling and labelling machine from Silenus Co under a finance lease. The cash price of the machine was $7,710 while the amount to be paid was $10,000. The agreement required the immediate payment of a $2,000 deposit with the balance being settled in four equal annual instalments commencing on 31 December 20X0. The charge of $2,290 represents interest of 15% per annum, calculated on the remaining balance of the liability during each accounting period. Depreciation on the plant is to be provided for at the rate of 20% per annum on a straight line basis assuming a residual value of nil.

Solution

Interest is calculated as 15% of the outstanding *capital* balance at the beginning of each year. The outstanding capital balance reduces each year by the capital element comprised in each instalment. The outstanding capital balance at 1 January 20X0 is $5,710 ($7,710 fair value less $2,000 deposit).

		$
Balance 1 January 20X0		5,710
Interest 15%		856
Instalment 31 December 20X0		(2,000)
Balance outstanding 31 December 20X0		4,566
Interest 15%		685
Instalment 31 December 20X1		(2,000)
Balance outstanding 31 December 20X1		3,251
Interest 15%		488
Instalment 31 December 20X2		(2,000)
Balance outstanding 31 December 20X2		1,739
Interest 15%		261
Instalment 31 December 20X3		(2,000)
		–

2.3 Disclosure requirements for lessees

The IFRS requires the following disclosures by lessees in respect of **finance leases**:

- The **net carrying amount** at the end of the reporting period for each class of asset

- The total of future minimum lease payments at the end of the reporting period for each of the following periods:

    - Not later than one year
    - Later than one year and not later than five years
    - Later than five years

2.4 Example: lessee disclosures

These disclosure requirements will be illustrated for Bacchus Co (above example). We will assume that Bacchus Co makes up its accounts to 31 December and uses the actuarial method to apportion finance charges.

Solution

The company's accounts for the first year of the lease, the year ended 31 December 20X0, would include the information given below.

STATEMENT OF FINANCIAL POSITION AS AT 31 DECEMBER 20X0 (EXTRACTS)

	$	$
Non-current assets		
Assets held under finance leases		
Plant and machinery at cost	7,710	
Less accumulated depreciation (20% × $7,710)	1,542	
		6,168
Non-current liabilities		
Obligations under finance leases		
(Balance at 31 December 20X1)		3,251
Current liabilities		
Obligations under finance leases (4,566 – 3,251)		1,315

(Notice that only the outstanding **capital** element is disclosed under liabilities, ie the total of the minimum lease payments with future finance charges separately deducted.)

STATEMENT OF COMPREHENSIVE INCOME
FOR THE YEAR ENDED 31 DECEMBER 20X0 (EXTRACT)

	$
Interest payable and similar charges	
Interest on finance leases	856

 ## 2.5 Example: 6-monthly payments

Now let us see what would change if Bacchus was not required to pay a deposit but had to pay $1,250 every 6 months for 4 years. We will use the same interest rate and calculate the amounts for the first year's financial statements.

	$
Balance 1 January 20X0	7,710
Interest to 30 June 20X0 (7,710 × 15% × 6/12)	578
Instalment paid 30 June 20X0	(1,250)
Balance 30 June 20X0	7,038
Interest to 31 December 20X0 (7,038 × 15% × 6/12)	528
Instalment paid 31 December 20X0	(1,250)
Balance 31 December 20X0	6,316
Interest to 30 June 20X1 (6,316 × 15% × 6/12)	478
Instalment paid 30 June 20X1	(1,250)
Balance 30 June 20X1	5,544
Interest to 31 December 20X1 (5,544 × 15% × 6/12)	416
Instalment paid 31 December 20X1	(1,250)
Balance 31 December 20X1	4,710

Financial statement extracts at 31 December 20X0:

	$
Non-current assets (as above)	6,168
Non-current liabilities	
Obligations under finance leases	4,710
Current liabilities	
Obligations under finance leases (6,316 – 4,710)	1,606
Income statement: interest payable (578 + 528)	1,106

2.6 Operating leases: disclosures

For **operating leases** the disclosures are as follows.

The total of future minimum lease payments under non-cancellable operating leases for each of the following periods:

(a)   Not later than one year
(b)   Later than one year and not later than five years
(c)   Later than five years

Unit Roundup

- A finance lease is a means of acquiring the long-term use of an asset whereas an operating lease is a short-term rental agreement. Substance over form is important in distinguishing between them.

- Under **finance leases**:
  - Assets acquired should be capitalised
  - Interest element of instalments should be charged against profit.

- **Operating leases** are **rental agreements** and all instalments are charged against profit.

- You must learn (through repeated practice) how to apply the actuarial method of **interest allocation**.

- You must also learn the **disclosure requirements** for lessees.

Quick Quiz

1   (a)   ....leases transfer substantially all the risks and rewards of ownership.

    (b)   ....leases are usually short-term rental agreements with the lessor being responsible for the repairs and maintenance of the asset.

2   A business acquires an asset under a finance lease. What is the double entry?

3   List the disclosures required for lessees.

4   A lorry has an expected useful life of six years. It is acquired under a four year finance lease. Over which period should it be depreciated?

5   A company leases a photocopier under an operating lease which expires in June 20X2. Its office is leased under an operating lease due to expire in January 20X3. How should past and future operating leases be disclosed in its 31 December 20X1 accounts?

1   (a)   Finance leases
     (b)   Operating leases

2   DEBIT   Asset account
     CREDIT   Lessor (liability) account

3   See Paras 2.4 and 2.6.

4   The four year term, being the shorter of the lease term and the useful life.

5   The total operating lease rentals charged though profit or loss should be disclosed. The payments committed to should be disclosed analysing them between those falling due in the next year and the second to fifth years.

Now try the question below

Hillcrest   36 mins

On 1 October 20X5 Hillcrest entered into a non-cancellable agreement whereby the business would lease a new machine. The terms of the agreement were that Hillcrest would pay 26 rentals of $3,000 quarterly in advance commencing on 1 October 20X5, and that after this initial period Hillcrest could continue, at its option, to use the machine for a nominal rental which is not material. The cash price of this asset would have been $61,570 and the asset has a useful life of 10 years. Hillcrest considers this lease to be a finance lease and charges a full year's depreciation in the year of purchase of an asset. The rate of interest implicit in the lease is 2% per quarter.

On 1 July 20X4 Hillcrest entered into another non-cancellable agreement to lease another piece of machinery for a period of 10 years at a rental of $5,000 half-yearly to be paid in advance, commencing on 1 July 20X4. Hillcrest considers this lease to be an operating lease.

Required

Show how these transactions would be reflected in the financial statements for the year ended 31 December 20X5.   (20 marks)

Answer

Hillcrest

STATEMENT OF COMPREHENSIVE INCOME (extract)

	$
Depreciation ($61,570/10)*	6,157
Operating lease rentals (2 × 5,000)	10,000
Finance costs (W)	1,171

STATEMENT OF FINANCIAL POSITION (extract)

Non-current assets	
Property, plant and equipment ($61,570 – $6,157)	55,413
Non-current liabilities	
Finance lease liabilities (W)	51,033
Current liabilities	
Finance lease liabilities (59,741 – 51,033 (W))	8,708

Working

Interest on finance lease

	$
Cash price	61,570
Instalment 1 October 20X5	(3,000)
	58,570
Interest October - December 20X5 (2%)	1,171
Balance 31 December 20X5	59,741
Instalment 1 January 20X6	(3,000)
	56,741
Interest January - March 20X6 (2%)	1,135
Balance 31 March 20X6	57,876
Instalment 1 April 20X6	(3,000)
	54,876
Interest April - June 20X6 (2%)	1,098
Balance 30 June 20X6	55,974
Instalment 1 July 20X6	(3,000)
	52,974
Interest July - September 20X6 (2%)	1,059
Balance 30 September 20X6	54,033
Instalment 1 October 20X6	(3,000)
	51,033

*As there is a secondary lease period for which only a nominal rental is payable we can assume that Hillcrest will keep the machine for the full 10 years of its useful life. If this were not the case it would be depreciated over the 6.5 years of the lease term.

Provisions, contingencies and events after the end of the reporting period

Unit topic list

1   Provisions
2   Provisions for restructuring
3   Contingent liabilities and contingent assets
4   Events after the reporting period

Assessment criteria

4   **Understand and apply IFRS for SMEs in the preparation of their financial statements**

4.14   Understand and apply section 21 of IFRS for SMEs when an SME has provisions and contingencies

4.22   Understand and apply section 32 of IFRS for SMEs when an SME accounts for events occurring after the end of the reporting period

1 Provisions

Under the IFRS for SMEs a provision should be recognised when:

- An entity has a **present obligation**, legal or constructive
- It is probable that a **transfer of resources embodying economic benefits** will be required to settle it
- A reliable estimate can be made of its amount.

1.1 Objective

The *IFRS for SMEs* aims to ensure that appropriate **recognition criteria** and **measurement bases** are applied to provisions, contingent liabilities and contingent assets and that **sufficient information** is disclosed in the **notes** to the financial statements to enable users to understand their nature, timing and amount.

Attention!

> **Important**
> The key aim is to ensure that **provisions are made only** where there are valid grounds for them.

The IFRS views a provision as a liability.

Key terms

> A **provision** is a **liability** of uncertain timing or amount.
>
> A **liability** is a present obligation of the entity arising from past events , the settlement of which is expected to result in an outflow from the entity of resources embodying economic benefits.
>
> *(IFRS for SMEs)*

The standard distinguishes provisions from other liabilities such as trade payables and accruals. This is on the basis that for a provision there is **uncertainty** about the timing or amount of the future expenditure. Whilst uncertainty is clearly present in the case of certain accruals the uncertainty is generally much less than for provisions.

1.2 Recognition

A provision should be **recognised** as a liability in the financial statements when:

- An entity has a **present obligation** (legal or constructive) as a result of a past event
- It is probable that an **outflow of resources embodying economic benefits** will be required to settle the obligation
- A **reliable estimate** can be made of the amount of the obligation

1.3 Meaning of obligation

It is fairly clear what a legal obligation is. However, you may not know what a **constructive obligation** is.

Key term

> A **constructive obligation** is
>
> 'An obligation that derives from an entity's actions where:
>
> - by an established pattern of past practice, published policies or a sufficiently specific current statement the entity has indicated to other parties that it will accept certain responsibilities; and
> - as a result, the entity has created a valid expectation on the part of those other parties that it will discharge those responsibilities.'

1.3.1 Probable transfer of resources

For the purpose of the IFRS, a transfer of resources embodying economic benefits is regarded as **'probable'** if the event is **more likely than not** to occur. This appears to indicate a probability of more than 50%. However, the standard makes it clear that where there are a number of similar obligations the probability should be based on considering the population as a whole, rather than one single item.

1.3.2 Example: transfer of resources

If a company has entered into a warranty obligation then the probability of transfer of resources embodying economic benefits may well be extremely small in respect of one specific item. However, when considering the population as a whole the probability of some transfer of resources is quite likely to be much higher. If there is a **greater than 50% probability** of some transfer of economic benefits then a **provision** should be made for the **expected amount**.

1.3.3 Measurement of provisions

Attention!

> **Important**
> The amount recognised as a provision should be the best estimate of the expenditure required to settle the present obligation at the end of the reporting period.

The estimates will be determined by the **judgement** of the entity's management supplemented by the experience of similar transactions.

Allowance is made for **uncertainty**. Where the provision being measured involves a large population of items, the obligation is estimated by weighting all possible outcomes by their associated probabilities, ie **expected value**.

Where the provision involves a single item, such as the outcome of a legal case, provision is made **in full** for the most likely outcome.

Activity

Parker Co sells goods with a warranty under which customers are covered for the cost of repairs of any manufacturing defect that becomes apparent within the first six months of purchase. The company's past experience and future expectations indicate the following pattern of likely repairs.

% of goods sold	Defects	Cost of repairs if all items suffered from these defects $m
75	None	–
20	Minor	1.0
5	Major	4.0

What is the provision required?

Answer

The cost is found using 'expected values' (75% × $nil) + (20% × $1.0m) + (5% × $4.0m) = $400,000.

Where the effect of the **time value of money** is material, the amount of a provision should be the **present value** of the expenditure required to settle the obligation. An appropriate **discount** rate should be used.

The discount rate should be a pre-tax rate that reflects current market assessments of the time value of money. The discount rate(s) should not reflect risks for which future cash flow estimates have been adjusted.

1.4 Example

A company knows that when it ceases a certain operation in 5 years time it will have to pay environmental cleanup costs of $5m.

The provision to be made now will be the present value of $5m in 5 years time.

The relevant discount rate in this case is 10%.

Therefore a provision will be made for:

	$
$5m × 0.62092*	3,104,600

* The discount rate for 5 years at 10%.

The following year the provision will be:

$5m × 0.68301	3,415,050
	310,540

The increase in the second year of $310,450 will be charged to profit or loss. It is referred to as the **unwinding** of the discount. This is accounted for as a finance cost.

1.4.1 Future events

Future events which are reasonably expected to occur (eg new legislation, changes in technology) may affect the amount required to settle the entity's obligation and should be taken into account.

1.4.2 Expected disposal of assets

Gains from the expected disposal of assets should not be taken into account in measuring a provision.

1.4.3 Reimbursements

Some or all of the expenditure needed to settle a provision may be expected to be recovered from a third party. If so, the reimbursement should be recognised only when it is virtually certain that reimbursement will be received if the entity settles the obligation.

- The reimbursement should be treated as a separate asset, and the amount recognised should not be greater than the provision itself.
- The provision and the amount recognised for reimbursement may be netted off in profit or loss.

1.4.4 Changes in provisions

Provisions should be reviewed at the end of each reporting period and adjusted to reflect the current best estimate. If it is no longer probable that a transfer of resources will be required to settle the obligation, the provision should be reversed.

1.4.5 Use of provisions

A provision should be used only for expenditures for which the provision was originally recognised. Setting expenditures against a provision that was originally recognised for another purpose would conceal the impact of two different events.

1.4.6 Future operating losses

Provisions should not be recognised for future operating losses. They do not meet the definition of a liability and the general recognition criteria set out in the standard.

1.4.7 Onerous contracts

If an entity has a contract that is onerous, the present obligation under the contract **should be recognised and measured** as a provision. An example might be vacant leasehold property. The entity is under an obligation to maintain the property but is receiving no income from it.

Key term

> An **onerous contract** is a contract entered into with another party under which the unavoidable costs of fulfilling the terms of the contract exceed any revenues expected to be received from the goods or services supplied or purchased directly or indirectly under the contract and where the entity would have to compensate the other party if it did not fulfil the terms of the contract.

Eg

1.5 Examples of possible provisions

It is easier to see what the IFRS is driving at if you look at examples of those items which are possible provisions under this standard. Some of these we have already touched on.

(a) **Warranties**. These are argued to be genuine provisions as on past experience it is probable, ie more likely than not, that some claims will emerge. The provision must be estimated, however, on the basis of the class as a whole and not on individual claims. There is a clear legal obligation in this case.

(b) **Major repairs**. In the past it has been quite popular for companies to provide for expenditure on a major overhaul to be accrued gradually over the intervening years between overhauls. Under current accounting standards this is no longer possible as it is argued that this is a mere intention to carry out repairs, not an obligation. The entity can always sell the asset in the meantime. The only solution is to treat major assets such as aircraft, ships, furnaces etc as a series of smaller assets where each part is depreciated over shorter lives. Thus any major overhaul may be argued to be replacement and therefore capital rather than revenue expenditure.

(c) **Self insurance**. A number of companies have created a provision for self insurance based on the expected cost of making good fire damage etc instead of paying premiums to an insurance company. Under the IFRS this provision is no longer justifiable as the entity has no obligation until a fire or accident occurs. No obligation exists until that time.

(d) **Environmental contamination**. If the company has an environmental policy such that other parties would expect the company to clean up any contamination or if the company has broken current environmental legislation then a provision for environmental damage must be made.

(e) **Decommissioning or abandonment costs**. When an oil company initially purchases an oilfield it is put under a legal obligation to decommission the site at the end of its life. Prior to current accounting standards most oil companies set up the provision gradually over the life of the field so that no one year would be unduly burdened with the cost.

The IFRS , however, insists that a legal obligation exists on the initial expenditure on the field and therefore a liability exists immediately. This would appear to result in a large charge to profit and loss in the first year of operation of the field. However, the IFRS takes the view that the cost of purchasing the field in the first place is not only the cost of the field itself but also the costs of putting it right again. Thus all the costs of decommissioning may be capitalised.

(f) **Restructuring**. This is considered in detail below.

2 Provisions for restructuring

> One of the main purposes of accounting standards in this area was to target abuses of provisions for restructuring. Accordingly, the *IFRS for SMEs* lays down **strict criteria** to determine when such a provision can be made. The IFRS defines a **restructuring** as:

Key term

> A programme that is planned and is controlled by management and materially changes one of two things.
>
> - The scope of a business undertaken by an entity
> - The manner in which that business is conducted

The question is whether or not an entity has an obligation – legal or constructive – at the end of the reporting period. For this to be the case:

- An entity must have a **detailed formal plan** for the restructuring
- It must have **raised a valid expectation** in those affected that it will carry out the restructuring by starting to implement that plan or announcing its main features to those affected by it

Attention!

> **Important**
> A **mere management decision is not normally sufficient**. Management decisions may sometimes trigger off recognition, but only if earlier events such as negotiations with employee representatives and other interested parties have been concluded subject only to management approval.

2.1 Disclosure

Disclosures for provisions fall into two parts.

- Disclosure of details of the **change in carrying value** of a provision from the beginning to the end of the year
- Disclosure of the **background** to the making of the provision and the uncertainties affecting its outcome

Activity

In which of the following circumstances might a provision be recognised?

(a) On 13 December 20X9 the board of an entity decided to close down a division. The accounting date of the company is 31 December. Before 31 December 20X9 the decision was not communicated to any of those affected and no other steps were taken to implement the decision.

(b) The board agreed a detailed closure plan on 20 December 20X9 and details were given to customers and employees.

(c) A company is obliged to incur clean up costs for environmental damage (that has already been caused).

(d) A company intends to carry out future expenditure to operate in a particular way in the future.

Answer

(a) No provision would be recognised as the decision has not been communicated.

(b) A provision would be made in the 20X9 financial statements.

(c) A provision for such costs is appropriate.

(d) No present obligation exists and under the IFRS no provision would be appropriate. This is because the entity could avoid the future expenditure by its future actions, maybe by changing its method of operation.

3 Contingent liabilities and contingent assets

An entity should not **recognise** a contingent asset or liability, but they should be **disclosed**.

Now you understand provisions it will be easier to understand contingent assets and liabilities.

A **contingent liability** is:

- A possible obligation that arises from past events and whose existence will be confirmed only by the occurrence or non-occurrence of one or more uncertain future events not wholly within the control of the entity; or

- A present obligation that arises from past events but is not recognised because:
  - It is not probable that an outflow of resources embodying economic benefits will be required to settle the obligation; or
  - The amount of the obligation cannot be measured with sufficient reliability.

As a rule of thumb, probable means more than 50% likely. If an obligation is probable, it is not a contingent liability – instead, a provision is needed.

3.1 Treatment of contingent liabilities

Contingent liabilities **should not be recognised in financial statements** but they **should be disclosed**. The required disclosures are:

- A brief description of the nature of the contingent liability
- An estimate of its financial effect
- An indication of the uncertainties that exist
- The possibility of any reimbursement

3.2 Contingent assets

A **contingent asset** is:

A possible asset that arises from past events and whose existence will be confirmed by the occurrence or non-occurrence of one or more uncertain future events not wholly within control of the entity.

A contingent asset must not be recognised. Only when the realisation of the related economic benefits is **virtually certain** should recognition take place. At that point, **the asset is no longer a contingent asset**!

3.2.1 Disclosure: contingent assets

Contingent assets must only be disclosed in the notes if they are **probable**. In that case a brief description of the contingent asset should be provided along with an estimate of its likely financial effect.

3.3 Flow chart

You must practise the questions below to get the hang of this area of the IFRS. But first, study the flow chart below which is a good summary of its requirements concerning provisions and contingent liabilities.

If you learn this flow chart you should be able to deal with most questions you are likely to meet in an exam.

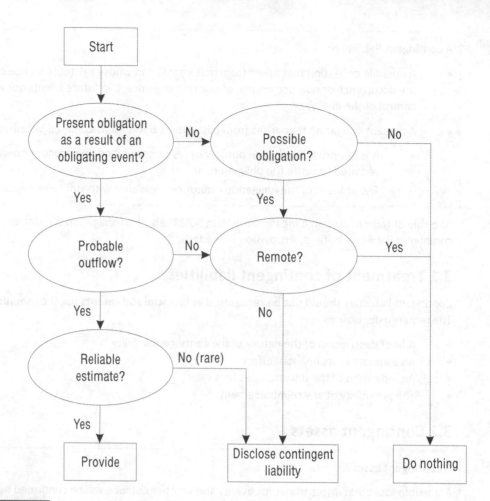

 Activity

During 20X0 Smack Co gives a guarantee of certain borrowings of Pony Co, whose financial condition at that time is sound. During 20X1, the financial condition of Pony Co deteriorates and at 30 June 20X1 Pony Co files for protection from its creditors.

What accounting treatment is required:

(a)   At 31 December 20X0?
(b)   At 31 December 20X1?

 Answer

(a)   *At 31 December 20X0*

There is a present obligation as a result of a past obligating event. The obligating event is the giving of the guarantee, which gives rise to a legal obligation. However, at 31 December 20X0 no transfer of resources is probable in settlement of the obligation.

No provision is recognised. The guarantee is disclosed as a contingent liability unless the probability of any transfer is regarded as remote.

(b)   *At 31 December 20X1*

As above, there is a present obligation as a result of a past obligating event, namely the giving of the guarantee.

At 31 December 20X1 it is probable that a transfer of resources will be required to settle the obligation. A provision is therefore recognised for the best estimate of the obligation.

Activity

Warren Co gives warranties at the time of sale to purchasers of its products. Under the terms of the warranty the manufacturer undertakes to make good, by repair or replacement, manufacturing defects that become apparent within a period of three years from the date of the sale. Should a provision be recognised?

Answer

Warren Co **cannot avoid** the cost of repairing or replacing all items of product that manifest manufacturing defects in respect of which warranties are given before the end of the reporting period, and a provision for the cost of this should therefore be made.

Warren Co is obliged to repair or replace items that fail within the entire warranty period. Therefore, in respect of **this year's sales**, the obligation provided for at the end of the reporting period should be the cost of making good items for which defects have been notified but not yet processed, **plus** an estimate of costs in respect of the other items sold for which there is sufficient evidence that manufacturing defects **will** manifest themselves during their remaining periods of warranty cover.

3.4 Section summary

- The objective of the IFRS in this area is to ensure that appropriate recognition criteria and measurement bases are applied to provisions and contingencies and that sufficient information is disclosed.
- The IFRS seeks to ensure that provisions are **only recognised** when a **measurable obligation** exists. It includes detailed rules that can be used to ascertain when an obligation exists and how to measure the obligation.
- The standard attempts to **eliminate** the **'profit smoothing'** which has gone on before it was issued.

4 Events after the reporting period

> **Events after the reporting period** which provide **additional evidence** of conditions existing at the reporting date, will cause **adjustments** to be made to the assets and liabilities in the financial statements.

The financial statements are significant indicators of a company's success or failure. It is important, therefore, that they include all the information necessary for an understanding of the company's position.

The *IFRS for SMEs* requires the provision of additional information in order to facilitate such an understanding and deals with events **after** the reporting date which may **affect the position at** the reporting date.

4.1 Definitions

Key terms

> Events after the reporting period are those events, both favourable and unfavourable, that occur between the reporting date and the date on which the financial statements are authorised for issue. Two types of events can be identified:
>
> - those that provide further evidence of conditions that existed at the reporting date (adjusting events); and
> - those that are indicative of conditions that arose subsequent to the reporting date (non-adjusting events).

Part B Reporting financial performance | 10: Provisions, contingencies and events after the end of the reporting period   131

4.2 Events after the reporting period

Between the reporting date and the date the financial statements are authorised (ie for issue outside the organisation), events may occur which show that assets and liabilities at the reporting date should be adjusted, or that disclosure of such events should be given.

4.3 Events requiring adjustment

> An entity shall adjust the amounts recognised in its financial statements to reflect adjusting events after the reporting period.

The IFRS requires adjustment of assets and liabilities where an event after the reporting period provides evidence of conditions that existed at the reporting date.

An **example** of additional evidence which becomes available after the reporting date is where a **customer goes bankrupt, thus confirming that the trade account receivable balance at the year end is uncollectable.**

4.4 Events not requiring adjustment

> An entity shall not adjust the amounts recognised in its financial statements to reflect non-adjusting events after the reporting period, but shall **disclose** them.

The financial statements are not adjusted for events which arose after the end of the reporting period and therefore do not provide evidence of conditions that existed at the reporting date.

The **example** given by the standard of such an event is where the **value of an investment falls between the reporting date and the date the financial statements are authorised** for issue. The fall in value represents circumstances during the current period, not conditions existing at the previous reporting date, so it is not appropriate to adjust the value of the investment in the financial statements. Disclosure is an aid to users, however, indicating 'unusual changes' in the state of assets and liabilities after the reporting date.

The rule for **disclosure** of events occurring after the reporting period which relate to conditions that arose after that date, is that disclosure should be made if non-disclosure would hinder the user's ability to made **proper evaluations** and decision based on the financial statements. An example might be the acquisition of another business.

4.5 Dividends

The declaration of a dividend after the end of the reporting period is a non-adjusting event and the dividend is not recognised as a liability at the reporting date.

4.6 Disclosures

The following **disclosure requirements** are given **for events** which occur after the reporting period which do *not* require adjustment. If disclosure of events occurring after the reporting period is required by this standard, the following information should be provided:

(a)   The nature of the event
(b)   An estimate of the financial effect, or a statement that such an estimate cannot be made

Exam focus point	Expect to be asked whether an item is adjusting or non-adjusting. You may well be asked to adjust for an adjusting item.

Activity

State whether the following events occurring after the reporting period require an adjustment to the assets and liabilities of the financial statements.

(a)   Purchase of an investment
(b)   A change in the rate of tax, applicable to the previous year
(c)   An increase in pension benefits
(d)   Losses due to fire
(e)   An irrecoverable debt suddenly being paid
(f)   The receipt of proceeds of sales or other evidence concerning the net realisable value of inventory
(g)   A sudden decline in the value of property held as a long-term asset

 Answer

(b), (e) and (f) require adjustment.

Of the other items, (a) would not need to be disclosed at all. Item (c) could need a disclosure if the cost to the company is likely to be material. Item (d) again would be disclosed if material, as would (g) if material.

Assuming that item (d) is material, it would be disclosed by way of the following note to the accounts. (The company year end is 31 December 20X8.)

Events after the reporting period

On 22 January 20X9, there was a fire at the company's warehouse. As a result, inventories costing a total of $250,000 were destroyed. These inventories are included in assets at the reporting date.

Unit Roundup

- Under the IFRS, a **provision** should be recognised

    –   When an entity has a **present obligation**, legal or constructive
    –   It is probable that a **transfer of resources embodying economic benefits** will be required to settle it
    –   A **reliable estimate** can be made of its amount

- One the main purposes of current accounting practice was to target abuses of provisions for restructuring. Accordingly, the IFRS lays down **strict criteria** to determine when such a provision can be made.

- An entity **should not recognise a contingent asset or liability**, but they **should be disclosed**.

- **Events after the reporting period** which provide **additional evidence** of conditions existing at the reporting date are classified as adjusting events.

- An entity shall adjust the amounts recognised in its financial statements to reflect adjusting events after the reporting period.

- **Events after the reporting period** which **do not affect the situation at the reporting date** are non-adjusting events.

- An entity shall not adjust the amounts recognised in its financial statements to reflect non-adjusting events after the **reporting period,** but should **disclose** them in the financial statements.

1   A provision is a .... of .... timing or amount.

2   A programme is undertaken by management which converts the previously wholly owned chain of restaurants they ran into franchises. Is this restructuring?

3   Define contingent asset and contingent liability.

4   How should decommissioning costs on an oilfield be accounted for under the IFRS?

5   'Provisions for major overhauls should be accrued for over the period between overhauls'. Is this correct?

6   When does an event after the reporting period require changes to the financial statements?

    A   Never
    B   If it provides further evidence of conditions existing at the reporting date

7   What disclosure is required when it is not possible to estimate the financial effect of an event not requiring adjustment?

    A   No disclosure
    B   A note to the accounts giving what information is available

8   Which of the following items are adjusting events?

    (i)   Inventory found to have deteriorated
    (ii)   Dividends declared after the year end
    (iii) A building destroyed by fire after the reporting date

    A   (i) only
    B   (ii) only
    C   (iii) only
    D   None of the above

9   Which of the following items are non-adjusting events?

    (i)   Inventory destroyed by flood two days before the reporting date

    (ii)   A customer goes bankrupt

    (iii) Fall in value of an investment between the reporting date and the date the financial statements are finalised

    A   (i) only
    B   (ii) only
    C   (iii) only
    D   None of the above

10   A receivable has been written off as irrecoverable. However the customer suddenly pays the written off amount after the reporting date. Is this event

    A   Adjusting
    B   Non-adjusting

1   Liability of uncertain timing or amount

2   Yes. The manner in which the business is conducted has changed

3   Refer to paragraphs 3.1 and 3.2

4   They should be capitalised as part of the initial expenditure on the oilfield.

5   No. It is not correct. See paragraph 1.5.

6   B   Assets and liabilities should be adjusted for events after the reporting period when these provide additional evidence for estimates existing at the reporting date.

7   B   A statement of the nature of the event and the fact that a financial estimate of the event cannot be made.

8   A

9   C

10 A

Now try the question below

Callow Co   18 mins

After a wedding in 20X0 ten people died, possibly as a result of food poisoning from products sold by Callow Co. Legal proceedings are started seeking damages from Callow but it disputes liability. Up to the date of approval of the financial statements for the year to 31 December 20X0, Callow's lawyers advise that it is probable that it will not be found liable. However, when Callow prepares the financial statements for the year to 31 December 20X1 its lawyers advise that, owing to developments in the case, it is probable that it will be found liable.

What is the required accounting treatment:

(a)   At 31 December 20X0?
(b)   At 31 December 20X1?

                                                               (10 marks)

Callow Co

(a) *At 31 December 20X0*

On the basis of the evidence available when the financial statements were approved, there is no obligation as a result of past events. No provision is recognised. The matter is disclosed as a contingent liability unless the probability of any transfer is regarded as remote.

(b) *At 31 December 20X1*

On the basis of the evidence available, there is a present obligation. A transfer of resources in settlement is probable.

A provision is recognised for the best estimate of the amount needed to settle the present obligation.

Income tax

11

Unit topic list

1 Current tax
2 Deferred tax
3 Taxable temporary differences
4 Deductible temporary differences
5 Measurement and recognition of deferred tax
6 Taxation in company accounts

Assessment criteria

4   Understand and apply IFRS for SMEs in the preparation of their financial statements

4.20 Understand and apply section 29 of IFRS for SMEs to account for income tax payable by an SME

1 Current tax

Current tax is the amount payable to the tax authorities in relation to the trading activities of the period.

1.1 Introduction

You may have assumed until now that accounting for income tax was a very simple matter for companies. You would calculate the amount of tax due to be paid on the company's taxable profits and you would:

DEBIT   Tax charge (statement of comprehensive income)
CREDIT   Tax liability (statement of financial position)

with this amount.

Indeed, this aspect of corporate taxation – **current tax** – *is* ordinarily straightforward. Complexities arise, however, when we consider the future tax consequences of what is going on in the accounts now. This is an aspect of tax called **deferred tax**, which we will look at in the next section.

1.2 Income taxes

The IFRS for SMEs covers both current and deferred tax. The parts relating to current tax are fairly brief, because this is the simple and uncontroversial area of tax.

1.3 Definitions

Key terms

- **Accounting profit**. Net profit or loss for a period before deducting tax expense.
- **Taxable profit (tax loss)**. The profit (loss) for a period, determined in accordance with the rules established by the taxation authorities, upon which income taxes are payable (recoverable).
- **Tax expense (tax income)**. The aggregate amount included in the determination of net profit or loss for the period in respect of current tax and deferred tax.
- **Current tax**. The amount of income taxes payable (recoverable) in respect of the taxable profit (tax loss) for a period.

Before we go any further, let us be clear about the difference between current and deferred tax.

(a)   **Current tax** is the amount *actually payable* to the tax authorities in relation to the trading activities of the entity during the period.

(b)   **Deferred tax** is an *accounting measure*, used to match the tax effects of transactions with their accounting impact and thereby produce less distorted results.

You should understand this a little better after working through Section 2.

1.4 Recognition of current tax liabilities and assets

The IFRS requires any **unpaid tax** in respect of the current or prior periods to be recognised as a **liability**.

Conversely, any **excess tax** paid in respect of current or prior periods over what is due should be recognised as an **asset**.

Activity

In 20X8 Darton Co had taxable profits of $120,000. In the previous year (20X7) income tax on 20X7 profits had been estimated as $30,000. The tax rate is 30%.

Required

Calculate tax payable and the charge for 20X8 if the tax due on 20X7 profits was subsequently agreed with the tax authorities as:

(a) $35,000; or
(b) $25,000.

Any under or over payments are not settled until the following year's tax payment is due.

Answer

(a)

	$
Tax due on 20X8 profits ($120,000 × 30%)	36,000
Underpayment for 20X7	5,000
Tax charge and liability	41,000

(b)

	$
Tax due on 20X8 profits (as above)	36,000
Overpayment for 20X7	(5,000)
Tax charge and liability	31,000

1.5 Example: tax losses carried back

In 20X7 Eramu Co paid $50,000 in tax on its profits. In 20X8 the company made tax losses of $24,000. The local tax authority rules allow losses to be carried back to offset against current tax of prior years.

Required

Show the tax charge and tax liability for 20X8. The tax rate is 30%.

Solution

Tax repayment due on tax losses = 30% × $24,000 = $7,200.

The double entry will be:

DEBIT	Tax receivable (statement of financial position)	$7,200	
CREDIT	Tax repayment (statement of comprehensive income)		$7,200

The tax receivable will be shown as an asset until the repayment is received from the tax authorities.

1.6 Measurement

Measurement of current tax liabilities (assets) for the current and prior periods is very simple. They are measured at the **amount expected to be paid to (recovered from) the tax authorities**. The tax rates (and tax laws) used should be those enacted (or substantively enacted) by the end of the reporting period.

1.7 Recognition of current tax

Normally, current tax is recognised as income or expense and included in the net profit or loss for the period, except for tax arising from a transaction or event which is recognised **directly in equity** (in the same or a different period).

1.8 Presentation

In the statement of financial position, **tax assets and liabilities** should be shown separately from other assets and liabilities.

Current tax assets and liabilities can be **offset**, but this should happen only when certain conditions apply.

(a)   The entity has a **legally enforceable right** to set off the recognised amounts.

(b)   The entity intends to settle the amounts on a **net basis**, or to realise the asset and settle the liability at the same time.

The **tax expense (income)** related to the profit or loss from ordinary activities should be shown in the statement of comprehensive income.

The **disclosure requirements** of the IFRS are extensive and we will look at these later in the chapter.

2 Deferred tax

Deferred tax is an accounting measure used to match the tax effects of transactions with their accounting impact. It is quite complex.

2.1 What is deferred tax?

When a company recognises an asset or liability, it expects to **recover or settle the carrying amount** of that asset or liability. In other words, it expects to sell or use up assets, and to pay off liabilities. What happens if that recovery or settlement is likely to make future tax payments larger (or smaller) than they would otherwise have been if the recovery or settlement had no tax consequences? In these circumstances, the IFRS requires companies to recognise a **deferred tax liability** (or **deferred tax asset**).

2.2 Definitions

Don't worry too much if you don't understand the concept of deferred tax yet; things should become clearer as you work through this section.

Key terms

Deferred tax liabilities are the amounts of income taxes payable in future periods in respect of taxable temporary differences.

Deferred tax assets are the amounts of income taxes recoverable in future periods in respect of:

*   Deductible temporary differences
*   The carry forward of unused tax losses
*   The carry forward of unused tax credits

Temporary differences are differences between the carrying amount of an asset or liability in the statement of financial position and its tax basis. Temporary differences may be either:

*   **Taxable temporary differences**, which are temporary differences that will result in taxable amounts in determining taxable profit (tax loss) of future periods when the carrying amount of the asset or liability is recovered or settled
*   **Deductible temporary differences**, which are temporary differences that will result in amounts that are deductible in determining taxable profit (tax loss) of future periods when the carrying amount of the asset or liability is recovered or settled

The **tax basis** of an asset or liability is the amount attributed to that asset or liability for tax purposes.

We need to look at some of these definitions in more detail.

2.3 Tax basis

We can expand on the definition given above by stating that the **tax basis of an asset** is the amount that will be deductible for tax purposes against any taxable economic benefits that will flow to the entity when it recovers the carrying value of the asset. Where those economic benefits are not taxable, the tax basis of the asset is the same as its carrying amount.

Activity

State the tax basis of each of the following assets.

(a)   A machine cost $10,000. For tax purposes, depreciation of $3,000 has already been deducted in the current and prior periods and the remaining cost will be deductible in future periods, either as depreciation or through a deduction on disposal. Revenue generated by using the machine is taxable, any gain on disposal of the machine will be taxable and any loss on disposal will be deductible for tax purposes.

(b)   Interest receivable has a carrying amount of $1,000. The related interest revenue will be taxed on a cash basis.

(c)   Trade receivables have a carrying amount of $10,000. The related revenue has already been included in taxable profit (tax loss).

(d)   A loan receivable has a carrying amount of $1m. The repayment of the loan will have no tax consequences.

Answer

(a)   The tax basis of the machine is $7,000.
(b)   The tax basis of the interest receivable is nil.
(c)   The tax basis of the trade receivables is $10,000.
(d)   The tax basis of the loan is $1m.

In the case of a **liability**, the tax basis will be its carrying amount, less any amount that will be deducted for tax purposes in relation to the liability in future periods. For revenue received in advance, the tax basis of the resulting liability is its carrying amount, less any amount of the revenue that will *not* be taxable in future periods.

Activity

State the tax basis of each of the following liabilities.

(a)   Current liabilities include accrued expenses with a carrying amount of $1,000. The related expense will be deducted for tax purposes on a cash basis.

(b)   Current liabilities include interest revenue received in advance, with a carrying amount of $10,000. The related interest revenue was taxed on a cash basis.

(c)   Current liabilities include accrued expenses with a carrying amount of $2,000. The related expense has already been deducted for tax purposes.

(d)   Current liabilities include accrued fines and penalties with a carrying amount of $100. Fines and penalties are not deductible for tax purposes.

(e)   A loan payable has a carrying amount of $1m. The repayment of the loan will have no tax consequences.

Answer

(a)   The tax basis of the accrued expenses is nil.
(b)   The tax basis of the interest received in advance is nil.
(c)   The tax basis of the accrued expenses is $2,000.
(d)   The tax basis of the accrued fines and penalties is $100.
(e)   The tax basis of the loan is $1m.

The following are examples of circumstances in which the carrying amount of an asset or liability will be **equal to its tax basis**.

- **Accrued expenses** which have already been deducted in determining an entity's current tax liability for the current or earlier periods.
- A **loan payable** is measured at the amount originally received and this amount is the same as the amount repayable on final maturity of the loan.
- **Accrued expenses** which will never be deductible for tax purposes.
- **Accrued income** which will never be taxable.

2.4 Temporary differences

You may have found the definition of temporary differences somewhat confusing. Remember that accounting profits form the basis for computing **taxable profits**, on which the tax liability for the year is calculated; however, accounting profits and taxable profits are different. There are two reasons for the differences.

(a) **Permanent differences**. These occur when certain items of revenue or expense are excluded from the computation of taxable profits (for example, client entertainment expenses may not be allowable for tax purposes).

(b) **Temporary differences**. These occur when items of revenue or expense are included in both accounting profits and taxable profits, but not for the same accounting period. For example, an expense which is allowable as a deduction in arriving at taxable profits for 20X7 might not be included in the financial accounts until 20X8 or later. In the long run, the total taxable profits and total accounting profits will be the same (except for permanent differences) so that temporary differences originate in one period and are capable of reversal in one or more subsequent periods. Deferred tax is the tax attributable to **temporary differences.**

2.5 Section summary

- Deferred tax is an **accounting device**. It does *not* represent tax payable to the tax authorities.
- The **tax basis** of an asset or liability is the value of that asset or liability for tax purposes.
- You should understand the difference between **permanent and temporary differences**.
- Deferred tax is the tax attributable to **temporary differences**.

3 Taxable temporary differences

Deferred tax assets and liabilities arise from taxable and deductible temporary differences.

Exam focus point

The rule to remember here is that:

'All taxable temporary differences give rise to a deferred tax liability.'

3.1 Examples

The following are examples of circumstances that give rise to taxable temporary differences.

3.1.1 Transactions that affect the statement of comprehensive income

(a) **Interest revenue** received in arrears and included in accounting profit on the basis of time apportionment. It is included in taxable profit, however, on a cash basis.

(b) **Sale of goods revenue** is included in accounting profit when the goods are delivered, but only included in taxable profit when cash is received.

(c) **Depreciation** of an asset is accelerated for tax purposes. When new assets are purchased, allowances may be available against taxable profits which exceed the amount of depreciation chargeable on the assets in the financial accounts for the year of purchase.

(d)   **Development costs** which have been capitalised will be amortised in the statement of comprehensive income, but they were deducted in full from taxable profit in the period in which they were incurred.

(e)   **Prepaid expenses** have already been deducted on a cash basis in determining the taxable profit of the current or previous periods.

3.1.2 Transactions that affect the statement of financial position

(a)   **Depreciation of an asset** is not deductible for tax purposes. No deduction will be available for tax purposes when the asset is sold/scrapped.

(b)   A borrower records a **loan** at proceeds received (amount due at maturity) less transaction costs. The carrying amount of the loan is subsequently increased by amortisation of the transaction costs against accounting profit. The transaction costs were, however, deducted for tax purposes in the period when the loan was first recognised.

3.1.3 Differences that do not give rise to a deferred tax liability

Remember the rule we gave you above, that all taxable temporary differences give rise to a deferred tax liability? There are **two circumstances** where this does *not* apply.

(a)   The deferred tax liability arises from **goodwill** for which amortisation is not deductible for tax purposes.

(b)   The deferred tax liability arises from the **initial recognition** of an asset or liability in a transaction which:

  (i)   Is *not* a business combination, *and*
  (ii)   At the time of the transaction affects neither accounting profit nor taxable profit

Try to **understand the reasoning** behind the recognition of deferred tax liabilities on taxable temporary differences.

(a)   When an **asset is recognised**, it is expected that its carrying amount will be recovered in the form of economic benefits that flow to the entity in future periods.

(b)   If the carrying amount of the asset is **greater than** its tax basis, then taxable economic benefits will also be greater than the amount that will be allowed as a deduction for tax purposes.

(c)   The difference is therefore a **taxable temporary difference** and the obligation to pay the resulting income taxes in future periods is a **deferred tax liability**.

(d)   As the entity recovers the carrying amount of the asset, the taxable temporary difference will **reverse** and the entity will have taxable profit.

(e)   It is then probable that economic benefits will flow from the entity in the form of **tax payments**, and so the recognition of all deferred tax liabilities (except those excluded above) is required.

3.2 Example: taxable temporary differences

A company purchased an asset costing $1,500. At the end of 20X8 the carrying amount is $1,000. The cumulative depreciation for tax purposes is $900 and the current tax rate is 25%.

Required

Calculate the deferred tax liability for the asset.

Solution

Firstly, what is the tax basis of the asset? It is $1,500 – $900 = $600.

In order to recover the carrying value of $1,000, the entity must earn taxable income of $1,000, but it will only be able to deduct $600 as a taxable expense. The entity must therefore pay income tax of $400 × 25% = $100 when the carrying value of the asset is recovered.

The entity must therefore recognise a deferred tax liability of $400 × 25% = $100, recognising the difference between the carrying amount of $1,000 and the tax basis of $600 as a taxable temporary difference.

3.3 Timing differences

Some temporary differences are often called **timing differences**, when income or expense is included in accounting profit in one period, but is included in taxable profit in a different period. The main types of taxable temporary differences which are timing differences and which result in deferred tax liabilities are included in the examples given above.

- **Interest received** which is accounted for on an accruals basis, but which for tax purposes is included on a cash basis.
- **Accelerated depreciation** for tax purposes.
- Capitalised and amortised **development costs**.

Activity

Jonquil Co buys equipment for $50,000 and depreciates it on a straight line basis over its expected useful life of five years. For tax purposes, the equipment is depreciated at 25% per annum on a straight line basis. Tax losses may be carried back against taxable profit of the previous five years. In year 20X0, the entity's taxable profit was $25,000. The tax rate is 40%.

Required

Assuming nil profits/losses after depreciation in years 20X1 to 20X5 show the current and deferred tax impact in years 20X1 to 20X5 of the acquisition of the equipment.

Answer

Jonquil Co will recover the carrying amount of the equipment by using it to manufacture goods for resale. Therefore, the entity's current tax computation is as follows.

	Year				
	20X1	*20X2*	*20X3*	*20X4*	*20X5*
	$	*$*	*$*	*$*	*$*
Taxable income*	10,000	10,000	10,000	10,000	10,000
Depreciation for tax purposes	12,500	12,500	12,500	12,500	0
Taxable profit (tax loss)	(2,500)	(2,500)	(2,500)	(2,500)	10,000
Current tax expense (income) at 40%	(1,000)	(1,000)	(1,000)	(1,000)	4,000

* ie nil profit plus $50,000 ÷ 5 depreciation add-back.

The entity recognises a current tax asset at the end of years 20X1 to 20X4 because it recovers the benefit of the tax loss against the taxable profit of year 20X0.

The temporary differences associated with the equipment and the resulting deferred tax asset and liability and deferred tax expense and income are as follows.

	Year				
	20X1	*20X2*	*20X3*	*20X4*	*20X5*
	$	*$*	*$*	*$*	*$*
Carrying amount	40,000	30,000	20,000	10,000	0
Tax basis	37,500	25,000	12,500	0	0
Taxable temporary difference	2,500	5,000	7,500	10,000	0
Opening deferred tax liability	0	1,000	2,000	3,000	4,000
Deferred tax expense (income): bal fig	1,000	1,000	1,000	1,000	(4,000)
Closing deferred tax liability @ 40%	1,000	2,000	3,000	4,000	0

The entity recognises the deferred tax liability in years 20X1 to 20X4 because the reversal of the taxable temporary difference will create taxable income in subsequent years. The entity's income statement is as follows.

	Year				
	20X1	20X2	20X3	20X4	20X5
	$	$	$	$	$
Income	10,000	10,000	10,000	10,000	10,000
Depreciation	10,000	10,000	10,000	10,000	10,000
Profit before tax	0	0	0	0	0
Current tax expense (income)	(1,000)	(1,000)	(1,000)	(1,000)	4,000
Deferred tax expense (income)	1,000	1,000	1,000	1,000	(4,000)
Total tax expense (income)	0	0	0	0	0
Net profit for the period	0	0	0	0	0

3.4 Section summary

- With one or two exceptions, all taxable temporary differences give rise to a **deferred tax liability**.
- Many taxable temporary differences are **timing differences**.
- Timing differences arise when income or an expense is included in accounting profit in one period, but in taxable profit in a **different period**.

4 Deductible temporary differences

4.1 Definition

Refer again to the definition given in Section 3 above.

Exam focus point

> The rule to remember here is that:
>
> 'All deductible temporary differences give rise to a deferred tax asset.'

There is a proviso, however. The deferred tax asset must also satisfy the **recognition criteria** which is that a deferred tax asset should be recognised for all deductible temporary differences to the extent that it is **probable that taxable profit will be available** against which it can be utilised. This is an application of prudence. Before we look at this issue in more detail, let us consider some examples of deductible temporary differences.

4.2 Transactions that affect the statement of comprehensive income

(a) **Retirement benefit costs** (pension costs) are deducted from accounting profit as service is provided by the employee. They are not deducted in determining taxable profit until the entity pays either retirement benefits or contributions to a fund. (This may also apply to similar expenses.)

(b) **Accumulated depreciation** of an asset in the financial statements is greater than the accumulated depreciation allowed for tax purposes up to the end of the reporting period.

(c) The **cost of inventories** sold before the end of the reporting period is deducted from accounting profit when goods/services are delivered, but is deducted from taxable profit when the cash is received. (*Note.* There is also a taxable temporary difference associated with the related trade receivable, as noted in Section 3 above.)

(d) The **NRV** of inventory, or the **recoverable amount** of an item of property, plant and equipment falls and the carrying value is therefore **reduced**, but that reduction is ignored for tax purposes until the asset is sold.

(e) **Research costs** (or organisation/other start-up costs) are recognised as an expense for accounting purposes but are not deductible against taxable profits until a later period.

(f) Income is **deferred** in the statement of financial position, but has already been included in taxable profit in current/prior periods.

4.3 Fair value adjustments

Current investments or **financial instruments** may be carried at fair value which is less than cost, but no equivalent adjustment is made for tax purposes.

4.4 Recognition of deductible temporary differences

We looked at the important recognition criteria in Section 4.1 above. As with temporary taxable differences, there are also circumstances where the overall rule for recognition of a deferred tax asset is *not* allowed.

(a) Where the deferred tax asset arises from **negative goodwill** which is treated as deferred income.

(b) Where the deferred tax asset arises from **initial recognition** of an asset or liability in a transaction which:

  (i) Is not a business combination, *and*

  (ii) At the time of the transaction, affects neither accounting nor taxable profit/tax loss.

Let us lay out the reasoning behind the recognition of deferred tax assets arising from deductible temporary differences.

(a) When a **liability is recognised**, it is assumed that its carrying amount will be settled in the form of outflows of economic benefits from the entity in future periods.

(b) When these resources flow from the entity, part or all may be deductible in determining taxable profits of a **period later** than that in which the liability is recognised.

(c) A **temporary tax difference** then exists between the carrying amount of the liability and its tax basis.

(d) A **deferred tax asset** therefore arises, representing the income taxes that will be recoverable in future periods when that part of the liability is allowed as a deduction from taxable profit.

(e) Similarly, when the carrying amount of an asset is **less than its tax basis**, the difference gives rise to a deferred tax asset in respect of the income taxes that will be recoverable in future periods.

4.5 Example: deductible temporary differences

Pargatha Co recognises a liability of $10,000 for accrued product warranty costs on 31 December 20X7. These product warranty costs will not be deductible for tax purposes until the entity pays claims. The tax rate is 25%.

Required

State the deferred tax implications of this situation.

Solution

What is the tax basis of the liability? It is nil (carrying amount of $10,000 less the amount that will be deductible for tax purposes in respect of the liability in future periods).

When the liability is settled for its carrying amount, the entity's future taxable profit will be reduced by $10,000 and so its future tax payments by $10,000 × 25% = $2,500.

The difference of $10,000 between the carrying amount ($10,000) and the tax basis (nil) is a deductible temporary difference. The entity should therefore recognise a deferred tax asset of $10,000 × 25% = $2,500 **provided that** it is probable that the entity will earn sufficient taxable profits in future periods to benefit from a reduction in tax payments.

4.6 Taxable profits in future periods

When can we be sure that sufficient taxable profit will be available against which a deductible temporary difference can be utilised? This will be assumed when sufficient **taxable temporary differences** exist which relate to the same taxation authority and the same taxable entity. These should be expected to reverse:

(a)   In the same period as the expected reversal of the deductible temporary difference, *or*

(b)   In periods into which a tax loss arising from the deferred tax asset can be carried back or forward.

Only in these circumstances is the deferred tax asset **recognised**, in the period in which the deductible temporary differences arise.

4.7 Unused tax losses and unused tax credits

An entity may have unused tax losses or credits (ie which it can offset against taxable profits) at the end of a period. Should a deferred tax asset be recognised in relation to such amounts? A deferred tax asset may be recognised in such circumstances **to the extent that it is probable future taxable profit will be available against which the unused tax losses/credits can be utilised**.

4.8 Section summary

- Deductible temporary differences give rise to a **deferred tax asset**.
- **Prudence** dictates that deferred tax assets can only be recognised when **sufficient future taxable profits** exist against which they can be utilised.

5 Measurement and recognition of deferred tax

5.1 Basis of provision of deferred tax

The IFRS adopts the **full provision** method of accounting for deferred tax.

The **full provision method** has the **advantage** that it recognises that each temporary difference at the end of the reporting period has an effect on future tax payments. If a company claims an accelerated tax allowance on an item of plant, future tax assessments will be bigger than they would have been otherwise. Future transactions may well affect those assessments still further, but that is not relevant in assessing the position at the end of the reporting period.

5.2 Example

Suppose that Girdo Co begins trading on 1 January 20X7. In its first year it makes profits of $5m, the depreciation charge is $1m and the tax allowances on those assets is $1.5m. The rate of income tax is 30%.

Solution: full provision

The tax liability is $1.35m (30% × $m(5.0 + 1.0 −1.5), but the debit to profit or loss is increased by the deferred tax liability of 30% × $0.5m = $150,000. The total charge to profit or loss is therefore $1.5m which is an effective tax rate of 30% on accounting profits (ie 30% × $5.0m).

5.3 Changes in tax rates

Where the corporate rate of income tax **fluctuates from one year to another**, a problem arises in respect of the amount of deferred tax to be credited (debited) to the statement of comprehensive income in later years.

The IFRS requires deferred tax assets and liabilities to be measured at the tax rates expected to apply in the period **when the asset is realised or liability settled**, based on tax rates and laws enacted (or substantively enacted) at the end of the reporting period. This is known as the **liability method**.

5.4 Discounting

Discounting is used to allow for the effect of the time value of money.

The IFRS states that deferred tax assets and liabilities **should not be discounted**.

5.5 Carrying amount of deferred tax assets

The carrying amount of deferred tax assets should be **reviewed at the end of each reporting period** and reduced where appropriate (insufficient future taxable profits). Such a reduction may be reversed in future years.

5.6 Recognition

As with current tax, deferred tax should normally be recognised as income or an expense and included in the net profit or loss for the period in the **statement of comprehensive income**. The exception is where the tax arises from a transaction or event which is recognised (in the same or a different period) **directly in equity**.

The figures shown for deferred tax in the statement of comprehensive income will consist of **two components**.

(a)   Deferred tax relating to **timing differences**.

(b)   Adjustments relating to **changes in the carrying amount of deferred tax assets/liabilities** (where there is no change in timing differences), eg changes in tax rates/laws, reassessment of the recoverability of deferred tax assets, or a change in the expected recovery of an asset.

Items in (b) will be recognised in profit or loss, *unless* they relate to items previously charged/credited to equity.

Deferred tax (and current tax) should be **charged/credited directly to equity** if the tax relates to items also charged/credited directly to equity (in the same or a different period).

5.7 Why do we recognise deferred tax?

(a)   Adjustments for deferred tax are made in accordance with the **accruals concept** and in accordance with the definition of a **liability** in the Framework, ie a past event has given rise to an obligation in the form of increased taxation which will be payable in the future. The amount can be reliably estimated. A deferred tax asset similarly meets the definition of an **asset**.

(b)   If the future tax consequences of transactions are not recognised, profit can be overstated, leading to overpayment of dividends and distortion of share price and EPS.

6 Taxation in company accounts

In the statement of financial position the liability for tax payable is the tax charge for the year. In the statement of comprehensive income the tax charge for the year is adjusted for transfers to or from deferred tax and for prior year under- or over-provisions.

We have now looked at the 'ingredients' of taxation in company accounts. There are two aspects to be learned:

(a)   Taxation on profits in the statement of comprehensive income.

(b)   Taxation payments due, shown as a liability in the statement of financial position.

6.1 Taxation in the statement of comprehensive income

The tax on profit on ordinary activities is calculated by **aggregating**:

(a)   **Income tax** on taxable profits

(b)   **Transfers to or from deferred taxation**

(c)   Any **under provision or overprovision** of income tax on profits of previous years

When income tax on profits is calculated, **the calculation is only an estimate of what the company thinks its tax liability will be. In subsequent dealings with the tax authorities, a different income tax charge might eventually be agreed.**

The difference between the estimated tax on profits for one year and the actual tax charge finally agreed for the year is made as an adjustment to taxation on profits in the following year, **resulting in the disclosure of either an underprovision or an overprovision of tax.**

6.2 Taxation in the statement of financial position

It should already be apparent from the previous examples that the income tax charge in the statement of comprehensive income will not be the same as income tax liabilities in the statement of financial position.

In the statement of financial position, there are several items which we might expect to find.

(a)   **Income tax may be payable** in respect of (say) interest payments paid in the last accounting return period of the year, or accrued.

(b)   If no tax is payable (or very little), then there might be an **income tax recoverable asset** disclosed in current assets (income tax is normally recovered by offset against the tax liability for the year).

(c)   There will usually be a **liability for tax**, possibly including the amounts due in respect of previous years but not yet paid.

(d)   We may also find a **liability on the deferred taxation account**. Deferred taxation is shown under 'non-current liabilities' in the statement of financial position.

 Activity

For the year ended 31 July 20X4 Norman Kronkest Co made taxable trading profits of $1,200,000 on which income tax is payable at 30%.

(a)   A transfer of $20,000 will be made to the deferred taxation account. The balance on this account was $100,000 before making any adjustments for items listed in this paragraph.

(b)   The estimated tax on profits for the year ended 31 July 20X3 was $80,000, but tax has now been agreed at $84,000 and fully paid.

(c)   Tax on profits for the year to 31 July 20X4 is payable on 1 May 20X5.

(d)   In the year to 31 July 20X4 the company made a capital gain of $60,000 on the sale of some property. This gain is taxable at a rate of 30%.

Required

(a)   Calculate the tax charge for the year to 31 July 20X4.

(b)   Calculate the tax liabilities in the statement of financial position of Norman Kronkest as at 31 July 20X4.

 Answer

(a)   *Tax charge for the year*

		$
(i)	Tax on trading profits (30% of $1,200,000)	360,000
	Tax on capital gain	18,000
	Deferred taxation	20,000
		398,000
	Underprovision of taxation in previous years $(84,000 – 80,000)	4,000
	Tax charge on profit for the period	402,000

(ii)   *Note.* The statement of comprehensive income will show the following.

	$
Profit before tax (1,200,000 + 60,000)	1,260,000
Income tax expense	(402,000)
Profit for the year	858,000

(b)

	$
Deferred taxation	
Balance brought forward	100,000
Transferred from profit or loss	20,000
Deferred taxation in the statement of financial position	120,000

The tax liability is as follows.

	$
Payable on 1 May 20X5	
Tax on profits (30% of $1,200,000)	360,000
Tax on capital gain (30% of $60,000)	18,000
Due on 1 May 20X5	378,000

	$
Summary	
Current liabilities	
Tax, payable on 1 May 20X5	378,000
Non-current liabilities	
Deferred taxation	120,000

Note. It may be helpful to show the journal entries for these items.

		$	$
DEBIT	Tax charge (statement of comprehensive income)	402,000	
CREDIT	Tax payable		*382,000
	Deferred tax		20,000

* This account will show a debit balance of $4,000 until the underprovision is recorded, since payment has already been made: (360,000 + 18,000 + 4,000). The closing balance will therefore be $378,000.

6.3 Presentation of tax assets and liabilities

These should be **presented separately** from other assets and liabilities in the statement of financial position. Deferred tax assets and liabilities should be distinguished from current tax assets and liabilities.

In addition, deferred tax assets/liabilities should *not* be classified as current assets/liabilities, where an entity makes such a distinction.

There are only limited circumstances where **current tax** assets and liabilities may be **offset**. This should only occur if two things apply

(a)   The entity has a legally enforceable right to set off the recognised amounts.

(b)   The entity intends either to settle on a net basis, or to realise the asset and settle the liability simultaneously.

Similar criteria apply to the **offset of deferred tax assets and liabilities**.

6.4 Presentation of tax expense

The tax expense or income related to the profit or loss for the period should be presented in the statement of comprehensive income.

Unit Roundup

- Taxation consists of **two components.**
  - Current tax
  - Deferred tax

- **Current tax** is the amount payable to the tax authorities in relation to the trading activities during the period. It is generally straightforward.

- **Deferred tax** is an accounting measure, used to match the tax effects of transactions with their accounting impact. It is quite complex.

- **Deferred tax assets and liabilities** arise from deductible and taxable temporary differences.

- In the statement of financial position the liability for tax payable is the tax charge for the year. In the statement of comprehensive income the tax charge for the year is adjusted for transfers to or from deferred tax and for prior year under- or over-provisions.

Quick quiz

1   The tax expense related to the profit for the period should be shown in the statement of comprehensive income.

    True ☐

    False ☐

2   Deferred tax liabilities are the amounts of income taxes payable in future periods in respect of
    ....

3   Give three examples of temporary differences.

4   An entity has a tax overprovision relating to the prior year of $3,000. Taxable temporary differences have increased by $6,000 and profit for the year is $150,000. Tax is at 30%.

    What is the charge to profit or loss?

Answers to quick quiz

1   True

2   Taxable temporary differences

3   Any three of:

- Interest revenue received in arrears
- Depreciation accelerated for tax purposes
- Development costs capitalised in the statement of financial position
- Prepayments
- Sale of goods revenue recognised before the cash is received

4     $43,800

	$
Tax on profit (150,000 × 30%)	45,000
Overprovision	(3,000)
Deferred tax increase (6,000 × 30%)	1,800
	43,800

Now try the question below

Neil Down Co   18 mins

In the accounting year to 31 December 20X3, Neil Down Co made an operating profit before taxation of $110,000.

Income tax on the operating profit has been estimated as $45,000. In the previous year (20X2) income tax on 20X2 profits had been estimated as $38,000 but it was subsequently agreed at $40,500.

A transfer to the credit of the deferred taxation account of $16,000 will be made in 20X3.

Required

(a)   Calculate the tax on profits for 20X3 for disclosure in the accounts.   **(7 marks)**

(b)   Calculate the amount of tax payable.   **(3 marks)**

       (Total = 10 marks)

Answer

Neil Down Co

(a)

	$
Income tax on profits (liability in the statement of FP)	45,000
Deferred taxation	16,000
Underprovision of tax in previous year $(40,500 − 38,000)	2,500
Tax on profits for 20X3 (income statement charge)	63,500

(b)

	$
Tax payable on 20X3 profits (liability)	45,000

Financial instruments

12

Unit topic list

1　Financial instruments
2　Recognition of financial instruments
3　Measurement of financial instruments

Assessment criteria

4　**Understand and apply IFRS for SMEs in the preparation of their financial statements**

4.5　Understand and apply section 11 of IFRS for SMEs when an SME has basic financial instruments

1 Financial instruments

Financial instruments can be very complex, particularly derivative instruments.

1.1 Introduction

Section 11 of the IFRS for SMEs deals with basic financial instruments and Section 12 deals with other financial instruments Section 11 is relevant to all entities and is examinable for this syllabus. Section 12 applies to more complex financial instruments and transactions and is not examinable for this syllabus.

An entity shall choose to apply either:

(a)   the provisions of both Section 11 and Section 12 in full, or

(b)   the recognition and measurement provisions of IAS 39 *Financial Instruments: Recognition and Measurement* and the disclosure requirements of Sections 11 and 12 to account for all of its financial instruments.

It is believed that most SMEs will choose to follow the *IFRS for SMEs* rather than the more complex IAS 39.

1.2 Definitions

Key terms

> - **Financial instrument.** Any contract that gives rise to both a financial asset of one entity and a financial liability or equity instrument of another entity.
>
> - **Financial asset.** Any asset that is:
>
>   (a)   cash
>
>   (b)   an equity instrument of another entity
>
>   (c)   a contractual right to receive cash or another financial asset from another entity; or to exchange financial instruments with another entity under conditions that are potentially favourable to the entity
>
> - **Financial liability.** Any liability that is:
>
>   (a)   a contractual obligation:
>
>   (i)   to deliver cash or another financial asset to another entity, or
>
>   (ii)   to exchange financial instruments with another entity under conditions that are potentially unfavourable
>
> - **Equity instrument.** Any contract that evidences a residual interest in the assets of an entity after deducting all of its liabilities.
>
> - **Fair value** is the amount for which an asset could be exchanged, or a liability settled, between knowledgeable, willing parties in an arm's length transaction.   *(IFRS for SMEs)*

We should clarify some points arising from these definitions. Firstly, one or two terms above should be themselves defined.

(a)   A '**contract**' need not be in writing, but it must comprise an agreement that has 'clear economic consequences' and which the parties to it cannot avoid, usually because the agreement is enforceable in law.

(b)   An '**entity**' here could be an individual, partnership, incorporated body or government agency.

The definitions of **financial assets** and **financial liabilities** may seem rather circular, referring as they do to the terms financial asset and financial instrument. The point is that there may be a chain of contractual rights and obligations, but it will lead ultimately to the receipt or payment of cash *or* the acquisition or issue of an equity instrument.

Examples of **financial assets** include:

(a) Trade receivables
(b) Options
(c) Shares (when held as an investment)

Examples of **financial liabilities** include:

(a) Trade payables
(b) Debenture loans payable
(c) Redeemable preference (non-equity) shares

2 Recognition of financial instruments

The IFRS for SMEs establishes principles for recognising and measuring financial assets and financial liabilities.

2.1 Scope

Section 11 of the *IFRS for SMEs* applies to the following financial instruments:

(a) Cash

(b) A debt instrument (such as an account, note, or loan receivable or payable) meeting the conditions below

(c) A commitment to receive a loan that:

    (i) cannot be settled net in cash, and
    (ii) when the commitment is executed, is expected to meet certain conditions

(d) An investment in non-convertible preference shares and non-puttable ordinary shares or preference shares.

Relevant debt instruments are those that satisfy all of the conditions in (a)–(d) below:

(a) Returns to the holder are

    (i) a fixed amount;
    (ii) a fixed rate of return over the life of the instrument;
    (iii) a variable return that, throughout the life of the instrument, is equal to a single referenced quoted or observable interest rate (such as LIBOR); or
    (iv) some combination of such fixed rate and variable rates (such as LIBOR plus 200 basis points), provided that both the fixed and variable rates are positive (eg an interest rate swap with a positive fixed rate and negative variable rate would not meet this criterion). For fixed and variable rate interest returns, interest is calculated by multiplying the rate for the applicable period by the principal amount outstanding during the period.

(b) There is no contractual provision that could, by its terms, result in the holder losing the principal amount or any interest attributable to the current period or prior periods. The fact that a debt instrument is subordinated to other debt instruments is not an example of such a contractual provision.

(c) Contractual provisions that permit the issuer (the debtor) to prepay a debt instrument or permit the holder (the creditor) to put it back to the issuer before maturity are not contingent on future events.

(d) There are no conditional returns or repayment provisions except for the variable rate return described in (a) and prepayment provisions described in (c).

Examples of financial instruments that would normally satisfy the conditions above are:

(a) Trade accounts and notes receivable and payable, and loans from banks or other third parties.

(b) Accounts payable in a foreign currency.

(c) Loans to or from subsidiaries or associates that are due on demand.

(d) A debt instrument that would become immediately receivable if the issuer defaults on an interest or principal payment

2.2 Initial recognition

A financial asset or financial liability should be recognised in the statement of financial position when the reporting entity becomes a party to the contractual provisions of the instrument.

Notice that this is **different** from the recognition criteria in the *Concepts and Pervasive Principles* chapter of the IFRS for SMEs and in most other standards. Items are normally recognised when there is a probable inflow or outflow of resources and the item has a cost or value that can be measured reliably.

2.3 Derecognition

Derecognition is the removal of a previously recognised financial instrument from an entity's statement of financial position.

An entity should derecognise a **financial asset** when:

(a) the **contractual rights** to the cash flows from the financial asset **expire**; or
(b) it transfers substantially all the risks and rewards of ownership of the financial asset to another party.

Exam focus point

The principle here is that of **substance over form**.

An entity should derecognise a **financial liability** when it is **extinguished** – ie, when the obligation specified in the contract is discharged or cancelled or expires.

It is possible for only **part** of a financial asset or liability to be derecognised. This is allowed if the part comprises:

(a) only specifically identified cash flows; or
(b) only a fully proportionate (pro rata) share of the total cash flows.

For example, if an entity holds a bond it has the right to two separate sets of cash inflows: those relating to the principal and those relating to the interest. It could sell the right to receive the interest to another party while retaining the right to receive the principal.

On derecognition, the amount to be included in net profit or loss for the period is calculated as follows:

	$	$
Carrying amount of asset/liability (or the portion of asset/liability) transferred		X
Less: Proceeds received/paid	X	
Any cumulative gain or loss reported in equity	X	
		(X)
Difference to net profit/loss		X

Where only part of a financial asset is derecognised, the carrying amount of the asset should be allocated between the part retained and the part transferred based on their relative fair values on the date of transfer. A gain or loss should be recognised based on the proceeds for the portion transferred.

3 Measurement of financial instruments

All financial assets should be initially measured at cost.

3.1 Initial measurement

Financial instruments are initially measured at the **fair value** of the consideration given or received (ie, **cost**) **plus** (in most cases) **transaction costs** that are **directly attributable** to the acquisition or issue of the financial instrument.

The **exception** to this rule is where a financial instrument is designated as **at fair value through profit or loss**. In this case, **transaction costs** are **not** added to fair value at initial recognition.

The fair value of the consideration is normally the transaction price or market prices. If market prices are not reliable, the fair value may be **estimated** using a valuation technique (for example, by discounting cash flows).

3.2 Examples – financial assets

1   For a long-term loan made to another entity, a receivable is recognised at the present value of cash receivable (including interest payments and repayment of principal) from that entity.

2   For goods sold to a customer on short-term credit, a receivable is recognised at the undiscounted amount of cash receivable from that entity, which is normally the invoice price.

3   For an item sold to a customer on two-year interest-free credit, a receivable is recognised at the current cash sale price for that item. If the current cash sale price is not known, it may be estimated as the present value of the cash receivable discounted using the prevailing market rate(s) of interest for a similar receivable.

4   For a cash purchase of another entity's ordinary shares, the investment is recognised at the amount of cash paid to acquire the shares.

3.3 Examples – financial liabilities

1   For a loan received from a bank, a payable is recognised initially at the present value of cash payable to the bank (eg including interest payments and repayment of principal).

2   For goods purchased from a supplier on short-term credit, a payable is recognised at the undiscounted amount owed to the supplier, which is normally the invoice price.

3.4 Subsequent measurement

At the end of each **reporting period**, financial instruments should be measured as follows:

(a)   Debt instruments shall be measured at **amortised cost** using the **effective interest method**.

(b)   Debt instruments that are classified as current assets or current liabilities shall be measured at the undiscounted amount of the cash or other consideration expected to be paid or received.

(c)   Commitments to receive a loan shall be measured at cost (which sometimes is nil) less impairment.

(d)   Investments in non-convertible preference shares and non-puttable ordinary or preference shares shall be measured as follows

(i)   if the shares are publicly traded or their fair value can otherwise be measured reliably, the investment shall be measured at fair value with changes in fair value recognised in profit or loss.

(ii)   all other such investments shall be measured at cost less impairment.

3.5 Example: amortised cost

On 1 January 20X1 Abacus Co purchases a debt instrument for its fair value of $1,000. The debt instrument is due to mature on 31 December 20X5. The instrument has a principal amount of $1,250 and the instrument carries fixed interest at 4.72% that is paid annually. The effective rate of interest is 10%.

How should Abacus Co account for the debt instrument over its five year term?

Solution

Abacus Co will receive interest of $59 (1,250 × 4.72%) each year and $1,250 when the instrument matures.

Abacus must allocate the discount of $250 and the interest receivable over the five year term at a constant rate on the carrying amount of the debt. To do this, it must apply the effective interest rate of 10%.

The following table shows the allocation over the years:

Year	Amortised cost at beginning of year	Income statement: Interest income for year (@10%)	Interest received during year (cash inflow)	Amortised cost at end of year
	$	$	$	$
20X1	1,000	100	(59)	1,041
20X2	1,041	104	(59)	1,086
20X3	1,086	109	(59)	1,136
20X4	1,136	113	(59)	1,190
20X5	1,190	119	(1,250+59)	–

Each year the carrying amount of the financial asset is increased by the interest income for the year and reduced by the interest actually received during the year.

Investments whose **fair value cannot be reliably measured** should be measured at **cost**.

3.6 Impairment and uncollectability of financial assets

At each reporting date, an entity should assess whether there is any objective evidence of impairment of any financial assets that are measured at cost or amortised cost.

Where there is objective evidence of impairment, the entity should **determine the amount** of any impairment loss and recognise it in profit or loss immediately.

3.6.1 Financial assets carried at amortised cost

The impairment loss is the **difference** between the asset's **carrying amount** and its **recoverable amount**. The asset's recoverable amount is the present value of estimated future cash flows, discounted at the financial instrument's **original** effective interest rate.

The amount of the loss should be **recognised in profit or loss.**

3.6.2 Financial assets carried at cost

The impairment loss is the difference between the asset's **carrying amount** and the **best estimate** of the amount that the entity would receive for the asset if it were to be sold at the reporting date.

3.7 Statement of financial position – categories of financial assets and financial liabilities

An entity shall disclose the carrying amounts of each of the following categories of financial assets and financial liabilities at the reporting date, in total, either in the statement of financial position or in the notes:

(a) Financial assets measured at fair value through profit or loss
(b) Financial assets that are debt instruments measured at amortised cost
(c) Financial assets that are equity instruments measured at cost less impairment
(d) Financial liabilities measured at fair value through profit or loss
(e) Financial liabilities measured at amortised cost
(f) Loan commitments measured at cost less impairment

Unit Roundup

- Financial instruments can be very complex, particularly derivative instruments
- *The IFRS for SMEs* establishes principles for recognising and measuring financial assets and financial liabilities.
- **All financial assets and liabilities** should be **recognised in the statement of financial position.**
- **Financial assets** should **initially** be measured at **cost = the fair value** of the consideration paid.
- Subsequently they should be **re-measured to either fair value** or amortised cost.

Quick Quiz

1   Define the following.

    (a)   Financial asset
    (b)   Financial liability

2   What is the critical feature used to identify a financial liability?

3   When should a financial asset be de-recognised?

4   How are financial instruments initially measured?

5   After initial recognition, all financial liabilities should be measured at amortised cost. True or false?

1   See Key Terms, paragraph 1.2

2   The contractual obligation to deliver cash or another financial asset to the holder

3   Financial assets should be derecognised when the rights to the cash flows from the asset expire or where substantially all the risks and rewards of ownership are transferred to another party.

4   At cost

5   False. See paragraph 3.5

Now try the question below

Galaxy Co
9 mins

Galaxy Co issues a bond for $503,778 on 1 January 20X2. No interest is payable on the bond, but it will be held to maturity and redeemed on 31 December 20X4 for $600,000. The bond has **not** been designated as at fair value through profit or loss. The effective interest rate is 6%.

Required

Calculate the charge to the income statement of Galaxy Co for the year ended 31 December 20X2 and the balance outstanding at 31 December 20X2.
(5 marks)

Answer

Galaxy Co

The bond is a 'deep discount' bond and is a financial liability of Galaxy Co. It is measured at amortised cost. Although there is no interest as such, the difference between the initial cost of the bond and the price at which it will be redeemed is a finance cost. This must be allocated over the term of the bond at a constant rate on the carrying amount. This is done by applying the effective interest rate.

The charge to the income statement is $30,226 (503,778 × 6%)

The balance outstanding at 31 December 20X2 is $534,004 (503,778 + 30,226)

Employee benefits

13

Unit topic list

1 Employee benefits
2 Post-employment benefits
3 Defined contribution plans
4 Defined benefit plans: recognition and measurement
5 Defined benefit plans: other matters
6 Share based payment

Assessment criteria

4   Understand and apply IFRS for SMEs in the preparation of their financial statements

4.18   Obtain an understanding of share-based payments and employee benefits as contained in section 26 and section 28 of the IFRS for SMEs

1 Employee benefits

1.1 The conceptual nature of employee benefit costs

When a company or other entity employs a new worker, that worker will be offered a **package of pay and benefits.** Some of these will be short-term and the employee will receive the benefit at about the same time as he or she earns it, for example basic pay, overtime etc. Other employee benefits are **deferred**, however, the main example being retirement benefits (ie a pension).

1.2 Accounting for employee benefit costs

Accounting for **short-term employee benefit costs** tends to be quite straightforward, because they are simply recognised as an expense in the employer's financial statements of the current period.

Accounting for the cost of **deferred employee benefits** is much more difficult. This is because of the large amounts involved, as well as the long time scale, complicated estimates and uncertainties. In the past, entities accounted for these benefits simply by charging profit or loss (the income statements) of the employing entity on the basis of actual payments made. This led to substantial variations in reported profits of these entities and disclosure of information on these costs was usually sparse.

1.3 IFRS for SMEs and employee benefits

The IFRS is intended to prescribe the following.

(a)   When the cost of employee benefits should be **recognised as a liability or an expense**
(b)   The **amount** of the liability or expense that should be recognised

As a basic rule, the IFRS states the following.

(a)   A **liability** should be recognised when an employee has provided a service in exchange for benefits to be received by the employee at some time in the future.

(b)   An **expense** should be recognised when the entity enjoys the economic benefits from a service provided by an employee regardless of when the employee received or will receive the benefits from providing the service.

The basic problem is therefore fairly straightforward. An entity will often enjoy the **economic benefits** from the services provided by its employees in advance of the employees receiving all the employment benefits from the work they have done, for example they will not receive pension benefits until after they retire.

1.4 Categories of employee benefits

The standard recognises four categories of employee benefits, and proposes a different accounting treatment for each. These four categories are as follows.

1   Short-term benefits including:
- Wages and salaries
- Social security contributions
- Paid annual leave
- Paid sick leave
- Paid maternity/paternity leave
- Profit shares and bonuses paid within 12 months of the year end
- Paid jury service
- Paid military service
- Non-monetary benefits, eg medical care, cars, free goods

2   Post-employment benefits, eg pensions and post-employment medical care

3   Other long-term benefits, eg profit shares, bonuses or deferred compensation payable later than 12 months after the year end, sabbatical leave, long-service benefits

4   Termination benefits, eg early retirement payments and redundancy payments

Benefits may be paid to the employees themselves, to their dependants (spouses, children, etc) or to third parties.

1.5 Definitions

There are a great many important definitions. They are grouped together here, but you should refer back to them as necessary as you work through the rest of this chapter.

Key terms

Employee benefits are all forms of consideration given by an entity in exchange for service rendered by employees.

Short-term employee benefits are employee benefits (other than termination benefits) which fall due wholly within twelve months after the end of the period in which the employees render the related service.

Post-employment benefits are employee benefits (other than termination benefits) which are payable after the completion of employment.

Post-employment benefit plans are formal or informal arrangements under which an entity provides post-employment benefits for one or more employees.

Defined contribution plans are post-employment benefit plans under which an entity pays fixed contributions into a separate entity (a fund) and will have no legal or constructive obligation to pay further contributions if the fund does not hold sufficient assets to pay all employee benefits relating to employee service in the current and prior periods.

Defined benefit plans are post-employment benefit plans other than defined contribution plans.

Multi-employer plans are defined contribution plans (other than state plans) or defined benefit plans (other than state plans) that:

(a) pool the assets contributed by various entities that are not under common control, and

(b) use those assets to provide benefits to employees of more than one entity, on the basis that contribution and benefit levels are determined without regard to the identity of the entity that employs the employees concerned.

Other long-term employee benefits are employee benefits (other than post-employment benefits and termination benefits) which do not fall due wholly within twelve months after the end of the period in which the employees render the related service.

Termination benefits are employee benefits payable as a result of either:

(a) an entity's decision to terminate an employee's employment before the normal retirement date, or

(b) an employee's decision to accept voluntary redundancy in exchange for those benefits.

Vested employee benefits are employee benefits that are not conditional on future employment.

The **present value of a defined benefit** obligation is the present value, without deducting any plan assets, of expected future payments required to settle the obligation resulting from employee service in the current and prior periods.

Current service cost is the increase in the present value of the defined benefit obligation resulting from employee service in the current period.

Interest cost is the increase during a period in the present value of a defined benefit obligation which arises because the benefits are one period closer to settlement.

Plan assets comprise:

(a) Assets held by a long-term employee benefit fund; and

(b) Qualifying insurance policies

The **return on plan assets** is interest, dividends and other revenue derived from the plan assets, together with realised and unrealised gains or losses on the plan assets, less any cost of administering the plan and loess any tax payable by the plan itself.

Actuarial gains and losses comprise:

(a) Experience adjustments (the effects of differences between the previous actuarial assumptions and what has actually occurred), and

(b) The effects of changes in actuarial assumptions.

Past service cost is the change in the present value of the defined benefit obligation for employee service in prior periods, resulting in the current period from the introduction of, or changes to, post-employment benefits or other long-term employee benefits. Past service cost may be either positive (when benefits are introduced or changed so that the present value of the defined benefit obligation increases) or negative (when existing benefits are changed so that the present value of the defined benefit obligation decreases).

2 Post-employment benefits

There are two types of post-employment benefit plan:

- Defined contribution plans
- Defined benefit plans

Defined contribution plans are simple to account for as the benefits are defined by the contributions made.

Defined benefit plans are much more difficult to deal with as the benefits are promised, they define the contributions to be made.

Many employers provide post-employment benefits for their employees after they have stopped working. **Pension schemes** are the most obvious example, but an employer might provide post-employment death benefits to the dependants of former employees, or post-employment medical care.

Post-employment benefit schemes are often referred to as **'plans'**. The 'plan' receives regular contributions from the employer (and sometimes from current employees as well) and the money is invested in assets, such as stocks and shares and other investments. The post-employment benefits are paid out of the income from the plan assets (dividends, interest) or from money from the sale of some plan assets.

There are two types or categories of post-employment benefit plan, as given in the definitions in Section 1 above.

(a) **Defined contribution plans**. With such plans, the employer (and possibly current employees too) pay regular contributions into the plan of a given or 'defined' amount each year. The contributions are invested, and the size of the post-employment benefits paid to former employees depends on how well or how badly the plan's investments perform. If the investments perform well, the plan will be able to afford higher benefits than if the investments performed less well.

(b) **Defined benefit plans**. With these plans, the size of the post-employment benefits is determined in advance, ie the benefits are 'defined'. The employer (and possibly current employees too) pay contributions into the plan, and the contributions are invested. The size of the contributions is set at an amount that is expected to earn enough investment returns to meet the obligation to pay the post-employment benefits. If, however, it becomes apparent that the assets in the fund are insufficient, the employer will be required to make additional contributions into the plan to make up the expected shortfall. On the other hand, if the fund's assets appear to be larger than they need to be, and in excess of what is required to pay the post-employment benefits, the employer may be allowed to take a 'contribution holiday' (ie stop paying in contributions for a while).

It is important to make a clear distinction between the following.

(a) **Funding** a defined benefit plan, ie paying contributions into the plan
(b) **Accounting for** the cost of funding a defined benefit plan

2.1 Multi-employer plans

These were defined above. The IFRS requires an entity to **classify** such a plan as a defined contribution plan or a defined benefit plan, depending on its terms (including any constructive obligation beyond those terms).

For a multi-employer plan that is a **defined benefit plan**, the entity should account for its proportionate share of the defined benefit obligation, plan assets and cost associated with the plan in the same way as for any other defined benefit plan and make full disclosure.

When there is **insufficient information** to use defined benefit accounting, then the multi-employer plan should be accounted for as a defined contribution plan and additional disclosures made (that the plan is in fact a defined benefit plan and information about any known surplus or deficit).

2.2 Section summary

- There are two categories of **post-retirement benefits**:
    - Defined contribution schemes
    - Defined benefit schemes
- **Defined contribution schemes** provide benefits commensurate with the fund available to produce them.
- **Defined benefit schemes** provide promised benefits and so contributions are based on estimates of how the fund will perform.
- **Defined contribution scheme costs** are easy to account for and this is covered in the next section.
- The rest of the chapter deals with the more difficult question of how **defined benefit scheme costs** are accounted for.

3 Defined contribution plans

Accounting for payments into defined contribution plans is straightforward.

(a) The **obligation** is determined by the amount paid into the plan in each period.

(b) There are no actuarial assumptions to make.

(c) If the obligation is settled in the current period (or at least no later than 12 months after the end of the current period) there is **no requirement for discounting**.

The IFRS requires the following.

(a) **Contributions** to a defined contribution plan should be recognised as an **expense** in the period they are payable (except to the extent that labour costs may be included within the cost of assets).

(b) Any liability for **unpaid contributions** that are due as at the end of the period should be recognised as a **liability** (accrued expense).

(c) Any **excess contributions** paid should be recognised as an asset (prepaid expense), but only to the extent that the prepayment will lead to, eg a reduction in future payments or a cash refund.

Disclosure requirements

(a) A **description** of the plan

(b) The amount recognised as an **expense** in the period

4 Defined benefit plans: recognition and measurement

Accounting for defined benefit plans is much more complex. The complexity of accounting for defined benefit plans stems largely from the following factors.

(a) The future benefits (arising from employee service in the current or prior years) **cannot be estimated exactly**, but whatever they are, the employer will have to pay them, and the liability should therefore be recognised now. To estimate these future obligations, it is necessary to use **actuarial assumptions**.

(b) The obligations payable in future years should be valued, by discounting, on a **present value** basis. This is because the obligations may be settled in many years' time.

(c) If actuarial assumptions change, the amount of required contributions to the fund will change, and there may be **actuarial gains or losses**. A contribution into a fund in any period is not necessarily the total for that period, due to actuarial gains or losses.

4.1 Outline of the method

There is a **six-step method** for accounting for the expenses and liability of a defined benefit pension plan.

An outline of the method used for an employer to account for the expenses and obligation of a defined benefit plan is given below. The stages will be explained in more detail later.

Step 1   **Actuarial assumptions** should be used to make a reliable estimate of the amount of future benefits employees have earned from service in relation to the current and prior years. Assumptions include, for example, assumptions about employee turnover, mortality rates, future increases in salaries (if these will affect the eventual size of future benefits such as pension payments).

Step 2   These **future benefits** should be attributed to service performed by employees in the current period, and in prior periods, using the **Projected Unit Credit Method**. This gives a total present value of future benefit obligations arising from past and current periods of service.

Step 3   The **fair value** of any plan assets should be established.

Step 4   The size of any **actuarial gains or losses** should be determined, and the amount of these that will be recognised.

Step 5   If the benefits payable under the plan have been improved, the **extra cost arising from past service** should be determined.

Step 6   If the **benefits payable** under the plan have been reduced or cancelled, the resulting gain should be determined.

4.2 The Projected Unit Credit Method

With this method, it is assumed that each period of service by an employee gives rise to an **additional unit of future benefits**. The present value of that unit of future benefits can be calculated, and attributed to the period in which the service is given. The units, each measured separately, build up to the overall obligation. The accumulated present value of (discounted) future benefits will incur interest over time, and an interest expense should be recognised.

In practice, the mathematics will be complex and you will not need to go into the detail in the exam.

For an SME this method is only used if it can be without undue cost or effort.

If an SME is not able, without undue cost or effort, to use the projected unit credit method to measure its obligation and cost under defined benefit plans, the entity is permitted to make the following simplifications in measuring its defined benefit obligation with respect to current employees:

(a)   ignore estimated future salary increases (ie assume current salaries continue until current employees are expected to begin receiving post-employment benefits);

(b)   ignore future service of current employees (ie assume closure of the plan for existing as well as any new employees); and

(c)   ignore possible in-service mortality of current employees between the reporting date and the date employees are expected to begin receiving post-employment benefits (ie assume all current employees will receive the post-employment benefits). However, mortality after service (ie life expectancy) will still need to be considered.

The IFRS does not require an entity to engage an independent actuary to perform the comprehensive actuarial valuation needed to calculate its defined benefit obligation. Nor does it require that a comprehensive actuarial valuation must be done annually. In the periods between comprehensive actuarial valuations, if the principal actuarial assumptions have not changed significantly the defined benefit obligation can be measured by adjusting the prior period measurement for changes in employee demographics such as number of employees and salary levels.

4.3 Interest cost

The interest cost in the statement of comprehensive income is the **present value of the defined benefit obligation** as at the start of the year multiplied by the discount rate.

Note that the interest charge is *not* the opening statement of financial position liability multiplied by the discount rate, because the liability is stated after deducting the market value of the plan assets and after making certain other adjustments, for example for actuarial gains or losses. Interest is the **obligation** multiplied by the discount rate.

4.4 The statement of financial position

In the statement of financial position, the amount recognised as a **defined benefit liability** (which may be a negative amount, ie an asset) should be the total of the following.

(a)   The **present value of the defined obligation** at the year end, **less**
(b)   The **fair value of the assets of the plan** as at the year end (if there are any) out of which the future obligations to current and past employees will be directly settled

If this total is a **negative amount**, there is an asset and this should be shown in the statement of financial position.

4.4.1 The statement of comprehensive income

The **expense** that should be recognised in the statement of comprehensive income (in profit or loss for the year) for post-employment benefits in a defined benefit plan is the net total of the following.

(a)   The current service cost
(b)   Interest
(c)   The expected return on any plan assets
(d)   The actuarial gains or losses, to the extent that they are recognised in profit or loss although they can be recognised in other comprehensive income
(e)   Past service cost
(f)   The effect of any curtailments or settlements

Activity

Under Hibbo Co's plan, all employees are paid a lump sum retirement benefit of $100,000. They must be still employed aged 55 after 20 years' service, *or* still employed at the age of 65, no matter what their length of service.

Required

State how this benefit should be attributed to service periods.

Answer

This answer is in three parts.

(a)   In the case of those employees joining before age 35, service first leads to benefits under this plan at the age of 35, because an employee could leave at the age of 30 and return at the age of 33, with no effect on the amount/timing of benefits. In addition, service beyond age 55 will lead to no further benefits. Therefore, for these employees Hibbo Co should allocate $100,000 ÷ 20 = $5,000 to each year between the ages of 35 and 55.
(b)   In the case of employees joining between the ages of 35 and 45, service beyond 20 years will lead to no further benefit. For these employees, Hibbo Co should allocate $100,000 ÷ 20 = $5,000 to each of the first 20 years.
(c)   Employees joining at 55 exactly will receive no further benefit past 65, so Hibbo Co should allocate $100,000 ÷ 10 = $10,000 to each of the first 10 years.

The current service cost and the present value of the obligation for all employees reflect the probability that the employee may not complete the necessary period of service.

4.5 Actuarial assumptions

Actuarial assumptions made should be unbiased and based on market expectations.

Discount rates used should be determined by reference to market yields on high-quality fixed-rate corporate bonds.

Actuarial assumptions are needed **to estimate the size of the future (post-employment) benefits** that will be payable under a defined benefits scheme. The main categories of actuarial assumptions are as follows.

(a) **Demographic assumptions** are about mortality rates before and after retirement, the rate of employee turnover, early retirement, claim rates under medical plans for former employees, and so on.

(b) **Financial assumptions** are the discount rate to apply, the expected return on plan assets, future salary levels (allowing for seniority and promotion as well as inflation) and the future rate of increase in medical costs (not just inflationary cost rises, but also cost rises specific to medical treatments and to medical treatments required given the expectations of longer average life expectancy).

The **discount rate** adopted should be determined by reference to **market yields** (at the year end) on high quality fixed-rate corporate bonds. In the absence of a 'deep' market in such bonds, the yields on comparable government bonds should be used as reference instead. The maturity of the corporate bonds that are used to determine a discount rate should have a term to maturity that is consistent with the expected maturity of the post-employment benefit obligations, although a single weighted average discount rate is sufficient.

The guidelines comment that there may be some difficulty in obtaining a **reliable yield for long-term maturities**, say 30 or 40 years from now. This should not, however, be a significant problem: the present value of obligations payable in many years time will be relatively small and unlikely to be a significant proportion of the total defined benefit obligation. The total obligation is therefore unlikely to be sensitive to errors in the assumption about the discount rate for long-term maturities (beyond the maturities of long-term corporate or government bonds).

4.6 Actuarial gains or losses

Actuarial gains and losses arise for several reasons, and the IFRS for SMEs requires that all such gains and losses are either shown in profit or loss or within other comprehensive income.

Actuarial gains or losses arise because of the following.

• **Actual events** (eg employee turnover, salary increases) differ from the actuarial assumptions that were made to estimate the defined benefit obligations.

• **Actuarial assumptions are revised** (eg a different discount rate is used, or a different assumption is made about future employee turnover, salary rises, mortality rates, and so on)

• **Actual returns on plan assets** differ from expected returns

The *IFRS for SMEs* requires that all actuarial gains and losses are recognised in full. This recognition can be in profit or loss or alternatively in other comprehensive income. This is a matter of accounting policy.

4.7 Past service cost

A past service cost arises when an entity either introduces a defined benefits plan or **improves the benefits payable** under an existing plan. As a result, the entity has taken on additional obligations that it has not hitherto provided for. For example, an employer might decide to introduce a medical benefits scheme for former employees. This will create a new defined benefit obligation, that has not yet been provided for. How should this obligation be accounted for?

The *IFRS for SMEs* requires that all past service costs are recognised immediately in profit or loss.

Activity

Watkins Co operates a pension plan that provides a pension of 2% of final salary for every year of service and the benefits become vested after five years' service. On 1 January 20X6 Watkins Co improved the pension to 2.5% of final salary for every year of service starting from 1 January 20X2.

At the date of improvement, the present value of the additional benefits for service from 1 January 20X2 to 1 January 20X6 is as follows.

	$m
Employees with more than 5 years' service at 1/11/X6	300
Employees with less than 5 years' service at 1/11/X6 (average period until vesting = 3 years	240
	540

Required

State the correct accounting treatment for past service costs.

Answer

Watkins Co should recognise $540m immediately in profit or loss.

4.8 Plan assets

The contributions into a plan by the employer (and employees) are invested, and the plan builds up assets in the form of stocks and shares, etc. The **fair value of these plan assets** are deducted from the defined benefits obligation, in calculating the liability in the statement of financial position. This makes sense, because the employer is not liable to the defined benefits scheme to the extent that the assets of the fund are sufficient to meet those obligations.

The standard includes the following specific requirements.

(a)   The fair value of the plan assets should be **net of any transaction costs** that would be incurred in selling them.

(b)   The plan assets should **exclude any contributions due** from the employer but not yet paid.

4.9 Return on plan assets

The difference between the expected return and actual return on plan assets must be calculated.

It is also necessary to recognise the distinction between:

(a)   the **expected return** on the plan assets, which is an actuarial assumption, and
(b)   the **actual return** made by the plan assets in a financial period.

The **expected return** on the plan assets is a component element in the income statement (in profit or loss), not the actual returns. The **difference between the expected return and the actual return** may also be included in profit or loss, but within the actuarial gains or losses.

4.10 Example: plan assets

At 1 January 20X2 the fair value of the assets of a defined benefit plan was valued at $1m.

On 31 December 20X2, the plan received contributions from the employer of $490,000 and paid out benefits of $190,000.

After these transactions, the fair value of the plan's assets at 31 December 20X2 was $1.5m. The present value of the defined benefit obligation was $1,479,200 and actuarial losses on the obligation for 20X2 were $6,000.

The expected return on the plan assets (net of investment transaction costs) is 8% per annum.

The reporting entity made the following estimates at 1 January 20X2, based on market prices at that date.

	%
Dividend/interest income (after tax payable by fund)	9.25
Realised and unrealised gains (after tax) on plan assets	2.00
Administration costs	(1.00)
	10.25

Required

Calculate the expected and actual return on plan assets, and calculate any actuarial gain or loss.

Solution

The expected and actual return for 20X2 are as follows.

	$
Return on $1m held for 12 months at 10.25%	102,500
Return on $(490,000 – 190,000) = $300,000	
for 6 months at 5% (ie 10.25% annually compounded every 6 months)	15,000
Expected return on plan assets	117,500

	$
Fair value of plan assets at 31/12/X2	1,500,000
Less fair value of plan assets at 1/1/X2	(1,000,000)
Less contributions received	(490,000)
Add benefits paid	190,000
Actual return on plan assets	200,000

Actuarial gain = $(200,000 – 117,500) = $82,500.

∴ Cumulative net actuarial gains = $(82,500 – 6,000) = $76,500.

5 Defined benefit plans: other matters

This section looks at the presentation and disclosure of defined benefit plans, but we begin here by looking at the special circumstances of curtailment and settlements.

5.1 Curtailments and settlements

You should know how to deal with **curtailments** and **settlements**.

A **curtailment** occurs when an entity cuts back on the benefits available under a defined benefit scheme, so that there is either a significant reduction in the number of employees eligible for the post-employment benefits (eg because a large number of staff have been made redundant due to a plant closure), or there is a reduction in the post-employment benefits that will be given for the future service of current employees.

A **settlement** occurs either when an employer pays off its post-employment benefit obligations in exchange for making a lump sum payment, or when an employer reduces the size of post-employment benefits payable in the future in respect of **past service**.

A curtailment and settlement might **happen together**, for example when an employer brings a defined benefit plan to an end by settling the obligation with a one-off lump sum payment and then scrapping the plan.

Gains or losses arising from the curtailment or settlement of a defined benefit plan should be **recognised in full in the financial year that they occur**. These gains or losses will comprise the following.

- Any **change in the present value of the future obligations** of the entity as a result of the curtailment or settlement
- Any **change in the fair value of the plan assets** as a consequence of the curtailment or settlement
- Any related **actuarial gains/losses** and **past service cost** that had not previously been recognised

An entity should **remeasure the obligation** (and the related plan assets, if any) using current actuarial assumptions, before determining the effect of a curtailment or settlement.

5.2 Suggested approach and questions

The suggested approach to defined benefit schemes is to deal with the change in the obligation and asset in the following order, building up the disclosure notes:

Step	Item	Recognition	
1	**Record opening figures:** • asset • obligation		
2	**Interest cost** • Based on discount rate and PV obligation at start of period. • Should also reflect any changes in obligation during period.	DEBIT CREDIT	*Interest cost (I/S)* *(x% × b/d obligation)* *PV defined benefit obligation (SOFP)*
3	**Expected return on plan assets** • Based on long-term expectations as advised by actuary and asset value at start of period. • Technically, the expected return is also time apportioned on contributions less benefits paid in the period.	DEBIT CREDIT	*Plan assets (SOFP)* *Exp'd return on plan assets (I/S)* *(y% × b/d assets)*
4	**Current service cost** Increase in the present value of the obligation resulting from employee service in the current period.	DEBIT CREDIT	*Current service cost (I/S)* *PV defined benefit obligation (SOFP)*
5	**Contributions** As advised by actuary.	DEBIT CREDIT	*Plan assets (SOFP)* *Company cash*
6	**Benefits** Actual pension payments made.	DEBIT CREDIT	*PV defined benefit obligation (SOFP)* *Plan assets (SOFP)*
7	**Past service cost** • Increase in PV obligation as a result of introduction or improvement of benefits. • Past service cost is *vested* when any minimum employment period has been completed.	DEBIT CREDIT	*Past service cost (I/S)* *PV defined benefit obligation (SOFP)*

Step	Item	Recognition
8	**Actuarial gains and losses** • Arising from annual valuations of obligation and asset. • On obligation, differences between actuarial assumptions and actual experience during the period, or changes in actuarial assumptions. • On assets, differences between expected and actual return.	Recognise in: – Profit or loss directly, *or* – other comprehensive income according to accounting policy.
9	**Disclose in accordance with the IFRS**	See comprehensive question.

Activity

During the year ended 30 November 20X3, the directors of Pole decided to form a defined benefit pension scheme for the employees of the company and contributed cash of $160 million to it. The following details relate to the scheme at 30 November 20X3:

	$m
Present value of obligation	208
Fair value of plan assets	200
Current service cost	176
Interest cost – scheme liabilities	32
Expected return on pension scheme assets	16

The only entry in the financial statements made to date is in respect of the cash contribution which has been included in trade receivables. The directors have been uncertain as to how to deal with the above pension scheme in the consolidated financial statements because of the significance of the potential increase in the charge to profit or loss (in the income statements) relating to the pension scheme. The accounting policy is to recognise actuarial gains or losses in profit or loss.

Required

Show how the defined benefit pension scheme should be dealt with in the financial statements for the year ended 30 November 20X3.

Answer

The pension scheme has a deficit of liabilities over assets:

	$m
Fair value of plan assets	200
Less: present value of obligation	(208)
	(8)

The deficit is reported as a liability in the statement of financial position.

The statement of comprehensive income for the year includes:

	$m
Current service cost	176
Interest cost	32
Expected return on plan assets	(16)
	192

	$m
Actuarial gain on defined benefit pension scheme assets (see below)	24

Adjustment to the financial statements:

DEBIT	Retained earnings	$168 million
CREDIT	Receivables	$160 million
CREDIT	Defined benefit pension scheme liability	$8 million

Working

	$m
Scheme assets:	
Contributions paid	160
Expected return on plan assets	16
Actuarial gain (balancing figure)	24
Fair value of plan assets	200
Scheme liabilities:	
Current service cost	176
Interest cost	32
Present value of obligation	208

6 Share based payment

Share-based payment transactions should be recognised in the financial statements. You need to understand and be able to advise on:

- Recognition
- Measurement
- Disclosure

of both equity settled and cash settled transactions.

6.1 Background

Transactions whereby entities purchase goods or services from other parties, such as suppliers and employees, by **issuing shares or share options** to those other parties are **increasingly common.** Share schemes are a common feature of director and executive remuneration and in some countries the authorities may offer tax incentives to encourage more companies to offer shares to employees. Companies whose shares or share options are regarded as a valuable 'currency' commonly use share-based payment to obtain employee and professional services.

The increasing use of share-based payment has raised questions about the accounting treatment of such transactions in company financial statements.

Share options are often granted to employees at an exercise price that is equal to or higher than the market price of the shares at the date the option is granted. Consequently the options have no intrinsic value and so **no transaction is recorded in the financial statements**.

This leads to an **anomaly:** if a company pays its employees in cash, an expense is recognised in profit or loss, but if the payment is in share options, no expense is recognised.

6.2 Objective and scope

The IFRS for SMEs requires an entity to **reflect the effects of share-based payment transactions** in its profit or loss and financial position.

The IFRS applies to all share-based payment transactions. There are three types.

(a) **Equity-settled share-based payment transactions**, in which the entity receives goods or services in exchange for equity instruments of the entity (including shares or share options)

(b) **Cash-settled share-based payment transactions**, in which the entity receives goods or services in exchange for amounts of cash that are based on the price (or value) of the entity's shares or other equity instruments of the entity

(c) Transactions in which the entity receives or acquires goods or services and either the entity or the supplier has a **choice** as to whether the entity settles the transaction in cash (or other assets) or by issuing equity instruments

Share-based payment transaction A transaction in which the entity receives goods or services as consideration for equity instruments of the entity (including shares or share options), or acquires goods or services by incurring liabilities to the supplier of those goods or services for amounts that are based on the price of the entity's shares or other equity instruments of the entity.

Share-based payment arrangement An agreement between the entity and another party (including an employee) to enter into a share-based payment transaction, which thereby entitles the other party to receive cash or other assets of the entity for amounts that are based on the price of the entity's shares or other equity instruments of the entity, or to receive equity instruments of the entity, provided the specified vesting conditions, if any, are met.

Equity instrument A contract that evidences a residual interest in the assets of an entity after deducting all of its liabilities.

Equity instrument granted The right (conditional or unconditional) to an equity instrument of the entity conferred by the entity on another party, under a share-based payment arrangement.

Share option A contract that gives the holder the right, but not the obligation, to subscribe to the entity's shares at a fixed or determinable price for a specified period of time.

Fair value The amount for which an asset could be exchanged, a liability settled, or an equity instrument granted could be exchanged, between knowledgeable, willing parties in an arm's length transaction.

Grant date The date at which the entity and another party (including an employee) agree to a share-based payment arrangement, being when the entity and the other party have a shared understanding of the terms and conditions of the arrangement. At grant date the entity confers on the other party (the counterparty) the right to cash, other assets, or equity instruments of the entity, provided the specified vesting conditions, if any, are met. If that agreement is subject to an approval process (for example, by shareholders), grant date is the date when that approval is obtained.

Intrinsic value The difference between the fair value of the shares to which the counterparty has the (conditional or unconditional) right to subscribe or which it has the right to receive, and the price (if any) the other party is (or will be) required to pay for those shares. For example, a share option with an exercise price of $15 on a share with a fair value of $20, has an intrinsic value of $5.

Measurement date The date at which the fair value of the equity instruments granted is measured. For transactions with employees and others providing similar services, the measurement date is grant date. For transactions with parties other than employees (and those providing similar services), the measurement date is the date the entity obtains the goods or the counterparty renders service.

Vest To become an entitlement. Under a share-based payment arrangement, a counterparty's right to receive cash, other assets, or equity instruments of the entity vests upon satisfaction of any specified vesting conditions.

Vesting conditions The conditions that must be satisfied for the counterparty to become entitled to receive cash, other assets or equity instruments of the entity, under a share-based payment arrangement. Vesting conditions include service conditions, which require the other party to complete a specified period of service, and performance conditions, which require specified performance targets to be met (such as a specified increase in the entity's profit over a specified period of time).

Vesting period The period during which all the specified vesting conditions of a share-based payment arrangement are to be satisfied.

6.3 Recognition: the basic principle

An entity should **recognise goods or services received or acquired in a share-based payment transaction when it obtains the goods or as the services are received.** Goods or services received or acquired in a share-based payment transaction **should be recognised as expenses unless they qualify for recognition as assets**. For example, services are normally recognised as expenses (because they are normally rendered immediately), while goods are recognised as assets.

If the goods or services were received or acquired in an **equity-settled** share-based payment transaction the entity should recognise **a corresponding increase in equity** (reserves).

If the goods or services were received or acquired in a **cash-settled** share-based payment transaction the entity should recognise a **liability.**

6.4 Equity-settled share-based payment transactions

6.4.1 Measurement

The issue here is how to measure the 'cost' of the goods and services received and the equity instruments (eg the share options) granted in return.

The general principle is that when an entity recognises the goods or services received and the corresponding increase in equity, it should measure these at the **fair value of the goods or services received**. Where the transaction is with **parties other than employees**, there is a rebuttable presumption that the fair value of the goods or services received can be estimated reliably.

If the fair value of the goods or services received cannot be measured reliably, the entity should measure their value by reference to the **fair value of the equity instruments granted.**

Where the transaction is with a party other than an employee fair value should be measured at the date the entity obtains the goods or the counterparty renders service.

Where shares, share options or other equity instruments are granted to **employees** as part of their remuneration package, it is not normally possible to measure directly the services received. For this reason, the entity should measure the fair value of the employee services received by reference to the **fair value of the equity instruments granted**. The fair value of those equity instruments should be measured at **grant date**.

6.4.2 Determining the fair value of equity instruments granted

Where a transaction is measured by reference to the fair value of the equity instruments granted, fair value is based on **market prices** if available, taking into account the terms and conditions upon which those equity instruments were granted.

If market prices are not available the entity's directors can use their judgement to determine a best estimate of fair value if there is no observable market price.

6.4.3 Transactions in which services are received

The issue here is **when** to recognise the transaction. When equity instruments are granted they may vest immediately, but often the counterparty has to meet specified conditions first. For example, an employee may have to complete a specified period of service. This means that the effect of the transaction normally has to be allocated over more than one accounting period.

If the equity instruments granted **vest immediately**, (ie, the counterparty is not required to complete a specified period of service before becoming unconditionally entitled to the equity instruments) it is presumed that the services have already been received (in the absence of evidence to the contrary). The entity should **recognise the services received in full**, with a corresponding increase in equity, **on the grant date**.

If the equity instruments granted do not vest until the counterparty completes a specified period of service, the entity should account for those services **as they are rendered** by the counterparty during the vesting period. For example if an employee is granted share options on condition that he or she completes three years' service, then the services to be rendered by the employee as consideration for the share options will be received in the future, over that three-year vesting period.

The entity should recognise an amount for the goods or services received during the vesting period based on the **best available estimate** of the **number of equity instruments expected to vest**. It should **revise** that estimate if subsequent information indicates that the number of equity instruments expected to vest differs from previous estimates. On **vesting date**, the entity should revise the estimate to **equal the number of equity instruments that actually vest**.

Once the goods and services received and the corresponding increase in equity have been recognised, the entity should make no subsequent adjustment to total equity after vesting date.

6.5 Example: Equity-settled share-based payment transaction

On 1 January 20X1 an entity grants 100 share options to each of its 400 employees. Each grant is conditional upon the employee working for the entity until 31 December 20X3. The fair value of each share option is $20.

During 20X1 20 employees leave and the entity estimates that 20% of the employees will leave during the three year period.

During 20X2 a further 25 employees leave and the entity now estimates that 25% of its employees will leave during the three year period.

During 20X3 a further 10 employees leave.

Required

Calculate the remuneration expense that will be recognised in respect of the share-based payment transaction for each of the three years ended 31 December 20X3.

Solution

The IFRS requires the entity to recognise the remuneration expense, based on the fair value of the share options granted, as the services are received during the three year vesting period.

In 20X1 and 20X2 the entity estimates the number of options expected to vest (by estimating the number of employees likely to leave) and bases the amount that it recognises for the year on this estimate.

In 20X3 it recognises an amount based on the number of options that actually vest. A total of 55 employees left during the three year period and therefore 34,500 options (400 − 55 × 100) vested.

The amount recognised as an expense for each of the three years is calculated as follows:

		Cumulative expense at year-end $	Expense for year $
20X1	40,000 × 80% × 20 × 1/3	213,333	213,333
20X2	40,000 × 75% × 20 × 2/3	400,000	186,667
20X3	34,500 × 20	690,000	290,000

Activity

During its financial year ended 31 January 20X6, TSQ issued share options to several of its senior employees. The options vest immediately upon issue.

Which *one* of the following describes the accounting entry that is required to recognise the options?

A	DEBIT the statement of changes in equity	CREDIT liabilities
B	DEBIT the statement of changes in equity	CREDIT equity
C	DEBIT profit or loss	CREDIT liabilities
D	DEBIT profit or loss	CREDIT equity

Answer

D   Under the IFRS for SMEs a charge must be made to profit or loss

Activity

On 1 January 20X3 an entity grants 250 share options to each of its 200 employees. The only condition attached to the grant is that the employees should continue to work for the entity until 31 December 20X6. Five employees leave during the year.

The market price of each option was $12 at 1 January 20X3 and $15 at 31 December 20X3.

Required

Show how this transaction will be reflected in the financial statements for the year ended 31 December 20X3.

Answer

The remuneration expense for the year is based on the fair value of the options granted at the grant date (1 January 20X3). As five of the 200 employees left during the year it is reasonable to assume that 20 employees will leave during the four year vesting period and that therefore 45,000 options (250 × 180) will actually vest.

Therefore the entity recognises a remuneration expense of $135,000 (45,000 × 12 × ¼) in the profit or loss and a corresponding increase in equity of the same amount.

6.6 Cash-settled share-based payment transactions

Examples of this type of transaction include:

(a)   **Share appreciation rights** granted to employees: the employees become entitled to a future cash payment (rather than an equity instrument), based on the increase in the entity's share price from a specified level over a specified period of time or

(b)   An entity might grant to its employees a right to receive a future cash payment by granting to them a **right to shares that are redeemable**

The basic principle is that the entity measures the goods or services acquired and the liability incurred at the **fair value of the liability**.

The entity should **remeasure** the fair value of the liability **at each reporting date** until the liability is settled **and at the date of settlement**. Any **changes** in fair value are recognised in **profit or loss** for the period.

The entity should recognise the services received, and a liability to pay for those services, **as the employees render service.** For example, if share appreciation rights do not vest until the employees have completed a specified period of service, the entity should recognise the services received and the related liability, over that period.

6.7 Example: cash-settled share-based payment transaction

On 1 January 20X1 an entity grants 100 cash share appreciation rights (SARs) to each of its 500 employees, on condition that the employees continue to work for the entity until 31 December 20X3.

During 20X1 35 employees leave. The entity estimates that a further 60 will leave during 20X2 and 20X3.

During 20X2 40 employees leave and the entity estimates that a further 25 will leave during 20X3.

During 20X3 22 employees leave.

At 31 December 20X3 150 employees exercise their SARs. Another 140 employees exercise their SARs at 31 December 20X4 and the remaining 113 employees exercise their SARs at the end of 20X5.

The fair values of the SARs for each year in which a liability exists are shown below, together with the intrinsic values at the dates of exercise.

	Fair value	Intrinsic value
	$	$
20X1	14.40	
20X2	15.50	
20X3	18.20	15.00
20X4	21.40	20.00
20X5		25.00

Required

Calculate the amount to be recognised in the profit or loss for each of the five years ended 31 December 20X5 and the liability to be recognised in the statement of financial position at 31 December for each of the five years.

Solution

For the three years to the vesting date of 31 December 20X3 the expense is based on the entity's estimate of the number of SARs that will actually vest (as for an equity-settled transaction). However, the fair value of the liability is **re-measured** at each year-end.

The intrinsic value of the SARs at the date of exercise is the amount of cash actually paid.

		Liability at year-end		Expense for Year
		$	$	$
20X1	Expected to vest (500 – 95):			
	405 × 100 × 14.40 × 1/3	194,400		194,400
20X2	Expected to vest (500 – 100):			
	400 × 100 × 15.50 × 2/3	413,333		218,933
20X3	Exercised:			
	150 ×100 × 15.00		225,000	
	Not yet exercised (500 – 97 – 150):			
	253 × 100 × 18.20	460,460	47,127	
				272,127
20X4	Exercised:			
	140 × 100 × 20.00		280,000	
	Not yet exercised (253 – 140):			
	113 × 100 × 21.40	241,820	(218,640)	
				61,360
20X5	Exercised:			
	113 × 100 × 25.00		282,500	
		Nil	(241,820)	
				40,680
				787,500

Transactions which either the entity or the other party has a choice of settling in cash or by issuing equity instruments

If the entity has incurred a liability to settle in cash or other assets it should account for the transaction as a cash-settled share-based payment transaction.

If no such liability has been incurred the entity should account for the transaction as an equity-settled share-based payment transaction.

Unit Roundup

- There are **two types of post-employment benefit plan**:
    - Defined contribution plans
    - Defined benefit plans

- **Defined contribution plans** are simple to account for as the benefits are defined by the contributions made.

- **Defined benefit plans** are much more difficult to deal with as the benefits are promised, they define the contributions to be made.

- There is a **six-step method** for accounting for the expenses and liability of a defined benefit pension plan.

- **Discount rates** used should be determined by reference to market yields on high-quality fixed-rate corporate bonds.

- **Actuarial gains and losses** arise for several reasons and they must be recognised in full in either profit or loss or other comprehensive income. This is an accounting policy choice.

- You should know how to deal with **curtailments** and **settlements**.

- **Share-based payment** transactions should be recognised in the financial statements. You need to understand and be able to advise on:
    - Recognition
    - Measurement
    - Disclosure

  of both equity settled and cash settled transactions.

Quick Quiz

1   What are the four categories of employee benefits given by the IFRS?

2   What is the difference between defined contribution and defined benefit plans?

3   How should a defined benefit expense be recognised in profit or loss for the year?

4   What causes actuarial gains or losses?

5   What is a cash-settled share based payment transaction?

6   What is grant date?

7   If an entity has entered into an equity settled share-based payment transaction, what should it recognise in its financial statements?

8   Where an entity has granted share options to its employees in return for services, how is the transaction measured?

1 • Short-term
   • Post-employment
   • Other long-term
   • Termination

2 See Paragraph 2

3 Current service cost + interest − expected return ± recognised actuarial gains/losses + past service cost + curtailments or settlements.

4 See Paragraph 4.6

5 A transaction in which the entity receives goods or services in exchange for amounts of cash that are based on the price (or value) of the entity's shares or other equity instruments of the entity.

6 The date at which the entity and another party (including an employee) agree to a share based payment arrangement, being when the entity and the other party have a shared understanding of the terms and conditions of the arrangement.

7 The goods or services received and a corresponding increase in equity.

8 By reference to the fair value of the equity instruments granted, measured at grant date.

Now try the question below

Defined benefit scheme   36 mins

For the sake of simplicity and clarity, all transactions are assumed to occur at the year end.

The following data applies to the post employment defined benefit compensation scheme of an entity.

Expected return on plan assets: 12% (each year)
Discount rate: 10% (each year)
Present value of obligation at start of 20X2: $1m
Market value of plan assets at start of 20X2: $1m

The following figures are relevant.

	20X4	20X3	20X2
	$'000	$'000	$'000
Current service cost	150	150	140
Benefits paid out	150	140	120
Contributions paid by entity	120	120	110
Present value of obligation at year end	1,700	1,600	1,200
Market value of plan assets at year end	1,610	1,450	1,250

Required

Show how the reporting entity should account for this defined benefit plan in each of years 20X2, 20X3 and 20X4. Actuarial gains and losses are to be recognised in full in profit or loss for the year. **(20 marks)**

Defined benefit scheme

The actuarial gain or loss is established as a balancing figure in the calculations, as follows.

Present value of obligation	20X4	20X3	20X2
	$'000	$'000	$'000
PV of obligation at start of year	1,600	1,200	1,000
Interest cost (10%)	160	120	100
Current service cost	150	150	140
Benefits paid	(150)	(140)	(120)
Actuarial (gain)/loss on obligation: balancing figure	(60)	270	80
PV of obligation at end of year	1,700	1,600	1,200

Market value of plan assets	20X4	20X3	20X2
	$'000	$'000	$'000
Market value of plan assets at start of year	1,450	1,250	1,000
Expected return on plan assets (12%)	174	150	120
Contributions	120	120	110
Benefits paid	(150)	(140)	(120)
Actuarial gain/(loss) on plan assets: balancing figure	16	70	140
Market value of plan assets at year end	1,610	1,450	1,250
Actuarial gain/(loss) for year: obligation	60	(270)	(80)
Actuarial gain/(loss) for year: plan assets	16	70	140
Net actuarial gain/loss	(64)	(140)	60

In the statement of financial position, the liability that is recognised is calculated as follows.

	20X4	20X3	20X2
	$'000	$'000	$'000
Present value of obligation	1,700	1,600	1,200
Market value of plan assets	1,610	1,450	1,250
Liability/(asset) in statement of financial position	90	150	(50)

The following will be recognised in profit or loss for the year:

	20X4	20X3	20X2
	$'000	$'000	$'000
Current service cost	150	150	140
Interest cost	160	120	100
Expected return on plan assets	(174)	(150)	(120)
Net actuarial (gain)/loss recognised in the year	64	140	(60)
Expense recognised in profit or loss	200	260	60

Related party
disclosures

Unit topic list

Assessment criteria

4   Understand and apply IFRS for SMEs in the preparation of their financial statements

4.23   Understand and apply section 33 of IFRS for SMEs for an SME which needs to consider related party disclosures

1 Related party disclosures

The requirements of the IFRS for SMEs for related parties are primarily about disclosure. It is concerned with improving the quality of information provided by published accounts and also to strengthen their stewardship role.

In the absence of information to the contrary, it is assumed that a reporting entity has **independent discretionary power** over its resources and transactions and pursues its activities independently of the interests of its individual owners, managers and others. Transactions are presumed to have been undertaken on an **arm's length basis**, ie on terms such as could have obtained in a transaction with an external party, in which each side bargained knowledgeably and freely, unaffected by any relationship between them.

These assumptions may not be justified when **related party relationships** exist, because the requisite conditions for competitive, free market dealings may not be present. Whilst the parties may endeavour to achieve arm's length bargaining the very nature of the relationship may preclude this occurring.

1.1 Objective

This is the related parties issue and it is tackled by ensuring that financial statements contain the disclosures necessary to draw attention to the possibility that the reported financial position and results may have been affected by the existence of related parties and by material transactions with them. In other words, this is a standard which is primarily concerned with **disclosure**.

1.2 Scope

The standard requires an entity to include in its financial statements the disclosures necessary to draw attention to the possibility that its financial position and profit or loss have been affected by the existence of related parties and by transactions and outstanding balances with such parties.

1.3 Definitions

Key terms

> **Related party**. A party is related to an entity if:
>
> (a) directly, or indirectly through one or more intermediaries, it:
>   (i) controls, is controlled by, or is under common control with, the entity (this includes parents, subsidiaries and fellow subsidiaries);
>   (ii) has an interest in the entity that gives it significant influence over the entity; or
>   (iii) has joint control over the entity;
>
> (b) it is an associate;
>
> (c) it is a joint venture in which the entity is a venturer;
>
> (d) it is a member of the key management personnel of the entity or its parent;
>
> (e) it is a close member of the family of any individual referred to in (a) or (d);
>
> (f) it is an entity that is controlled, jointly controlled or significantly influenced by; or for which significant voting power in such entity resides with, directly or indirectly, any individual referred to in (d) or (e); or
>
> (g) it is a post-employment benefit plan for the benefit of employees of the entity, or of any entity that is a related party of the entity.
>
> **Related party transaction**. A transfer of resources, services or obligations between related parties, regardless of whether a price is charged.
>
> **Control** is the power to govern the financial and operating policies of an entity so as to obtain benefits from its activities.

Significant influence is the power to participate in the financial and operating policy decisions of an entity, but is not control over these policies. Significant ownership may be gained by share ownership, statute or agreement.

Joint control is the contractually agreed sharing of control over an economic activity.

Key management personnel are those persons having authority and responsibility for planning, directing and controlling the activities of the entity, directly or indirectly, including any director (whether executive or otherwise) of that entity.

Close members of the family of an individual are those family members who may be expected to influence, or be influenced by, that individual in their dealings with the entity. They may include:

(a)   the individual's domestic partner and children;
(b)   children of the domestic partner; and
(c)   dependants of the individual or the domestic partner.

The most important point to remember here is that, when considering each possible related party relationship, attention must be paid to the **substance of the relationship, not merely the legal form**.

The IFRS lists the following which are **not necessarily related parties**.

(a)   **Two entities simply because they have a director or other key management in common** (notwithstanding the definition of related party above, although it is necessary to consider how that director would affect both entities)

(b)   **Two venturers, simply because they share joint control over a joint venture**.

(c)   Certain other bodies, simply as a result of their **role in normal business dealings** with the entity

     (i)   Providers of finance
     (ii)   Trade unions
     (iii)   Public utilities
     (iv)   Government departments and agencies

(d)   **Any single customer, supplier, franchisor, distributor, or general agent** with whom the entity transacts a significant amount of business, simply by virtue of the resulting economic dependence.

1.4 Examples of relevant transactions

IAS 24 lists some **examples** of transactions that are disclosed if they are with a related party. These are not reproduced in the IFRS for SMES but are still relevant:

- Purchases or sales of goods (finished or unfinished)
- Purchases or sales of property and other assets
- Rendering or receiving of services
- Leases
- Transfer of research and development
- Transfers under licence agreements
- Provision of finance (including loans and equity contributions in cash or in kind)
- Provision of guarantees and collateral security
- Settlement of liabilities on behalf of the entity or by the entity on behalf of another party.

1.5 Disclosure

As noted above, the requirement of the IFRS is almost entirely concerned with disclosure and its provisions are meant to **supplement** those disclosure requirements required by national company legislation and other sections of the IFRS for SMEs.

1.5.1 Disclosure of parent subsidiary relationships

Relationships between **parents and subsidiaries** must be **disclosed irrespective** of **whether** any **transactions** have **taken place between** the related parties. An entity must disclose the **name** of its **parent** and, if different, the **ultimate controlling party**. This will enable a reader of the financial statements to be able to form a view about the effects of a related party relationship on the reporting entity.

If neither the parent nor the ultimate controlling party produces financial statements available for public use, the name of the next most senior parent that does so shall also be disclosed.

1.5.2 Disclosure of key management personnel compensation

An entity should disclose key management personnel compensation including all employee benefits and share-based payments. Key management personnel compensation should be disclosed in total.

1.5.3 Disclosure of related party transactions

If an entity has related party transactions, it must disclose the nature of the related party relationship as well as information about the transactions, outstanding balances and commitments necessary for an understanding of the potential effect of the relationship on the financial statements.

As a minimum disclosure must include:

(a)   the amount of the transactions

(b)   the amount of outstanding balances

(c)   any allowance for receivables related to outstanding balances

(d)   the expense recognised in the period in respect of bad or doubtful debts due from related parties.

The disclosure should be made separately for each of the following categories:

(a)   entities with control, joint control or significant influence over the entity

(b)   entities over which the reporting entity has control, joint control or significant influence

(c)   key management personnel of the entity (in aggregate)

(d)   other related parties.

2 Question

Try this long question on related parties.

Activity

Discuss whether the following events would require disclosure in the financial statements of the RP Group.

The RP Group, merchant bankers, has a number of subsidiaries, associates and joint ventures in its group structure. During the financial year to 31 October 20X9 the following events occurred.

(a)   The company agreed to finance a management buyout of a group company, AB. In addition to providing loan finance, the company has retained a 25% equity holding in the company and has a main board director on the board of AB. RP received management fees, interest payments and dividends from AB.

(b)   On 1 July 20X9, RP sold a wholly owned subsidiary, X, to Z . During the year RP supplied X with second hand office equipment and X leased its factory from RP. The transactions were all contracted for at market rates.

(c)   The retirement benefit scheme of the group is managed by another merchant bank. An investment manager of the group retirement benefit scheme is also a non-executive director of the RP Group and received an annual fee for his services of $25,000 which is not material in the group context. The company pays $16m per annum into the scheme and occasionally transfers assets into the scheme. In 20X9, property, plant and equipment of $10m were transferred into the scheme and a recharge of administrative costs of $3m was made.

(a) The IFRS does not require disclosure of transactions between companies and providers of finance in the ordinary course of business. As RP is a merchant bank, no disclosure is needed between RP and AB. However, RP owns 25% of the equity of AB and it would seem significant influence exists, **greater than 20% existing holding means significant influence is presumed**, and therefore AB could be an associate of RP. The IFRS regards associates as related parties.

The decision as to associate status depends upon the ability of RP to exercise significant influence especially as the other 75% of votes are owned by the management of AB.

Merchant banks tend to regard companies which would qualify for associate status as trade investments since the relationship is designed to provide finance.

The IFRS presumes that a party owning or able to exercise control over 20% of voting rights is a related party. So an investor with a 25% holding and a director on the board would be expected to have significant influence over operating and financial policies in such a way as to inhibit the pursuit of separate interests. If it can be shown that this is not the case, there is no related party relationship.

If it is decided that there is a related party situation then **all material transactions** should be disclosed including **management fees, interest, dividends and the terms of the loan**.

(b) **The IFRS does *not* require intragroup transactions and balances eliminated** on **consolidation to be disclosed**. The IFRS does not deal with the situation where an undertaking becomes, or ceases to be, a subsidiary during the year.

Best practice indicates that related party transactions should be disclosed for the period when X was not part of the group. Transactions between RP and X should be disclosed between 1 July 20X9 and 31 October 20X9 but transactions prior to 1 July will have been eliminated on consolidation.

There is no related party relationship between RP and Z since it is a normal business transaction unless either parties interests have been influenced or controlled in some way by the other party.

(c) **Employee retirement benefit schemes** of the reporting entity are included in the definition of **related parties**.

The contributions paid, the non current asset transfer ($10m) and the charge of administrative costs ($3m) must be disclosed.

The **pension investment manager** would **not normally** be **considered** a **related party. However,** the manager is **key management personnel** by virtue of his **non-executive directorship.**

Directors are deemed to be related parties , and the manager receives a $25,000 fee. The IFRS requires the disclosure of **compensation paid to key management personnel** and the fee falls within the definition of compensation. Therefore it must be disclosed.

Unit Roundup

- The requirements of the IFRS for SMEs for related party transactions are largely about disclosure. It is concerned with improving the quality of information provided by published accounts and also to strengthen their stewardship role.

Quick Quiz

1   What is a related party transaction?

2   A managing director of a company is a related party.

    True ☐

    False ☐

3   What are the minimum disclosures required in respect of related party transactions?

1   A transfer of resources, services or obligations between related parties, regardless of whether a price is charged.

2   True. A member of the key management personnel of an entity is a related party of that entity.

3   (a)   Amount of transactions

(b)   Amount of outstanding balances

(c)   Allowance for receivables in relation to outstanding balances

(d)   Bad and doubtful debt expense in relation to related parties.

Now try the question below

Fancy Feet Co   18 mins

Fancy Feet Co is a UK company which supplies handmade leather shoes to a chain of high street shoe shops. The company is also the sole importer of some famous high quality Greek stoneware which is supplied to an upmarket shop in London's West End.

Fancy Feet Co was set up 30 years ago by Georgios Kostades who left Greece when he fell out with the local government. The company is owned and run by Mr Kostades and his three children.

The shoes are purchased from a French company, the shares of which are owned by the Kostades Family Trust (Monaco).

Required

Identify the financial accounting issues arising out of the above scenario.   **(10 marks)**

Fancy Feet Co

Issues

(a)   The basis on which Fancy Feet trades with the Greek supplier and the French company owned by the Kostades family trust.

(b)   Whether the overseas companies trade on commercial terms with the UK company or do the foreign entities control the UK company.

(c)   Who owns the Greek company: is this a related party?

(d)   Should the nature of trade suggest a related party controls Fancy Feet Co? Detailed disclosures will be required in the accounts.

Part C

Group accounts

Group accounts

Basic consolidation principles

15

Unit topic list

1   Group accounts
2   Consolidated and separate financial statements
3   Content of group accounts and group structure

Assessment criteria

4   Understand and apply IFRS for SMEs in the preparation of their financial statements

4.3   Preparation of consolidated and separate financial statements as per section 9 of the IFRS for SMEs

1 Group accounts

Many large businesses consist of several companies controlled by one central or administrative company. Together these companies are called a **group**. The controlling company, called the parent or **holding company**, will own some or all of the shares in the other companies, called subsidiaries.

1.1 Introduction

There are many reasons for businesses to operate as groups; for the goodwill associated with the names of the subsidiaries, for tax or legal purposes and so forth. In many countries, company law requires that the results of a group should be presented as a whole. Unfortunately, it is not possible simply to add all the results together and this chapter and those following will teach you how to **consolidate** all the results of companies within a group.

In traditional accounting terminology, a **group of companies** consists of a **parent company** and one or more **subsidiary companies** which are controlled by the parent company.

1.2 Definitions

We will look at some of these definitions in more detail later, but they are useful here in that they give you an overview of all aspects of group accounts.

Exam focus point

All the definitions relating to group accounts are extremely important. You must **learn them** and **understand** their meaning and application.

Key terms

- **Control**. The power to govern the financial and operating policies of an entity so as to obtain benefits from its activities.

- **Subsidiary**. An entity that is controlled by another entity (known as the parent).

- **Parent**. An entity that has one or more subsidiaries.

- **Group**. A parent and all its subsidiaries.

- **Associate**. An entity, including an unincorporated entity such as a partnership, in which an investor has significant influence and which is neither a subsidiary nor a joint venture of the investor.

- **Significant influence** is the power to participate in the financial and operating policy decisions of an investee or an economic activity but is not control or joint control over those policies.

We can summarise the different types of investment *and* the required accounting for them as follows.

Investment	Criteria	Required treatment in group accounts
Subsidiary	Control	Full consolidation
Associate	Significant influence	Equity accounting (see unit 18)
Investment which is none of the above	Asset held for accretion of wealth	As for single company accounts per IFRS for SMEs section 11 Basic Financial Instruments

1.3 Investments in subsidiaries

The important point here is **control**. In most cases, this will involve the holding company or parent owning a majority of the ordinary shares in the subsidiary (to which normal voting rights are attached). There are circumstances, however, when the parent may own only a minority of the voting power in the subsidiary, *but* the parent still has control.

The IFRS for SMEs states that control can usually be assumed to exist when the parent **owns more than half (ie over 50%) of the voting power** of an entity *unless* it can be clearly shown that **such ownership does not constitute control** (these situations will be very rare).

What about situations where this ownership criterion does not exist? The IFRS lists the following situations where control exists, even when the parent owns only 50% or less of the voting power of an entity.

(a) The parent has power over more than 50% of the voting rights by virtue of **agreement with other investors**

(b) The parent has power to **govern the financial and operating policies** of the entity by statute or under an agreement

(c) The parent has the power to **appoint or remove a majority of members of the board of directors** (or equivalent governing body)

(d) The parent has power to cast a **majority of votes at meetings of the board of directors**

Exam focus point

You should learn the contents of the above paragraph as you may be asked to apply them in the exam.

1.3.1 Accounting treatment in parent company accounts

The IFRS for SMEs requires that a parent company accounts for its investment in a subsidiary at either:

- Cost less impairment, or
- Fair value, with changes in fair value recognised in profit or loss

The same accounting policy must be applied to all subsidiaries.

1.3.2 Accounting treatment in group accounts

The IFRS requires a parent to present consolidated financial statements, in which the accounts of the parent and subsidiary (or subsidiaries) are combined and presented **as a single entity**.

1.4 Investments in associates

This type of investment is something less than a subsidiary, but more than a simple investment. The key criterion here is **significant influence**. This is defined as the 'power to participate', but *not* to 'control' (which would make the investment a subsidiary).

Significant influence can be determined by the holding of voting rights (usually attached to shares) in the entity. The IFRS states that if an investor holds **20% or more** of the voting power of the investee, it can be presumed that the investor has significant influence over the investee, *unless* it can be clearly shown that this is not the case.

Significant influence can be presumed *not* to exist if the investor holds **less than 20%** of the voting power of the investee, unless it can be demonstrated otherwise.

The **existence of significant influence** is evidenced in one or more of the following ways.

(a) Representation on the **board of directors** (or equivalent) of the investee
(b) Participation in the **policy making process**
(c) **Material transactions** between investor and investee
(d) Interchange of management personnel
(e) Provision of essential technical information

1.4.1 Accounting treatment in parent company accounts

The IFRS for SMEs requires that a parent company accounts for its investment in an associate at either:

- Cost less impairment, or
- Fair value, with changes in fair value recognised in profit or loss

The same accounting policy must be applied to all associates.

1.4.2 Accounting treatment in group accounts

The IFRS requires the use of the **equity method, the cost model or the fair value model** of accounting for investments in associates. This will be explained in detail in Unit 18.

2 Consolidated and separate financial statements

The IFRS for SMEs requires a parent to present **consolidated** financial statements.

2.1 Introduction

Consolidated financial statements. The financial statements of a group presented as those of a single economic entity.

When a parent issues consolidated financial statements, it should consolidate **all subsidiaries**, both foreign and domestic. This includes any special purpose entity created to accomplish a particular objective and controlled in substance by the parent company.

2.2 Exemption from preparing group accounts

A parent **need not present** consolidated financial statements if

(a) Both of the following conditions are met:

    (i) the parent itself is a subsidiary, and

    (ii) its ultimate parent produces consolidated general purpose financial statements that comply with either full IFRS or the IFRS for SMEs.

(b) It has no subsidiaries other than one that was acquired with the intention of selling or disposing of it within one year.

2.3 Potential voting rights

An entity may own share warrants, share call options, or other similar instruments that are **convertible into ordinary shares** in another entity. If these are exercised or converted they may give the entity voting power or reduce another party's voting power over the financial and operating policies of the other entity (potential voting rights). The **existence and effect** of potential voting rights, including potential voting rights held by another entity, should be considered when assessing whether an entity has control over another entity (and therefore has a subsidiary).

In assessing whether potential voting rights give rise to control, the entity examines all facts and circumstances that affect the rights (for example, terms and conditions), except the intention of management and the financial ability to exercise the rights or convert them into equity shares.

2.4 Exclusion of a subsidiary from consolidation

The rules on exclusion of subsidiaries from consolidation are necessarily strict, because this is a common method used by entities to manipulate their results. If a subsidiary which carries a large amount of debt can be excluded, then the gearing of the group as a whole will be improved. In other words, this is a way of taking debt **out of the statement of financial position**.

Under the IFRS for SMEs there are no reasons for a subsidiary to be excluded from consolidation.

2.5 Different reporting dates

In most cases, all group companies will prepare accounts to the same reporting date. However this is not required by the IFRS for SMEs if this is impracticable.

2.6 Uniform accounting policies

Consolidated financial statements should be prepared using **the same accounting policies** for like transactions and other events in similar circumstances.

Adjustments must be made where members of a group use different accounting policies, so that their financial statements are suitable for consolidation.

2.7 Date of inclusion/exclusion

The results of subsidiary undertakings are included in the consolidated financial statements from:

(a)   the date of 'acquisition', ie the **date control passes to the parent**, to
(b)   the date of 'disposal', ie the **date control passes from the parent**.

Once an investment is no longer a subsidiary, it should be treated as an associate (if applicable) or as an investment.

2.8 Disclosure

The following disclosures should be made in consolidated financial statements:

(a)   the fact that the statements are consolidated financial statements

(b)   the basis for concluding that control exists when the parent does not own more than half of the voting power

(c)   any difference in the reporting date of the financial statements of the parent and its subsidiaries used in the preparation of the consolidated financial statements

(d)   the nature and extent of any significant restrictions on the ability of subsidiaries to transfer funds to the parent in the form of cash dividends or to repay loans.

When a parent prepares separate financial statements in addition to consolidated financial statements, the separate financial statements must disclose:

(a)   The fact that the statements are separate financial statements

(b)   a description of the methods used to account for investments in subsidiaries, joint ventures and associates.

2.9 Section summary

The IFRS for SMEs covers the basic rules and definitions of the parent-subsidiary relationship. You should learn:

- **Definitions**
- Rules for **exemption** from preparing consolidated financial statements
- **Disclosure**

3 Content of group accounts and group structure

It is important to distinguish between the parent company individual accounts and the group accounts.

3.1 Introduction

The information contained in the individual statements of a parent company and each of its subsidiaries does not give a picture of the group's total activities. A **separate set of group statements** can be prepared from the individual ones. Remember that a group has no separate (legal) existence, except for accounting purposes.

Consolidated accounts are one form of group accounts which combines the information contained in the separate accounts of a holding company and its subsidiaries as if they were the accounts of a single entity. 'Group accounts' and 'consolidated accounts' are terms often used synonymously.

In simple terms a set of consolidated accounts is prepared by **adding together** the assets and liabilities of the parent company and each subsidiary. The **whole** of the assets and liabilities of each company are included, even though some subsidiaries may be only partly owned. The 'equity and liabilities' section of the statement of financial position will indicate how much of the net assets are attributable to the group and how much to outside investors in partly owned subsidiaries. These **outside investors** are known as the **non-controlling interest**.

Non-controlling interest should be presented in the consolidated statement of financial position **within equity, separately from the parent shareholders' equity**.

Most parent companies present their own individual accounts and their group accounts in a single **package**. The package typically comprises the following.

- **Consolidated statement of financial position**
- **Consolidated statement of comprehensive income** (or separate income statement)
- **Consolidated statement of cash flows**

3.2 Group structure

With the difficulties of definition and disclosure dealt with, let us now look at group structures. The simplest are those in which a parent company has only a **direct interest** in the shares of its subsidiary companies. For example:

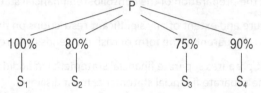

S_1 Co is a wholly owned subsidiary of P Co. S_2 Co, S_3 Co and S_4 Co are partly owned subsidiaries; a proportion of the shares in these companies is held by outside investors.

Often a parent will have **indirect holdings** in its subsidiary companies. This can lead to more complex group structures.

P Co owns 51% of the equity shares in S Co, which is therefore its subsidiary. S Co in its turn owns 51% of the equity shares in SS Co. SS Co is therefore a subsidiary of S Co and consequently a subsidiary of P Co. SS Co would describe S Co as its parent (or holding) company and P Co as its ultimate parent company.

Note that although P Co can control the assets and business of SS Co by virtue of the chain of control, its interest in the assets of SS Co is only 26%. This can be seen by considering a dividend of $100 paid by SS Co: as a 51% shareholder, S Co would receive $51; P Co would have an interest in 51% of this $51 = $26.01.

Unit Roundup

- Many large businesses consist of several companies controlled by one central or administrative company. Together these companies are called a **group**. The controlling company, called the **parent** or **holding company** will own some or all of the shares in the other companies, called **subsidiaries**.

- The IFRS for SMEs requires a parent to present consolidated financial statements.

- It is important to distinguish between the parent company **individual accounts** and the **group accounts.**

Quick Quiz

1   Define a 'subsidiary'.

2   When can control be assumed?

3   How should a parent company account for the investment in a subsidiary?

4   When is a parent exempted from preparing consolidated financial statements?

5   Under what circumstances should subsidiary undertakings be excluded from consolidation?

6   What is a non-controlling interest?

Answers to Quick Quiz

1   An entity that is controlled by another entity.

2   When the parent owns more than half (ie over 50%) of the voting power of an entity, **unless** it can be clearly shown that such ownership does not constitute control.

3   The parent company can choose whether to record a subsidiary at cost or fair value in its individual financial statements.

4   When the parent is itself a subsidiary and the ultimate parent company prepares consolidated general purpose financial statements that comply with full IFRS or the IFRS for SMEs, or

   When there are no subsidiaries other than one that was acquired with the intention of disposing of it within one year.

5   Never.

6   The equity in a subsidiary not attributable, directly or indirectly, to a parent.

Now try the question below

Useful   18 mins

Explain why consolidated financial statements are useful to the users of financial statements (as opposed to just the parent company's separate (entity) financial statements).   **(10 marks)**

Answer

Useful

The main reason for preparing consolidated accounts is that groups operate as a single economic unit, and it is not possible to understand the affairs of the parent company without taking into account the financial position and performance of all the companies that it controls. The directors of the parent company should be held fully accountable for all the money they have invested on their shareholders behalf, whether that has been done directly by the parent or via a subsidiary.

There are also practical reasons why parent company accounts cannot show the full picture. The parent company's own financial statements only show the original cost of the investment and the dividends received from the subsidiary. As explained below, this hides the true value and nature of the investment in the subsidiary, and, without consolidation, could be used to manipulate the reported results of the parent.

- The cost of the investment will include a premium for goodwill, but this is only quantified and reported if consolidated accounts are prepared.

- A controlling interest in a subsidiary can be achieved with a 51% interest. The full value of the assets controlled by the group is only shown through consolidation when the non-controlling interest is taken into account.

- Without consolidation, the assets and liabilities of the subsidiary are disguised.
    - A subsidiary could be very highly geared, making its liquidity and profitability volatile.
    - A subsidiary's assets might consist of intangible assets, or other assets with highly subjective values.

- The parent company controls the dividend policy of the subsidiary, enabling it to smooth out profit fluctuations with a steady dividend. Consolidation reveals the underlying profits of the group.

- Over time the net assets of the subsidiary should increase, but the cost of the investment will stay fixed and will soon bear no relation to the true value of the subsidiary.

Consolidated statement of financial position

16

Unit topic list

1　Summary of consolidation procedures
2　Non-controlling interests
3　Dividends paid by a subsidiary
4　Goodwill arising on consolidation
5　Comprehensive question
6　Intra-group trading
7　Intra-group sales of non-current assets
8　Summary: consolidated statement of financial position
9　Acquisition of a subsidiary during its accounting period
10　Dividends and pre-acquisition profits
11　Fair values in acquisition accounting

Assessment criteria

4　Understand and apply IFRS for SMEs in the preparation of their financial statements

4.3　Preparation of consolidated and separate financial statements as per section 9 of the IFRS for SMEs

4.12　Understand and apply section 19 of IFRS for SMEs when the SME carries on a business combination and how to treat goodwill

1 Summary of consolidation procedures

How are consolidated financial statements prepared? The IFRS for SMEs lays out the basic procedures and we will consider these in this chapter.

1.1 Basic procedure

The financial statements of a parent and its subsidiaries are **combined on a line-by-line basis** by adding together like items of assets, liabilities, equity, income and expenses.

The following steps are then taken, in order that the consolidated financial statements should **show financial information about the group as if it was a single entity**.

(a)   The carrying amount of the parent's **investment in each subsidiary** and the parent's **portion of equity** of each subsidiary are **eliminated or cancelled**

(b)   **Non-controlling interests in the net income of consolidated subsidiaries** are adjusted against group income, to arrive at the net income attributable to the owners of the parent

(c)   **Non-controlling interests** in the net assets of consolidated subsidiaries should be presented separately in the consolidated statement of financial position

Other matters to be dealt with include the following.

(a)   **Goodwill on consolidation** should be dealt with according to the IFRS for SMEs (see later in this unit)

(b)   **Dividends paid** by a subsidiary must be accounted for

All intragroup balances and transactions, and the resulting **unrealised profits**, should be **eliminated in full**. **Unrealised losses** resulting from intragroup transactions should also be eliminated *unless* cost can be recovered. This will be explained later in this unit.

1.2 Cancellation and part cancellation

The preparation of a consolidated statement of financial position, in a very simple form, consists of two procedures.

(a)   Take the individual accounts of the parent company and each subsidiary and **cancel out items** which appear as an asset in one company and a liability in another.

(b)   Add together all the uncancelled assets and liabilities throughout the group.

Items requiring cancellation may include the following.

(a)   The asset **'shares in subsidiary companies'** which appears in the parent company's accounts will be matched with the liability 'share capital' in the subsidiaries' accounts.

(b)   There may be **intra-group trading** within the group. For example, S Co may sell goods on credit to P Co. P Co would then be a receivable in the accounts of S Co, while S Co would be a payable in the accounts of P Co.

1.3 Example: cancellation

P Co regularly sells goods to its one subsidiary company, S Co, which it has owned since S Co's incorporation. The statement of financial position of the two companies on 31 December 20X6 are given below.

STATEMENT OF FINANCIAL POSITION AS AT 31 DECEMBER 20X6

	P Co $	S Co $
Assets		
Non-current assets		
Property, plant and equipment	35,000	45,000
Investment in 40,000 $1 shares in S Co at cost	40,000	
	75,000	
Current assets		
Inventories	16,000	12,000
Receivables: S Co	2,000	
Other	6,000	9,000
Cash at bank	1,000	
Total assets	100,000	66,000
Equity and liabilities		
Equity		
40,000 $1 ordinary shares		40,000
70,000 $1 ordinary shares	70,000	
Retained earnings	16,000	19,000
	86,000	59,000
Current liabilities		
Bank overdraft		3,000
Payables: P Co		2,000
Payables: Other	14,000	2,000
Total equity and liabilities	100,000	66,000

Required

Prepare the consolidated statement of financial position of P Co at 31 December 20X6.

Solution

The cancelling items are:

(a) P Co's asset 'investment in shares of S Co' ($40,000) cancels with S Co's liability 'share capital' ($40,000);

(b) P Co's asset 'receivables: S Co' ($2,000) cancels with S Co's liability 'payables: P Co' ($2,000).

The remaining assets and liabilities are added together to produce the following consolidated statement of financial position.

P CO
CONSOLIDATED STATEMENT OF FINANCIAL POSITION AS AT 31 DECEMBER 20X6

	$	$
Assets		
Non-current assets		
Property, plant and equipment		80,000
Current assets		
Inventories	28,000	
Receivables	15,000	
Cash at bank	1,000	
		44,000
Total assets		124,000

	$	$
Equity and liabilities		
Equity		
70,000 $1 ordinary shares	70,000	
Retained earnings	35,000	
		105,000
Current liabilities		
Bank overdraft	3,000	
Payables	16,000	
		19,000
Total equity and liabilities		124,000

Note the following.

(a) P Co's bank balance is **not netted off** with S Co's bank overdraft. To offset one against the other would be less informative and would conflict with the principle that assets and liabilities should not be netted off.

(b) The share capital in the consolidated statement of financial position is the **share capital of the parent company alone**. This must *always* be the case, no matter how complex the consolidation, because the share capital of subsidiary companies must *always* be a wholly cancelling item.

1.4 Part cancellation

An item may appear in the statements of financial position of a parent company and its subsidiary, but not at the same amounts.

(a) The parent company may have acquired **shares in the subsidiary** at a price **greater or less than their par value**. The asset will appear in the parent company's accounts at cost, while the liability will appear in the subsidiary's accounts at par value. This raises the issue of **goodwill**, which is dealt with later in this unit.

(b) Even if the parent company acquired shares at par value, it **may not** have **acquired all the shares of the subsidiary** (so the subsidiary may be only partly owned). This raises the issue of **non-controlling interests**, which are also dealt with later in this unit.

(c) The inter-company trading balances may be out of step because of **goods or cash in transit**.

(d) One company may have **issued loan stock** of which a **proportion only** is taken up by the other company.

The following question illustrates the techniques needed to deal with items (c) and (d) above. The procedure is to **cancel as far as possible**. The remaining uncancelled amounts will appear in the consolidated statement of financial position.

(a) **Uncancelled loan stock** will appear as a **liability of the group**.

(b) **Uncancelled balances on intra-group accounts** represent **goods or cash in transit**, which will appear in the consolidated statement of financial position.

 Activity

The statements of financial position of P Co and of its subsidiary S Co have been made up to 30 June. P Co has owned all the ordinary shares and 40% of the loan stock of S Co since its incorporation.

P CO
STATEMENT OF FINANCIAL POSITION AS AT 30 JUNE

	$	$
Assets		
Non-current assets		
Property, plant and equipment	120,000	
Investment in S Co, at cost		
80,000 ordinary shares of $1 each	80,000	
$20,000 of 12% loan stock in S Co	20,000	
		220,000
Current assets		
Inventories	50,000	
Receivables	40,000	
Current account with S Co	18,000	
Cash	4,000	
		112,000
Total assets		332,000
Equity and liabilities		
Equity		
Ordinary shares of $1 each, fully paid	100,000	
Retained earnings	95,000	
		195,000
Non-current liabilities		
10% loan stock		75,000
Current liabilities		
Payables	47,000	
Taxation	15,000	
		62,000
Total equity and liabilities		332,000

S CO
STATEMENT OF FINANCIAL POSITION AS AT 30 JUNE

	$	$
Assets		
Property, plant and equipment		100,000
Current assets		
Inventories	60,000	
Receivables	30,000	
Cash	6,000	
		96,000
Total assets		196,000
Equity and liabilities		
Equity		
80,000 ordinary shares of $1 each, fully paid	80,000	
Retained earnings	28,000	
		108,000
Non-current liabilities		
12% loan stock		50,000
Current liabilities		
Payables	16,000	
Taxation	10,000	
Current account with P Co	12,000	
		38,000
Total equity and liabilities		196,000

The difference on current account arises because of goods in transit.

Required

Prepare the consolidated statement of financial position of P Co.

Answer

P CO
CONSOLIDATED STATEMENT OF FINANCIAL POSITION AS AT 30 JUNE

	$	$
Assets		
Non-current assets		
Property, plant and equipment (120,000 + 100,000)		220,000
Current assets		
Inventories (50,000 + 60,000)	110,000	
Goods in transit (18,000 – 12,000)	6,000	
Receivables (40,000 + 30,000)	70,000	
Cash (4,000 + 6,000)	10,000	
		196,000
Total assets		416,000
Equity and liabilities		
Equity		
Ordinary shares of $1 each, fully paid (parent)	100,000	
Retained earnings (95,000 + 28,000)	123,000	
		223,000
Non-current liabilities		
10% loan stock	75,000	
12% loan stock (50,000 × 60%)	30,000	
		105,000
Current liabilities		
Payables (47,000 + 16,000)	63,000	
Taxation (15,000 + 10,000)	25,000	
		88,000
Total equity and liabilities		416,000

Note especially how:

(a)   The uncancelled loan stock in S Co becomes a liability of the group
(b)   The goods in transit is the difference between the current accounts ($18,000 – $12,000)
(c)   The investment in S Co's shares is cancelled against S Co's share capital

2 Non-controlling interests

In the consolidated statement of financial position it is necessary to distinguish non-controlling interests from those net assets attributable to the group and financed by shareholders' equity.

2.1 Introduction

It was mentioned earlier that the total assets and liabilities of subsidiary companies are included in the consolidated statement of financial position, even in the case of subsidiaries which are only partly owned. A proportion of the net assets of such subsidiaries in fact belongs to investors from outside the group (**non-controlling interests**).

The following example shows how the non-controlling interest is calculated at its proportionate share of the subsidiary's net assets.

2.2 Example: non-controlling interest

P Co has owned 75% of the share capital of S Co since the date of S Co's incorporation. Their latest statements of financial position are given below.

P CO
STATEMENT OF FINANCIAL POSITION

	$	$
Assets		
Non-current assets		
Property, plant and equipment	50,000	
30,000 $1 ordinary shares in S Co at cost	30,000	
		80,000
Current assets		45,000
Total assets		125,000
Equity and liabilities		
Equity		
80,000 $1 ordinary shares	80,000	
Retained earnings	25,000	
		105,000
Current liabilities		20,000
Total equity and liabilities		125,000

S CO
STATEMENT OF FINANCIAL POSITION

	$	$
Assets		
Property, plant and equipment		35,000
Current assets		35,000
Total assets		70,000
Equity and liabilities		
Equity		
40,000 $1 ordinary shares	40,000	
Retained earnings	10,000	
		50,000
Current liabilities		20,000
Total equity and liabilities		70,000

Required

Prepare the consolidated statement of financial position.

Solution

All of S Co's net assets are consolidated despite the fact that the company is only 75% owned. The amount of net assets attributable to non-controlling interests is calculated as follows.

	$
Non-controlling share of share capital (25% × $40,000)	10,000
Non-controlling share of retained earnings (25% × $10,000)	2,500
	12,500

Of S Co's share capital of $40,000, $10,000 is included in the figure for non-controlling interest, while $30,000 is cancelled with P Co's asset 'investment in S Co'.

The consolidated statement of financial position can now be prepared.

P GROUP
CONSOLIDATED STATEMENT OF FINANCIAL POSITION

	$	$
Assets		
Property, plant and equipment		85,000
Current assets		80,000
Total assets		165,000
Equity and liabilities		
Equity attributable to owners of the parent		
Share capital	80,000	
Retained earnings $(25,000 + (75\% \times \$10,000))$	32,500	
		112,500
Non-controlling interest		12,500
		125,000
Current liabilities		40,000
Total equity and liabilities		165,000

2.3 Procedure

(a) Aggregate the assets and liabilities in the statement of financial position ie 100% P + 100% S irrespective of how much P actually owns.

This shows the amount of net assets **controlled** by the group.

(b) Share capital is that of the parent only.

(c) Balance of subsidiary's reserves are consolidated (after cancelling any intra-group items).

(d) Calculate the non-controlling interest share of the subsidiary's net assets (share capital plus reserves).

Activity

Set out below are the draft statement of financial position of P Co and its subsidiary S Co. You are required to prepare the consolidated statement of financial position.

P CO

	$	$
Assets		
Non-current assets		
Property, plant and equipment		31,000
Investment in S Co		
12,000 $1 ordinary shares at cost	12,000	
$8,000 10% loan stock at cost	8,000	
		20,000
		51,000
Current assets		21,000
Total assets		72,000
Equity and liabilities		
Equity		
Ordinary shares of $1 each	40,000	
Retained earnings	22,000	
		62,000
Current liabilities		10,000
Total equity and liabilities		72,000

S CO

	$	$
Assets		
Property, plant and equipment		34,000
Current assets		32,000
Total assets		66,000
Equity and liabilities		
Equity		
Ordinary shares of $1 each	20,000	
Revaluation surplus	6,000	
Retained earnings	4,000	
		30,000
Non-current liabilities		
10% loan stock		26,000
Current liabilities		10,000
Total equity and liabilities		66,000

 Answer

The group structure is:

P Co
|
| 60%
↓
S Co

Partly cancelling items are the components of P Co's investment in S Co, ie ordinary shares, loan stock. Non-controlling shareholders have an interest in 40% (8,000/20,000) of S Co's ordinary shares, including reserves.

You should now aggregate the assets and liabilities and produce workings for non-controlling interest, revaluation surplus and retained earnings as follows.

Workings

1   Revaluation surplus

	$
P Co	–
Share of S Co's revaluation surplus (60% × 6,000)	3,600
	3,600

2   Retained earnings

	$
P Co	22,000
Share of S Co's retained earnings (60% × 4,000)	2,400
	24,400

3   Non-controlling interest

	$
S Co's net assets (66,000 – 36,000)	30,000
× 40%	12,000

The results of the workings are now used to construct the consolidated statement of financial position.

P GROUP
CONSOLIDATED STATEMENT OF FINANCIAL POSITION

	$	$
Assets		
Property, plant and equipment		65,000
Current assets		53,000
Total assets		118,000
Equity and liabilities		
Equity attributable to owners of the parent		
Ordinary shares of $1 each	40,000	
Revaluation surplus (W1)	3,600	
Retained earnings (W2)	24,400	
		68,000
Non-controlling interest (W3)		12,000
		80,000
Non-current liabilities		
10% loan stock (26,000 – 8,000)		18,000
Current liabilities		20,000
Total equity and liabilities		118,000

Notes

(a) S Co is a subsidiary of P Co because P Co owns 60% of its ordinary capital.

(b) As always, the share capital in the consolidated statement of financial position is that of the parent company alone. The share capital in S Co's statement of financial position was partly cancelled against the investment shown in P Co's statement of financial position, while the uncancelled portion was credited to non-controlling interest.

(c) The figure for non-controlling interest comprises the interest of outside investors in the share capital and reserves of the subsidiary. The uncancelled portion of S Co's loan stock is not shown as part of non-controlling interest but is disclosed separately as a liability of the group.

3 Dividends paid by a subsidiary

When a subsidiary company pays a **dividend** during the year the accounting treatment is not difficult. Suppose S Co, a 60% subsidiary of P Co, pays a dividend of $1,000 on the last day of its accounting period. Its total reserves before paying the dividend stood at $5,000.

(a) $400 of the dividend is paid to non-controlling shareholders. The cash leaves the group and will not appear anywhere in the consolidated statement of financial position.

(b) The parent company receives $600 of the dividend, debiting cash and crediting profit or loss. This will be cancelled on consolidation.

(c) The remaining balance of retained earnings in S Co's statement of financial position ($4,000) will be consolidated in the normal way. The group's share (60% × $4,000 = $2,400) will be included in group retained earnings in the statement of financial position; the non-controlling interest share (40% × $4,000 = $1,600) is credited to the non-controlling interest account in the statement of financial position.

However, the situation is more complicated when a subsidiary pays a dividend shortly after acquisition and some of that dividend is deemed to have been paid from pre-acquisition profits. This situation is considered in Section 10.

4 Goodwill arising on consolidation

In the examples we have looked at so far the cost of shares acquired by the parent company has always been equal to the par value of those shares. This is seldom the case in practice and we must now consider some more complicated examples.

4.1 Accounting

To begin with, **we will examine the entries made by the parent company in its own statement of financial position when it acquires shares.**

When a company P Co wishes to **purchase shares** in a company S Co it must pay the previous owners of those shares. The most obvious form of payment would be in **cash**. Suppose P Co purchases all 40,000 $1 shares in S Co and pays $60,000 cash to the previous shareholders in consideration. The entries in P Co's books would be:

DEBIT	Investment in S Co at cost	$60,000	
CREDIT	Bank		$60,000

However, the previous shareholders might be prepared to accept some other form of consideration. For example, they might accept an agreed number of **shares** in P Co. P Co would then issue new shares in the agreed number and allot them to the former shareholders of S Co. This kind of deal might be attractive to P Co since it avoids the need for a heavy cash outlay. The former shareholders of S Co would retain an indirect interest in that company's profitability via their new holding in its parent company.

Continuing the example, suppose that instead of $60,000 cash the shareholders of S Co agreed to accept one $1 ordinary share in P Co for every two $1 ordinary shares in S Co. P Co would then need to issue and allot 20,000 new $1 shares. How would this transaction be recorded in the books of P Co?

The former shareholders of S Co have presumably agreed to accept 20,000 shares in P Co because they consider each of those shares to have a value of $3. This gives us the following method of recording the transaction in P Co's books.

DEBIT	Investment in S Co	$60,000	
CREDIT	Share capital		$20,000
	Share premium account		$40,000

The amount which P Co records in its books as the cost of its investment in S Co may be more or less than the book value of the assets it acquires. Suppose that S Co in the previous example has nil reserves and nil liabilities, so that its share capital of $40,000 is balanced by tangible assets with a book value of $40,000. For simplicity, assume that the book value of S Co's assets is the same as their market or fair value.

Now when the directors of P Co agree to pay $60,000 for a 100% investment in S Co they must believe that, in addition to its tangible assets of $40,000, S Co must also have intangible assets worth $20,000. This amount of $20,000 paid over and above the value of the tangible assets acquired is called **goodwill arising on consolidation** (sometimes **premium on acquisition**).

Following the normal cancellation procedure the $40,000 share capital in S Co's statement of financial position could be cancelled against $40,000 of the 'investment in S Co' in the statement of financial position of P Co. This would leave a $20,000 debit uncancelled in the parent company's accounts and this $20,000 would appear in the consolidated statement of financial position under the caption 'Intangible non-current assets: goodwill arising on consolidation'.

4.2 Goodwill and pre-acquisition profits

Up to now we have assumed that S Co had nil retained earnings when its shares were purchased by P Co. Assuming instead that S Co had earned profits of $8,000 in the period before acquisition, its statement of financial position just before the purchase would look as follows.

	$
Total assets	48,000
Share capital	40,000
Retained earnings	8,000
	48,000

If P Co now purchases all the shares in S Co it will acquire total assets worth $48,000 at a cost of $60,000. Clearly in this case S Co's intangible assets (goodwill) are being valued at $12,000. It should be apparent that any earnings retained by the subsidiary **prior to its acquisition** by the parent company must be **incorporated in the cancellation** process so as to arrive at a figure for goodwill arising on consolidation. In other words, not only S Co's share capital, but also its **pre-acquisition** retained earnings, must be cancelled against the asset 'investment in S Co' in the accounts of the parent company. The uncancelled balance of $12,000 appears in the consolidated statement of financial position.

The consequence of this is that **any pre-acquisition retained earnings of a subsidiary company are not aggregated with the parent company's retained earnings** in the consolidated statement of financial position. The figure of consolidated retained earnings comprises the retained earnings of the parent company plus the **post-acquisition retained earnings only of subsidiary companies**. The post-acquisition retained earnings are simply retained earnings now *less* retained earnings at acquisition.

4.3 Example: goodwill and pre-acquisition profits

Sing Co acquired the ordinary shares of Wing Co on 31 March when the draft statements of financial position of each company were as follows.

SING CO
STATEMENT OF FINANCIAL POSITION AS AT 31 MARCH

	$
Assets	
Non-current assets	
Investment in 50,000 shares of Wing Co at cost	80,000
Current assets	40,000
Total assets	120,000
Equity and liabilities	
Equity	
Ordinary shares	75,000
Retained earnings	45,000
Total equity and liabilities	120,000

WING CO
STATEMENT OF FINANCIAL POSITION AS AT 31 MARCH

	$
Current assets	60,000
Equity	
50,000 ordinary shares of $1 each	50,000
Retained earnings	10,000
	60,000

Prepare the consolidated statement of financial position as at 31 March.

Solution

The technique to adopt here is to produce a new working: 'Goodwill'. A proforma working is set out below.

Goodwill

	$	$
Consideration transferred		X
Net assets acquired as represented by:		
Ordinary share capital	X	
Share premium	X	
Retained earnings on acquisition	X	
		(X)
Goodwill		X

Applying this to our example the working will look like this.

	$	$
Consideration transferred		80,000
Net assets acquired as represented by:		
Ordinary share capital	50,000	
Retained earnings on acquisition	10,000	
		(60,000)
Goodwill		20,000

SING CO
CONSOLIDATED STATEMENT OF FINANCIAL POSITION AS AT 31 MARCH

	$
Assets	
Non-current assets	
Goodwill arising on consolidation (W)	20,000
Current assets (40,000 + 60,000)	100,000
	120,000
Equity	
Ordinary shares	75,000
Retained earnings	45,000
	120,000

4.4 Goodwill and non-controlling interest

Now let us look at what would happen if Sing Co had obtained less than 100% of the shares of Wing Co.

If Sing Co had paid $70,000 for 40,000 shares in Wing Co, the goodwill working would be as follows:

	$
Consideration transferred	70,000
Net assets acquired (60,000 × 80%)	(48,000)
Goodwill	22,000

4.5 Amortisation of goodwill

Goodwill arising on consolidation is subjected to an annual amortisation charge. If it is not possible to make a reliable estimate for the life of the goodwill then it will be presumed to be 10 years. The double entry to write off the amortisation is:

DEBIT Group retained earnings   CREDIT Goodwill

4.6 Worked example

P acquired 75% of the shares in S on 1 January 20X7 when S had retained earnings of $15,000. The market price of S's shares just before the date of acquisition was $1.60. P values non-controlling interest at fair value. The useful life of goodwill cannot be reliably estimated.

The statements of financial position of P and S at 31 December 20X7 were as follows:

	P	S
	$	$
Property, plant and equipment	60,000	50,000
Shares in S	68,000	–
	128,000	50,000
Current assets	52,000	35,000
	180,000	85,000

	P	S
Share capital – $1 shares	100,000	50,000
Retained earnings	70,000	25,000
	170,000	75,000
Current liabilities	10,000	10,000
	180,000	85,000

Prepare the consolidated statement of financial position of the P Group as at 31 December 20X7.

Solution

CONSOLIDATED STATEMENT OF FINANCIAL POSITION AS AT 31 DECEMBER 20X7

	$
Assets	
Property plant and equipment (60,000 + 50,000)	110,000
Goodwill (W1)	17,325
Current assets (52,000 + 35,000)	87,000
Total assets	214,325
Equity and liabilities	
Equity attributable to the owners of P	
Share capital	100,000
Retained earnings (W2)	75,575
	175,575
Non-controlling interest (W3)	18,750
Total equity	194,325
Current liabilities (10,000 + 10,000)	20,000
Total equity and liabilities	214,325

Workings

1   *Goodwill*

	Group
	$
Consideration transferred	68,000
Group share of net assets of S at acq'n (50,000 + 15,000)	(48,750)
Goodwill	19,250
Amortisation x 1/10	(1,925)
Goodwill reported in CSFP	17,325

2   *Retained earnings*

	P	S
	$	$
Per statement of financial position	70,000	25,000
Less pre-acquisition		(15,000)
		10,000
Group share of S (10,000 × 75%)	7,500	
Amortisation of goodwill	(1,925)	
Group retained earnings	75,575	

3   *Non-controlling interest at year end*

	$
Share of net assets of S (75,000 × 25%)	18,750

4.7 Gain on a bargain purchase

Goodwill arising on consolidation is one form of **purchased goodwill**, and is governed by the IFRS.

Goodwill arising on consolidation is the difference between the cost of an acquisition and the value of the subsidiary's net assets acquired. This difference can be **negative**: the aggregate of the fair values of the separable net assets acquired may **exceed** what the parent company paid for them. The IFRS refers to this as a 'bargain purchase'. In this situation:

(a)   An entity should first **re-assess** the amounts at which it has measured both the cost of the combination and the acquiree's identifiable net assets. This exercise should **identify any errors.**

(b)   Any **excess remaining** should be **recognised immediately in profit or loss**.

4.8 Cost of combination

The cost of a business combination may include consideration in a number of different forms and this will affect the calculation of goodwill. Here are some examples:

4.8.1 Contingent consideration

The parent acquired 60% of the subsidiary's $100m share capital on 1 Jan 20X6 for a cash payment of $150m and a further payment of $50m on 31 March 20X7 if the subsidiary's post acquisition profits have exceeded an agreed figure by that date.

In the financial statements for the year to 31 December 20X6 $50m will be added to the cost of the combination, discounted as appropriate.

The IFRS requires that contingent consideration is recognised as part of the consideration for the acquiree where it will probably be paid and can be measured reliably..

The acquirer may be required to pay contingent consideration in the form of equity or of a debt instrument or cash . Contingent consideration can also be an asset, if the consideration has already been transferred and the acquirer has the right to return of some of it, if certain considerations are met.

4.8.2 Deferred consideration

An agreement may be made that part of the consideration for the combination will be paid at a future date. This consideration will therefore be discounted to its present value using the acquiring entity's cost of capital.

The parent acquired 75% of the subsidiary's 80m $1 shares on 1 Jan 20X7. It paid $3.50 per share and agreed to pay a further $108m on 1 Jan 20X8.

The parent company's cost of capital is 8%.

As at 1 January 20X7 the cost of the combination will be as follows:

	$m
80m shares × 75% × $3.50	210
Deferred consideration:	
$108m × 1/1.08	100
Total consideration	310

At 31 December 20X7, the cost of the combination will be unchanged but $8m will be charged to finance costs, being the unwinding of the discount on the deferred consideration.

4.8.3 Share exchange

The parent has acquired 12,000 $1 shares in the subsidiary by issuing 5 of its own $1 shares for every 4 shares in the subsidiary. The market value of the parent company's shares is $6.

Cost of the combination:

	$
12,000 × 5/4 × $6	90,000

Note that this is credited to the share capital and share premium of the parent company as follows:

	DR	CR
	$	$
Investment in subsidiary	90,000	
Share capital ($12,000 × 5/4)		15,000
Share premium ($12,000 × 5/4 × 5)		75,000

4.8.4 Incidental costs of acquisition

The IFRS for SMEs includes any costs directly attributable to the business combination as part of the cost of acquisition for the purposes of calculating goodwill.

4.9 Adjustments to goodwill

At the date of acquisition the parent recognises the assets, liabilities and contingent liabilities of the subsidiary at their fair value at the date when control is acquired. It may be that some of these assets or liabilities had not previously been recognised by the acquiree.

For instance, the subsidiary may have tax losses brought forward, but had not recognised these as an asset because it could not foresee future profits against which they could be offset. If it now appears that taxable profits will be forthcoming, the deferred tax asset can be recognised.

An entity has acquired a 60% interest in another entity which has brought forward tax losses unutilised of $200,000. The tax losses can now be utilised.

The adjustment will be:

	DR	CR
Deferred tax (subsidiary)	$200,000	
Goodwill (effectively)		$200,000

5 Comprehensive question

Now we will look at a full consolidation question including non-controlling interest.

Activity

The draft statements of financial position of Ping Co and Pong Co on 30 June 20X8 were as follows.

PING CO
STATEMENT OF FINANCIAL POSITION AS AT 30 JUNE 20X8

	$	$
Assets		
Non-current assets		
Property, plant and equipment	50,000	
20,000 ordinary shares in Pong Co at cost	30,000	
		80,000
Current assets		
Inventory	3,000	
Receivables	16,000	
Cash	2,000	
		21,000
Total assets		101,000
Equity and liabilities		
Equity		
Ordinary shares of $1 each	45,000	
Revaluation surplus	12,000	
Retained earnings	26,000	
		83,000
Current liabilities		
Owed to Pong Co	8,000	
Trade payables	10,000	
		18,000
Total equity and liabilities		101,000

PONG CO
STATEMENT OF FINANCIAL POSITION AS AT 30 JUNE 20X8

	$	$
Assets		
Property, plant and equipment		40,000
Current assets		
Inventory	8,000	
Owed by Ping Co	10,000	
Receivables	7,000	
		25,000
Total assets		65,000
Equity and liabilities		
Equity		
Ordinary shares of $1 each	25,000	
Revaluation surplus	5,000	
Retained earnings	28,000	
		58,000
Current liabilities		
Trade payables		7,000
Total equity and liabilities		65,000

Ping Co acquired its investment in Pong Co on 1 July 20X7 when the retained earnings of Pong Co stood at $6,000. The agreed consideration was $30,000 cash and a further $10,000 on 1 July 20X9 if Pong Co attained certain profit targets. It appears likely that these targets will be met. Ping Co's cost of capital is 7%. Pong Co has an internally-developed brand name – 'Pongo' – which was valued at $5,000 at the date of acquisition. There have been no changes in the share capital or revaluation surplus of Pong Co since that date. At 30 June 20X4 Pong Co had invoiced Ping Co for goods to the value of $2,000 which had not been received by Ping Co.

The goodwill is to be amortised over a period of 10 years.

Prepare the consolidated statement of financial position of Ping Co as at 30 June 20X8.

Answer

1   **Agree current accounts.**

Ping Co has goods in transit of $2,000 making its total inventory $3,000 + $2,000 = $5,000 and its liability to Pong Co $8,000 + $2,000 = $10,000.

Cancel common items: these are the current accounts between the two companies of $10,000 each.

2   **Calculate goodwill.**

Goodwill

		Group
	$	$
Consideration transferred (W3)		38,734
Net assets acquired as represented by:		
Ordinary share capital	25,000	
Revaluation surplus on acquisition	5,000	
Retained earnings on acquisition	6,000	
Intangible asset – brand name	5,000	
	41,000	
Group %		(32,800)
Goodwill		5,934
Amortisation (1/10)		(593)
Goodwill in CSFP		5,341

3   **Consideration transferred**

	$
Cash paid	30,000
Contingent consideration: $10,000 \times 1/(1.07^2)$*	8,734
	38,734

* Note that the contingent consideration has been discounted at 7% for two years (1 July 20X7 to 1 July 20X9).

However, at the date of the current financial statements, 30 June 20X8, the discount for one year has unwound. The amount of the discount unwound is

	$
$(10,000 \times 1/1.07) - 8,734$	618

So this amount will be charged to finance costs in the consolidated financial statements and the contingent consideration under liabilities will be shown as $9,352 (8,734 + 618).

4   **Calculate consolidated reserves.**

Consolidated revaluation surplus

	$
Ping Co	12,000
Share of Pong Co's post acquisition revaluation surplus	–
	12,000

Consolidated retained earnings

	Ping	Pong
	$	$
Retained earnings per question	26,000	28,000
Amortisation of goodwill	(593)	
Less pre-acquisition		(6,000)
Discount unwound – finance costs	(618)	22,000
Share of Pong: 80% × $22,000	17,600	
	42,389	

5   **Calculate non-controlling interest at year end**

	$
Pong Co's net assets per question (65,000 – 7,000)	58,000
Intangible asset (brand name)	5,000
	63,000
NCI share 20%	12,600

6   Prepare the consolidated statement of financial position.

PING CO
CONSOLIDATED STATEMENT OF FINANCIAL POSITION AS AT 30 JUNE 20X8

	$	$
Assets		
Non-current assets		
Property, plant and equipment ($50,000 + $40,000)		90,000
Intangible assets: goodwill (W2)		5,341
Brand name		5,000
Current assets		
Inventories ($5,000 + $8,000)	13,000	
Receivables ($16,000 + $7,000)	23,000	
Cash	2,000	
		38,000
Total assets		138,341

	$	$
Equity and liabilities		
Equity		
Ordinary shares of $1 each	45,000	
Revaluation surplus (W4)	12,000	
Retained earnings (W4)	42,389	
		99,389
Non-controlling interest (W5)		12,600
		111,989
Current liabilities		
Trade payables ($10,000 + $7,000)		17,000
Contingent consideration (W3)		9,352
Total equity and liabilities		138,341

6 Intra-group trading

We have already come across cases where one company in a group engages in trading with another group company. Any profit made is eliminated on consolidation.

6.1 Unrealised profit

Any receivable/payable balances outstanding between the companies are cancelled on consolidation. No further problem arises if all such intra-group transactions are **undertaken at cost**, without any mark-up for profit.

However, each company in a group is a separate trading entity and may wish to treat other group companies in the same way as any other customer. In this case, a company (say A Co) may buy goods at one price and sell them at a higher price to another group company (B Co). The accounts of A Co will quite properly include the profit earned on sales to B Co; and similarly B Co's statement of financial position will include inventories at their cost to B Co, ie at the amount at which they were purchased from A Co.

This gives rise to two problems.

(a) Although A Co makes a profit as soon as it sells goods to B Co, the group does not make a sale or achieve a profit until an outside customer buys the goods from B Co.

(b) Any purchases from A Co which remain unsold by B Co at the year end will be included in B Co's inventory. Their value in the statement of financial position will be their cost to B Co, which is not the same as their cost to the group.

The objective of consolidated accounts is to present the financial position of several connected companies as that of a single entity, the group. This means that **in a consolidated statement of financial position the only profits recognised should be those earned by the group** in providing goods or services to outsiders; and similarly, inventory in the consolidated statement of financial position should be valued at cost to the group.

Suppose that a holding company P Co buys goods for $1,600 and sells them to a wholly owned subsidiary S Co for $2,000. The goods are in S Co's inventory at the year end and appear in S Co's statement of financial position at $2,000. In this case, P Co will record a profit of $400 in its individual accounts, but from the group's point of view the figures are:

Cost	$1,600
External sales	nil
Closing inventory at cost	$1,600
Profit/loss	nil

If we add together the figures for retained earnings and inventory in the individual statements of financial position of P Co and S Co the resulting figures for consolidated retained earnings and consolidated inventory will each be overstated by $400. A **consolidation adjustment** is therefore necessary as follows.

DEBIT   Group retained earnings
CREDIT   Group inventory (statement of financial position)

with the amount of **profit unrealised** by the group.

Activity

P Co acquired all the shares in S Co one year ago when the reserves of S Co stood at $10,000. Draft statements of financial position for each company are as follows.

	P Co $	P Co $	S Co $	S Co $
Assets				
Non-current assets				
Property, plant and equipment	80,000			40,000
Investment in S Co at cost	46,000			
		126,000		
Current assets		40,000		30,000
Total assets		166,000		70,000
Equity and liabilities				
Equity				
Ordinary shares of $1 each	100,000		30,000	
Retained earnings	45,000		22,000	
		145,000		52,000
Current liabilities		21,000		18,000
Total equity and liabilities		166,000		70,000

During the year S Co sold goods to P Co for $50,000, the profit to S Co being 20% of selling price. At the end of the reporting period, $15,000 of these goods remained unsold in the inventories of P Co. At the same date, P Co owed S Co $12,000 for goods bought and this debt is included in the trade payables of P Co and the receivables of S Co. The goodwill arising on consolidation is amortised over a period of 10 years.

Required

Prepare a draft consolidated statement of financial position for P Co.

Answer

1	*Goodwill*	$	$
	Consideration transferred		46,000
	Net assets acquired as represented by		
	Share capital	30,000	
	Retained earnings	10,000	
			(40,000)
	Goodwill		6,000
	Amortisation (1/10)		(600)
	Goodwill in CSFP		5,400

2   *Retained earnings*

	P Co $	S Co $
Retained earnings per question	45,000	22,000
Unrealised profit: 20% × $15,000		(3,000)
Pre-acquisition		(10,000)
		9,000
Share of S Co	9,000	
Goodwill amortisation	(600)	
	53,400	

P CO
CONSOLIDATED STATEMENT OF FINANCIAL POSITION

	$	$
Assets		
Non-current assets		
Property, plant and equipment	120,000	
Goodwill (6,000 – 1,500)	5,400	
		125,400
Current assets (W1)		55,000
Total assets		180,400
Equity and liabilities		
Equity		
Ordinary shares of $1 each	100,000	
Retained earnings	53,400	
		153,400
Current liabilities (W2)		27,000
Total equity and liabilities		180,400

Workings

1   *Current assets*

	$	$
In P Co's statement of financial position		40,000
In S Co's statement of financial position	30,000	
Less S Co's current account with P Co cancelled	(12,000)	
		18,000
		58,000
Less unrealised profit excluded from inventory valuation		(3,000)
		55,000

2   *Current liabilities*

	$
In P Co's statement of financial position	21,000
Less P Co's current account with S Co cancelled	(12,000)
	9,000
In S Co's statement of financial position	18,000
	27,000

6.2 Non-controlling interests in unrealised intra-group profits

A further problem occurs where a subsidiary company which is **not wholly owned is involved in intra-group trading** within the group. If a subsidiary S Co is 75% owned and sells goods to the parent company for $16,000 cost plus $4,000 profit, ie for $20,000 and if these items are unsold by P Co at the end of the reporting period, the 'unrealised' profit of $4,000 earned by S Co and charged to P Co will be partly owned by the non-controlling interest of S Co. As far as the non-controlling interest of S Co is concerned, their share (25% of $4,000) amounting to $1,000 of profit on the sale of goods would appear to have been fully realised. It is only the group that has not yet made a profit on the sale.

The correct treatment of these intragroup profits is to remove the whole profit, charging the non-controlling interest with their proportion.

DEBIT	Group retained earnings
DEBIT	Non-controlling interest
CREDIT	Group inventory (statement of financial position)

6.3 Example: non-controlling interests and intra-group profits

P Co has owned 75% of the shares of S Co since the incorporation of that company. During the year to 31 December 20X2, S Co sold goods costing $16,000 to P Co at a price of $20,000 and these goods were still unsold by P Co at the end of the year. Draft statements of financial position of each company at 31 December 20X2 were as follows.

	P Co		S Co	
Assets	$	$	$	$
Non-current assets				
Property, plant and equipment	125,000		120,000	
Investment: 75,000 shares in S Co at cost	75,000		–	
		200,000		120,000
Current assets				
Inventories	50,000		48,000	
Trade receivables	20,000		16,000	
		70,000		64,000
Total assets		270,000		184,000
Equity and liabilities				
Equity				
Ordinary shares of $1 each fully paid	80,000		100,000	
Retained earnings	150,000		60,000	
		230,000		160,000
Current liabilities		40,000		24,000
Total equity and liabilities		270,000		184,000

Required

Prepare the consolidated statement of financial position of P Co at 31 December 20X2.

Solution

The profit earned by S Co but unrealised by the group is $4,000 of which $3,000 (75%) is attributable to the group and $1,000 (25%) to the non-controlling interest. Remove the whole of the profit loading, charging the non-controlling interest with their proportion.

	P Co	S Co
	$	$
Retained earnings		
Per question	150,000	60,000
Less unrealised profit		(4,000)
		56,000
Share of S Co: $56,000 × 75%	42,000	
	192,000	
Non-controlling interest		
S Co's net assets (184,000 – 24,000)		160,000
Unrealised profit		(4,000)
		156,000
× 25%		39,000

P CO
CONSOLIDATED STATEMENT OF FINANCIAL POSITION AS AT 31 DECEMBER 20X2

	$	$
Assets		
Property, plant and equipment		245,000
Current assets		
Inventories $(50,000 + 48,000 – 4,000)$	94,000	
Trade receivables	36,000	
		130,000
Total assets		375,000
Equity and liabilities		
Equity		
Ordinary shares of $1 each	80,000	
Retained earnings	192,000	
		272,000
Non-controlling interest		39,000
		311,000
Current liabilities		64,000
Total equity and liabilities		375,000

7 Intra-group sales of non-current assets

As well as engaging in trading activities with each other, group companies may on occasion wish to **transfer non-current assets**.

7.1 Accounting treatment

In their individual accounts the companies concerned will treat the transfer just like a sale between unconnected parties: the selling company will record a profit or loss on sale, while the purchasing company will record the asset at the amount paid to acquire it, and will use that amount as the basis for calculating depreciation.

On consolidation, the usual **'group entity' principle applies**. The consolidated statement of financial position must show assets at their cost to the group, and any depreciation charged must be based on that cost. Two consolidation adjustments will usually be needed to achieve this.

(a) An adjustment to alter retained earnings and non-current assets cost so as to remove any element of unrealised profit or loss. This is similar to the adjustment required in respect of unrealised profit in inventory.

(b) An adjustment to alter retained earnings and accumulated depreciation is made so that consolidated depreciation is based on the asset's cost to the group.

In practice, these steps are combined so that the retained earnings of the entity making the unrealised profit are debited with the unrealised profit less the additional depreciation.

The double entry is as follows.

(a) Sale by parent

DEBIT   Group retained earnings
CREDIT   Non-current assets

with the profit on disposal, less the additional depreciation.

(b) Sale by subsidiary

DEBIT   Group retained earnings (P's share of S)
DEBIT   Non-controlling interest (NCI's share of S)
CREDIT   Non-current assets

with the profit on disposal, less additional depreciation

7.2 Example: intra-group sale of non-current assets

P Co owns 60% of S Co and on 1 January 20X1 S Co sells plant costing $10,000 to P Co for $12,500. The companies make up accounts to 31 December 20X1 and the balances on their retained earnings at that date are:

P Co after charging depreciation of 10% on plant	$27,000
S Co including profit on sale of plant	$18,000

Required

Show the working for consolidated retained earnings.

Solution

Retained earnings

	P Co $	S Co $
Per question	27,000	18,000
Disposal of plant		
Profit		(2,500)
Depreciation: 10% × $2,500		250
		15,750
Share of S Co: $15,750 × 60%	9,450	
	36,450	

Notes

1. The non-controlling interest in the retained earnings of S Co is 40% × $15,750 = $6,300.

2. The asset is written down to cost and depreciation and the 'profit' element is removed. The group profit for the year is thus reduced by a net (($2,500 − $250) × 60%) = $1,350.

8 Summary: consolidated statement of financial position

Purpose	To show the net assets which P controls and the ownership of those assets.
Net assets	Always 100% P plus 100% S providing P holds a majority of voting rights.
Share capital	P only.
Reason	Simply reporting to the parent company's shareholders in another form.
Retained earnings	100% P plus group share of post-acquisition retained earnings of S less consolidation adjustments.
Reason	To show the extent to which the group actually owns total assets less liabilities.
Non-controlling interest	NCI share of S's consolidated net assets.
Reason	To show the equity in a subsidiary not attributable to the parent.

9 Acquisition of a subsidiary during its accounting period

When a parent company acquires a subsidiary during its accounting period the only accounting entries made at the time will be those recording the **cost of acquisition in the parent company's books**.

9.1 Accounting problem

As we have already seen, at the end of the accounting year it will be necessary to prepare consolidated accounts.

The subsidiary company's accounts to be consolidated will show the subsidiary's profit or loss for the whole year. For consolidation purposes, however, it will be necessary to distinguish between:

(a) Profits earned before acquisition
(b) Profits earned after acquisition

In practice, a subsidiary company's profit may not accrue evenly over the year; for example, the subsidiary might be engaged in a trade, such as toy sales, with marked seasonal fluctuations. Nevertheless, the assumption can be made that **profits accrue evenly** whenever it is impracticable to arrive at an accurate split of pre– and post-acquisition profits.

Once the amount of pre-acquisition profit has been established the appropriate consolidation workings (goodwill, retained earnings) can be produced.

Bear in mind that in calculating **non-controlling interests** at the year end, the distinction between pre– and post-acquisition profits is irrelevant. The non-controlling shareholders are simply credited with their share of the subsidiary's total net assets at the end of the reporting period.

It is worthwhile to summarise what happens on consolidation to the retained earnings figures extracted from a subsidiary's statement of financial position. Suppose the accounts of S Co, a 60% subsidiary of P Co, show retained earnings of $20,000 at the end of the reporting period, of which $14,000 were earned prior to acquisition. The figure of $20,000 will appear in the consolidated statement of financial position as follows.

	$
Non-controlling interests working:	8,000
their share of total retained earnings at the end of the reporting period (40% × $20,000)	
Goodwill working: group share of pre-acquisition retained earnings (60% × $14,000)	8,400
Consolidated retained earnings working:	
group share of post-acquisition retained earnings (60% × $6,000)	3,600
	20,000

Activity

Hinge Co acquired 80% of the ordinary shares of Singe Co on 1 April 20X5. On 31 December 20X4 Singe Co's accounts showed a share premium account of $4,000 and retained earnings of $15,000. The statements of financial position of the two companies at 31 December 20X5 are set out below. Neither company has paid any dividends during the year. You are required to prepare the consolidated statement of financial position of Hinge Co at 31 December 20X5. In this example we will ignore the requirement to amortise goodwill.

HINGE CO
STATEMENT OF FINANCIAL POSITION AS AT 31 DECEMBER 20X5

	$	$
Assets		
Non-current assets		
Property, plant and equipment	32,000	
16,000 ordinary shares of 50c each in Singe Co	50,000	
		82,000
Current assets		85,000
Total assets		167,000
Equity and liabilities		
Equity		
Ordinary shares of $1 each	100,000	
Share premium account	7,000	
Retained earnings	40,000	
		147,000
Current liabilities		20,000
Total equity and liabilities		167,000

SINGE CO
STATEMENT OF FINANCIAL POSITION AS AT 31 DECEMBER 20X5

	$	$
Assets		
Property, plant and equipment		30,000
Current assets		43,000
Total assets		73,000
Equity and liabilities		
Equity		
20,000 ordinary shares of 50c each	10,000	
Share premium account	4,000	
Retained earnings	39,000	
		53,000
Current liabilities		20,000
Total equity and liabilities		73,000

 ## Answer

Singe Co has made a profit of $24,000 ($39,000 – $15,000) for the year. In the absence of any direction to the contrary, this should be assumed to have arisen evenly over the year; $6,000 in the three months to 31 March and $18,000 in the nine months after acquisition. The company's pre-acquisition retained earnings are therefore as follows.

	$
Balance at 31 December 20X4	15,000
Profit for three months to 31 March 20X5	6,000
Pre-acquisition retained earnings	21,000

The balance of $4,000 on share premium account is all pre-acquisition.

The consolidation workings can now be drawn up.

1   Goodwill

	$	$
Consideration transferred		50,000
Net assets acquired		
represented by		
Ordinary share capital	10,000	
Retained earnings (pre-acquisition)	21,000	
Share premium	4,000	
	35,000	
Group share 80%		(28,000)
Goodwill		22,000

2   Retained earnings

	Hinge Co $	Singe Co $
Per question	40,000	39,000
Pre-acquisition (see above)		(21,000)
		18,000
Share of Singe: $18,000 × 80%	14,400	
	54,400	

3   Non-controlling interest at reporting date

	$
Singe Co net assets (73,000 – 20,000)	53,000
× 20%	10,600

4   *Share premium account*

	$
Hinge Co	7,000
Share of Singe Co's post-acquisition share premium	–
	7,000

HINGE CO
CONSOLIDATED STATEMENT OF FINANCIAL POSITION AS AT 31 DECEMBER 20X5

	$	$
Assets		
Property, plant and equipment		62,000
Goodwill (W1)		22,000
Current assets		128,000
Total assets		212,000
Equity and liabilities		
Equity		
Ordinary shares of $1 each	100,000	
Share premium account (W4)	7,000	
Retained earnings (W2)	54,400	
		161,400
Non-controlling interest (W3)		10,600
		172,000
Current liabilities		40,000
Total equity and liabilities		212,000

9.2 Example: pre-acquisition losses of a subsidiary

As an illustration of the entries arising when a subsidiary has pre-acquisition *losses*, suppose P Co acquired all 50,000 $1 ordinary shares in S Co for $20,000 on 1 January 20X1 when there was a debit balance of $35,000 on S Co's retained earnings. In the years 20X1 to 20X4 S Co makes profits of $40,000 in total, leaving a credit balance of $5,000 on retained earnings at 31 December 20X4. P Co's retained earnings at the same date are $70,000.

Solution

The consolidation workings would appear as follows.

1   *Goodwill*

	$	$
Consideration transferred		20,000
Net assets acquired as represented by		
Ordinary share capital	50,000	
Retained earnings	(35,000)	
		(15,000)
Goodwill		5,000

2   *Retained earnings*

	P Co	S Co
	$	$
At the end of the reporting period	70,000	5,000
Pre-acquisition loss		35,000
		40,000
S Co – share of post-acquisition retained earnings		
(40,000 × 100%)	40,000	
	110,000	

10 Dividends and pre-acquisition profits

A further problem in consolidation occurs when a subsidiary pays out **a dividend soon after acquisition**.

10.1 Pre-acquisition profits

The parent company, as a member of the subsidiary, is entitled to its share of the dividends paid but it is necessary to decide whether or not these dividends come out of the pre-acquisition profits of the subsidiary.

If the dividends come from **post-acquisition** profits there is no problem. The holding company simply **credits** the relevant amount to its **own statement of comprehensive income**, as with any other dividend income. The dividend received by the parent and paid by the subsidiary are then cancelled upon consolidation. The double entry is quite different, however, if the dividend is paid from **pre-acquisition profits**, being as follows.

DEBIT	Cash
CREDIT	Investment in subsidiary

Where the dividend is paid from pre-acquisition profits, it **reduces** the cost of the parent company's investment.

10.2 Is the dividend paid from pre-acquisition profits?

We need next to consider how it is decided whether a dividend is paid from pre-acquisition profits. The simplest example is where a parent acquires a subsidiary on the first day of an accounting period and the dividend was in respect of the previous accounting period. Clearly, the dividend was paid from profits earned in the period before acquisition.

The position is less straightforward if shares are acquired **during the subsidiary's accounting period**. The usual method of dealing with this is by **time-apportionment**.

10.3 Example

P acquires a 60% interest in S on 1 September 20X0. S's year end is 31 December. On 10 January 20X1 S pays a dividend of $10,000 in respect of 20X0. P's share of the dividend is $6,000. However, as it relates to the year of acquisition, $2,000 ($6,000 \times {}^4/_{12}$ is treated as being from post-acquisition profits and $4,000 ($6,000 \times {}^8/_{12}$) is treated as being from pre-acquisition profits.

Why do we make this distinction? If we consider the situation of a holding company deciding whether to invest in a subsidiary, we can see the significance of a dividend paid from pre-acquisition profits. If the prospective subsidiary's financial statements disclose that it proposes to pay a dividend in the near future, the prospective holding company knows that if it invests in the shares some of its investment will be returned to it very soon. Also, a dividend paid out of pre-acquisition profits cannot be regarded as a return on the company's investment because it relates to the period before the investment was made. So we treat it as what it effectively is – a reduction in the cost of the investment.

10.4 Example

To continue the example of P and S above, P has paid $175,000 for its 60% shareholding in S. At the date of acquisition S had share capital of $100,000 and retained earnings of $70,000.

In 20X1 S pays a $10,000 dividend of which P receives $6,000. $4,000 is deemed to be from pre-acquisition profits. The goodwill calculation at 31 December 20X1 is as follows:

	$	$
Consideration transferred		175,000
Less pre-acquisition dividend		(4,000)
		171,000
Net assets acquired:		
Share capital	100,000	
Retained earnings	70,000	
	170,000	
Group share 60%		(102,000)
Goodwill		69,000

11 Fair values in acquisition accounting

Fair values are very important in calculating goodwill.

11.1 Goodwill

To understand the importance of fair values in the acquisition of a subsidiary consider again what we mean by goodwill.

Key term

> **Goodwill**. Any excess of the consideration transferred over the acquirer's interest in the fair value of the identifiable assets and liabilities acquired as at the date of the exchange transaction.

The **statement of financial position of a subsidiary company** at the date it is acquired may not be a guide to the fair value of its net assets. For example, the market value of a freehold building may have risen greatly since it was acquired, but it may appear in the statement of financial position at historical cost less accumulated depreciation.

11.2 What is fair value?

Fair value is defined as follows by the IFRS – it is an important definition.

Key term

> **Fair value**. The amount for which an asset could be exchanged, or a liability settled, between knowledgeable, willing parties in an arm's length transaction.

We will look at the requirements of the IFRS regarding fair value in more detail below. First let us look at some practical matters.

11.3 Fair value adjustment calculations

Until now we have calculated goodwill as the difference between the consideration transferred and the **book value** of net assets acquired by the group. If this calculation is to comply with the definition above we must ensure that the book value of the subsidiary's net assets is the same as their **fair value**.

There are two possible ways of achieving this.

(a)   The **subsidiary company** might **incorporate any necessary revaluations** in its own books of account. In this case, we can proceed directly to the consolidation, taking asset values and reserves figures straight from the subsidiary company's statement of financial position.

(b)   The **revaluations** may be made as a **consolidation adjustment without being incorporated** in the subsidiary company's books. In this case, we must make the necessary adjustments to the subsidiary's statement of financial position as a working. Only then can we proceed to the consolidation.

Note. Remember that when depreciating assets are revalued there may be a corresponding alteration in the amount of depreciation charged and accumulated.

11.4 Example: fair value adjustments

P Co acquired 75% of the ordinary shares of S Co on 1 September 20X5. At that date the fair value of S Co's non-current assets was $23,000 greater than their carrying amount, and the balance of retained earnings was $21,000. The statements of financial position of both companies at 31 August 20X6 are given below. S Co has not incorporated any revaluation in its books of account.

P CO
STATEMENT OF FINANCIAL POSITION AS AT 31 AUGUST 20X6

	$	$
Assets		
Non-current assets		
Property, plant and equipment	63,000	
Investment in S Co at cost	51,000	
		114,000
Current assets		82,000
Total assets		196,000
Equity and liabilities		
Equity		
Ordinary shares of $1 each	80,000	
Retained earnings	96,000	
		176,000
Current liabilities		20,000
Total equity and liabilities		196,000

S CO
STATEMENT OF FINANCIAL POSITION AS AT 31 AUGUST 20X6

	$	$
Assets		
Property, plant and equipment		28,000
Current assets		43,000
Total assets		71,000
Equity and liabilities		
Equity		
Ordinary shares of $1 each	20,000	
Retained earnings	41,000	
		61,000
Current liabilities		10,000
Total equity and liabilities		71,000

If S Co had revalued its non-current assets at 1 September 20X5, an addition of $3,000 would have been made to the depreciation charged for 20X5/X6. Amortisation of goodwill is to be ignored in this example.

Required

Prepare P Co's consolidated statement of financial position as at 31 August 20X6.

Solution

P CO CONSOLIDATED STATEMENT OF FINANCIAL POSITION AS AT 31 AUGUST 20X6

	$	$
Non-current assets		
Property, plant and equipment $(63,000 + 48,000)*	111,000	
Goodwill (W1)	3,000	
		114,000
Current assets		125,000
		239,000

	$	$
Equity and liabilities		
Equity		
Ordinary shares of $1 each	80,000	
Retained earnings (W2)	108,750	
		188,750
Non-controlling interest (W3)		20,250
		209,000
Current liabilities		30,000
		239,000

* (28,000 + 23,000 – 3,000)

1 Goodwill

		Group
	$	$
Consideration transferred		51,000
Net assets acquired as represented by		
Ordinary share capital	20,000	
Retained earnings	21,000	
Fair value adjustment	23,000	
	64,000	
Group		(48,000)
Goodwill		3,000

2 Retained earnings

	P Co	S Co
	$	$
Per question	96,000	41,000
Pre acquisition profits		(21,000)
Depreciation adjustment		(3,000)
Post acquisition S Co		17,000
Group share in S Co		
($17,000 × 75%)	12,750	
Group retained earnings	108,750	

3 Non-controlling interest at reporting date

	$
S Co's net assets (71,000 – 10,000)	61,000
Fair value adjustment (23,000 – 3,000)	20,000
	81,000
× 25%	20,250

Activity

An asset is recorded in S Co's books at its historical cost of $4,000. On 1 January 20X5 P Co bought 80% of S Co's equity. Its directors attributed a fair value of $3,000 to the asset as at that date. It had been depreciated for two years out of an expected life of four years on the straight line basis. There was no expected residual value. On 30 June 20X5 the asset was sold for $2,600. What is the profit or loss on disposal of this asset to be recorded in S Co's accounts and in P Co's consolidated accounts for the year ended 31 December 20X5?

Answer

S Co: carrying amount at disposal (at historical cost) = $4,000 × 1½/4 = $1,500
∴ Profit on disposal = $1,100 (depreciation charge for the year = $500)

P Co: carrying amount at disposal (at fair value) = $3,000 × 1½/2 = $2,250
∴ Profit on disposal for consolidation = $350 (depreciation for the year = $750).

The non-controlling interest would be credited with 20% of both the profit on disposal and the depreciation charge as part of the one line entry in the consolidated statement of comprehensive income.

The **general principles** for arriving at the fair values of a subsidiary's assets and liabilities are that the acquirer should recognise the acquiree's identifiable assets, liabilities and contingent liabilities at the acquisition date only if they satisfy the following criteria.

(a) In the case of an **asset** other than an intangible asset, it is **probable** that any associated **future economic benefits** will flow to the acquirer, and its fair value can be **measured reliably.**

(b) In the case of a **liability** other than a contingent liability, it is probable that an **outflow** of resources embodying economic benefits will be required to settle the obligation, and its fair value can be **measured reliably**.

(c) In the case of an **intangible asset** or a **contingent liability**, its fair value can be **measured reliably**.

The acquiree's identifiable assets and liabilities might include assets and liabilities **not previously recognised** in the acquiree's financial statements. For example, a tax benefit arising from the acquiree's tax losses that was not recognised by the acquiree may be recognised by the group if the acquirer has future taxable profits against which the unrecognised tax benefit can be applied.

11.4.1 Restructuring and future losses

An acquirer **should not recognise liabilities for future losses** or other costs expected to be incurred as a result of the business combination.

A plan to restructure a subsidiary following an acquisition is not a present obligation of the acquiree at the acquisition date. Neither does it meet the definition of a contingent liability. Therefore an acquirer **should not recognise a liability for** such **a restructuring plan** as part of allocating the cost of the combination unless the subsidiary was already committed to the plan before the acquisition.

This **prevents creative accounting**. An acquirer cannot set up a provision for restructuring or future losses of a subsidiary and then release this to the profit or loss in subsequent periods in order to reduce losses or smooth profits.

11.4.2 Intangible assets

The acquiree may have **intangible assets**, such as development expenditure. These can be recognised separately from goodwill only if they are **identifiable**. An intangible asset is identifiable only if it:

(a) Is **separable**, ie capable of being separated or divided from the entity and sold, transferred, or exchanged, either individually or together with a related contract, asset or liability, or

(b) Arises from contractual or other legal rights

11.4.3 Contingent liabilities

Contingent liabilities of the acquirer are **recognised** if their **fair value can be measured reliably**.

11.4.4 Cost of a business combination

The general principle is that the acquirer should measure the cost of a business combination as the total of the **fair values**, at the date of exchange, **of assets given**, liabilities incurred or assumed, and equity instruments issued by the acquirer, in exchange for control of the acquiree.

Sometimes all or part of the cost of an acquisition is deferred (ie, does not become payable immediately). The fair value of any deferred consideration is determined by **discounting** the amounts payable to their **present value** at the date of exchange.

Where equity instruments (eg ordinary shares) of a quoted entity form part of the cost of a combination, the **published price** at the date of exchange normally provides the best evidence of the instrument's fair value and except in rare circumstances this should be used.

Future losses or other costs expected to be incurred as a result of a combination should not be included in the cost of the combination.

Costs **attributable** to the combination, for example professional fees and administrative costs are included as part of the cost of the combination.

Activity

On 1 September 20X7 Tyzo Co acquired 6 million $1 shares in Kono Co at $2.00 per share. At that date Kono Co produced the following interim financial statements.

	$m		$m
Property, plant and equipment		Trade payables	3.2
(note 1)	16.0	Taxation	0.6
Inventories (note 2)	4.0	Bank overdraft	3.9
Receivables	2.9	Long-term loans	4.0
Cash in hand	1.2	Share capital ($1 shares)	8.0
		Retained earnings	4.4
	24.1		24.1

Notes

1   The following information relates to the property, plant and equipment of Kono Co at 1 September 20X7.

	$m
Gross replacement cost	28.4
Net replacement cost (gross replacement cost less depreciation)	16.6
Economic value	18.0
Net realisable value	8.0

2   The inventories of Kono Co which were shown in the interim financial statements are raw materials at cost to Kono Co of $4 million. They would have cost $4.2 million to replace at 1 September 20X7.

3   On 1 September 20X7 Tyzo Co took a decision to rationalise the group so as to integrate Kono Co. The costs of the rationalisation were estimated to total $3.0 million and the process was due to start on 1 March 20X8. No provision for these costs has been made in the financial statements given above.

Required

Compute the goodwill on consolidation of Kono Co that will be included in the consolidated financial statements of the Tyzo Co group for the year ended 31 December 20X7, explaining your treatment of the items mentioned above.

Answer

Goodwill on consolidation of Kono Co

	$m	$m
Consideration ($2.00 × 6m)		12.0
Fair value of net assets acquired		
Share capital	8.0	
Pre-acquisition reserves	4.4	
Fair value adjustments		
Property, plant and equipment (16.6 – 16.0)	0.6	
Inventories (4.2 – 4.0)	0.2	
	13.2	
Group share 75%		(9.9)
Goodwill		2.1

Notes on treatment

(a) Share capital and pre-acquisition profits represent the book value of the net assets of Kono Co at the date of acquisition. Adjustments are then required to this book value in order to give the fair value of the net assets at the date of acquisition. For short-term monetary items, fair value is their carrying value on acquisition.

(b) The fair value of property, plant and equipment should be determined by market value or, if information on a market price is not available (as is the case here), then by reference to depreciated replacement cost, reflecting normal business practice. The net replacement cost (ie $16.6m) represents the gross replacement cost less depreciation based on that amount, and so further adjustment for extra depreciation is unnecessary.

(c) Raw materials should be valued at replacement cost. In this case that amount is $4.2m.

(d) The rationalisation costs cannot be reported in pre-acquisition results as they are not a liability of Kono Co at the acquisition date.

11.4.5 Example: cost of a business combination

Rather than pay cash for Kono Co's shares, Tyzo has funded the acquisition by issuing 4.5m of its own shares to Kono Co's shareholders.

Tyzo's shares have a market value of $3. The costs of the share issue amounted to $500,000 and Tyzo paid a total of $750,000 to lawyers and accountants to carry out the combination.

Calculate the goodwill.

Solution

	$m
Consideration:	
Share issue (4.5m × $3)	13.5
Net assets acquired (as above)	(9.9)
Goodwill	3.6

Note. The share issue costs are debited to share premium and the $750,000 expenses are written off.

Unit Roundup

- The IFRS for SMEs lays out the basic procedures for preparing consolidated financial statements.

- In the consolidated statement of financial position it is necessary to distinguish **non-controlling interests** from those net assets attributable to the group and financed by shareholders' equity.

- **Goodwill** arises where the consideration transferred by the parent company is not equal to the group share of net assets at acquisition.

- Intra-group trading can give rise to **unrealised profit** which is eliminated on consolidation.

- As well as engaging in trading activities with each other, group companies may on occasion wish to **transfer non-current assets**.

- When a parent company acquires a subsidiary during its accounting period, the reserves of the subsidiary at the date of the acquisition must be calculated in order to perform a consolidation.

- A further problem in consolidation occurs when a subsidiary pays out a **dividend soon after acquisition**.

- **Fair values** are very important in calculating goodwill.

Quick Quiz

1   Chicken Co owns 80% of Egg Co. Egg Co sells goods to Chicken Co at cost plus 50%. The total invoiced sales to Chicken Co by Egg Co in the year ended 31 December 20X9 were $900,000 and, of these sales, goods which had been invoiced at $60,000 were held in inventory by Chicken Co at 31 December 20X9. What is the reduction in aggregate group gross profit?

2   Major Co, which makes up its accounts to 31 December, has an 80% owned subsidiary Minor Co. Minor Co sells goods to Major Co at a mark-up on cost of 33.33%. At 31 December 20X8, Major had $12,000 of such goods in its inventory and at 31 December 20X9 had $15,000 of such goods in its inventory.

   What is the amount by which the consolidated profit attributable to Major Co's shareholders should be adjusted in respect of the above?

   Ignore taxation

   A $1,000 Debit
   B $800 Credit
   C $750 Credit
   D $600 Debit

3   What are the components making up the figure of non-controlling interest in a consolidated statement of financial position?

4   Goodwill is always positive. True or false?

5   A parent company can assume that, for a subsidiary acquired during its accounting period, profits accrue evenly during the year. True or false?

6   What entries are made in the workings to record the pre-acquisition profits of a subsidiary?

7   What entries are made in the parent company's accounts to record a dividend received from a subsidiary's pre-acquisition profits?

8   Describe the requirement in relation to the revaluation of a subsidiary company's assets to fair value at the acquisition date.

1    $60,000 \times \dfrac{50}{150} = \$20,000$

2   D $(15,000 - 12,000) \times \dfrac{33.3}{133.3} \times 80\%$

3   The non-controlling interests' share of ordinary shares, reserves and retained earnings

4   False. Goodwill can be negative if the purchaser has 'got a bargain'.

5   Not necessarily – the examiner will advise you on this.

6   See paragraph 4.2

7   DEBIT   Cash
          CREDIT   Investment in subsidiary

8   See paragraph 11.3

Now try the question below

Boo and Goose
45 mins

Boo has owned 80% of Goose's equity since Goose's incorporation. On 31 December 20X8 Boo despatched goods which cost $80,000 to Goose, at an invoiced cost of $100,000. Goose received the goods on 2 January 20X9 and recorded the transaction then. The two companies' draft statements of financial position as at 31 December 20X8 are shown below.

STATEMENTS OF FINANCIAL POSITION AT 31 DECEMBER 20X8

	Boo $'000	Goose $'000
Assets		
Non-current assets	2,000	200
Current assets		
Inventories	500	120
Trade receivables	650	40
Bank and cash	390	35
	1,540	195
Total assets	3,540	395
Equity and liabilities		
Equity		
Share capital	2,000	100
Retained earnings	500	240
	2,500	340
Current liabilities		
Trade payables	910	30
Tax	130	25
	1,040	55
Total equity and liabilities	3,540	395

Required

Prepare a draft consolidated statement of financial position.

(25 marks)

Boo and Goose

BOO GROUP
CONSOLIDATED STATEMENT OF FINANCIAL POSITION AS AT 31 DECEMBER 20X8

	$'000	$'000
Assets		
Non-current assets (2,000 + 200 – 80 (cost of investment in Goose))		2,120
Current assets		
Inventory (500 + 120 + 80)	700	
Trade receivables (650 – 100 + 40)	590	
Bank and cash (390 + 35)	425	
		1,715
Total assets		3,835
Equity and liabilities		
Equity attributable to owners of the parent		
Share capital (Boo only)		2,000
Retained earnings (W2)		672
		2,672
Non-controlling interest (W3)		68
Total equity		2,740
Current liabilities		
Trade payables (910 + 30)	940	
Tax (130 + 25)	155	
		1,095
Total equity and liabilities		3,835

Workings

1 *Group structure*

Boo

80% since incorporation

Goose

2 *Retained earnings*

	Boo	Goose
	$'000	$'000
Per question	500	240
Unrealised profit (100 – 80)	(20)	
	480	
Less pre acquisition		–
		240
Goose: 80% × 240	192	
Total	672	

3 *Non-controlling interest*

	$'000
NCI at acquisition (SC 100 × 20%)	20
NCI share of post acquisition retained earnings (240 × 20%)	48
	68

Step 1: Record Goose's purchase

DEBIT Purchases	$100,000	
CREDIT Payables		$100,000
DEBIT Closing inventory (SOFP)	$100,000	
CREDIT Closing inventory I/S (COS)		$100,000

Step 2: Cancel unrealised profit

DEBIT COS (and retained earnings) in Boo	$20,000	
CREDIT Inventory (SOFP)		$20,000

Step 3: Cancel intragroup transaction

DEBIT Revenue	$100,000	
CREDIT Cost of sales		$100,000

Step 4: Cancel intragroup balances

DEBIT Receivables	$100,000	
CREDIT Payables		$100,000

Consolidated statement of comprehensive income

17

Unit topic list

1   The consolidated statement of comprehensive income

Assessment criteria

4   Understand and apply IFRS for SMEs in the preparation of their financial statements

4.3   Preparation of consolidated and separate financial statements as per section 9 of the IFRS for SMEs

4.12   Understand and apply section 19 of IFRS for SMEs when the SME carries on a business combination
        and how to treat goodwill

1 The consolidated statement of comprehensive income

The source of the consolidated statement of comprehensive income is the individual accounts of the separate companies in the group.

1.1 Consolidation procedure

It is customary in practice to prepare a working paper (known as a **consolidation schedule**) on which the individual statement of comprehensive incomes are set out side by side and totalled to form the basis of the consolidated statement of comprehensive income.

Exam focus point

In an examination it is very much quicker not to do this. Use workings to show the calculation of complex figures such as the non-controlling interest and show the derivation of others on the face of the statement of comprehensive income, as shown in our examples.

In the consolidated statement of comprehensive income non-controlling interest is brought in as a one-line adjustment.

1.2 Simple example: consolidated statement of comprehensive income

P Co acquired 75% of the ordinary shares of S Co on that company's incorporation in 20X3. The summarised statements of comprehensive income and movement on retained earnings of the two companies for the year ending 31 December 20X6 are set out below.

	P Co $	S Co $
Sales revenue	75,000	38,000
Cost of sales	30,000	20,000
Gross profit	45,000	18,000
Administrative expenses	14,000	8,000
Profit before tax	31,000	10,000
Income tax expense	10,000	2,000
Profit for the year	21,000	8,000

Note: Movement on retained earnings

Retained earnings brought forward	87,000	17,000
Profit for the year	21,000	8,000
Retained earnings carried forward	108,000	25,000

Required

Prepare the consolidated statement of comprehensive income and extract from the statement of changes in equity showing retained earnings and non-controlling interest.

Solution

P CO
CONSOLIDATED STATEMENT OF COMPREHENSIVE INCOME
FOR THE YEAR ENDED 31 DECEMBER 20X6

	$
Sales revenue (75 + 38)	113,000
Cost of sales (30 + 20)	50,000
Gross profit	63,000
Administrative expenses (14 + 8)	22,000
Profit before tax	41,000
Income tax expense	12,000
Profit for the year	29,000

		$
Profit attributable to:		
Owners of the parent		27,000
Non-controlling interest ($8,000 × 25%)		2,000
		29,000

STATEMENT OF CHANGES IN EQUITY (EXTRACT)

	Retained Earnings $	Non-controlling Interest $	Total Equity $
Balance at 1 January 20X6	99,750	4,250	104,000
Total comprehensive income for the year	27,000	2,000	29,000
Balance at 31 December 20X6	126,750	6,250	133,000

Notice how the non-controlling interest is dealt with.

(a) Down to the line **'profit for the year'** the **whole** of S Co's results is included without reference to group share or non-controlling share. A **one-line adjustment** is then inserted to deduct the non-controlling share of S Co's profit.

(b) The non-controlling share ($4,250) of S Co's retained earnings brought forward (17,000 × 25%) is **excluded** from group retained earnings. This means that the carried forward figure of $126,750 is the figure which would appear in the statement of financial position for group retained earnings.

This last point may be clearer if we construct the working for group retained earnings.

Group retained earnings

	P Co $	S Co $
At reporting date	108,000	25,000
Less pre-acquisition retained earnings		–
		25,000
S Co – share of post acquisition retained earnings (25,000 × 75%)	18,750	
	126,750	

The non-controlling share of S Co's retained earnings comprises the non-controlling interest in the $17,000 profits brought forward plus the non-controlling interest ($2,000) in $8,000 retained profits for the year.

We will now look at the complications introduced by **inter-company trading**, **inter-company dividends** and **pre-acquisition profits** in the subsidiary.

1.3 Intra-group trading

Intra-group sales and purchases are eliminated from the consolidated statement of comprehensive income.

Like the consolidated statement of financial position, the consolidated statement of comprehensive income should deal with the results of the group as those of a single entity. When one company in a group sells goods to another an identical amount is added to the sales revenue of the first company and to the cost of sales of the second. Yet as far as the entity's dealings with outsiders are concerned no sale has taken place.

The consolidated figures for sales revenue and cost of sales should represent **sales to**, and **purchases from, outsiders**. An adjustment is therefore necessary to reduce the sales revenue and cost of sales figures by the value of intra-group sales during the year.

We have also seen in an earlier unit that any unrealised profits on intra-group trading should be excluded from the figure for group profits. This will occur whenever goods sold at a profit within the group remain in the inventory of the purchasing company at the year end. The best way to deal with this is to **calculate the unrealised profit on unsold inventories at the year end and reduce consolidated gross profit by this amount**. Cost of sales will be the balancing figure.

1.4 Example: intra-group trading

Suppose in our earlier example that S Co had recorded sales of $5,000 to P Co during 20X6. S Co had purchased these goods from outside suppliers at a cost of $3,000. One half of the goods remained in P Co's inventory at 31 December 20X6. Prepare the revised consolidated statement of comprehensive income.

Solution

The consolidated statement of comprehensive income for the year ended 31 December 20X6 would now be as follows.

	$
Sales revenue (75 + 38 – 5)	108,000
Cost of sales (30 + 20 – 5 + 1*)	(46,000)
Gross profit (45 + 18 – 1*)	62,000
Administrative expenses	(22,000)
Profit before taxation	40,000
Income tax expense	(12,000)
Profit for the year	28,000
Profit attributable to:	
Owners of the parent	26,250
Non-controlling interest (8,000 – 1,000) × 25%	1,750
	28,000
Note:	
Retained earnings brought forward	99,750
Profit for the year	26,250
Retained earnings carried forward	126,000

*Unrealised profit: ½ × ($5,000 – $3,000)

An adjustment will be made for the unrealised profit against the inventory figure in the consolidated statement of financial position.

1.5 Intra-group dividends

In our example so far we have assumed that S Co retains all of its after-tax profit. It may be, however, that S Co distributes some of its profits as dividends. As before, the **non-controlling interest** in the subsidiary's profit should be calculated immediately after the figure of after-tax profit. For this purpose, no account need be taken of how much of the non-controlling interest is to be distributed by S Co as dividend.

Note that group retained earnings are only adjusted for dividends paid to the parent company shareholders. Dividends paid by the subsidiary to the parent are cancelled on consolidation and dividends paid to the non-controlling interest are replaced by the allocation to the non-controlling interest of their share of the profit for the year of the subsidiary.

1.6 Pre-acquisition profits

Only the **post acquisition** profits of the subsidiary are brought into the consolidated statement of comprehensive income.

As explained above, the figure for retained earnings carried forward must be the same as the figure for retained earnings in the consolidated statement of financial position. We have seen in the previous unit that retained earnings in the consolidated statement of financial position comprise:

(a)   The **whole of the parent company's** retained earnings

(b)   A **proportion of the subsidiary company's** retained earnings. The proportion is the **group's share of post-acquisition retained earnings** in the subsidiary. From the total retained earnings of the subsidiary we must therefore **exclude** both the **non-controlling share** of total retained earnings and the **group's share of pre-acquisition** retained earnings.

A **similar procedure is necessary in the consolidated statement of comprehensive income** if it is to link up with the consolidated statement of financial position. Previous examples have shown how the non-controlling share of profits is excluded in the statement of comprehensive income. Their share of profits for the year is deducted from profit after tax, while the figure for profits brought forward in the consolidation schedule includes only the group's proportion of the subsidiary's profits.

In the same way, when considering examples which include pre-acquisition profits in a subsidiary, the figure for profits brought forward should include only the group's share of the post-acquisition retained profits. If the subsidiary is **acquired during the accounting year**, it is therefore necessary to apportion its profit for the year between pre-acquisition and post-acquisition elements. The part year method is used.

With the part-year method, the entire statement of comprehensive income of the subsidiary is split between pre-acquisition and post-acquisition proportions. Only the post-acquisition figures are included in the consolidated statement of comprehensive income.

Activity

P Co acquired 60% of the $100,000 equity of S Co on 1 April 20X5. The statements of comprehensive income of the two companies for the year ended 31 December 20X5 are set out below.

	P Co	S Co	S Co ($^9/_{12}$)
	$	$	$
Sales revenue	170,000	80,000	60,000
Cost of sales	65,000	36,000	27,000
Gross profit	105,000	44,000	33,000
Other income – dividend received S Co	3,600		
Administrative expenses	43,000	12,000	9,000
Profit before tax	65,600	32,000	24,000
Income tax expense	23,000	8,000	6,000
Profit for the year	42,600	24,000	18,000
Note			
Dividends (paid 31 December)	12,000	6,000	
Profit retained	30,600	18,000	
Retained earnings brought forward	81,000	40,000	
Retained earnings carried forward	111,600	58,000	

Prepare the consolidated statement of comprehensive income and the retained earnings and non-controlling interest extracts from the statement of changes in equity.

Answer

The shares in S Co were acquired three months into the year. Only the post-acquisition proportion (9/12ths) of S Co's statement of comprehensive income is included in the consolidated statement of comprehensive income. This is shown above for convenience.

P CO CONSOLIDATED STATEMENT OF COMPREHENSIVE INCOME
FOR THE YEAR ENDED 31 DECEMBER 20X5

	$
Sales revenue (170 + 60)	230,000
Cost of sales (65 + 27)	(92,000)
Gross profit	138,000
Administrative expenses (43 + 9)	(52,000)
Profit before tax	86,000
Income tax expense (23 + 6)	(29,000)
Profit for the year	57,000
Profit attributable to:	
Owners of the parent	49,800
Non-controlling interest (18 × 40%)	7,200
	57,000

STATEMENT OF CHANGES IN EQUITY

	Retained earnings $	Non-controlling interest $
Balance at 1 January 20X5	81,000	–
Dividends paid (6,000 – 3,600)	(12,000)	(2,400)
Total comprehensive income for the year	49,800	7,200
Added on acquisition of subsidiary (W)	–	58,400
Balance at 31 December 20X5	118,800	63,200

* All of S Co's profits brought forward are pre-acquisition.

Working

	$
Added on acquisition of subsidiary:	
Share capital	100,000
Retained earnings brought forward	40,000
Profits Jan-March 20X5 (24,000 – 18,000)	6,000
	146,000
Non-controlling share 40%	58,400

Activity

The following information relates to Brodick Co and its subsidiary Lamlash Co for the year to 30 April 20X7.

	Brodick Co $'000	Lamlash Co $'000
Sales revenue	1,100	500
Cost of sales	(630)	(300)
Gross profit	470	200
Administrative expenses	(105)	(150)
Dividend from Lamlash Co	24	–
Profit before tax	389	50
Income tax expense	(65)	(10)
Profit for the year	324	40
Note		
Dividends paid	200	30
Profit retained	124	10
Retained earnings brought forward	460	106
Retained earnings carried forward	584	116

Additional information

(a) The issued share capital of the group was as follows.

    Brodick Co   : 5,000,000 ordinary shares of $1 each.
    Lamlash Co   : 1,000,000 ordinary shares of $1 each.

(b) Brodick Co purchased 80% of the issued share capital of Lamlash Co in 20X0. At that time, the retained earnings of Lamlash stood at $56,000.

Required

Insofar as the information permits, prepare the Brodick group consolidated statement of comprehensive income for the year to 30 April 20X7, and extracts from the statement of changes in equity showing retained earnings and non-controlling interest.

Answer

BRODICK GROUP
CONSOLIDATED STATEMENT OF COMPREHENSIVE INCOME
FOR THE YEAR TO 30 APRIL 20X7

	$'000
Sales revenue (1,100 + 500)	1,600
Cost of sales (630 + 300)	(930)
Gross profit	670
Administrative expenses (105 + 150)	(255)
Profit before tax	415
Income tax expense (65 + 10)	(75)
Profit for the year	340

Profit attributable to:

Owners of the parent	332
Non-controlling interest (W1)	8
	340

STATEMENT OF CHANGES IN EQUITY

	Non-controlling interest $'000	Retained earnings $'000
Balance brought forward (W2)	–	500
Dividends paid (30,000 – 24,000)	(6)	(200)
Total comprehensive income for the year	8	332
Added on acquisition of subsidiary (W3)	211	–
Balance carried forward	213	632

Workings

1 *Non-controlling interests*

	$'000
In Lamlash (20% × 40)	8

2 *Retained earnings brought forward*

	Brodick Co $'000	Lamlash Co $'000
Per question	460	106
Less pre-aqn		(56)
		50
Share of Lamlash: 80% × 50	40	
	500	

3 *Added on acquisition of subsidiary*

	$'000
Share capital	1,000
Retained earnings	56
	1,056
Non-controlling share 20%	211

1.7 Section summary

The table below summarises the main points about the consolidated statement of comprehensive income.

Purpose	To show the results of the group for an accounting period as if it were a single entity.
Sales revenue to profit for year	100% P + 100% S (excluding adjustments for inter-company transactions).
Reason	To show the results of the group which were controlled by the parent company.
Intra-group sales	Strip out inter-company activity from both sales revenue and cost of sales.
Unrealised profit on intra-group sales	(a) Goods sold by P. Increase cost of sales by unrealised profit. (b) Goods sold by S. Increase cost of sales by full amount of unrealised profit and decrease non-controlling interest by their share of unrealised profit.
Depreciation	If the value of S's non-current assets have been subjected to a fair value uplift then any additional depreciation must be charged in the consolidated statement of comprehensive income. The non-controlling interest will need to be adjusted for their share.
Transfer of non-current assets	Expenses must be increased by any profit on the transfer and reduced by any additional depreciation arising from the increased carrying value of the asset.

Non-controlling interests	S's profit after tax (PAT) X
	 Less: * unrealised profit (X)
	        * profit on disposal of non-current assets (X)
	        additional depreciation following FV uplift (X)
	 Add: ** additional depreciation following disposal of non-current assets X
	                                                  X
	 NCI% X
	
	 * Only applicable if sales of goods and non-current assets made by subsidiary.
	
	 ** Only applicable if sale of non-current assets made by subsidiary.

Reason	To show the extent to which profits generated through P's control are in fact owned by other parties.
Reserves carried forward	As per the calculations for the statement of financial position.

Unit Roundup

- The source of the consolidated statement of comprehensive income is the individual accounts of the separate companies in the group.

- In the consolidated statement of comprehensive income non-controlling interest is brought in as a one-line adjustment after 'profit for the year'.

- Intra-group sales and purchases are eliminated from the consolidated statement of comprehensive income.

- Only the **post acquisition** profits of the subsidiary are brought into the consolidated statement of comprehensive income.

Quick Quiz

1   Where does unrealised profit on intra-group trading appear in the statement of comprehensive income?

2   At the beginning of the year a 75% subsidiary transfers a non-current asset to the parent for $500,000. Its carrying value was $400,000 and it has 4 years of useful life left. How is this accounted for at the end of the year in the consolidated statement of comprehensive income?

Answers to Quick Quiz

1   As a deduction from consolidated gross profit.

2

	$
Unrealised profit	100,000
Additional depreciation (100 ÷ 4)	(25,000)
Net charge to statement of comprehensive income	75,000

	DR $	CR $
Non-current asset		100,000
Additional depreciation	25,000	
Group profit (75%)	56,250	
Non-controlling interest (25%)	18,750	
	100,000	100,000

Haworth

45 mins

Haworth purchased 75% of the issued share capital of Steeton on 1 April 20X9.

Details of the purchase consideration given at the date of purchase are a share exchange of 2 shares in Haworth for every 3 shares in Steeton plus an issue to the shareholders of Steeton 8% loan notes redeemable at par on 30 June 20Y1 on the basis of $100 loan note for every 250 shares held in Steeton.

The summarised statements of comprehensive income for the two companies for the year to 30 September 20X9 are:

	Haworth $000	Steeton $000
Revenue	75,000	40,700
Cost of Sales	(47,400)	(19,700)
Gross Profit	27,600	21,000
Operating expenses	(10,480)	(9,000)
Operating Profit	17,120	12,000
Interest expense	(170)	
Profit before tax	16,950	12,000
Income tax expense	(4,800)	(3,000)
Profit for year	12,150	9,000

The following information is relevant:

(i) A fair value exercise was carried out for Steeton at the date of its acquisition with the following results:

	Book value $'000	Fair value $'000
Land	20,000	23,000
Plant	25,000	30,000

The fair values have not been reflected in Steeton's financial statements. The increase in the fair value of the plant would create additional depreciation of $500,000 in the post acquisition period in the consolidated financial statements to 30 September 20X9.

Depreciation of plant is charged to cost of sales.

(ii) The details of each company's share capital and reserves at 1 October 2008 are:

	Haworth $'000	Steeton $'000
Equity shares of $1 each	20,000	10,000
Share premium	5,000	4,000
Retained earnings	18,000	7,500

(iii) In the post acquisition period Haworth sold goods to Steeton for $10 million. Haworth made a profit of $4 million on these sales. One-quarter of these goods were still in the inventory of Steeton at 30 September 20X9.

(iv) The goodwill in Steeton is amortised over 10 years

Required

(a) Calculate the goodwill arising on the purchase of the shares in Steeton at 1 April 20X9 and 30 September 20X9. **(10 marks)**

(b) Prepare a consolidated income statement for the Haworth Group for the year to 30 September 20X9. **(15 marks)**

(Total = 25 marks)

Haworth

(a) Goodwill

		$000
Consideration		
Shares: (10,000 × 75%) × 2/3 × $6		30,000
Loan note: (10,000 × 75%) /250 × $100		3,000
		33,000
Fair value of net assets of Steeton at acquisition (W2)		(34,000)
Share capital	10,000	
Share premium	4,000	
Retained earnings (7,500 + (9,000 × 6/12))	12,000	
FV Adjustment land	3,000	
FV adjustment plant	5,000	
Group share x 75%		(25,500)
Goodwill at 1 April 20X9		7,500
Amortisation 7,500/10 x 6/12		(375)
Goodwill at 30 September 20X9		7,125

(b) Consolidated statement of comprehensive income for Haworth for the year
ended 30 September 20X9

	$000
Revenue (75,000 + 20,350 – 10,000)	85,350
Cost of sales (W1)	(48,750)
Gross profit	36,600
Operating expenses (10,480 + 4,500 + 375 (a))	(15,355)
Interest expense	(170)
Profit before tax	21,075
Income tax expense (4,800 + 1,500)	(6,300)
Profit for the year	14,775
Attributable to:	
Owners of the parent (β)	13,775
Non-controlling interest (W2)	1,000

(W1) Cost of sales	$000
Haworth	47,400
Steeton (19,700 × 6/12)	9,850
Extra depreciation	500
Intercompany sales	(10,000)
PUP (25% × 4,000)	1,000
	48,750

(W2) Non-controlling interest	
6m of Steeton's profits	4,500
Fair value adjustment depreciation	(500)
	4,000
NCI share 25%	1,000

18

Associates and joint ventures

Unit topic list

Assessment criteria

4   Understand and apply IFRS for SMEs in the preparation of their financial statements

4.7   Understand and apply section 14 of IFRS for SMEs when an SME is required to account for an investment in associates

4.8   Understand and apply section 15 of IFRS for SMEs when an SME is required to account for an investment in joint ventures

1 Accounting for associates

> The investing company does not have control of an associate, as it does with a subsidiary, but it does have **significant influence**.

1.1 Definitions

We looked at some of the important definitions in Unit 15; these are repeated here with some additional important terms.

Key terms

> - **Associate**. An entity, including an unincorporated entity such as a partnership, over which an investor has significant influence and which is neither a subsidiary nor an interest in a joint venture.
> - **Significant influence** is the power to participate in the financial and operating policy decisions of the investee but is not control or joint control over those policies.
> - **Equity method**. A method of accounting whereby the investment is initially recorded at cost and adjusted thereafter for the post-acquisition change in the investor's share of net assets of the investee. The profit or loss of the investor includes the investor's share of the profit or loss of the investee.

We have already looked at how the **status** of an investment in an associate should be determined. Go back to Section 1 of Unit 15 to revise it. (Note that, as for an investment in a subsidiary, any **potential voting rights** should be taken into account in assessing whether the investor has **significant influence** over the investee.)

An investor shall account for all of its investments in associates using one of the following:

(a)   The cost model (see below)
(b)   The equity method (see section 2 of this unit)
(c)   The fair value model (see below)

1.2 The cost model

An investor shall measure its investments in associates, other than those for which there is a published price quotation, at cost less any accumulated **impairment losses.**

The investor shall recognise dividends and other distributions received from the investment as income without regard to whether the distributions are from accumulated profits of the associate arising before or after the date of acquisition.

However if there is a published price quotation for the investment in the associate then an investor must use the fair value model.

1.3 The fair value model

If the fair value model is to be used then on initial recognition the investment in an associate is measured at the transaction price which excludes transaction costs.

At each subsequent reporting date the investment is measured at fair value with the changes in fair value being taken to profit or loss. If it is impracticable to measure fair value reliably without undue cost or effort then the cost model should be used.

1.4 Separate financial statements of the investor

If an investor **issues consolidated financial statements** (because it has subsidiaries), an investment in an associate should be *either*:

(a)   Accounted for at **cost**, or
(b)   At fair value

in its separate financial statements.

If an investor that does **not issue consolidated financial statements** (ie it has no subsidiaries) but has an investment in an associate this should similarly be included in the financial statements of the investor either at cost, or fair value.

2 The equity method

2.1 Application of the equity method: consolidated accounts

Many of the procedures required to apply the equity method are the same as are required for full consolidation. In particular, **intra-group unrealised profits** must be excluded.

2.1.1 Consolidated statement of comprehensive income

The basic principle is that the investing company (X Co) should take account of its **share of the earnings** of the associate, Y Co, whether or not Y Co distributes the earnings as dividends. X Co achieves this by adding to consolidated profit the group's share of Y Co's profit after tax.

Notice the difference between this treatment and the **consolidation** of a subsidiary company's results. If Y Co were a subsidiary X Co would take credit for the whole of its sales revenue, cost of sales etc and would then make a one-line adjustment to remove any non-controlling share.

Under equity accounting, the associate's sales revenue, cost of sales and so on are *not* amalgamated with those of the group. Instead the group share only of the associate's profit after tax for the year is added to the group profit.

2.1.2 Consolidated statement of financial position

A figure for **investment in associates** is shown which at the time of the acquisition must be stated at cost. This amount will increase (decrease) each year by the amount of the group's share of the associated company's profit (loss) for the year.

2.2 Example: associate

P Co, a company with subsidiaries, acquires 25,000 of the 100,000 $1 ordinary shares in A Co for $60,000 on 1 January 20X8. In the year to 31 December 20X8, A Co earns profits after tax of $24,000, from which it pays a dividend of $6,000.

How will A Co's results be accounted for in the individual and consolidated accounts of P Co for the year ended 31 December 20X8, assuming that the cost model is adopted in the individual accounts and the equity method in the consolidated accounts?

Solution

In the **individual accounts** of P Co, the investment will be recorded on 1 January 20X8 at cost. Unless there is an impairment in the value of the investment (see below), this amount will remain in the individual statement of financial position of P Co permanently. The only entry in P Co's individual income statement will be to record dividends received. For the year ended 31 December 20X8, P Co will:

DEBIT	Cash	$1,500	
CREDIT	Income from shares in associates		$1,500

In the **consolidated accounts** of P Co equity accounting principles will be used to account for the investment in A Co. Consolidated profit after tax will include the group's share of A Co's profit after tax (25% × $24,000 = $6,000). To the extent that this has been distributed as dividend, it is already included in P Co's individual accounts and will automatically be brought into the consolidated results. That part of the group's share of profit in the associate which has not been distributed as dividend ($4,500) will be brought into consolidation by the following adjustment.

DEBIT	Investment in associates	$4,500	
CREDIT	Share of profit of associates		$4,500

The asset 'Investment in associates' is then stated at $64,500, being cost plus the group share of post-acquisition retained profits.

3 Financial statements

3.1 Consolidated statement of comprehensive income

> In the **consolidated statement of comprehensive income** the investing group takes credit for its **share of the after-tax profits** of associates whether or not they are distributed as dividends.

A **consolidation schedule** may be used to prepare the consolidated income statement of a group with associates. The treatment of associates' profits in the following example should be studied carefully.

3.2 Illustration

The following **consolidation schedule** relates to the P Co group, consisting of the parent company, an 80% owned subsidiary (S Co) and an associate (A Co) in which the group has a 30% interest.

CONSOLIDATION SCHEDULE

	Group $'000	P Co $'000	S Co $'000	A Co $'000
Sales revenue	1,400	600	800	300
Cost of sales	770	370	400	120
Gross profit	630	230	400	180
Administrative expenses	290	110	180	80
	340	120	220	100
Interest receivable	30	30	–	–
	370	150	220	100
Interest payable	(20)	–	(20)	–
Share of profit of associate (57× 30%)	17	–	–	–
Profit before tax	367	150	200	100
Income tax expense				
Group	(145)	(55)	(90)	
Associate	–	–	–	(43)
Profit for the year	222	95	110	57
Non-controlling interest (110× 20%)	(22)			
	200			

Note the following

(a) Group sales revenue, group gross profit and costs such as depreciation etc exclude the sales revenue, gross profit and costs etc of associated companies.

(b) The group share of the associated company profits is credited to the group income statement. If the associated company has been acquired during the year, it would be necessary to deduct the pre-acquisition profits (remembering to allow for tax on current year profits).

(c) The non-controlling interest will only ever apply to subsidiary companies.

3.3 Pro-forma consolidated statement of comprehensive income

The following is a **suggested layout** (using the figures given in the illustration above) for the consolidated statement of comprehensive income for a company having subsidiaries as well as associated companies.

	$'000
Sales revenue	1,400
Cost of sales	(770)
Gross profit	630
Other income: interest receivable	30
Administrative expenses	(290)
Finance costs	(20)
Share of profit of associate	17
Profit before tax	367
Income tax expense	(145)
Profit for the year	222
Profit attributable to:	
Owners of the parent	200
Non-controlling interest	22
	222

3.4 Consolidated statement of financial position

In the consolidated statement of financial position the investment in associates should be shown as:

- Cost of the investment in the associate; plus
- Group share of post acquisition profits; less
- Any amounts paid out as dividends; less
- Any amount written off the investment

As explained earlier, the consolidated statement of financial position will contain an **asset 'Investment in associates'**. The amount at which this asset is stated will be its original cost plus the group's share of any **profits earned since acquisition** which have not been distributed as dividends.

3.5 Example: consolidated statement of financial position

On 1 January 20X6 the net tangible assets of A Co amount to $220,000, financed by 100,000 $1 ordinary shares and revenue reserves of $120,000. P Co, a company with subsidiaries, acquires 30,000 of the shares in A Co for $75,000. During the year ended 31 December 20X6 A Co's profit after tax is $30,000, from which dividends of $12,000 are paid.

Show how P Co's investment in A Co would appear in the consolidated statement of financial position at 31 December 20X6.

Solution

CONSOLIDATED STATEMENT OF FINANCIAL POSITION
AS AT 31 DECEMBER 20X6 (extract)

	$
Non-current assets	
Investment in associated company	
Cost	75,000
Group share of post-acquisition retained profits	
(30% × $18,000)	5,400
	80,400

Activity

Set out below are the draft accounts of Parent Co and its subsidiaries and of Associate Co. Parent Co acquired 40% of the equity capital of Associate Co three years ago when the latter's reserves stood at $40,000.

SUMMARISED STATEMENTS OF FINANCIAL POSITION

	Parent Co & subsidiaries $'000	Associate Co $'000
Tangible non-current assets	220	170
Investment in Associate at cost	60	–
Loan to Associate Co	20	–
Current assets	100	50
Loan from Parent Co	–	(20)
	400	200
Share capital ($1 shares)	250	100
Retained earnings	150	100
	400	200

SUMMARISED STATEMENTS OF COMPREHENSIVE INCOME

	Parent Co & subsidiaries $'000	Associate Co $'000
Profit before tax	95	80
Income tax expense	35	30
Net profit for the year	60	50

You are required to prepare the summarised consolidated accounts of Parent Co.

Notes

(1)   Assume that the associate's assets/liabilities are stated at fair value.
(2)   Assume that there are no non-controlling interests in the subsidiary companies.

Answer

PARENT CO
CONSOLIDATED STATEMENT OF COMPREHENSIVE INCOME

	$'000
Net profit	95
Share of profits of associated company (50 × 40%)	20
Profit before tax	115
Income tax expense	(35)
Profit attributable to the members of Parent Co	80

PARENT CO
CONSOLIDATED STATEMENT OF FINANCIAL POSITION

	$'000
Assets	
Tangible non-current assets	220
Investment in associate (see note)	104
Current assets	100
Total assets	424
Equity and liabilities	
Share capital	250
Retained earnings (W)	174
Total equity and liabilities	424

Note

	$'000
Investment in associate	
Cost of investment	60
Share of post-acquisition retained earnings (W)	24
Loan to associate	20
	104

Working		
	Parent &	
Retained earnings	Subsidiaries	Associate
	$'000	$'000
Per question	150	100
Pre-acquisition		40
Post-acquisition		60
Group share in associate		
($60 × 40%)	24	
Group retained earnings	174	

Activity

Alfred Co bought a 25% shareholding on 31 December 20X8 in Grimbald Co at a cost of $38,000.

During the year to 31 December 20X9 Grimbald Co made a profit before tax of $82,000 and the taxation charge on the year's profits was $32,000. A dividend of $20,000 was paid on 31 December out of these profits.

Calculate the entries for the associate which would appear in the consolidated accounts of the Alfred group, in accordance with the requirements of the IFRS.

Answer

CONSOLIDATED STATEMENT OF COMPREHENSIVE INCOME

	$
Group share of profit of associate (82,000 × 25%)	20,500
Less taxation (32,000 × 25%)	(8,000)
Share of profit of associate	12,500

CONSOLIDATED STATEMENT OF FINANCIAL POSITION

	$
Investment in associate	45,500

Working

	$
Cost of investment	38,000
Share of post-acquisition retained earnings ((82,000 – 32,000 – 20,000) × 25%)	7,500
	45,500

The following points are also relevant and are similar to a parent-subsidiary consolidation situation.

(a) Use financial statements drawn up to the **same reporting date** unless impracticable.

(b) If this is impracticable, adjust the financial statements for **significant transactions/ events** in the intervening period.

(c) Use **uniform accounting policies** for like transactions and events in similar circumstances, adjusting the associate's statements to reflect group policies unless this is impracticable.

3.6 'Upstream' and 'downstream' transactions

'Upstream' transactions are, for example, sales of assets from an associate to the investor. 'Downstream' transactions are, for example, sales of assets from the investor to an associate.

Profits and losses resulting from 'upstream' and 'downstream' transactions between an investor (including its consolidated subsidiaries) and an associate are eliminated to the extent of the investor's interest in the associate. This is very similar to the procedure for eliminating intra-group transactions between a parent and a subsidiary. The important thing to remember is that **only the group's share is eliminated.**

3.7 Example: downstream transaction

A Co, a parent with subsidiaries, holds 25% of the equity shares in B Co. During the year, A Co makes sales of $1,000,000 to B Co at cost plus a 25% mark-up. At the year-end, B Co has all these goods still in inventories.

Solution

A Co has made an unrealised profit of $200,000 (1,000,000 × 25/125) on its sales to the associate. The group's share (25%) of this must be eliminated:

DEBIT	Cost of sales (consolidated income statement)	$50,000
CREDIT	Investment in associate (consolidated statement of financial position)	$50,000

Because the sale was made to the associate, the group's share of the unsold inventory forms part of the investment in the associate at the year-end. If the associate had made the sale to the parent, the adjustment would have been:

DEBIT	Cost of sales (consolidated income statement)	$50,000
CREDIT	Inventories (consolidated statement of financial position)	$50,000

3.8 Associate's losses

When the equity method is being used and the investor's share of losses of the associate equals or exceeds its interest in the associate, the investor should **discontinue** including its share of further losses. The investment is reported at nil value. The interest in the associate is normally the carrying amount of the investment in the associate, but it also includes any other long-term interests, for example, long term receivables or loans.

After the investor's interest is reduced to nil, **additional losses** should only be recognised where the investor has incurred obligations or made payments on behalf of the associate (for example, if it has guaranteed amounts owed to third parties by the associate).

3.9 Impairment losses

In the case of an associate, any impairment loss will be deducted from the carrying value in the statement of financial position.

The working would be as follows.

	$
Cost of investment	X
Share of post-acquisition retained earnings	X
	X
Impairment loss	(X)
Investment in associate	X

4 Joint ventures

4.1 Definitions

Joint control is the contractually agreed sharing of **control** over an economic activity, and exists only when the strategic financial and operating decisions relating to the activity require the unanimous consent of the parties sharing control.

A joint venture is a contractual arrangement whereby two or more parties undertake an economic activity that is subject to joint control. Joint ventures can take the form of jointly controlled operations, jointly controlled assets, or **jointly controlled entities**.

4.2 Jointly controlled operations

The operation of some joint ventures involves the use of the assets and other resources of the venturers rather than the establishment of a corporation, partnership or other entity.

Each venturer uses its own property, plant and equipment and carries its own inventories. It also incurs its own expenses and liabilities and raises its own finance, which represent its own obligations. The joint venture activities may be carried out by the venturer's employees alongside the venturer's similar activities. The joint venture agreement usually provides a means by which the revenue from the sale of the joint product and any expenses incurred in common are shared among the venturers.

In respect of its interests in jointly controlled operations, a venturer shall recognise in its financial statements:

(a)   the assets that it controls and the liabilities that it incurs, and

(b)   the expenses that it incurs and its share of the income that it earns from the sale of goods or services by the joint venture.

4.3 Jointly controlled assets

Some joint ventures involve the joint control, and often the joint ownership, by the venturers of one or more assets contributed to, or acquired for the purpose of, the joint venture and dedicated to the purposes of the joint venture.

A venturer shall recognise in its financial statements:

(a)   its share of the jointly controlled assets, classified according to the nature of the assets;

(b)   any liabilities that it has incurred;

(c)   its share of any liabilities incurred jointly with the other venturers in relation to the joint venture;

(d)   any income from the sale or use of its share of the output of the joint venture, together with its share of any expenses incurred by the joint venture; and

(e)   any expenses that it has incurred in respect of its interest in the joint venture.

4.4 Jointly controlled entities

A jointly controlled entity is a joint venture that involves the establishment of a corporation, partnership or other entity in which each venturer has an interest. The entity operates in the same way as other entities, except that a contractual arrangement between the venturers establishes joint control over the economic activity of the entity.

A venturer shall account for all of its interests in jointly controlled entities using one of the following:

(a)   the cost model
(b)   the equity method
(c)   the fair value model

The accounting treatment for each of these methods/models is the same as that for associates considered earlier in this unit.

Unit Roundup

- The investing company does not have control of an associate, as it does with a subsidiary, but it does have **significant influence.**

- The IFRS for SMEs requires that, in consolidated accounts, **associates** should be accounted for using the cost model, the fair value model or **equity accounting principles**.

- Under the cost model the investment is recognised at cost less any accumulated impairment losses.

- Using the fair value model the investment is recognised at fair value at each reporting date with changes in fair value being taken to profit or loss.

- Using the equity method in the **consolidated statement of comprehensive income** the investing group takes credit for its **share of the after-tax profits** of associates, whether or not they are distributed as dividends.

- In the **consolidated statement of financial position**, the investment in associates should be shown as:
    - Cost of the investment in the associate; plus
    - Group share of post-acquisition profits; less
    - Any amounts paid out as dividends and any amounts written off.

- There are three types of joint venture:
    - jointly controlled operations
    - jointly controlled assets
    - jointly controlled entities

- A jointly controlled entity is accounted for in the same way as an associate.

Quick Quiz

1   Define an associate.

2   What are the three possible methods of accounting for an associate in an entity's consolidated financial statements?

3   What is the effect of the equity method on the consolidated statement of comprehensive income and statement of financial position?

4   What are the three types of joint venture recognised in the IFRS for SMEs?

Answers to Quick Quiz

1   An entity in which an investor has a significant influence, but which is not a subsidiary or a joint venture of the investor.

2   The cost model, the fair value model or the equity method.

3   (a)   *Statement of comprehensive income.* Investing company includes its share of the earnings of the associate, by adding its share of profit after tax.

    (b)   *Statement of financial position.* Investment in associates is initially included in assets at cost. This will increase or decrease each year according to whether the associated company makes a profit or loss.

4   Jointly controlled operations, jointly controlled assets and jointly controlled entities.

J Group

45 mins

The statements of financial position of J Co and its investee companies, P Co and S Co, at 31 December 20X5 are shown below.

STATEMENTS OF FINANCIAL POSITION AS AT 31 DECEMBER 20X5

	J Co $'000	P Co $'000	S Co $'000
Non-current assets			
Freehold property	1,950	1,250	500
Plant and machinery	795	375	285
Investments	1,500	–	–
	4,245	1,625	785
Current assets			
Inventory	575	300	265
Trade receivables	330	290	370
Cash	50	120	20
	955	710	655
Total assets	5,200	2,335	1,440
Equity and liabilities			
Equity			
Share capital – $1 shares	2,000	1,000	750
Retained earnings	1,460	885	390
	3,460	1,885	1,140
Non-current liabilities			
12% loan stock	500	100	
Current liabilities			
Trade payables	680	350	300
Bank overdraft	560	–	–
	1,240	350	300
Total equity and liabilities	5,200	2,335	1,440

Additional information

(a) J Co acquired 600,000 ordinary shares in P Co on 1 January 20X0 for $1,000,000 when the retained earnings of P Co were $200,000.

(b) At the date of acquisition of P Co, the fair value of its freehold property was considered to be $400,000 greater than its value in P Co's statement of financial position. P Co had acquired the property in January 20W0 and the buildings element (comprising 50% of the total value) is depreciated on cost over 50 years.

(c) J Co acquired 225,000 ordinary shares in S Co on 1 January 20X4 for $500,000 when the retained earnings of S Co were $150,000.

(d) P Co manufactures a component used by both J Co and S Co. Transfers are made by P Co at cost plus 25%. J Co held $100,000 inventory of these components at 31 December 20X5 and S Co held $80,000 at the same date.

(e) The goodwill in P Co is being amortised over 5 years. An impairment loss of $92,000 is to be recognised on the investment in S Co.

Required

Prepare, in a format suitable for inclusion in the annual report of the J Group, the consolidated statement of financial position at 31 December 20X5. **(25 marks)**

Answer

J Group

J GROUP CONSOLIDATED STATEMENT OF FINANCIAL POSITION AS AT 31 DECEMBER 20X5

	$'000
Non-current assets	
Freehold property (W2)	3,570.00
Plant and machinery (795 + 375)	1,170.00
Investment in associate (W9)	475.20
	5,215.20
Current assets	
Inventory (W3)	855.00
Receivables (W4)	620.00
Cash (50 + 120)	170.00
	1,645.00
Total assets	6,860.20
Equity and liabilities	
Equity	
Share capital	2,000.00
Retained earnings (W10)	1,778.12
	3,778.12
Non-controlling interest (W11)	892.08
	4,670.20
Non-current liabilities	
12% loan stock (500 + 100)	600.00
Current liabilities (W5)	1,590.00
Total equity and liabilities	6,860.20

Workings

1   Group structure

```
                        J
              ╱                   ╲
   1.1.X0   60%                  30%   1.1.X4
 (6 years ago)                       (2 years ago)
            P                         S
```

2   Freehold property

	$'000
J Co	1,950
P Co	1,250
Fair value adjustment	400
Additional depreciation (400 × 50% ÷ 40) × 6 years (20X0-20X5)	(30)
	3,570

3   Inventory

	$'000
J Co	575
P Co	300
PUP (100 × $^{25}/_{125}$)	(20)
	855

4   Receivables

	$'000
J Co	330
P Co	290
	620

5 *Current liabilities*

		$'000
J Co:	bank overdraft	560
	trade payables	680
P Co:	trade payables	350
		1,590

6 *Unrealised profit (PUP)*

	$'000
On sales to J (parent co) 100 × 25/125	20.0
On sales to S (associate) 80 × 25/125 × 30%	4.8
	24.8

7 *Fair value adjustments*

	Difference at acquisition $'000	Difference now $'000
Property	400	400
Additional depreciation: 200 × 6/40	–	(30)
	400	370

∴ Charge $30,000 to retained earnings

8 *Goodwill*

	$'000	$'000
P Co		
Consideration transferred		1,000
Net assets acquired		
Share capital	1,000	
Retained earnings	200	
Fair value adjustment	400	
	1,600	
Group share 60%		(960)
Goodwill at acquisition		40
Amortised (in full)		(40)
		0

9 *Investment in associate*

	$'000
Cost of investment	500.00
Share of post-acquisition profit (390 – 150) × 30%	72.00
Less PUP	(4.80)
Less impairment loss	(92.00)
	475.20

10 *Retained earnings*

	J $'000	P $'000	S $'000
Retained earnings per question	1,460.0	885.0	390.0
Adjustments			
Unrealised profit (W6)		(24.8)	
Fair value adjustments (W7)		(30.0)	
		830.2	390.0
Less pre-acquisition reserves		(200.0)	(150.0)
	1,460.0	630.2	240.0
P: 60% × 630.2	378.1		
S: 30% × 240	72.0		
Goodwill amortisation	(40.0)		
Less impairment losses in S	(92.0)		
	1,778.1		

11 *Non-controlling interest at reporting date*

	$'000
Net assets of P Co	1,885.0
Fair value adjustment (W7)	370.0
Less PUP: sales to J Co	(20.0)
sales to S Co $(80 \times {}^{25}/_{125} \times 30\%)$	(4.8)
	2,230.2
Non-controlling interest (40%)	892.08

Foreign currency

Unit topic list

1 Foreign currency translation
2 Individual company stage
3 Consolidated financial statements stage

Assessment criteria

4   Understand and apply IFRS for SMEs in the preparation of their financial statements

4.21   Understand and apply section 30 of IFRS for SMEs when an SME is required to account for foreign currency

1 Foreign currency translation

If a company trades overseas, it will buy or sell assets in foreign currencies. For example, an Indian company might buy materials from Canada, and pay for them in US dollars, and then sell its finished goods in Germany, receiving payment in €, or perhaps in some other currency. If the company owes money in a foreign currency at the end of the accounting year, or holds assets which were bought in a foreign currency, those liabilities or assets must be translated into the local currency (in this Study Guide $), in order to be shown in the books of account.

A company might have a subsidiary abroad (ie a foreign entity that it owns), and the subsidiary will trade in its own local currency. The subsidiary will keep books of account and prepare its annual accounts in its own currency. However, at the year end, the holding company must 'consolidate' the results of the overseas subsidiary into its group accounts, so that somehow, the assets and liabilities and the annual profits of the subsidiary must be translated from the foreign currency into $.

If foreign currency exchange rates remained constant, there would be no accounting problem. As you will be aware, however, foreign exchange rates are continually changing, and it is not inconceivable for example, that the rate of exchange between the Polish zlotych and sterling might be Z6.2 to £1 at the start of the accounting year, and Z5.6 to £1 at the end of the year (in this example, a 10% increase in the relative strength of the zlotych).

There are two distinct types of foreign currency transaction, conversion and translation.

1.1 Conversion gains and losses

Conversion is the process of exchanging amounts of one foreign currency for another. For example, suppose a local company buys a large consignment of goods from a supplier in Germany. The order is placed on 1 May and the agreed price is €124,250. At the time of delivery the rate of foreign exchange was €3.50 to $1. The local company would record the amount owed in its books as follows.

DEBIT	Purchases account (124,250 ÷ 3.5)	$35,500	
CREDIT	Payables account		$35,500

When the local company comes to pay the supplier, it needs to obtain some foreign currency. By this time, however, if the rate of exchange has altered to €3.55 to $1, the cost of raising €124,250 would be (÷ 3.55) $35,000. The company would need to spend only $35,000 to settle a debt for inventories 'costing' $35,500. Since it would be administratively difficult to alter the value of the inventories in the company's books of account, it is more appropriate to record a profit on conversion of $500.

DEBIT	Payables account	$35,500	
CREDIT	Cash		$35,000
CREDIT	Profit on conversion		$500

Profits (or losses) on conversion would be included in profit or loss for the year in which conversion (whether payment or receipt) takes place.

Suppose that another home company sells goods to a Chinese company, and it is agreed that payment should be made in Chinese Yuan at a price of Y116,000. We will further assume that the exchange rate at the time of sale is Y10.75 to $1, but when the debt is eventually paid, the rate has altered to Y10.8 to $1. The company would record the sale as follows.

DEBIT	Receivables account (116,000 ÷ 10.75)	$10,800	
CREDIT	Sales account		$10,800

When the Y116,000 are paid, the local company will convert them into $, to obtain (÷ 10.8) $10,750. In this example, there has been a loss on conversion of $50 which will be written off to profit of loss for the year:

DEBIT	Cash	$10,750	
DEBIT	Loss on conversion	$50	
CREDIT	Payables account		$10,800

There are **no accounting difficulties** concerned with foreign currency conversion gains or losses, and the procedures described above are uncontroversial.

1.2 Translation

Foreign currency translation, as distinct from conversion, does not involve the act of exchanging one currency for another. **Translation is required at the end of an accounting period when a company still holds assets or liabilities in its statement of financial position which were obtained or incurred in a foreign currency.**

These assets or liabilities might consist of any of the following.

(a)   An individual home company holding individual **assets** or **liabilities** originating in a foreign currency 'deal'.

(b)   An individual home company with a separate **branch** of the business operating abroad which keeps its own books of account in the local currency.

(c)   A home company which wishes to consolidate the **results of a foreign subsidiary**.

There has been great **uncertainty** about the method which should be used to translate the following.

- Value of assets and liabilities from a foreign currency into $ for the year end statement of financial position

- Profits of an independent foreign branch or subsidiary into $ for the annual statement of comprehensive income

Suppose, for example, that a Belgian subsidiary purchases a piece of property for €210,000 on 31 December 20X7. The rate of exchange at this time was €7.0 to $1. During 20X8, the subsidiary charged depreciation on the building of €1,680, so that at 31 December 20X8, the subsidiary recorded the asset as follows.

	€
Property at cost	210,000
Less accumulated depreciation	1,680
Carrying amount	208,320

At this date, the rate of exchange has changed to €6.0 to $1.

The local holding company must translate the asset's value into $, but there is a **choice of exchange rates**.

(a)   Should the rate of exchange for translation be the rate which existed at the date of purchase, which would give a carrying amount of 208,320 ÷ 7.0 = $29,760?

(b)   Should the rate of exchange for translation be the rate existing at the end of 20X8 (the closing rate of €6.0 to $1)? This would give a carrying amount of $34,720.

Similarly, should depreciation be charged to group profit or loss at the rate of €7.0 to $1 (the historical rate), €6.0 to $1 (the closing rate), or at an average rate for the year (say, €6.4 to $1)?

1.3 Consolidated accounts

If a parent has a subsidiary whose accounts are presented in a foreign currency, those accounts must be translated into the local currency before they can be included in the consolidated financial statements.

- Should the subsidiary's accounts be translated as if the subsidiary is an extension of the parent?
- Or should they be translated as if the subsidiary is a separate business?

Where the affairs of a foreign operation are very closely interlinked with those of the investing company, it should be included in the consolidated financial statements as if the transactions had been entered into by the investing company in its own currency. Non-monetary assets and depreciation are translated at **historical rate** and sales, purchase and expenses at **average rate**. **Exchange differences** arising on retranslation are reported as part of **profit or loss** on ordinary activities.

Where a foreign operation is effectively a separate business, the **closing rate** is used for most items in the financial statements. **Exchange differences** are taken **directly** to **equity**.

We will look at the consolidation of foreign subsidiaries in much more detail in Section 3 of this unit.

2 Individual company stage

The questions discussed above are addressed by *the IFRS for SMEs*. We will examine those matters which affect single company accounts here.

2.1 Definitions

These are some of the definitions.

> **Foreign currency**. A currency other than the functional currency of the entity.
>
> **Functional currency**. The currency of the primary economic environment in which the entity operates.
>
> **Presentation currency**. The currency in which the financial statements are presented.
>
> **Exchange rate**. The ratio of exchange for two currencies.
>
> **Exchange difference**. The difference resulting from translating a given number of units of one currency into another currency at different exchange rates.
>
> **Closing rate**. The spot exchange rate at the year end date.
>
> **Spot exchange rate**. The exchange rate for immediate delivery.
>
> **Monetary items**. Units of currency held and assets and liabilities to be received or paid in a fixed or determinable number of units of currency.

Each entity – whether an individual company, a parent of a group, or an operation within a group (such as a subsidiary, associate or branch) – should determine its **functional currency** and **measure its results and financial position in that currency**.

For most individual companies the functional currency will be the currency of the country in which they are located and in which they carry out most of their transactions. Determining the functional currency is much more likely to be an issue where an entity operates as part of a group. The IFRS contains detailed guidance on how to determine an entity's functional currency and we will look at this in more detail in Section 3.

An entity can present its financial statements in any currency (or currencies) it chooses. The IFRS deals with the situation in which financial statements are presented in a currency other than the functional currency.

Again, this is unlikely to be an issue for most individual companies. Their presentation currency will normally be the same as their functional currency (the currency of the country in which they operate). A company's presentation currency may be different from its functional currency if it operates within a group and we will look at this in Section 3.

2.2 Foreign currency transactions: initial recognition

The IFRS states that a foreign currency transaction should be recorded, on initial recognition in the functional currency, by applying the exchange rate between the reporting currency and the foreign currency **at the date of the transaction** to the foreign currency amount.

An **average rate** for a period may be used if exchange rates do not fluctuate significantly.

2.3 Reporting at subsequent year ends

The following rules apply at each subsequent year end.

(a) Report foreign currency **monetary items** using the **closing rate**

(b) Report **non-monetary items** (eg non-current assets, inventories) which are carried at **historical cost** in a foreign currency using the **exchange rate at the date of the transaction** (historical rate)

(c) Report **non-monetary items** which are carried at **fair value** in a foreign currency using the exchange rates that existed **when the values were determined.**

2.4 Recognition of exchange differences

Exchange differences occur when there is a **change in the exchange rate** between the transaction date and the date of settlement of monetary items arising from a foreign currency transaction.

Exchange differences arising on the settlement of monetary items (receivables, payables, loans and cash in a foreign currency) or on translating an entity's monetary items at rates different from those at which they were translated initially, or reported in previous financial statements, should be **recognised in profit or loss** in the period in which they arise.

There are two situations to consider.

(a) The transaction is **settled in the same period** as that in which it occurred: all the exchange difference is recognised in that period.

(b) The transaction is **settled in a subsequent accounting period**: the exchange difference recognised in each intervening period up to the period of settlement is determined by the change in exchange rates during that period.

In other words, where a monetary item has not been settled at the end of a period, it should be **restated using the closing exchange rate** and any exchange difference recognised in profit or loss.

Activity

White Cliffs Co, whose year end is 31 December, buys some goods from Rinka SA of France on 30 September. The invoice value is €40,000 and is due for settlement in equal instalments on 30 November and 31 January. The exchange rate moved as follows.

	€= $1
30 September	1.60
30 November	1.80
31 December	1.90
31 January	1.85

Required

State the accounting entries in the books of White Cliffs Co.

Answer

The purchase will be recorded in the books of White Cliffs Co using the rate of exchange ruling on 30 September.

DEBIT	Purchases	$25,000	
CREDIT	Trade payables		$25,000

Being the $ cost of goods purchased for €40,000 (€40,000 ÷ €1.60/$1)

On 30 November, White Cliffs must pay €20,000. This will cost €20,000 ÷ €1.80/$1 = $11,111 and the company has therefore made an exchange gain of $12,500 – $11,111 = $1,389.

DEBIT	Trade payables	$12,500	
CREDIT	Exchange gains (profit or loss)		$1,389
CREDIT	Cash		$11,111

On 31 December, the year end, the outstanding liability will be recalculated using the rate applicable to that date: €20,000 ÷ €1.90/$1 = $10,526. A further exchange gain of $1,974 has been made and will be recorded as follows.

DEBIT	Trade payables	$1,974	
CREDIT	Exchange gains (profit or loss)		$1,974

The total exchange gain of $3,363 will be included in the operating profit for the year ending 31 December.

On 31 January, White Cliffs must pay the second instalment of €20,000. This will cost them $10,811 (€20,000 ÷ €1.85/$1).

DEBIT	Trade payables	$10,526	
	Exchange losses	$285	
CREDIT	Cash		$10,811

When a gain or loss on a non-monetary item is recognised **directly in equity** any **related exchange differences** should also be **recognised directly in equity.**

3 Consolidated financial statements stage

3.1 Definitions

The following definitions are relevant here.

Key terms

Foreign operation. A subsidiary, associate, joint venture or branch of a reporting entity, the activities of which are based or conducted in a country or currency other than those of the reporting entity.

Net investment in a foreign operation. The amount of the reporting entity's interest in the net assets of that operation.

3.2 Determining functional currency

You may have to make the decision yourself as to whether the subsidiary has the same functional currency as the parent or a different functional currency from the parent. This determines whether the subsidiary is treated as an **extension of the parent** or as a **net investment.**

A holding or parent company with foreign operations must **translate the financial statements** of those operations into its own reporting currency before they can be consolidated into the group accounts. There are two methods: **the method used depends** upon **whether** the foreign operation has the **same functional currency as the parent**.

The IFRS states that an entity should consider the following factors in determining its functional currency:

(a) The currency that mainly **influences sales prices** for goods and services (often the currency in which prices are denominated and settled)

(b) The currency of the **country whose competitive forces and regulations** mainly determine the sales prices of its goods and services

(c) The currency that mainly **influences labour, material and other costs** of providing goods or services (often the currency in which prices are denominated and settled)

Sometimes the functional currency of an entity is not immediately obvious. Management must then exercise judgement and may also need to consider:

(a) The currency in which **funds from financing activities** (raising loans and issuing equity) are generated

(b) The currency in which **receipts from operating activities** are usually retained

Where a parent has a foreign operation a number of factors are considered:

(a) Whether the activities of the foreign operation are carried out as an **extension of the parent**, rather than being carried out with a **significant degree of autonomy**.

(b) Whether **transactions with the parent** are a high or a low proportion of the foreign operation's activities.

(c) Whether **cash flows** from the activities of the foreign operation **directly affect the cash flows of the parent** and are readily available for remittance to it.

(d) Whether the activities of the foreign operation are **financed from its own cash flows** or by **borrowing from the parent**.

3.2.1 Same functional currency as the reporting entity

In this situation, the foreign operation normally carries on its business as though it were an **extension of the reporting entity's operations.** For example, it may only sell goods imported from, and remit the proceeds directly to, the reporting entity.

Any **movement in the exchange rate** between the reporting currency and the foreign operation's currency will have an **immediate impact** on the reporting entity's cash flows from the foreign operations. In other words, changes in the exchange rate affect the **individual monetary items** held by the foreign operation, *not* the reporting entity's net investment in that operation.

3.2.2 Different functional currency from the reporting entity

In this situation, although the reporting entity may be able to exercise control, the foreign operation normally operates in a **semi-autonomous** way. It accumulates cash and other monetary items, generates income and incurs expenses, and may also arrange borrowings, all **in its own local currency**.

A change in the exchange rate will produce **little or no direct effect on the present and future cash flows** from operations of either the foreign operation or the reporting entity. Rather, the change in exchange rate affects the reporting entity's **net investment** in the foreign operation, not the individual monetary and non-monetary items held by the foreign operation.

Exam focus point

> Where the foreign operation's functional currency is different from the parent's, the financial statements need to be translated before consolidation.

3.3 Accounting treatment: different functional currency from the reporting entity

The financial statements of the foreign operation must be translated to the functional currency of the parent. Different procedures must be followed here, because the functional currency of the parent is the **presentation currency** of the foreign operation.

(a) The **assets and liabilities** shown in the foreign operation's statement of financial position are translated at the **closing rate** at the year end, regardless of the date on which those items originated. The balancing figure in the translated statement of financial position represents the reporting entity's net investment in the foreign operation.

(b) Amounts in the **statement of comprehensive income** should be translated at the rate ruling at the date of the transaction (an **average rate** will usually be used for practical purposes).

(c) **Exchange differences** arising from the re-translation at the end of each year of the parent's net investment should be **recognised in other comprehensive income**, not in profit or loss for the year, until the disposal of the net investment.

3.4 Example: different functional currency from the reporting entity

A dollar-based company, Stone Co, set up a foreign subsidiary on 30 June 20X7. Stone subscribed €24,000 for share capital when the exchange rate was €2 = $1. The subsidiary, Brick Inc, borrowed €72,000 and bought a non-monetary asset for €96,000. Stone Co prepared its accounts on 31 December 20X7 and by that time the exchange rate had moved to €3 = $1. As a result of highly unusual circumstances, Brick Inc sold its asset early in 20X8 for €96,000. It repaid its loan and was liquidated. Stone's capital of €24,000 was repaid in February 20X8 when the exchange rate was €3 = $1.

Required

Account for the above transactions as if the entity has a different functional currency from the parent.

Solution

From the above it can be seen that Stone Co will record its initial investment at $12,000 which is the starting cost of its shares. The statement of financial position of Brick Inc at 31 December 20X7 is summarised below.

	€'000
Non-monetary asset	96
Share capital	24
Loan	72
	96

This may be translated as follows.

	$'000
Non-monetary asset	
(€3 = $1)	32
Share capital and reserves (retained earnings) (balancing figure)	8
Loan (€3 = $1)	24
	32
Exchange gain/(loss) for 20X7	(4)

The exchange gain and loss are the differences between the value of the original investment ($12,000) and the total of share capital and reserves (retained earnings) as disclosed by the above statements of financial position.

On liquidation, Stone Co will receive $8,000 (€24,000 converted at €3 = $1). No gain or loss will arise in 20X8.

3.5 Some practical points

The following points apply.

(a) For consolidation purposes calculations are simpler if a subsidiary's share capital is translated at the **historical rate** (the rate when the investing company acquired its interest) and reserves are found as a balancing figure.

(b) **Dividends declared** by a subsidiary should always be translated at the **closing rate** in the statement of changes in equity and at the actual rate on the date of payment. This is because the investing company will record the items at these rates in its own books.

You must be able to calculate **exchange differences**.

Practising examination questions is the best way of learning this topic.

3.6 Summary of method

A summary of the translation method is given below, which shows the main steps to follow in the consolidation process.

Exam focus point

You should learn this summary.

Translation	
Step 1 Translate the **closing statement of financial position** (net assets/ shareholders' funds) and use this for preparing the consolidated statement of financial position in the normal way.	Use the **closing rate** at the year end for all items.

Step 2

Translate the **statement of comprehensive income**.

(In all cases, dividends should be translated at the rate ruling when the dividend was paid or, in the case of proposed dividends, the closing rate at the year end.)

Use the **average rate** for the year for all items (but see comment on dividends). The figures obtained can then be used in preparing the consolidated income statement.

Step 3

Translate the **shareholders' funds** (net assets) at the beginning of the year.

Use the **closing rate** at the beginning of the year (the opening rate for the current year).

Step 4

Calculate the **total exchange difference** for the year as follows.

	$
Closing net assets at closing rate (Step 1)	X
Less opening net assets at opening rate (Step 3)	X
	X
Less retained profit per translated income statement (Step 2)	X
Exchange differences	X
Group share (%)	X

It may be necessary to adjust for any profits or losses taken direct to reserves during the year.

This stage will be **unnecessary** unless you are asked to state the total exchange differences or are asked to prepare a statement of the movement on reserves, where the exchange difference will be shown.

For **exam purposes** you can translate the closing shareholders' funds as follows.

(a) Share capital + pre-acquisition reserves at historical rate.

(b) Post-acquisition reserves as a balancing figure.

As mentioned above, the share capital may be translated at the historical rate. The reserves will then be the balancing figure. The advantage of this method is that it simplifies the 'cancellation' of the share capital on consolidation.

3.7 Analysis of exchange differences

The exchange differences in the above exercise could be reconciled by splitting them into their component parts.

The exchange difference consists of those exchange gains/losses arising from:

- Translating **income/expense items** at the exchange rates at the date of transactions, whereas **assets/liabilities** are translated at the closing rate.
- Translating the **opening net investment** (opening net assets) in the foreign entity at a closing rate different from the closing rate at which it was previously reported.

This can be demonstrated numerically.

Suppose we have the following opening statement of financial position and translating at €2 = $1 and €1 = $1 gives the following.

	€2 = $1	€1 = $1	Difference
	$	$	$
Non-current assets at carrying amount	170	340	170
Inventories	60	120	60
Net current monetary liabilities	(25)	(50)	(25)
	205	410	205

	€2 = $1	€1 = $1	Difference
	$	$	$
Equity	150	300	150
Loans	55	110	55
	205	410	205

Translating the income statement part of the statement of comprehensive income using €1.60 = $1 and €1 = $1 gives the following results.

	€1.60 = $1	€1 = $1	Difference
	$	$	$
Profit before tax, depreciation and increase in inventory values	75	120	45
Increase in inventory values	50	80	30
	125	200	75
Depreciation	(25)	(40)	(15)
	100	160	60
Tax	(50)	(80)	(30)
Profit after tax, retained	50	80	30

The overall position is then:

	$	$
Gain on non-current assets ($170 – $15)		155
Loss on loan		(55)
Gain on inventories ($60 + $30)	90	
Loss on net monetary current assets/ Liabilities (all other differences) ($45 – $30 – $25)	(10)	
		80
Net exchange gain		180

3.8 Further matters relating to foreign operations

3.8.1 Goodwill and fair value adjustments

Goodwill and fair value adjustments arising on the acquisition of a foreign operation should be treated as assets and liabilities of the acquired entity. This means that they should be expressed in the functional currency of the foreign operation and translated at the **closing rate**.

Here is a layout for calculating goodwill and the exchange gain or loss. The parent holds 90% of the shares.

Goodwill

	F'000	F'000	Rate	$'000
Consideration transferred (12,000 × 6)		72,000		
Less:				
Less share capital	40,000			
Pre acquisition retained earnings	26,000			
Group share x 90%		(59,400)		
At 1.4.X1		12,600	6*	2,100
Foreign exchange gain		–	Balance	420
At 31.3.X7		12,600	5**	2,520

* Historic rate
** Closing rate

3.8.2 Consolidation procedures

Follow normal consolidation procedures, except that where an exchange difference arises on **long- or short-term intra-group monetary items**, these cannot be offset against other intra-group balances. This is because these are commitments to convert one currency into another, thus exposing the reporting entity to a gain or loss through currency fluctuations.

If the foreign operation's **reporting date** is different from that of the parent, it is acceptable to use the accounts made up to that date for consolidation, as long as adjustments are made for any significant changes in rates in the interim.

3.9 Change in functional currency

The functional currency of an entity can be changed only if there is a change to the underlying transactions, events and conditions that are relevant to the entity. For example, an entity's functional currency may change if there is a change in the currency that mainly influences the sales price of goods and services.

Where there is a change in an entity's functional currency, the entity translates all items into the new functional currency **prospectively** (ie, from the date of the change) using the exchange rate at the date of the change.

3.10 Section summary

- Where the functional currency of a foreign operation is **different** from that of the parent/reporting entity, they need to be translated before consolidation

    - Operation is semi-autonomous
    - Translate assets and liabilities at **closing rate**
    - Translate income statement at **average rate**
    - Exchange differences through **reserves/equity**

Unit Roundup

- There are two main aspects to dealing with foreign currency – translating individual transactions that a single company enters into and translating the financial statements of a foreign subsidiary.

- You may have to make the decision yourself as to whether the subsidiary has the same functional currency as the parent or a different functional currency from the parent. This determines whether the subsidiary is treated as an **extension of the parent** or as a **net investment**.

- You must be able to calculate exchange differences.

Quick Quiz

1   What is the difference between conversion and translation?

2   Define 'monetary' items.

3   How should foreign currency transactions be recognised initially in an individual entity's accounts?

4   What factors must management take into account when determining the functional currency of a foreign operation?

5   How should goodwill and fair value adjustments be treated on consolidation of a foreign operation?

6   When can an entity's functional currency be changed?

1   (a)   Conversion is the process of exchanging one currency for another.

       (b)   Translation is the restatement of the value of one currency in another currency.

2   Money held and assets and liabilities to be received or paid in fixed or determinable amounts of money.

3   Use the exchange rate at the date of the transaction. An average rate for a period can be used if the exchange rates did not fluctuate significantly.

4   See paragraph 3.2

5   Treat as assets/liabilities of the foreign operation and translate at the closing rate.

6   Only if there is a change to the underlying transactions relevant to the entity.

Darius Co

45 mins

The abridged statements of financial position and income statements of Darius Co and its foreign subsidiary, Xerxes Inc, appear below.

DRAFT STATEMENT OF FINANCIAL POSITION AS AT 31 DECEMBER 20X9

	Darius Co		Xerxes Inc	
	$	$	€	€
Assets				
Non-current assets				
Plant at cost	600		500	
Less depreciation	(250)		(200)	
		350		300
Investment in Xerxes				
100 €1 shares		25		–
		375		300
Current assets				
Inventories	225		200	
Receivables	150		100	
		375		300
		750		600
Equity and liabilities				
Equity				
Ordinary $1/€1 shares	300		100	
Retained earnings	300		280	
		600		380
Long-term loans		50		110
Current liabilities		100		110
		750		600

STATEMENTS OF COMPREHENSIVE INCOME
FOR THE YEAR ENDED 31 DECEMBER 20X9

	Darius Co	Xerxes Inc
	$	€
Profit before tax	200	160
Tax	100	80
Profit after tax, retained	100	80

The following further information is given.

(a) Darius Co has had its interest in Xerxes Inc since the incorporation of the company.

(b) Depreciation is 8% per annum on cost.

(c) There have been no loan repayments or movements in non-current assets during the year. The opening inventory of Xerxes Inc was €120. Assume that inventory turnover times are very short.

(d) Exchange rates: €4 to $1 when Xerxes Inc was incorporated
€2.5 to $1 when Xerxes Inc acquired its non-current assets
€2 to $1 on 31 December 20X8
€1.6 to $1 average rate of exchange year ending 31 December 20X9
€1 to $1 on 31 December 20X9.

Required

Prepare the summarised consolidated financial statements of Darius Co. **(25 marks)**

Darius Co

Step 1   The statement of financial position of Xerxes Inc at 31 December 20X9, other than share capital and retained earnings, should be translated at €1 = $1.

SUMMARISED STATEMENT OF FINANCIAL POSITION AT 31 DECEMBER 20X9

	$	$
Non-current assets (carrying amount)		300
Current assets		
Inventories	200	
Receivables	100	
		300
		600
Non-current liabilities		110
Current liabilities		110

∴ Equity = 600 – 110 – 110 = $380

Since Darius Co acquired the whole of the issued share capital on incorporation, the post-acquisition retained earnings including exchange differences will be the value of shareholders' funds arrived at above, less the original cost to Darius Co of $25. Post-acquisition retained earnings = $380 – $25 = $355.

SUMMARISED CONSOLIDATED STATEMENT OF FINANCIAL POSITION AS AT 31 DECEMBER 20X9

		$	$
Assets			
Non-current assets	$(350 + 300)		650
Current assets			
Inventories	$(225 + 200)	425	
Receivables	$(150 + 100)	250	
			675
			1,325
Equity and liabilities			
Equity			
Ordinary $1 shares (Darius only)			300
Retained earnings	$(300 + 355)		655
			955
Non-current liabilities: loans	$(50 + 110)		160
Current liabilities	$(100 + 110)		210
			1,325

Note. It is quite unnecessary to know the amount of the exchange differences when preparing the consolidated statement of financial position.

Step 2   The income statement should be translated at average rate (€1.6 = $1).

SUMMARISED STATEMENT OF COMPREHENSIVE INCOME OF XERXES INC
FOR THE YEAR ENDED 31 DECEMBER 20X9

	$
Profit before tax	100
Tax	50
Profit after tax, retained	50

Step 3   The equity interest at the beginning of the year can be found as follows.

	€
Equity value at 31 December 20X9	380
Retained profit for year	80
Equity value at 31 December 20X8	300
Translated at €2 = $1, this gives	$150

Step 4   The exchange difference can now be calculated.

	$
Equity interest at 31 December 20X9 (step 1)	380
Equity interest at 1 January 20X9 (step 3)	150
	230
Less retained profit (step 2)	50
Exchange gain	180

SUMMARISED CONSOLIDATED STATEMENT OF COMPREHENSIVE INCOME
FOR THE YEAR ENDED 31 DECEMBER 20X9

		$
Profit before tax	$(200 + 100)	300
Tax	$(100 + 50)	150
Profit after tax, retained	$(100 + 50)	150
Other comprehensive income		
Exchange gains		
Total comprehensive income		

CONSOLIDATED STATEMENT OF MOVEMENTS ON RESERVES
FOR THE YEAR ENDED 31 DECEMBER 20X9

	$
Consolidated reserves at 31 December 20X8	325
Total comprehensive income	330
Consolidated reserves at 31 December 20X9	655

(*Note*. The post-acquisition reserves of Xerxes Inc at the beginning of the year must have been $150 – $25 = $125 and the reserves of Darius Co must have been $300 – $100 = $200. The consolidated reserves must therefore have been $325.)

Part D

Interpretation of financial statements

Interpretation of financial
statements

Statement of cash flows

Unit topic list

1   Statement of cash flows
2   Preparing a statement of cash flows
3   Interpretation of statements of cash flows

Assessment criteria

3   **Financial statement presentation – the information that should be shown and how it should be presented**

3.11   Understand the information to be presented in the statement of cash flows – operating activities, investing activities, financing activities

3.12   Understand that there are two methods of reporting cash flows from operating activities – indirect and direct methods

3.13   Understand and apply the treatment and presentation of foreign currency cash flows, interest and dividends, income tax and non-cash transactions in a statement of cash flows

4   **Understand and apply IFRS for SMEs in the preparation of their financial statements**

4.2   Preparation of statements of cash flow using direct and indirect methods; also interpretation of these statements per section 7 of the IFRS for SMEs

1 Statement of cash flows

A statement of cash flows is a useful addition to a company's financial statements as a measure of performance.

1.1 Introduction

It has been argued that 'profit' does not always give a useful or meaningful picture of a company's operations. Readers of a company's financial statements might even be **misled by a reported profit figure**.

(a) Owners might believe that if a company makes a profit after tax, of say, $100,000 then this is the amount which it could afford to **pay as a dividend**. Unless the company has **sufficient cash** available to stay in business and also to pay a dividend, the owners' expectations would be wrong.

(b) Employees might believe that if a company makes profits, it can afford to **pay higher wages** next year. This opinion may not be correct: the ability to pay wages depends on the **availability of cash**.

(c) Survival of a business entity depends not so much on profits as on its **ability to pay its debts when they fall due**. Such payments might include 'revenue' items such as material purchases, wages, interest and taxation etc, but also capital payments for new non-current assets and the repayment of loan capital when this falls due (for example on the redemption of debentures).

From these examples, it may be apparent that a company's performance and prospects depend not so much on the 'profits' earned in a period, but more realistically on liquidity or **cash flows**.

1.2 Funds flow and cash flow

Some countries, either currently or in the past, have required the disclosure of additional statements based on **funds flow** rather than cash flow. However, the definition of 'funds' can be very vague and such statements often simply require a rearrangement of figures already provided in the statement of financial position and statement of comprehensive income. By contrast, a statement of cash flows is unambiguous and provides information which is additional to that provided in the rest of the accounts. It also lends itself to organisation by activity and not by classification in the statement of financial position.

Statements of cash flows are given as an **additional statement**, supplementing the statement of financial position, statement of comprehensive income and related notes. The group aspects of statements of cash flows (and certain complex matters) have been excluded as they are beyond the scope of your syllabus.

1.3 Objective of a statement of cash flows

The aim of *IFRS for SMEs* is to provide information to users of financial statements about the entity's **ability to generate cash and cash equivalents**, as well as indicating the cash needs of the entity. The statement of cash flows provides *historical* information about cash and cash equivalents, classifying cash flows between operating, investing and financing activities.

1.4 Scope

A statement of cash flows should be presented as an **integral part** of an entity's financial statements. All types of entity can provide useful information about cash flows as the need for cash is universal, whatever the nature of their revenue-producing activities. Therefore **all entities are required by the standard to produce a statement of cash flows**.

1.5 Benefits of cash flow information

The use of statements of cash flows is very much **in conjunction** with the rest of the financial statements. Users can gain further appreciation of the change in net assets, of the entity's financial position (liquidity and solvency) and the entity's ability to adapt to changing circumstances by affecting the amount and timing of cash flows. Statements of cash flows **enhance comparability** as they are not affected by differing accounting policies used for the same type of transactions or events.

Cash flow information of a historical nature can be used as an indicator of the amount, timing and certainty of future cash flows. Past forecast cash flow information can be **checked for accuracy** as actual figures emerge. The relationship between profit and cash flows can be analysed as can changes in prices over time.

1.6 Definitions

Key terms

> - **Cash** comprises cash on hand and demand deposits.
>
> - **Cash equivalents** are short-term, highly liquid investments that are readily convertible to known amounts of cash and which are subject to an insignificant risk of changes in value.
>
> - **Cash flows** are inflows and outflows of cash and cash equivalents.
>
> - **Operating activities** are the principal revenue-producing activities of the entity and other activities that are not investing or financing activities.
>
> - **Investing activities** are the acquisition and disposal of non-current assets and other investments not included in cash equivalents.
>
> - **Financing activities** are activities that result in changes in the size and composition of the equity capital and borrowings of the entity.

1.7 Cash and cash equivalents

The standard expands on the definition of cash equivalents: they are not held for investment or other long-term purposes, but rather to meet short-term cash commitments. To fulfil the above definition, an investment's **maturity date should normally be within three months from its acquisition date**. It would usually be the case then that equity investments (ie shares in other companies) are *not* cash equivalents. An exception would be where preferred shares were acquired with a very close maturity date.

Loans and other borrowings from banks are classified as investing activities. In some countries, however, **bank overdrafts** are repayable on demand and are treated as part of an entity's total cash management system. In these circumstances an overdrawn balance will be included in cash and cash equivalents. Such banking arrangements are characterised by a balance which fluctuates between overdrawn and credit.

Movements between different types of cash and cash equivalent are not included in cash flows. The investment of surplus cash in cash equivalents is part of cash management, not part of operating, investing or financing activities.

1.8 Presentation of a statement of cash flows

The IFRS requires statements of cash flows to report cash flows during the period classified by **operating, investing and financing activities.**

The manner of presentation of cash flows between operating, investing and financing activities **depends on the nature of the entity**. By classifying cash flows between different activities in this way users can see the impact on cash and cash equivalents of each one, and their relationships with each other. We can look at each in more detail.

1.8.1 Operating activities

This is perhaps the key part of the statement of cash flows because it shows whether, and to what extent, companies can **generate cash from their operations**. It is these operating cash flows which must, in the end pay for all cash outflows relating to other activities, ie paying loan interest, dividends and so on.

Most of the components of cash flows from operating activities will be those items which **determine the net profit or loss of the entity**, ie they relate to the main revenue-producing activities of the entity. The standard gives the following as examples of cash flows from operating activities.

(a) Cash receipts from the sale of goods and the rendering of services
(b) Cash receipts from royalties, fees, commissions and other revenue
(c) Cash payments to suppliers for goods and services
(d) Cash payments to and on behalf of employees

Certain items may be included in the net profit or loss for the period which do *not* relate to operational cash flows, for example the profit or loss on the sale of a piece of plant will be included in net profit or loss, but the cash flows will be classed as **investing**.

1.8.2 Investing activities

The cash flows classified under this heading show the extent of new investment in **assets which will generate future profit and cash flows**. The standard gives the following examples of cash flows arising from investing activities.

(a) Cash payments to acquire property, plant and equipment, intangibles and other non-current assets, including those relating to capitalised development costs and self-constructed property, plant and equipment
(b) Cash receipts from sales of property, plant and equipment, intangibles and other non-current assets
(c) Cash payments to acquire shares or debentures of other entities
(d) Cash receipts from sales of shares or debentures of other entities
(e) Cash advances and loans made to other parties
(f) Cash receipts from the repayment of advances and loans made to other parties

1.8.3 Financing activities

This section of the statement of cash flows shows the share of cash which the entity's capital providers have claimed during the period. This is an indicator of **likely future interest and dividend payments**. The standard gives the following examples of cash flows which might arise under this heading.

(a) Cash proceeds from issuing shares
(b) Cash payments to owners to acquire or redeem the entity's shares
(c) Cash proceeds from issuing debentures, loans, notes, bonds, mortgages and other short or long-term borrowings
(d) Principal repayments of amounts borrowed under finance leases

Item (d) needs more explanation. Where the reporting entity uses an asset held under a finance lease, the amounts to go in the statement of cash flows as **financing activities** are repayments of the **principal (capital)** rather than the **interest**. The interest paid will be shown under **operating activities**.

1.9 Example: finance lease rental

The notes to the financial statements of Hayley Co show the following in respect of obligations under finance leases.

Year ended 30 June	20X5 $'000	20X4 $'000
Amounts payable within one year	12	8
Within two to five years	110	66
	122	74
Less finance charges allocated to future periods	(14)	(8)
	108	66

Additions to tangible non-current assets acquired under finance leases were shown in the non-current asset note at $56,000.

Required

Calculate the capital repayment to be shown in the statement of cash flows of Hayley Co for the year to 30 June 20X5.

Solution

OBLIGATIONS UNDER FINANCE LEASES

	$'000		$'000
Capital repayment (bal fig)	14	Bal 1.7.X4	66
Bal 30.6.X5	108	Additions	56
	122		122

1.10 Reporting cash flows from operating activities

The standard offers a choice of method for this part of the statement of cash flows.

(a) **Direct method:** disclose major classes of gross cash receipts and gross cash payments

(b) **Indirect method**: net profit or loss is adjusted for the effects of transactions of a non-cash nature, any deferrals or accruals of past or future operating cash receipts or payments, and items of income or expense associated with investing or financing cash flows

1.10.1 Using the direct method

There are different ways in which the **information about gross cash receipts and payments** can be obtained. The most obvious way is simply to extract the information from the accounting records. This may be a laborious task, however, and the indirect method below may be easier. The example and question above used the direct method.

1.10.2 Using the indirect method

This method is undoubtedly **easier** from the point of view of the preparer of the statement of cash flows. The net profit or loss for the period is adjusted for the following.

(a) Changes during the period in inventories, operating receivables and payables

(b) Non-cash items, eg depreciation, provisions, profits/losses on the sales of assets

(c) Other items, the cash flows from which should be classified under investing or financing activities.

A **proforma** of such a calculation is as follows and this method may be more common in the exam.

	$
Cash flows from operating activities	
Profit before taxation	X
Adjustments for:	
Depreciation	X
Foreign exchange loss	X
Investment income	(X)
Interest expense	X
	X
Increase in trade and other receivables	(X)
Decrease in inventories	X
Decrease in trade payables	(X)
Cash generated from operations	X
Interest paid	(X)
Income taxes paid	(X)
Net cash from operating activities	X

It is important to understand why **certain items are added and others subtracted**. Note the following points.

(a) Depreciation is not a cash expense, but is deducted in arriving at profit. It makes sense, therefore, to eliminate it by adding it back.

(b) By the same logic, a loss on a disposal of a non-current asset (arising through underprovision of depreciation) needs to be added back and a profit deducted.

(c) An increase in inventories means less cash – you have spent cash on buying inventory.

(d) An increase in receivables means the company's debtors have not paid as much, and therefore there is less cash.

(e) If we pay off payables, causing the figure to decrease, again we have less cash.

1.10.3 Indirect versus direct

The direct method is encouraged where the necessary information is not too costly to obtain, but the IFRS does not require it. In practice the indirect method is more commonly used, since it is quicker and easier.

1.11 Interest and dividends

Cash flows from interest and dividends received and paid should each be **disclosed separately**. Each should be classified in a consistent manner from period to period as either operating, investing or financing activities.

Dividends paid by the entity can be classified in **one of two ways**.

(a) As a **financing cash flow**, showing the cost of obtaining financial resources.

(b) As a component of **cash flows from operating activities** so that users can assess the entity's ability to pay dividends out of operating cash flows.

1.12 Taxes on income

Cash flows arising from taxes on income should be **separately disclosed** and should be classified as cash flows from operating activities *unless* they can be specifically identified with financing and investing activities.

Taxation cash flows are often **difficult to match** to the originating underlying transaction, so most of the time all tax cash flows are classified as arising from operating activities.

1.13 Components of cash and cash equivalents

The components of cash and cash equivalents should be disclosed and a **reconciliation** should be presented, showing the amounts in the statement of cash flows reconciled with the equivalent items reported in the statement of financial position.

1.14 Other disclosures

All entities should disclose, together with a **commentary by management**, any other information likely to be of importance, for example:

(a) Restrictions on the use of or access to any part of cash equivalents

(b) The amount of undrawn borrowing facilities which are available

(c) Cash flows which increased operating capacity compared to cash flows which merely maintained operating capacity

(d) Cash flows arising from each reported industry and geographical segment

1.15 Example of a statement of cash flows

In the next section we will look at the procedures for preparing a statement of cash flows. First, look at this **example**.

1.15.1 Direct method

STATEMENT OF CASH FLOWS (DIRECT METHOD)
YEAR ENDED 31 DECEMBER 20X7

	$m	$m
Cash flows from operating activities		
Cash receipts from customers	30,330	
Cash paid to suppliers and employees	(27,600)	
Cash generated from operations	2,730	
Interest paid	(270)	
Income taxes paid	(900)	
Net cash from operating activities		1,560
Cash flows from investing activities		
Purchase of property, plant and equipment	(900)	
Proceeds from sale of equipment	20	
Interest received	200	
Dividends received	200	
Net cash used in investing activities		(480)
Cash flows from financing activities		
Proceeds from issue of share capital	250	
Proceeds from long-term borrowings	250	
Dividends paid*	(1,290)	
Net cash used in financing activities		(790)
Net increase in cash and cash equivalents		290
Cash and cash equivalents at beginning of period (Note)		120
Cash and cash equivalents at end of period (Note)		410

* This could also be shown as an operating cash flow

1.15.2 Indirect method

STATEMENT OF CASH FLOWS (INDIRECT METHOD)
YEAR ENDED 31 DECEMBER 20X7

	$m	$m
Cash flows from operating activities		
Profit before taxation	3,570	
Adjustments for:		
Depreciation	450	
Investment income	(500)	
Interest expense	400	
	3,920	
Increase in trade and other receivables	(500)	
Decrease in inventories	1,050	
Decrease in trade payables	(1,740)	
Cash generated from operations	2,730	
Interest paid	(270)	
Income taxes paid	(900)	
Net cash from operating activities		1,560
Cash flows from investing activities		
Purchase of property, plant and equipment	(900)	
Proceeds from sale of equipment	20	
Interest received	200	
Dividends received	200	
Net cash used in investing activities		(480)

	$m	$m
Cash flows from financing activities		
Proceeds from issue of share capital	250	
Proceeds from long-term borrowings	250	
Dividends paid*	(1,290)	
Net cash used in financing activities		(790)
Net increase in cash and cash equivalents		290
Cash and cash equivalents at beginning of period		120
Cash and cash equivalents at end of period		410

* This could also be shown as an operating cash flow

2 Preparing a statement of cash flows

You must be able to prepare a statement of cash flows by both the indirect and the direct methods.

2.1 Introduction

In essence, preparing a statement of cash flows is very straightforward. You should therefore simply learn the format and apply the steps noted in the example below. Note that the following items are treated in a way that might seem confusing, but the treatment is logical if you **think in terms of cash**.

(a)   **Increase in inventory** is treated as **negative** (in brackets). This is because it represents a cash **outflow**; cash is being spent on inventory.

(b)   An **increase in receivables** would be treated as **negative** for the same reasons; more receivables means less cash.

(c)   By contrast an **increase in payables is positive** because cash is being retained and not used to settle accounts payable. There is therefore more of it.

2.2 Example: preparation of a statement of cash flows

Kane Co's statement of comprehensive income for the year ended 31 December 20X2 and statements of financial position at 31 December 20X1 and 31 December 20X2 were as follows.

KANE CO
STATEMENT OF COMPREHENSIVE INCOME FOR THE YEAR ENDED 31 DECEMBER 20X2

	$'000	$'000
Sales		720
Raw materials consumed	70	
Staff costs	94	
Depreciation	118	
Loss on disposal of non-current asset	18	
		300
Operating profit		420
Interest payable		28
Profit before tax		392
Taxation		124
Profit for the year		268

KANE CO
STATEMENTS OF FINANCIAL POSITION AS AT 31 DECEMBER

	20X2 $'000	20X1 $'000
Non-current assets		
Cost	1,596	1,560
Depreciation	(318)	(224)
	1,278	1,336
Current assets		
Inventory	24	20
Trade receivables	76	58
Bank	48	56
	148	134
Total assets	1,426	1,470
Equity and liabilities		
Equity		
Share capital	360	340
Share premium	36	24
Retained earnings	716	514
	1,112	878
Non-current liabilities		
Long-term loans	200	500
Current liabilities		
Trade payables	12	6
Taxation	102	86
	114	92
Total equity and liabilities	1,426	1,470

Dividends paid were $66,000

During the year, the company paid $90,000 for a new piece of machinery.

Required

Prepare a statement of cash flows for Kane Co for the year ended 31 December 20X2 in accordance with the requirements of the IFRS, using the indirect method.

Solution

Step 1 **Set out the proforma statement of cash flows** with the headings required by the IFRS. You should leave plenty of space. Ideally, use three or more sheets of paper, one for the main statement, one for the notes and one for your workings. It is obviously essential to know the formats very well.

Step 2 Begin with the **cash flows from operating activities** as far as possible. When preparing the statement from statements of financial position, you will usually have to calculate such items as depreciation, loss on sale of non-current assets, profit for the year and tax paid (see Step 4). Note that you may not be given the tax charge in the statement of comprehensive income. You will then have to assume that the tax paid in the year is last year's year-end provision and calculate the charge as the balancing figure.

Step 3 Calculate the cash flow figures for **purchase or sale of non-current assets, issue of shares and repayment of loans** if these are not already given to you (as they may be).

Step 4 If you are not given the profit figure, open up a **working for profit or loss**. Using the opening and closing balances of retained earnings, the taxation charge and dividends paid and proposed, you will be able to calculate profit for the year as the balancing figure to put in the cash flows from operating activities section.

Step 5 You will now be able to **complete the statement** by slotting in the figures given or calculated.

KANE CO
STATEMENT OF CASH FLOWS FOR THE YEAR ENDED 31 DECEMBER 20X2

	$'000	$'000
Cash flows from operating activities		
Profit before tax	392	
Depreciation charges	118	
Loss on sale of tangible non-current assets	18	
Interest expense	28	
Increase in inventories	(4)	
Increase in receivables	(18)	
Increase in payables	6	
Cash generated from operations	540	
Interest paid	(28)	
Dividends paid	(66)	
Tax paid (86 + 124 – 102)	(108)	
Net cash from operating activities		338
Cash flows from investing activities		
Payments to acquire tangible non-current assets	(90)	
Receipts from sales of tangible non-current assets (W)	12	
Net cash used in investing activities		(78)
Cash flows from financing activities		
Issues of share capital (360 + 36 – 340 – 24)	32	
Long-term loans repaid (500 – 200)	(300)	
Net cash used in financing activities		(268)
Decrease in cash and cash equivalents		(8)
Cash and cash equivalents at 1.1.X2		56
Cash and cash equivalents at 31.12.X2		48

Working: non-current asset disposals

COST

	$'000		$'000
At 1.1.X2	1,560	At 31.12.X2	1,596
Purchases	90	Disposals (balance)	54
	1,650		1,650

ACCUMULATED DEPRECIATION

	$'000		$'000
At 31.12.X2	318	At 1.1.X2	224
Depreciation on disposals		Charge for year	118
(balance)	24		
	342		342

	$'000
Carrying amount of disposals	30
Net loss reported	(18)
Proceeds of disposals	12

3 Interpretation of statements of cash flows

A statement of cash flows was introduced on the basis that it would provide better, more comprehensive and more useful information than what was already shown in the financial statements.

3.1 Introduction

So what kind of information does the statement of cash flows, along with its notes, provide?

Some of the main areas where a statement of cash flows should provide information not found elsewhere in the financial statements are as follows.

(a) The **relationships between profit and cash** can be seen clearly and analysed accordingly.

(b) **Cash equivalents** are highlighted, giving a better picture of the liquidity of the company.

(c) **Financing inflows and outflows must be shown, rather than simply passed through reserves**.

One of the most important things to realise at this point is that it is wrong to try to assess the health or predict the death of a reporting entity solely on the basis of a single indicator. When analysing cash flow data, the **comparison should not just be between cash flows and profit, but also between cash flows over a period of time** (say three to five years).

Cash is not synonymous with profit on an annual basis, but you should also remember that the 'behaviour' of profit and cash flows will be very different. **Profit is smoothed out** through accruals, prepayments, provisions and other accounting conventions. This does not apply to cash, so the **cash flow figures** are likely to be **'lumpy'** in comparison. You must distinguish between this 'lumpiness' and the trends which will appear over time.

The **relationship between profit and cash flows will vary constantly**. Note that healthy companies do not always have reported profits exceeding operating cash flows. Similarly, unhealthy companies can have operating cash flows well in excess of reported profit. The value of comparing them is in determining the extent to which earned profits are being converted into the necessary cash flows.

Profit is not as important as the extent to which a company can **convert its profits into cash on a continuing basis.** This process should be judged over a period longer than one year. The cash flows should be compared with profits over the same periods to decide how successfully the reporting entity has converted earnings into cash.

Cash flow figures should also be considered in terms of their specific relationships with each other over time. A form of **'cash flow gearing'** can be determined by comparing operating cash flows and financing flows, particularly borrowing, to establish the extent of dependence of the reporting entity on external funding.

Other relationships can be examined.

(a) Operating cash flows and investment flows can be related to match cash recovery from investment to investment.

(b) Investment can be compared to distribution to indicate the proportion of total cash outflow designated specifically to investor return and reinvestment.

(c) A comparison of tax outflow to operating cash flow minus investment flow will establish a 'cash basis tax rate'.

The 'ratios' mentioned above can be monitored **inter- and intra-firm** and the analyses can be undertaken in monetary, general price-level adjusted, or percentage terms.

3.2 The advantages of cash flow accounting

The advantages of cash flow accounting are as follows.

(a) Survival in business depends on the **ability to generate** cash. Cash flow accounting directs attention towards this critical issue.

(b) Cash flow is **more comprehensive** than 'profit' which is dependent on accounting conventions and concepts.

(c) **Creditors** (long and short-term) are more interested in an entity's ability to repay them than in its profitability. Whereas 'profits' might indicate that cash is likely to be available, cash flow accounting is more direct with its message.

(d) Cash flow reporting provides a better means of **comparing the results** of different companies than traditional profit reporting.

(e) Cash flow reporting **satisfies the needs of all users** better.

    (i) For **management**, it provides the sort of information on which decisions should be taken (in management accounting, 'relevant costs' to a decision are future cash flows); traditional profit accounting does not help with decision-making.

(ii)   For **shareholders and auditors**, cash flow accounting can provide a satisfactory basis for stewardship accounting.

(iii)   As described previously, the information needs of **creditors and employees** will be better served by cash flow accounting.

(f)   Cash flow forecasts are **easier to prepare**, as well as more useful, than profit forecasts.

(g)   They can in some respects be **audited more easily** than accounts based on the accruals concept.

(h)   The accruals concept is confusing, and cash flows are **more easily understood**.

(i)   Cash flow accounting should be both retrospective, and also include a forecast for the future. This is of **great information value** to all users of accounting information.

(j)   **Forecasts** can subsequently be **monitored** by the publication of variance statements which compare actual cash flows against the forecast.

 Activity

Can you think of some possible disadvantages of cash flow accounting?

 Answer

The main disadvantages of cash accounting are essentially the advantages of accruals accounting (proper matching of related items). There is also the practical problem that few businesses keep historical cash flow information in the form needed to prepare a historical statement of cash flows and so extra record keeping is likely to be necessary.

Unit Roundup

- **Statements of cash flows** are a useful addition to the financial statements of companies because it is recognised that accounting profit is not the only indicator of a company's performance.

- Statements of cash flows concentrate on the sources and uses of cash and are a useful indicator of a company's **liquidity and solvency**.

- You need to be aware of the **format** of the statement as laid out in the *IFRS for SMEs*; setting out the format is an essential first stage in preparing the statement, so this format must be learnt.

- Remember the **step-by-step preparation procedure** and use it for all the questions you practise.

- Note that you may be expected to **analyse** or **interpret** a statement of cash flows.

Quick quiz

1   What is the aim of a statement of cash flows?

2   The standard headings in the *IFRS for SMEs* are:

- O................. a.................

- I.................. a...................

- F................... a.....................

- Net.................. in C..................... and ....

3   Cash equivalents are current asset investments which will mature or can be redeemed within three months of the year end.

   True   ☐

   False   ☐

4   Why are you more likely to encounter the indirect method as opposed to the direct method?

5   List five advantages of cash flow accounting.

1   To indicate an entity's ability to generate cash and cash equivalents.

2   • Operating activities
       • Investing activities
       • Financing activities
       • Net increase (decrease) in cash and cash equivalents

3   False. See the definition in paragraph 1.6 if you are not sure about this.

4   The indirect method utilises figures which appear in the financial statements. The figures required for the direct method may not be readily available.

5   See paragraph 3.2

Now try the question below

Emma Co   45 mins

Set out below are the financial statements of Emma Co. You are the financial controller, faced with the task of preparing the statement of cash flows for the year.

EMMA CO
STATEMENT OF COMPREHENSIVE INCOME FOR THE YEAR ENDED 31 DECEMBER 20X2

	$'000
Revenue	2,553
Cost of sales	(1,814)
Gross profit	739
Other income: interest received	25
Distribution costs	(125)
Administrative expenses	(264)
Finance costs	(75)
Profit before tax	300
Income tax expense	(140)
Profit for the year	160

EMMA CO
STATEMENTS OF FINANCIAL POSITION AS AT 31 DECEMBER

	20X2	20X1
	$'000	$'000
Assets		
Non-current assets		
Property, plant and equipment	380	305
Intangible assets	250	200
Investments	–	25
Current assets		
Inventories	150	102
Receivables	390	315
Short-term investments	50	–
Cash in hand	2	1
Total assets	1,222	948
Equity and liabilities		
Equity		
Share capital ($1 ordinary shares)	200	150
Share premium account	160	150
Retained earnings	260	180
Non-current liabilities		
Long-term loan	170	50

Current liabilities			
Trade payables		127	119
Bank overdraft		185	189
Taxation		120	110
Total equity and liabilities		1,222	948

The following information is available.

(a)   The proceeds of the sale of non-current asset investments amounted to $30,000.

(b)   Fixtures and fittings, with an original cost of $85,000 and a carrying amount of $45,000, were sold for $32,000 during the year.

(c)   The following information relates to property, plant and equipment.

	31.12.20X2	31.12.20X1
	$'000	$'000
Cost	720	595
Accumulated depreciation	340	290
Carrying amount	380	305

(d)   50,000 $1 ordinary shares were issued during the year at a premium of 20c per share.

(e)   The short-term investments are highly liquid and are close to maturity.

(f)   Dividends of $80,000 were paid during the year.

Required

Prepare a statement of cash flows for the year to 31 December 20X2 using the format laid out in the IFRS for SMEs.   **(25 marks)**

Answer

Emma Co

EMMA CO
STATEMENT OF CASH FLOWS FOR THE YEAR ENDED 31 DECEMBER 20X2

	$'000	$'000
Cash flows from operating activities		
Profit before tax	300	
Depreciation charge (W1)	90	
Loss on sale of property, plant and equipment (45 – 32)	13	
Profit on sale of non-current asset investments	(5)	
Interest expense (net)	50	
(Increase)/decrease in inventories	(48)	
(Increase)/decrease in receivables	(75)	
Increase/(decrease) in payables	8	
	333	
Interest paid	(75)	
Dividends paid	(80)	
Tax paid (110 + 140 – 120)	(130)	
Net cash from operating activities		48
Cash flows from investing activities		
Payments to acquire property, plant and equipment (W2)	(210)	
Payments to acquire intangible non-current assets	(50)	
Receipts from sales of property, plant and equipment	32	
Receipts from sale of non-current asset investments	30	
Interest received	25	
Net cash used in investing activities		(173)
Cash flows from financing activities		
Issue of share capital	60	
Long-term loan	120	
Net cash from financing activities		180
Increase in cash and cash equivalents		55
Cash and cash equivalents at 1.1.X2		(188)
Cash and cash equivalents at 31.12.X2		(133)

Workings

1 *Depreciation charge*

	$'000	$'000
Depreciation at 31 December 20X2		340
Depreciation 31 December 20X1	290	
Depreciation on assets sold (85 – 45)	40	
		250
Charge for the year		90

2 Purchase of property, plant and equipment (cost)

	$'000		$'000
1.1.X2 Balance b/d	595	Disposals	85
Purchases (bal fig)	210	31.12.X2 Balance c/d	720
	805		805

Note. In the exam you may have a number of issues to deal with in the statement of cash flows. Examples are:

- Share capital issues. The proceeds will be split between share capital and share premium.

- Bonus issues. These do *not* involve cash.

- Movement on deferred tax. This must be taken into account in calculating tax paid.

- Finance leases. Assets acquired under finance leases must be adjusted for in non-current asset calculations and the amount paid under the finance lease must appear as a cash flow.

21

Interpretation of financial statements

Unit topic list

1 The broad categories of ratios
2 Profitability and return on capital
3 Liquidity, gearing/leverage and working capital
4 Presentation of financial performance
5 Limitations of financial statements
6 Accounting policies and the limitations of ratio analysis

Assessment criteria

5 **Analyse and evaluate financial statements**

5.1 Calculation of a range of ratios over time, between different businesses and against bench marks

5.2 Be able to communicate the limitations of ratio analysis when writing a report to users

5.3 Communicate findings and conclusions in a professional written manner

1 The broad categories of ratios

Your syllabus requires you to calculate ratios and to communicate your findings about a business.

If you were to look at a statement of financial position or statement of comprehensive income, how would you decide whether the company was doing well or badly? Or whether it was financially strong or financially vulnerable? And what would you be looking at in the figures to help you to make your judgement?

Ratio analysis involves **comparing one figure against another** to produce a ratio, and assessing whether the ratio indicates a weakness or strength in the company's affairs.

1.1 The broad categories of ratios

Broadly speaking, basic ratios can be grouped into five categories.

- Profitability and return
- Long-term solvency and stability
- Short-term solvency and liquidity
- Efficiency (turnover ratios)
- Shareholders' investment ratios

Within each heading we will identify a number of standard measures or ratios that are normally calculated and generally accepted as meaningful indicators. One must stress however that each individual business must be considered separately, and a ratio that is meaningful for a manufacturing company may be completely meaningless for a financial institution. **Try not to be too mechanical** when working out ratios and constantly think about what you are trying to achieve.

The key to obtaining meaningful information from ratio analysis is **comparison**. This may involve comparing ratios over time within the same business to establish whether things are improving or declining, and comparing ratios between similar businesses to see whether the company you are analysing is better or worse than average within its specific business sector.

It must be stressed that ratio analysis on its own is not sufficient for interpreting company accounts, and that there are **other items of information** which should be looked at, for example:

(a) The content of any **accompanying commentary** on the accounts and other statements

(b) The age and nature of the **company's assets**

(c) **Current and future developments** in the company's markets, at home and overseas, recent acquisitions or disposals of a subsidiary by the company

(d) **Unusual** items separately disclosed in the statement of comprehensive income

(e) Any other **noticeable features** of the report and accounts, such as events after the end of the reporting period, contingent liabilities, a qualified auditors' report, the company's taxation position, and so on

1.2 Example: calculating ratios

To illustrate the calculation of ratios, the following **draft** statement of financial position and statement of comprehensive income figures will be used. We are using a separate statement of comprehensive income for this example as no items of other comprehensive income are involved.

FURLONG CO STATEMENT OF COMPREHENSIVE INCOME
FOR THE YEAR ENDED 31 DECEMBER 20X8

	Notes	20X8 $	20X7 $
Revenue	1	3,095,576	1,909,051
Operating profit	1	359,501	244,229
Interest	2	17,371	19,127
Profit before taxation		342,130	225,102
Income tax expense		74,200	31,272
Profit for the year		267,930	193,830

FURLONG CO STATEMENT OF FINANCIAL POSITION
AS AT 31 DECEMBER 20X8

	Notes	20X8 $	20X7 $
Assets			
Non-current assets			
Property, plant and equipment		802,180	656,071
Current assets			
Inventory		64,422	86,550
Receivables	3	1,002,701	853,441
Cash at bank and in hand		1,327	68,363
		1,068,450	1,008,354
Total assets		1,870,630	1,664,425
Equity and liabilities			
Equity			
Ordinary shares 10c each	5	210,000	210,000
Share premium account		48,178	48,178
Retained earnings		651,721	410,591
		909,899	668,769
Non-current liabilities			
10% loan stock 20X4/20Y0		100,000	100,000
Current liabilities	4	860,731	895,656
Total equity and liabilities		1,870,630	1,664,425

NOTES TO THE ACCOUNTS

		20X8 $	20X7 $
1	Sales revenue and profit		
	Sales revenue	3,095,576	1,909,051
	Cost of sales	2,402,609	1,441,950
	Gross profit	692,967	467,101
	Administration expenses	333,466	222,872
	Operating profit	359,501	244,229
	Depreciation charged	151,107	120,147
2	Interest		
	Payable on bank overdrafts and other loans	8,115	11,909
	Payable on loan stock	10,000	10,000
		18,115	21,909
	Receivable on short-term deposits	744	2,782
	Net payable	17,371	19,127
3	Receivables		
	Amounts falling due within one year		
	Trade receivables	905,679	807,712
	Prepayments and accrued income	97,022	45,729
		1,002,701	853,441

		20X8	20X7
		$	$
4	*Current liabilities*		
	Trade payables	627,018	545,340
	Accruals and deferred income	81,279	280,464
	Corporate taxes	108,000	37,200
	Other taxes	44,434	32,652
		860,731	895,656
5	*Called-up share capital*		
	Authorised ordinary shares of 10c each	1,000,000	1,000,000
	Issued and fully paid ordinary shares of 10c each	210,000	210,000
6	Dividends paid	20,000	–

2 Profitability and return on capital

Return on capital employed (ROCE) may be used by the shareholders or the Board to assess the performance of management.

In our example, the company made a profit in both 20X8 and 20X7, and there was an increase in profit between one year and the next:

(a) Of 52% before taxation
(b) Of 39% after taxation

Profit before taxation is generally thought to be a better figure to use than profit after taxation, because there might be unusual variations in the tax charge from year to year which would not affect the underlying profitability of the company's operations.

Another profit figure that should be calculated is PBIT, **profit before interest and tax**. This is the amount of profit which the company earned before having to pay interest to the providers of loan capital, such as loan notes and medium-term bank loans, which will be shown in the statement of financial position as non-current liabilities.

Formula to learn

Profit before interest and tax is therefore:

(a) the profit on ordinary activities before taxation; **plus**
(b) interest charges on loan capital.

Published accounts do not always give sufficient detail on interest payable to determine how much is interest on long-term finance. We will assume in our example that the whole of the interest payable ($18,115, note 2) relates to long-term finance.

PBIT in our example is therefore:

	20X8	20X7
	$	$
Profit on ordinary activities before tax	342,130	225,102
Interest payable	18,115	21,909
PBIT	360,245	247,011

This shows a 46% growth between 20X7 and 20X8.

2.1 Return on capital employed (ROCE)

It is impossible to assess profits or profit growth properly without relating them to the **amount of funds (capital) that were employed in making the profits**. The most important profitability ratio is therefore return on capital employed (ROCE), which states the profit as a percentage of the amount of capital employed.

ROCE = $\dfrac{\text{Profit before interest and taxation}}{\text{Total assets less current liabilites}} \times 100\%$

Capital employed = Shareholders' equity plus non-current liabilities
(*or* total assets less current liabilities)

The underlying principle is that we must **compare like with like**, and so if capital means share capital and reserves plus non-current liabilities and debt capital, profit must mean the profit earned by all this capital together. This is PBIT, since interest is the return for loan capital.

In our example, capital employed =   20X8 $1,870,630 – $860,731 = $1,009,899
20X7 $1,664,425 – $895,656 = $768,769

These total figures are the total assets less current liabilities figures for 20X8 and 20X7 in the statement of financial position.

	20X8	*20X7*
ROCE	$\dfrac{\$360,245}{\$1,009,899} = 35.7\%$	$\dfrac{\$247,011}{\$768,769} = 32\%$

What does a business's ROCE tell us? What should we be looking for? There are three comparisons that can be made.

(a)   The **change in ROCE from one year to the next** can be examined. In this example, there has been an increase in ROCE by about 4 percentage points from its 20X7 level.

(b)   The **ROCE being earned by other businesses**, if this information is available, can be compared with the ROCE of this company. Here the information is not available.

(c)   A comparison of the ROCE with **current market borrowing rates** may be made.

(i)   What would be the cost of extra borrowing to the company if it needed more loans, and is it earning a ROCE that suggests it could make profits to make such borrowing worthwhile?

(ii)   Is the company making a ROCE which suggests that it is getting value for money from its current borrowing?

(iii)   Companies are in a risk business and commercial borrowing rates are a good independent yardstick against which company performance can be judged.

In this example, if we suppose that current market interest rates, say, for medium-term borrowing from banks, are around 10%, then the company's actual ROCE of 36% in 20X8 would not seem low. On the contrary, it might seem high.

However, it is easier to spot a low ROCE than a high one, because there is always a chance that the company's non-current assets, especially property, are **undervalued** in its statement of financial position, and so the capital employed figure might be unrealistically low. If the company had earned a ROCE, not of 36%, but of, say only 6%, then its return would have been below current borrowing rates and so disappointingly low.

2.2 Return on equity (ROE)

Return on equity gives a more restricted view of capital than ROCE, but it is based on the same principles.

ROE = $\dfrac{\text{Profit after tax and preference dividend}}{\text{Equity shareholders funds}} \times 100\%$

In our example, ROE is calculated as follows.

	20X8	*20X7*
ROE	$\dfrac{\$267,930}{\$909,899} = 29.4\%$	$\dfrac{\$193,830}{\$668,769} = 29\%$

ROE is **not a widely-used ratio**, however, because there are more useful ratios that give an indication of the return to shareholders, such as earnings per share, dividend per share, dividend yield and earnings yield, which are described later.

2.3 Analysing profitability and return in more detail: the secondary ratios

We often sub-analyse ROCE, to find out more about why the ROCE is high or low, or better or worse than last year. There are two factors that contribute towards a return on capital employed, both related to sales revenue.

(a)   **Profit margin**. A company might make a high or low profit margin on its sales. For example, a company that makes a profit of 25c per $1 of sales is making a bigger return on its revenue than another company making a profit of only 10c per $1 of sales.

(b)   **Asset turnover**. Asset turnover is a measure of how well the assets of a business are being used to generate sales. For example, if two companies each have capital employed of $100,000 and Company A makes sales of $400,000 per annum whereas Company B makes sales of only $200,000 per annum, Company A is making a higher revenue from the same amount of assets (twice as much asset turnover as Company B) and this will help A to make a higher return on capital employed than B. Asset turnover is expressed as 'x times' so that assets generate x times their value in annual sales. Here, Company A's asset turnover is 4 times and B's is 2 times.

Profit margin and asset turnover together explain the ROCE and if the ROCE is the primary profitability ratio, these other two are the secondary ratios. The relationship between the three ratios can be shown mathematically.

Profit margin × Asset turnover = ROCE

$$\therefore \quad \frac{\text{PBIT}}{\text{Sales}} \times \frac{\text{Sales}}{\text{Capital employed}} = \frac{\text{PBIT}}{\text{Capital employed}}$$

In our example:

		Profit margin		Asset turnover		ROCE
(a)	20X8	$\dfrac{\$360,245}{\$3,095,576}$	×	$\dfrac{\$3,095,576}{\$1,009,899}$	=	$\dfrac{\$360,245}{\$1,009,899}$
		11.64%	×	3.06 times	=	35.6%

		Profit margin		Asset turnover		ROCE
(b)	20X7	$\dfrac{\$247,011}{\$1,909,051}$	×	$\dfrac{\$1,909,051}{\$768,769}$	=	$\dfrac{\$247,011}{\$768,769}$
		12.94%	×	2.48 times	=	32.1%

In this example, the company's improvement in ROCE between 20X7 and 20X8 is attributable to a higher asset turnover. Indeed the profit margin has fallen a little, but the higher asset turnover has more than compensated for this.

It is also worth commenting on the change in sales revenue from one year to the next. You may already have noticed that Furlong achieved sales growth of over 60% from $1.9 million to $3.1 million between 20X7 and 20X8. This is very strong growth, and this is certainly one of the most significant items in the statement of comprehensive income and statement of financial position.

2.3.1 A warning about comments on profit margin and asset turnover

It might be tempting to think that a high profit margin is good, and a low asset turnover means sluggish trading. In broad terms, this is so. But there is a trade-off between profit margin and asset turnover, and you cannot look at one without allowing for the other.

(a) A **high profit margin** means a high profit per $1 of sales, but if this also means that sales prices are high, there is a strong possibility that sales revenue will be depressed, and so asset turnover lower.

(b) A **high asset turnover** means that the company is generating a lot of sales, but to do this it might have to keep its prices down and so accept a low profit margin per $1 of sales.

Consider the following.

Company A		*Company B*	
Sales revenue	$1,000,000	Sales revenue	$4,000,000
Capital employed	$1,000,000	Capital employed	$1,000,000
PBIT	$200,000	PBIT	$200,000

These figures would give the following ratios.

ROCE $= \dfrac{\$200,000}{\$1,000,000} = 20\%$ ROCE $= \dfrac{\$200,000}{\$1,000,000} = 20\%$

Profit margin $= \dfrac{\$200,000}{\$1,000,000} = 20\%$ Profit margin $= \dfrac{\$200,000}{\$4,000,000} = 5\%$

Asset turnover $= \dfrac{\$1,000,000}{\$1,000,000} = 1$ Asset turnover $= \dfrac{\$4,000,000}{\$1,000,000} = 4$

The companies have the same ROCE, but it is arrived at in a very different fashion. Company A operates with a low asset turnover and a comparatively high profit margin whereas company B carries out much more business, but on a lower profit margin. Company A could be operating at the luxury end of the market, whilst company B is operating at the popular end of the market.

2.4 Gross profit margin, net profit margin and profit analysis

Depending on the format of the statement of comprehensive income, you may be able to calculate the gross profit margin as well as the net profit margin. **Looking at the two together** can be quite informative.

For example, suppose that a company has the following summarised statement of comprehensive income for two consecutive years.

	Year 1	Year 2
	$	$
Revenue	70,000	100,000
Cost of sales	42,000	55,000
Gross profit	28,000	45,000
Expenses	21,000	35,000
Net profit	7,000	10,000

Although the net profit margin is the same for both years at 10%, the gross profit margin is not.

In year 1 it is: $\dfrac{\$28,000}{\$70,000} = 40\%$

and in year 2 it is: $\dfrac{\$45,000}{\$100,000} = 45\%$

The improved gross profit margin has not led to an improvement in the net profit margin. This is because expenses as a percentage of sales have risen from 30% in year 1 to 35% in year 2.

3 Liquidity, gearing/leverage and working capital

Banks and other lenders will be interested in a company's gearing level.

3.1 Long-term solvency: debt and gearing ratios

Debt ratios are concerned with **how much the company owes in relation to its size**, whether it is getting into heavier debt or improving its situation, and whether its debt burden seems heavy or light.

(a) When a company is heavily in debt banks and other potential lenders may be unwilling to advance further funds.

(b) When a company is earning only a modest profit before interest and tax, and has a heavy debt burden, there will be very little profit left over for shareholders after the interest charges have been paid. And so if interest rates were to go up (on bank overdrafts and so on) or the company were to borrow even more, it might soon be incurring interest charges in excess of PBIT. This might eventually lead to the liquidation of the company.

These are two big reasons why companies should keep their debt burden under control. There are four ratios that are particularly worth looking at, the debt ratio, gearing ratio, interest cover and cash flow ratio.

3.2 Debt ratio

Formula to learn

The **debt ratio** is the ratio of a company's total debts to its total assets.

(a) Assets consist of non-current assets at their carrying value, plus current assets.

(b) Debts consist of all payables, whether they are due within one year or after more than one year.

You can ignore other non-current liabilities, such as deferred taxation.

There is no absolute guide to the maximum safe debt ratio, but as a very general guide, you might regard 50% as a safe limit to debt. In practice, many companies operate successfully with a higher debt ratio than this, but 50% is nonetheless a helpful benchmark. In addition, if the debt ratio is over 50% and getting worse, the company's debt position will be worth looking at more carefully.

In the case of Furlong the debt ratio is as follows.

	20X8	20X7
Total debts	$ (860,731 + 100,000)	$ (895,656 + 100,000)
Total assets	$1,870,630	$1,664,425
	= 51%	= 60%

In this case, the debt ratio is quite high, mainly because of the large amount of current liabilities. However, the debt ratio has fallen from 60% to 51% between 20X7 and 20X8, and so the company appears to be improving its debt position.

3.3 Gearing/leverage

Gearing or leverage is concerned with a company's **long-term capital structure**. We can think of a company as consisting of non-current assets and net current assets (ie working capital, which is current assets minus current liabilities). These assets must be financed by long-term capital of the company, which is one of two things.

(a) Issued share capital which can be divided into:

    (i) Ordinary shares plus other equity (eg reserves)

    (ii) Non-redeemable preference shares (unusual)

(b) Long-term debt including redeemable preference shares.

The **capital gearing ratio** is a measure of the proportion of a company's capital that is debt. It is measured as follows.

Formula to learn

$$\text{Gearing} = \frac{\text{Interest bearing debt}}{\text{Shareholers' equity} + \text{interest bearing debt}} \times 100\%$$

As with the debt ratio, there is **no absolute limit** to what a gearing ratio ought to be. A company with a gearing ratio of more than 50% is said to be high-geared (whereas low gearing means a gearing ratio of less than 50%). Many companies are high geared, but if a high geared company is becoming increasingly high geared, it is likely to have difficulty in the future when it wants to borrow even more, unless it can also boost its shareholders' capital, either with retained profits or by a new share issue.

Leverage is an alternative term for gearing; the words have the same meaning. Note that leverage (or gearing) can be looked at conversely, by calculating the proportion of total assets financed by equity, and which may be called the equity to assets ratio. It is calculated as follows.

Equity to assets ratio = $\dfrac{\text{Shareholders' equity}}{\text{Shareholders' equity} + \text{interest bearing debt}} \times 100\%$

or $\dfrac{\text{Shareholders' equity}}{\text{Total assets less current liabilities}}$

In the example of Furlong, we find that the company, although having a high debt ratio because of its current liabilities, has a low gearing ratio. It has no preference share capital and its only long-term debt is the 10% loan stock. The equity to assets ratio is therefore high.

		20X8	20X7
Gearing ratio	=	$\dfrac{\$100,000}{\$1,009,899}$	$\dfrac{\$100,000}{\$768,769}$
		= 10%	= 13%
Equity to assets ratio	=	$\dfrac{\$909,899}{\$1,009,899}$	$\dfrac{\$668,769}{\$768,769}$
		= 90%	= 87%

As you can see, the equity to assets ratio is the mirror image of gearing.

3.4 The implications of high or low gearing/leverage

We mentioned earlier that **gearing or leverage** is, amongst other things, an attempt to **quantify the degree of risk involved in holding equity shares in a company**, risk both in terms of the company's ability to remain in business and in terms of expected ordinary dividends from the company. The problem with a highly geared company is that by definition there is a lot of debt. Debt generally carries a fixed rate of interest (or fixed rate of dividend if in the form of preference shares), hence there is a given (and large) amount to be paid out from profits to holders of debt before arriving at a residue available for distribution to the holders of equity. The riskiness will perhaps become clearer with the aid of an example.

	Company A	Company B	Company C
	$'000	$'000	$'000
Ordinary shares	600	400	300
Retained earnings	300	300	300
	900	700	600
6% preference shares (redeemable)	–	–	100
10% loan stock	100	300	300
Capital employed	1,000	1,000	1,000
Gearing ratio	10%	30%	40%
Equity to assets ratio	90%	70%	60%

Now suppose that each company makes a profit before interest and tax of $50,000, and the rate of tax on company profits is 30%. Amounts available for distribution to equity shareholders will be as follows.

	Company A	Company B	Company C
	$'000	$'000	$'000
Profit before interest and tax	50	50	50
Interest/preference dividend	10	30	36
Taxable profit	40	20	14
Taxation at 30%	12	6	6
Profit for the period	28	14	8

If in the subsequent year profit before interest and tax falls to $40,000, the amounts available to ordinary shareholders will become as follows.

	Company A $'000	Company B $'000	Company C $'000
Profit before interest and tax	40	40	40
Interest/preference dividend	10	30	36
Taxable profit	30	10	4
Taxation at 30%	9	3	3
Profit for the period	21	7	1

Note the following.

Gearing ratio	10%	30%	40%
Equity to assets ratio	90%	70%	60%
Change in PBIT	−20%	−20%	−20%
Change in profit available for ord shareholders	−25%	−50%	−87.5%

The more highly geared the company, the greater the risk that little (if anything) will be available to distribute by way of dividend to the ordinary shareholders. The example clearly displays this fact in so far as the more highly geared the company, the greater the percentage change in profit available for ordinary shareholders for any given percentage change in profit before interest and tax. The relationship similarly holds when profits increase, and if PBIT had risen by 20% rather than fallen, you would find that once again the largest percentage change in profit available for ordinary shareholders (this means an increase) will be for the highly geared company. This means that there will be greater *volatility* of amounts available for ordinary shareholders, and presumably therefore greater volatility in dividends paid to those shareholders, where a company is highly geared. That is the risk: you may do extremely well or extremely badly without a particularly large movement in the PBIT of the company.

The risk of a company's ability to remain in business was referred to earlier. Gearing or leverage is relevant to this. A highly geared company has a large amount of interest to pay annually (assuming that the debt is external borrowing rather than preference shares). If those borrowings are **'secured'** in any way (and loan notes in particular are secured), then the **holders of the debt are perfectly entitled to force the company** to **realise assets to pay their interest** if funds are not available from other sources. Clearly the more highly geared a company the more likely this is to occur when and if profits fall.

3.5 Interest cover

The interest cover ratio shows whether a company is earning enough profits before interest and tax to pay its interest costs comfortably, or whether its interest costs are high in relation to the size of its profits, so that a fall in PBIT would then have a significant effect on profits available for ordinary shareholders.

Formula to learn

$$\text{Interest cover} = \frac{\text{Profit before interest and tax}}{\text{Interest charges}}$$

An interest cover of 2 times or less would be low, and should really exceed 3 times before the company's interest costs are to be considered within acceptable limits.

Returning first to the example of Companies A, B and C, the interest cover was as follows.

		Company A	Company B	Company C
(a)	When PBIT was $50,000 =	$\dfrac{\$50,000}{\$10,000}$	$\dfrac{\$50,000}{\$30,000}$	$\dfrac{\$50,000}{\$30,000}$
		5 times	1.67 times	1.67 times
(b)	When PBIT was $40,000 =	$\dfrac{\$40,000}{\$10,000}$	$\dfrac{\$40,000}{\$30,000}$	$\dfrac{\$40,000}{\$30,000}$
		4 times	1.33 times	1.33 times

Both B and C have a low interest cover, which is a warning to ordinary shareholders that their profits are highly vulnerable, in percentage terms, to even small changes in PBIT.

Activity

Returning to the example of Furlong in Paragraph 1.2, what is the company's interest cover?

Answer

Interest payments should be taken gross, from the note to the accounts, and not net of interest receipts as shown in the statement of comprehensive income.

	20X8	20X7
PBIT	360,245	247,011
Interest payable	18,115	21,909
	= 20 times	= 11 times

Furlong has more than sufficient interest cover. In view of the company's low gearing, this is not too surprising and so we finally obtain a picture of Furlong as a company that does not seem to have a debt problem, in spite of its high (although declining) debt ratio.

3.6 Cash flow ratio

The cash flow ratio is the ratio of a company's **net cash inflow to its total debts**.

(a)   **Net cash inflow** is the amount of cash which the company has coming into the business from its operations. A suitable figure for net cash inflow can be obtained from the statement of cash flows.

(b)   **Total debts** are short-term and long-term payables, including provisions. A distinction can be made between debts payable within one year and other debts and provisions.

Obviously, a company needs to be earning enough cash from operations to be able to meet its foreseeable debts and future commitments, and the cash flow ratio, and changes in the cash flow ratio from one year to the next provide a **useful indicator of a company's cash position**.

3.7 Short-term solvency and liquidity

Profitability is of course an important aspect of a company's performance and gearing or leverage is another. Neither, however, addresses directly the key issue of *liquidity*.

Key term

Liquidity is the amount of cash a company can put its hands on quickly to settle its debts (and possibly to meet other unforeseen demands for cash payments too).

Liquid funds consist of:

(a)   Cash

(b)   Short-term investments for which there is a ready market

(c)   Fixed-term deposits with a bank or other financial institution, for example, a six month high-interest deposit with a bank

(d)   Trade receivables (because they will pay what they owe within a reasonably short period of time)

In summary, **liquid assets are current asset items that will or could soon be converted into cash, and cash itself.** Two common definitions of liquid assets are:

- All current assets without exception
- All current assets with the exception of inventories

A company can obtain liquid assets from sources other than sales of goods and services, such as the issue of shares for cash, a new loan or the sale of non-current assets. But a company cannot rely on these at all times, and in general, obtaining liquid funds depends on making sales revenue and profits. Even so, profits do not always lead to increases in liquidity. This is mainly because funds generated from trading may be immediately invested in non-current assets or paid out as dividends.

The reason why a company needs liquid assets is so that it can meet its debts when they fall due. Payments are continually made for operating expenses and other costs, and so there is a **cash cycle** from trading activities of cash coming in from sales and cash going out for expenses.

3.8 The cash cycle

To help you to understand liquidity ratios, it is useful to begin with a brief explanation of the cash cycle. The cash cycle describes **the flow of cash out of a business and back into it again as a result of normal trading operations.**

Cash goes out to pay for supplies, wages and salaries and other expenses, although payments can be delayed by taking some credit. A business might hold inventory for a while and then sell it. Cash will come back into the business from the sales, although customers might delay payment by themselves taking some credit.

The main points about the cash cycle are as follows.

(a)   The timing of cash flows in and out of a business does not coincide with the time when sales and costs of sales occur. **Cash flows out can be postponed by taking credit. Cash flows in can be delayed by having receivables.**

(b)   **The time between making a purchase and making a sale also affects cash flows**. If inventories are held for a long time, the delay between the cash payment for inventory and cash receipts from selling it will also be a long one.

(c)   **Holding inventories and having receivables can therefore be seen as two reasons why cash receipts are delayed.** Another way of saying this is that if a company invests in working capital, its cash position will show a corresponding decrease.

(d)   Similarly, **taking credit from creditors can be seen as a reason why cash payments are delayed**. The company's liquidity position will worsen when it has to pay the suppliers, unless it can get more cash in from sales and receivables in the meantime.

The liquidity ratios and working capital turnover ratios are used to test a company's liquidity, length of cash cycle, and investment in working capital.

3.9 Liquidity ratios: current ratio and quick ratio

The 'standard' test of liquidity is the **current ratio**. It can be obtained from the statement of financial position.

$$\text{Current ratio} = \frac{\text{Current assets}}{\text{Current liabilities}}$$

The idea behind this is that a company should have enough current assets that give a promise of 'cash to come' to meet its future commitments to pay off its current liabilities. Obviously, a **ratio in excess of 1 should be expected**. Otherwise, there would be the prospect that the company might be unable to pay its debts on time. In practice, a ratio comfortably in excess of 1 should be expected, but what is 'comfortable' varies between different types of businesses.

Companies are not able to convert all their current assets into cash very quickly. In particular, some manufacturing companies might hold large quantities of raw material inventories, which must be used in production to create finished goods inventory. These might be warehoused for a long time, or sold on lengthy credit. In such businesses, where inventory turnover is slow, most inventories are not very 'liquid' assets, because the cash cycle is so long. For these reasons, we calculate an additional liquidity ratio, known as the quick ratio or acid test ratio.

The **quick ratio**, or **acid test ratio**, is calculated as follows.

Formula to learn

$$\text{Quick ratio} = \frac{\text{Current assets less inventory}}{\text{Current liabilities}}$$

This ratio should ideally be **at least 1** for companies with a slow inventory turnover. For companies with a fast inventory turnover, a quick ratio can be comfortably less than 1 without suggesting that the company could be in cash flow trouble.

Both the current ratio and the quick ratio offer an indication of the company's liquidity position, but the absolute figures **should not be interpreted too literally**. It is often theorised that an acceptable current ratio is 1.5 and an acceptable quick ratio is 0.8, but these should only be used as a guide. Different businesses operate in very different ways. A supermarket group for example might have a current ratio of 0.52 and a quick ratio of 0.17. Supermarkets have low receivables (people do not buy groceries on credit), low cash (good cash management), medium inventories (high inventories but quick turnover, particularly in view of perishability) and very high payables.

Compare this with a manufacturing and retail organisation, with a current ratio of 1.44 and a quick ratio of 1.03. Such businesses operate with liquidity ratios closer to the standard.

What is important is the **trend** of these ratios. From this, one can easily ascertain whether liquidity is improving or deteriorating. If a supermarket has traded for the last 10 years (very successfully) with current ratios of 0.52 and quick ratios of 0.17 then it should be supposed that the company can continue in business with those levels of liquidity. If in the following year the current ratio were to fall to 0.38 and the quick ratio to 0.09, then further investigation into the liquidity situation would be appropriate. It is the relative position that is far more important than the absolute figures.

Don't forget the other side of the coin either. A current ratio and a quick ratio can get **bigger than they need to be**. A company that has large volumes of inventories and receivables might be over-investing in working capital, and so tying up more funds in the business than it needs to. This would suggest poor management of receivables (credit) or inventories by the company.

3.10 Efficiency ratios: control of receivables and inventories

A rough measure of the average length of time it takes for a company's customers to pay what they owe is the accounts receivable collection period.

Formula to learn

The estimated average accounts receivable collection period is calculated as:

$$\frac{\text{Trade receivables}}{\text{Sales}} \times 365 \, \text{days}$$

The figure for sales should be taken as the sales revenue figure in the statement of comprehensive income. Note that any **cash sales should be excluded** – this ratio only uses credit sales. The trade receivables are not the total figure for receivables in the statement of financial position, which includes prepayments and non-trade receivables. The trade receivables figure will be itemised in an analysis of the receivable total, in a note to the accounts.

The estimate of the accounts receivable collection period is **only approximate**.

(a)   The value of receivables in the statement of financial position might be abnormally high or low compared with the 'normal' level the company usually has.

(b)   Sales revenue in the statement of comprehensive income is exclusive of sales taxes, but receivables in the statement of financial position are inclusive of sales tax. We are not strictly comparing like with like.

Sales are usually made on 'normal credit terms' of payment within 30 days. A collection period significantly in excess of this might be representative of poor management of funds of a business. However, some companies must allow generous credit terms to win customers. Exporting companies in particular may have to carry large amounts of receivables, and so their average collection period might be well in excess of 30 days.

The **trend of the collection period over time** is probably the best guide. If the collection period is increasing year on year, this is indicative of a poorly managed credit control function (and potentially therefore a poorly managed company).

3.11 Accounts receivable collection period: examples

Using the same types of company as examples, the collection period for each of the companies was as follows.

Company	Trade receivables / Sales	Collection period ($\times 365$)	Previous year	Collection period ($\times 365$)
Supermarket	$\dfrac{\$5,016K}{\$284,986K} =$	6.4 days	$\dfrac{\$3,977K}{\$290,668K} =$	5.0 days
Manufacturer	$\dfrac{\$458.3m}{\$2,059.5m} =$	81.2 days	$\dfrac{\$272.4m}{\$1,274.2m} =$	78.0 days
Sugar refiner and seller	$\dfrac{\$304.4m}{\$3,817.3m} =$	29.3 days	$\dfrac{\$287.0m}{\$3,366.3m} =$	31.1 days

The differences in collection period reflect the differences between the types of business. Supermarkets have hardly any trade receivables at all, whereas the manufacturing companies have far more. The collection periods are fairly constant from the previous year for all three companies.

3.12 Inventory turnover period

Another ratio worth calculating is the inventory turnover period. This is another estimated figure, obtainable from published accounts, which indicates the average number of days that items of inventory are held for. As with the average receivable collection period, however, it is only an approximate estimated figure, but one which should be reliable enough for comparing changes year on year.

<table>
<tr><td>Formula to learn</td><td>The inventory turnover period is calculated as:

$$\dfrac{\text{Inventory}}{\text{Cost of sales}} \times 365 \,\text{days}$$</td></tr>
</table>

This is another measure of how vigorously a business is trading. A lengthening inventory turnover period from one year to the next indicates:

(a)   a slowdown in trading; or

(b)   a build-up in inventory levels, perhaps suggesting that the investment in inventories is becoming excessive.

Generally the **higher the inventory turnover the better**, ie the lower the turnover period the better, but several aspects of inventory holding policy have to be balanced.

(a)   Lead times
(b)   Seasonal fluctuations in orders
(c)   Alternative uses of warehouse space
(d)   Bulk buying discounts
(e)   Likelihood of inventory perishing or becoming obsolete

If we add together the inventory turnover period and receivables collection period, this should give us an indication of how soon inventory is converted into cash. Both receivables collection period and inventory turnover period therefore give us a further indication of the company's liquidity.

3.13 Inventory turnover period: example

The estimated inventory turnover periods for a supermarket are as follows.

Company	Inventory / Cost of sales	Inventory turnover period (days $\times 365$)	Previous year

| Supermarket | $\dfrac{\$15{,}554K}{\$254{,}571K}$ | 22.3 days | $\dfrac{\$14{,}094K}{\$261{,}368K} \times$ | 365 = 19.7 days |

3.14 Accounts payable payment period

Accounts payable payment period is ideally calculated by the formula:

$$\frac{\text{Trade accounts payable}}{\text{Purchases}} \times 365 \text{ days}$$

It is rare to find purchases disclosed in published accounts and so **cost of sales serves as an approximation**. The payment period often helps to assess a company's liquidity; an increase is often a sign of lack of long-term finance or poor management of current assets, resulting in the use of extended credit from suppliers, increased bank overdraft and so on.

Activity

Calculate liquidity and working capital ratios from the accounts of TEB Co, a business which provides service support (cleaning etc) to customers worldwide. Comment on the results of your calculations.

	20X7 $m	20X6 $m
Sales revenue	2,176.2	2,344.8
Cost of sales	1,659.0	1,731.5
Gross profit	517.2	613.3
Current assets		
Inventories	42.7	78.0
Receivables (note 1)	378.9	431.4
Short-term deposits and cash	205.2	145.0
	626.8	654.4
Current liabilities		
Loans and overdrafts	32.4	81.1
Tax on profits	67.8	76.7
Accruals	11.7	17.2
Payables (note 2)	487.2	467.2
	599.1	642.2
Net current assets	27.7	12.2
Notes		
1 Trade receivables	295.2	335.5
2 Trade payables	190.8	188.1

Answer

	20X7	20X6
Current ratio	$\dfrac{626.8}{599.1} = 1.05$	$\dfrac{654.4}{642.2} = 1.02$
Quick ratio	$\dfrac{584.1}{599.1} = 0.97$	$\dfrac{576.4}{642..2} = 0.90$
Accounts receivable collection period	$\dfrac{295.2}{2{,}176.2} \times 365 = 49.5 \text{ days}$	$\dfrac{335.5}{2{,}344.8} \times 365 = 52.2 \text{ days}$
Inventory turnover period	$\dfrac{42.7}{1{,}659.0} \times 365 = 9.4 \text{ days}$	$\dfrac{78.0}{1{,}731.5} \times 365 = 16.4 \text{ days}$
Accounts payable payment period	$\dfrac{190.8}{1{,}659.0} \times 365 = 42.0 \text{ days}$	$\dfrac{188.1}{1{,}731.5} \times 365 = 40.0 \text{ days}$

The company's current ratio is a little lower than average but its quick ratio is better than average and very little less than the current ratio. This suggests that inventory levels are strictly controlled, which is reinforced by the low inventory turnover period. It would seem that working capital is tightly managed, to avoid the poor liquidity which could be caused by a long receivables collection period and comparatively high payables.

The company in the exercise is a service company and hence it would be expected to have very low inventory and a very short inventory turnover period. The similarity of receivables collection period and payables payment period means that the company is passing on most of the delay in receiving payment to its suppliers.

 Activity

(a) Calculate the operating cycle for Moribund for 20X2 on the basis of the following information.

		$
Inventory:	raw materials	150,000
	work in progress	60,000
	finished goods	200,000
Purchases		500,000
Trade accounts receivable		230,000
Trade accounts payable		120,000
Sales		900,000
Cost of goods sold		750,000

Tutorial note. You will need to calculate inventory turnover periods (total year end inventory over cost of goods sold), receivables as daily sales, and payables in relation to purchases, all converted into 'days'.

(b) List the steps which might be taken in order to improve the operating cycle.

 Answer

(a) The operating cycle can be found as follows.

Inventory turnover period: $\dfrac{\text{Total closing inventory} \times 365}{\text{Cost of goods sold}}$

plus

Accounts receivable collection period: $\dfrac{\text{Closing trade receivables} \times 365}{\text{Sales}}$

less

Accounts payable payment period: $\dfrac{\text{Closing trade payables} \times 365}{\text{Purchases}}$

	20X2
Total closing inventory ($)	410,000
Cost of goods sold ($)	750,000
Inventory turnover period	199.5 days
Closing receivables ($)	230,000
Sales ($)	900,000
Receivables collection period	93.3 days
Closing payables ($)	120,000
Purchases ($)	500,000
Payables payment period	(87.6 days)
Length of operating cycle (199.5 + 93.3 − 87.6)	205.2 days

(b)   The steps that could be taken to reduce the operating cycle include the following.

(i)   Reducing the raw material inventory turnover period.

(ii)   Reducing the time taken to produce goods. However, the company must ensure that quality is not sacrificed as a result of speeding up the production process.

(iii) Increasing the period of credit taken from suppliers. The credit period already seems very long – the company is allowed three months credit by its suppliers, and probably could not be increased. If the credit period is extended then the company may lose discounts for prompt payment.

(iv)   Reducing the finished goods inventory turnover period.

(v)   Reducing the receivables collection period. The administrative costs of speeding up debt collection and the effect on sales of reducing the credit period allowed must be evaluated. However, the credit period does already seem very long by the standards of most industries. It may be that generous terms have been allowed to secure large contracts and little will be able to be done about this in the short term.

4 Presentation of financial performance

You should begin your report with a heading showing who it is from, the name of the addressee, the subject of the report and a suitable date.

A good approach is often to head up a **'schedule of ratios and statistics'** which will form an appendix to the main report. Calculate the ratios in a logical sequence, dealing in turn with operating and profitability ratios, use of assets (eg turnover period for inventories, collection period for receivables), liquidity and gearing/leverage.

As you calculate the ratios you are likely to be struck by **significant fluctuations and trends**. These will form the basis of your comments in the body of the report. The report should begin with some introductory comments, setting out the scope of your analysis and mentioning that detailed figures have been included in an appendix. You should then go on to present your analysis under any categories called for by the question (eg separate sections for management, shareholders and creditors, or separate sections for profitability and liquidity).

Finally, look out for opportunities to **suggest remedial action** where trends appear to be unfavourable. Questions sometimes require you specifically to set out your advice and recommendations.

4.1 Planning your answers

This is as good a place as any to stress the importance of planning your answers. This is particularly important for 'wordy' questions. While you may feel like breathing a sigh of relief after all that number crunching, you should not be tempted to 'waffle'. The best way to avoid going off the point is to **prepare an answer plan**. This has the advantage of making you think before you write and structure your answer logically.

The following approach may be adopted when preparing an answer plan.

(a)   Read the question **requirements**.

(b)   **Skim through the question** to see roughly what it is about.

(c)   Read through the question carefully, **underlining any key words**.

(d)   Set out the **headings** for the main parts of your answer. Leave space to insert points within the headings.

(e)   **Jot down points** to make within the main sections, underlining points on which you wish to expand.

(f)   Write your **full answer**.

You should allow yourself the full time allocation for written answers, that is 1.8 minutes per mark. If, however, you run out of time, a clear answer plan with points in note form will earn you more marks than an introductory paragraph written out in full.

 Activity

The following information has been extracted from the recently published accounts of DG.

EXTRACTS FROM THE STATEMENTS OF COMPREHENSIVE INCOME TO 30 APRIL

	20X9	20X8
	$'000	$'000
Sales	11,200	9,750
Cost of sales	8,460	6,825
Net profit before tax	465	320
This is after charging:		
Depreciation	360	280
Loan note interest	80	60
Interest on bank overdraft	15	9
Audit fees	12	10

STATEMENTS OF FINANCIAL POSITION AS AT 30 APRIL

	20X9		20X8	
	$'000	$'000	$'000	$'000
Assets				
Non-current assets		1,850		1,430
Current assets				
Inventory	640		490	
Receivables	1,230		1,080	
Cash	80		120	
		1,950		1,690
Total assets		3,800		3,120
Equity and liabilities				
Equity				
Ordinary share capital	800		800	
Retained earnings	1,310		930	
		2,110		1,730
Non-current liabilities				
10% loan stock		800		600
Current liabilities				
Bank overdraft	110		80	
Payables	750		690	
Taxation	30		20	
		890		790
Total equity and liabilities		3,800		3,120

The following ratios are those calculated for DG, based on its published accounts for the previous year, and also the latest industry average ratios:

	DG	Industry
	30 April 20X8	average
ROCE (capital employed = equity and debentures)	16.70%	18.50%
Profit/sales	3.90%	4.73%
Asset turnover	4.29	3.91
Current ratio	2.00	1.90
Quick ratio	1.42	1.27
Gross profit margin	30.00%	35.23%
Accounts receivable collection period	40 days	52 days
Accounts payable payment period	37 days	49 days
Inventory turnover (times)	13.90	18.30
Gearing	26.37%	32.71%

Required

(a) Calculate comparable ratios (to two decimal places where appropriate) for DG for the year ended 30 April 20X9. All calculations must be clearly shown.

(b) Write a report to your board of directors analysing the performance of DG, comparing the results against the previous year and against the industry average.

Answer

(a)

	20X8	20X9	Industry average
ROCE	$\dfrac{320+60}{2,330}=16.30\%$	$\dfrac{465+80}{2,910}=18.72\%$	18.50%
Profit/sales	$\dfrac{320+60}{9,750}=3.90\%$	$\dfrac{465+80}{11,200}=4.87\%$	4.73%
Asset turnover	$\dfrac{9,750}{2,330}=4.18x$	$\dfrac{11,200}{2,910}=3.85x$	3.91x
Current ratio	$\dfrac{1,690}{790}=2.10$	$\dfrac{1,950}{890}=2.20$	1.90
Quick ratio	$\dfrac{1,080+120}{790}=1.52$	$\dfrac{1,230+80}{890}=1.47$	1.27
Gross profit margin	$\dfrac{9,750-6,825}{9,750}=30.00\%$	$\dfrac{11,200-8,460}{11,200}=24.46\%$	35.23%
Accounts receivable collection period	$\dfrac{1,080}{9,750}\times365=40\text{days}$	$\dfrac{1,230}{11,200}\times365=40\text{days}$	52 days
Accounts payable payment period	$\dfrac{690}{6,825}\times365=37\text{days}$	$\dfrac{750}{8,460}\times365=32\text{days}$	49 days
Inventory turnover (times)	$\dfrac{6,825}{490}=13.9x$	$\dfrac{8,460}{640}=13.2x$	18.30x
Gearing	$\dfrac{600}{2,330}=25.75\%$	$\dfrac{800}{2,910}=27.5\%$	32.71%

(b) REPORT

To: Board of Directors
From: Accountant   Date: xx/xx/xx
Subject: Analysis of performance of DG

This report should be read in conjunction with the appendix attached which shows the relevant ratios (from part (a)).

(i) Trading and profitability

Return on capital employed has improved considerably between 20X8 and 20X9 and is now higher than the industry average.

Net income as a proportion of sales has also improved noticeably between the years and is also now marginally ahead of the industry average. Gross margin, however, is considerably lower than in the previous year and is only some 70% of the industry average. This suggests either that there has been a change in the cost structure of DG or that there has been a change in the method of cost allocation between the periods. Either way, this is a marked change that requires investigation. The company may be in a period of transition as sales have increased by nearly 15% over the year and it would appear that new non-current assets have been purchased.

Asset turnover has declined between the periods although the 20X9 figure is in line with the industry average. This reduction might indicate that the efficiency with which assets are used has deteriorated or it might indicate that the assets acquired in 20X9 have not yet fully contributed to the business. A longer term trend would clarify the picture.

(ii)   Liquidity and working capital management

The current ratio has improved slightly over the year and is marginally higher than the industry average. It is also in line with what is generally regarded as satisfactory (2:1).

The quick ratio has declined marginally but is still better than the industry average. This suggests that DG has no short term liquidity problems and should have no difficulty in paying its debts as they become due.

Receivables as a proportion of sales is unchanged from 20X8 and are considerably lower than the industry average. Consequently, there is probably little opportunity to reduce this further and there may be pressure in the future from customers to increase the period of credit given. The period of credit taken from suppliers has fallen from 37 days' purchases to 32 days' and is much lower than the industry average; thus, it may be possible to finance any additional receivables by negotiating better credit terms from suppliers.

Inventory turnover has fallen slightly and is much slower than the industry average and this may partly reflect stocking up ahead of a significant increase in sales. Alternatively, there is some danger that the inventory could contain certain obsolete items that may require writing off. The relative increase in the level of inventory has been financed by an increased overdraft which may reduce if the inventory levels can be brought down.

The high levels of inventory, overdraft and receivables compared to that of payables suggests a labour intensive company or one where considerable value is added to bought-in products.

(iii)   Gearing

The level of gearing has increased only slightly over the year and is below the industry average. Since the return on capital employed is nearly twice the rate of interest on the loan stock, profitability is likely to be increased by a modest increase in the level of gearing.

Signed: Accountant

5 Limitations of financial statements

Financial statements are affected by the obvious shortcomings of historic cost information and are also subject to manipulation.

Financial statements are intended to give a fair presentation of the financial performance of an entity over a period and its financial position at the end of that period. The IASB *Framework* and the *IFRS for SMEs* are there to ensure as far as possible that they do. However, there are a number of reasons why the information in financial statements should not just be taken at its face value.

5.1 Problems of historic cost information

Historic cost information is reliable and can be verified, but it becomes less relevant as time goes by. The value shown for assets carried in the statement of financial position at historic cost may bear no relation whatever to what their current value is and what it may cost to replace them. The corresponding depreciation charge will also be low, leading to the overstatement of profits in real terms. The financial statements do not show the real cost of using such assets.

This is particularly misleading when attempting to predict future performance. It could be that a major asset will need to be replaced in two years time, at vastly more than the original cost of the asset currently shown in the statement of financial position. This will then entail much higher depreciation and interest payments (if a loan or finance lease is used). In addition, overstatement of profit due to the low depreciation charge can have led to too much profit having been distributed, increasing the likelihood of new asset purchases having to be financed by loans. This information could not have been obtained just from looking at the financial statements.

In a period of inflation, financial statements based on historic cost are subject to an additional distortion. Sales revenue will be keeping pace with inflation and so will the cost of purchases. However, using FIFO (and to some degree the weighted average method) inventory being used will be valued as the earliest (and therefore cheapest) purchases. This leads to understatement of cost of sales and overstatement of profits. This is the result of inventory carried at historic cost.

5.2 Creative accounting

Companies may produce their financial statements which show investors what they are expecting to see. For instance, a steady rise in profits, with no peaks or troughs, is reassuring to potential investors. Companies could sometimes achieve this by using provisions to smooth out the peaks and troughs although this is no longer allowed by IFRS, but companies can still achieve similar effects by delaying or advancing invoicing or manipulating cut-offs or accruals. Directors who are paid performance bonuses will favour the steady rise (enough to secure the bonus each year, rather than up one year, down the next) while those who hold share options may be aiming for one spectacular set of results just before they sell.

An important aspect of improving the appearance of the statement of financial position is keeping gearing as low as possible. Investors know that interest payments reduce the amount available for distribution and potential lenders will be less willing to lend to a company which is already highly geared.

A number of creative accounting measures are aimed at reducing gearing. In the past parent companies could find reasons to exclude highly-geared subsidiaries from the consolidation and could obtain loans in the first place via such 'quasi subsidiaries', so that the loan never appeared in the consolidated statement of financial position. This loophole has been effectively closed by IFRS, but other means of keeping debt out of the statement of financial position exist. Finance leases can be treated as operating leases, so that the asset and the loan are kept off-balance sheet. Assets can be 'sold' under a sale and leaseback agreement, which is in effect a disguised loan. And if all else fails, a last minute piece of 'window dressing' can be undertaken. For instance, a loan can be repaid just before the year end and taken out again at the beginning of the next year.

5.3 The effect of related parties

One objective of the *IFRS for SMEs* is to "ensure that an entity's financial statements contain the disclosures necessary to draw attention to the possibility that its financial position and profit or loss may have been affected by the existence of related parties and by transactions and outstanding balances with such parties".

Related parties are a normal feature of business. It is common for entities to carry on activities with or through subsidiaries and associates, or occasionally to engage in transactions with directors or their families. The point is that such transactions cannot be assumed to have been engaged in 'at arm's length' or in the best interests of the entity itself, which is why investors and potential investors need to be made aware of them. Transfer pricing can be used to transfer profit from one company to another and inter-company loans and transfers of non-current assets can also be used in the same way.

Despite the IFRS, companies which wish to disguise a related party relationship can probably still find complex ways to do it (the Enron scandal revealed the existence of numerous related party transactions) and financial statements do not show the unseen effects of such a relationship. For instance, a subsidiary may not have been allowed to tender for a contract in competition with another group company. Its shareholders will never know about such missed opportunities.

5.4 Seasonal trading

This is another issue that can distort reported results. Many companies whose trade is seasonal position their year end after their busy period, to minimise time spent on the inventory count. At this point in time, the statement of financial position will show a healthy level of cash and/or receivables and a low level of trade payables, assuming most of them have been paid. Thus the position is reported at the moment when the company is at its most solvent. A statement of financial position drawn up a few months earlier, or even perhaps a few months later, when trade is still slack but fixed costs still have to be paid, may give a very different picture.

5.5 Asset acquisitions

Major asset acquisitions just before the end of an accounting period can also distort results. The statement of financial position will show an increased level of assets and corresponding liabilities (probably a loan or lease payable), but the income which will be earned from utilisation of the asset will not yet have materialised. This will adversely affect the company's return on capital employed.

6 Accounting policies and the limitations of ratio analysis

The choice of accounting policy and the effect of its implementation are almost as important as its disclosure in that the results of a company can be altered significantly by the choice of accounting policy.

6.1 Changes in accounting policy

The effect of a change of accounting policy is treated as a prior year adjustment according to the IFRS (see Unit 4). This just means that the comparative figures are adjusted for the change in accounting policy for comparative purposes and an adjustment is put through retained earnings.

Under **consistency of presentation** any change in policy may only be made if it can be justified on the grounds that the new policy is preferable to the one it replaces because it will give a fairer presentation of the result and of the financial position of a reporting entity.

The problem with this situation is that the directors may be able to **manipulate the results** through change(s) of accounting policies. This would be done to avoid the effect of an old accounting policy or gain the effect of a new one. It is likely to be done in a sensitive period, perhaps when the company's profits are low or the company is about to announce a rights issue. The management would have to convince the auditors that the new policy was much better, but it is not difficult to produce reasons in such cases.

The effect of such a change is very **short-term**. Most sophisticated users will discount its effect immediately, except to the extent that it will affect any dividend (because of the effect on distributable profits). It may help to avoid breaches of banking covenants because of the effect on certain ratios.

Obviously, the accounting policy for any item in the accounts could only be changed once in quite a long period of time. Auditors would not allow another change, even back to the old policy, unless there was a wholly exceptional reason.

The managers of a company can choose accounting policies **initially** to suit the company or the type of results they want to get. Any changes in accounting policy must be justified, but some managers might try to change accounting policies just to manipulate the results.

6.2 Limitations of ratio analysis

The consideration of how accounting policies may be used to manipulate company results leads us to some of the other limitations of ratio analysis.

The most important ones are:

- In a company's first year of trading there will be no comparative figures. So there will be no indication of whether or not a ratio is improving.

- Comparison against industry averages may not be that revealing. A business may be subject to factors which are not common in the industry.

- Ratios based on historic cost accounts are subject to the distortions described above. In particular, undervalued assets will distort ROCE and exaggerate gearing.

- Financial statements are subject to manipulation and so are the ratios based on them. Creative accounting is undertaken with key ratios in mind.

- Inflation over a period will distort results and ratios. Net profit, and therefore ROCE, can be inflated where FIFO is applied during an inflationary period.

- No two companies, even operating in the same industry, will have the same financial and business risk profile. For instance, one may have better access to cheap borrowing than the other and so may be able to sustain a higher level of gearing.

6.3 Other issues

Are there other issues which should be looked at when assessing an entity's performance? Factors to consider are:

- How technologically advanced is it? If it is not using the latest equipment and processes it risks being pushed out of the market at some point or having to undertake a high level of capital expenditure.
- What are its environmental policies? Is it in danger of having to pay for cleanup if the law is tightened? Does it appeal to those seeking 'ethical investment'?
- What is the reputation of its management? If it has attracted good people and kept them, that is a positive indicator.
- What is its mission statement? To what degree does it appear to be fulfilling it?
- What is its reputation as an employer? Do people want to work for this company? What are its labour relations like?
- What is the size of its market? Does it trade in just one or two countries or worldwide?
- How strong is its competition? Is it in danger of takeover?

You can probably think of other factors that you would consider important. In some cases you can also look at the quality of the product that a company produces.

Activity

Analyse a company that you know something about against these criteria.

Unit Roundup

- This lengthy chapter has gone into quite a lot of detail about basic ratio analysis. The ratios you should be able to calculate and/or comment on are as follows.

    - **Profitability ratios**

        - Return on capital employed
        - Net profit as a percentage of sales
        - Asset turnover ratio
        - Gross profit as a percentage of sales

    - **Debt and gearing/leverage ratios**

        - Debt ratio
        - Gearing ratio/leverage
        - Interest cover
        - Cash flow ratio

    - **Liquidity and working capital ratios**

        - Current ratio
        - Quick ratio (acid test ratio)
        - Accounts receivable collection period
        - Accounts payable payment period
        - Inventory turnover period

- Ratios provide information through **comparison**.

    - **Trends** in a company's ratios from **one year to the next**, indicating an improving or worsening position.
    - In some cases, **against a 'norm' or 'standard'**.
    - In some cases, **against the ratios of other companies**, although differences between one company and another should often be expected.

- You must realise that, however many ratios you can find to calculate, **numbers alone will not answer a question**. You *must* interpret all the information available to you and support your interpretation with ratio calculations.

- Financial statements are affected by the obvious shortcoming of historic cost information and are also subject to manipulation.

- The choice of accounting policy and the effect of its implementation are almost as important as its disclosure, in that the results of a company can be altered significantly by the choice of accounting policy.

Quick quiz

1 List the main categories of ratio.

2 ROCE is $\dfrac{\text{Profit before interest and tax}}{\text{Capital employed}} \times 100\%$

    True ☐

    False ☐

3 Company Q has a profit margin of 7%. Briefly comment on this.

4 The debt ratio is a company's long-term debt divided by its net assets.

    True ☐

    False ☐

5 The cash flow ratio is the ratio of:

    A   Gross cash inflow to total debt
    B   Gross cash inflow to net debt
    C   Net cash inflow to total debt
    D   Net cash inflow to net debt

6 List the formulae for:

    (a)   Current ratio   (c)   Accounts receivable collection period
    (b)   Quick ratio   (d)   Inventory turnover period

7 What is the effect of inventory carried at historical cost in a period of inflation?

8 What is 'window dressing'?

9 How can companies attempt to transfer profits from one group company to another?

10 Will two companies in the same industry have the same ROCE?

1   See paragraph 1.1.

2   True

3   You should be careful here. You have very little information. This is a low margin but you need to know what industry the company operates in. 7% may be good for a major retailer.

4   False (see paragraph 3.2)

5   C (see paragraph 3.6)

6   See paragraphs 3.9, 3.10 and 3.12.

7   Overstatement of profits.

8   An accounting adjustment made just before the year end to improve the appearance of the financial statements.

9   Transfer pricing, intercompany loans, transfers of non-current assets.

10   Probably not, there may be many other differences between them.

Now try the question below

Reactive   45 mins

Reactive is a company that assembles domestic electrical goods which it then sells to both wholesale and retail customers. Reactive's management were disappointed in the company's results for the year ended 31 March 20X5. In an attempt to improve performance the following measures were taken early in the year ended 31 March 20X6:

–   A national advertising campaign was undertaken,

–   Rebates to all wholesale customers purchasing goods above set quantity levels were introduced,

–   The assembly of certain lines ceased and was replaced by bought in completed products. This allowed Reactive to dispose of surplus plant.

Reactive's summarised financial statements for the year ended 31 March 20X6 are set out below:

STATEMENT OF COMPREHENSIVE INCOME

	$million
Revenue (25% cash sales)	4,000
Cost of sales	(3,450)
Gross profit	550
Operating expenses	(370)
	180
Profit on disposal of plant (note (i))	40
Finance charges	(20)
Profit before tax	200
Income tax expense	(50)
Profit for the year	150

STATEMENT OF FINANCIAL POSITION

	$million	$million
Non-current assets		
Property, plant and equipment (note (i))		550
Current assets		
Inventory	250	
Trade receivables	360	
Bank	nil	610
Total assets		1,160

Equity and liabilities

Equity shares of 25 cents each		100
Retained earnings		380
		480

Non-current liabilities

8% loan notes		200

Current liabilities

Bank overdraft	10	
Trade payables	430	
Current tax payable	40	480
Total equity and liabilities		1,160

Below are ratios calculated for the year ended 31 March 20X5.

Return on year end capital employed (profit before interest and tax over total assets less current liabilities)	28.1%
Net asset (equal to capital employed) turnover	4 times
Gross profit margin	17%
Net profit (before tax) margin	6.3%
Current ratio	1.6:1
Closing inventory holding period	46 days
Trade receivables' collection period	45 days
Trade payables' payment period	55 days
Dividend yield	3.75%
Dividend cover	2 times

Notes

(i)   Reactive received $120 million from the sale of plant that had a carrying amount of $80 million at the date of its sale.

(ii)   The market price of Reactive's shares throughout the year averaged $3.75 each.

(iii)   There were no issues or redemption of shares or loans during the year.

(iv)   Dividends paid during the year ended 31 March 20X6 amounted to $90 million, maintaining the same dividend paid in the year ended 31 March 20X5.

Required

(a)   Calculate ratios for the year ended 31 March 20X6 (showing your workings) for Reactive, equivalent to those provided above.   **(10 marks)**

(b)   Analyse the financial performance and position of Reactive for the year ended 31 March 20X6 compared to the previous year.   **(15 marks)**

(Total = 25 marks)

Reactive

(a)   ROCE = 220/680 × 100 = 32.3%

Net asset turnover = 4,000/680 = 5.9 times

Gross profit margin = 550/4,000 × 100 = 13.8%

Net profit margin = 200/4,000 × 100 = 5%

Current ratio = 610/480 = 1.3:1

Closing inventory holding period = 250/3,450 × 365 = 26 days

Trade receivables collection period = 360/3,000* ×365 = 44 days

* credit sales

Trade payables payment period = 430/3450 × 365 = 45 days

Dividend yield = 22.5/375* × 100 = 6%

* Dividend per share(90/400)/market price of share

Dividend cover = 150/90 = 1.67 times

(b)   Analysis of the comparative financial performance and position of Reactive for the year ended 31 March 20X6

The first thing to notice about Reactive's results is that the ROCE has increased by 4.2 percentage points, from 28.1 to 32.3. On the face of it, this is impressive. However, we have to take into account the fact that the capital employed has been reduced by the plant disposal and the net profit has been increased by the profit on disposal. So the ROCE has been inflated by this transaction and we should look at what the ROCE would have been without the disposal. Taking out the effects of the disposal gives us the following ratios:

ROCE = 180/ (680 + 80) × 100 = 23.7%

Net asset turnover = 4,000/760 = 5.3 times

Net profit margin = 160/4,000 × 100 = 4%

Comparing these ratios to those for the period ended 31 March 20X5 we can see that ROCE has fallen. This fall has been occasioned by a fall in the net profit margin. The asset turnover has improved on the previous year even after adding back the disposal.

The net profit margin can be analysed into two factors – the gross profit margin and the level of expenses. The **gross profit percentage is 3.2% down** on the previous year. This is probably due to the rebates offered to wholesale customers, which will have increased sales at the expense of profitability. The replacement of some production lines by bought in products will probably also have reduced profit margins. Sales may have been increased by the advertising campaign, but this has been additional expense charged against net profit. It looks as if management have sought to boost revenue by any available means. The plant disposal has served to mask the effect on profits.

Reactive's **liquidity has also declined** over the current year. The current ratio has gone down from 1.6 to 1.3. However, there has also been a sharp decline in the inventory holding period, probably due to holding less raw material for production. It could be that the finished goods can be delivered direct to the wholesalers from the supplier. This will have served to reduce the current ratio. The receivables collection period has remained fairly constant but the payables payment period has gone down by 10 days. It looks as if, in return for prompt delivery, the finished goods supplier demands prompt payment. This fall in the payables period will have served to improve the current ratio. We do not have details of cash balances last year, but Reactive currently has no cash in the bank and a $10m overdraft. Without the $120m from the sale of plant the liquidity situation would obviously have been much worse.

The **dividend yield has increased** from 3.75% to 6%, which looks good as far as potential investors are concerned. But we are told that the dividend amount is the same as last year. As there have been no share issues, this means that the dividend per share is the same as last year. Therefore the increase in dividend yield can only have come about through a fall in the share price. The market is not that impressed by Reactive's results. At the same time the dividend cover has declined. So the same dividend has been paid on less profit (last year's dividend cover was 2.0, so profit must have been $180m). Management decided it was important to maintain the dividend, but this was not sufficient to hold the share price up.

To conclude, we can say that **Reactive's position and performance is down** on the previous year and any apparent improvement is due to the disposal of plant.

Part E

Audit requirements

Statutory audit requirements

Unit topic list

1 Objective of statutory audits and the audit opinion
2 Regulation of auditors
3 International Standards on Auditing

Assessment criteria

6 Understand audit requirements for SMEs

6.1 Understand what an external audit involves and understand International Auditing and Assurance Standards

6.2 Understand the audit thresholds relating to an SME

6.3 Understand the appropriate audit report for an SME

1 Objective of statutory audits and the audit opinion

Many companies are required to have an external audit by law, but some small companies are exempt. The outcome of the audit is the **audit report**, which sets out the auditor's **opinion** on the financial statements.

1.1 The statutory audit opinion

The purpose of an audit is for the auditor to express an opinion on the financial statements.

The audit opinion may also **imply** certain things are true, because otherwise the audit report would have mentioned them. For example, in the UK, such implications include the following:

- **Adequate accounting records** have been kept.
- **Returns** adequate for the audit have been received from branches not visited.
- The **accounts agree** with the **accounting records** and **returns**.
- **All information and explanations** have been **received** that the auditor believes are necessary for the purposes of the audit.
- **Details** of **directors' emoluments** and **other benefits** have been correctly **disclosed** in the financial statements.
- Particulars of **loans** and **other transactions** in favour of **directors** and others have been correctly in the financial statements.

1.2 Small company audit exemption

Many companies are required by national law to have an audit. A key exception to this requirement is that given to small companies. Many EC countries have a small company exemption from audit that is based on the annual sales turnover and total assets at the year-end.

In the UK the audit exemption threshold for small companies is annual turnover of £6.5 million and a balance sheet (statement of financial position) total of £3.26 million.

In most countries, the majority of companies are very small, employing few staff (if any) and are often owner-managed. This is very different from a large business where the owners (the shareholders) devolve the day-to-day running of the business to a group of managers or directors.

Key term

> A **small entity** is any enterprise in which:
>
> (a)   There is concentration of ownership and management in a small number of individuals (often a single individual), and
>
> (b)   One or more of the following are also found:
>
>   (i)   Few sources of income and uncomplicated activities
>
>   (ii)   Unsophisticated record-keeping
>
>   (iii) Limited internal controls together with the potential for management override of internal controls

There has long been a debate over the benefits of audit to small entities. Where such entities are owned by the same people that manage them, there is significantly less value in an independent review of the stewardship of the managers than where management and ownership are separate.

The case for retaining the small company audit rests on the value of the statutory audit to those who have an interest in audited accounts, that is, the users of the accounts. From the viewpoint of each type of user, the arguments for and against abolition are as follows.

(a) Shareholders	
Against change	Shareholders not involved in management need the reassurance given by audited accounts. Furthermore, the existence of the audit deters the directors from treating the company's assets as their own to the detriment of minority shareholders. Audited financial statements are invaluable in arriving at a fair valuation of the shares in an unquoted company either for taxation or other purposes.
For change	Where all the shareholders are also executive directors or closely related to them, the benefit gained from an audit may not be worth its cost.

(b) Banks and other institutional creditors	
Against change	Banks rely on accounts for the purposes of making loans and reviewing the value of security.
For change	There is doubt whether banks rely on the audited accounts of companies to a greater extent than those of unincorporated associations of a similar size which have not been audited. A review of the way in which the bank accounts of the company have been conducted and of forecasts and management accounts are at least as important to the banks as the appraisal of the audited accounts. There is no reason why a bank should not make an audit a precondition of granting a loan.

(c) Trade creditors	
Against change	Creditors and potential creditors should have the opportunity to assess the strength of their customers by examining audited financial statements.
For change	In practice, only limited reliance is placed on the accounts available from the regulatory authority as they are usually filed too late to be of use in granting credit.

(d) Tax authorities	
Against change	The authorities rely on accounts for computing corporation tax and checking returns.
For change	There is little evidence to suggest that the tax authorities rely on audited accounts to a significantly greater extent than those which, whilst being unaudited, have been prepared by an independent accountant.

(e) Employees	
Against change	Employees are entitled to be able to assess audited accounts when entering wage negotiations and considering the future viability of their employer.
For change	There is little evidence to suggest that such assessments are made in small companies.

(f) Management	
Against change	The audit provides management with a useful independent check on the accuracy of the accounting systems and the auditor is frequently able to recommend improvements to those systems.
For change	If the law were changed, the management of a company could still elect to have an independent audit. It is likely, however, that a systems review accompanied by a management consultancy report would represent a greater benefit for a similar cost.

1.3 Auditor rights and duties

The law gives auditors both rights and duties. This allows auditors to have sufficient power to carry out an independent and effective audit.

The audit is primarily a statutory concept, and eligibility to conduct an audit is often set down in statute. Similarly, the rights and duties of auditors can be set down in law, to ensure that the auditors have sufficient power to carry out an effective audit. In this section we look at the rights and duties of auditors in the **UK as an example** (but bear in mind that these may be different in other jurisdictions). The relevant legislation in the UK is the **Companies Act 2006**.

1.3.1 Duties

The auditors are required to report on every balance sheet (statement of financial position) and profit and loss account (statement of comprehensive income) laid before the company in general meeting.

The auditors must consider the following.

Compliance with legislation	Whether the accounts have been prepared in accordance with the relevant legislation
Truth and fairness of accounts	Whether the balance sheet shows a true and fair view of the company's affairs at the end of the period and the profit and loss account (and cash flow statement) show a true and fair view of the results for the period
Adequate accounting records and returns	Whether adequate accounting records have been kept and returns adequate for the audit received from branches not visited by the auditor
Agreement of accounts to records	Whether the accounts are in agreement with the accounting records and returns
Consistency of other information	Whether the information in the directors' report is consistent with the accounts
Directors' benefits	Whether disclosure of directors' benefits has been made in accordance with Companies Act 2006 regulations

1.3.2 Rights

The auditors must have certain rights to enable them to carry out their duties effectively.

The principal rights auditors should have, excepting those dealing with resignation or removal, are set out in the table below.

Access to records	A right of access at all times to the books, accounts and vouchers of the company (in whatever form they are held)
Information and explanations	A right to require from the company's officers such information and explanations as they think necessary for the performance of their duties as auditors
Attendance at/notices of general meetings	A right to attend any general meetings of the company and to receive all notices of and other communications relating to such meetings which any member of the company is entitled to receive
Attendance at/notices of general meetings	A right to be heard at general meetings which they attend on any part of the business that concerns them as auditors
Rights in relation to written resolutions	A right to receive a copy of any written resolution proposed

If auditors have not received all the information and explanations they consider necessary, they should state this fact in their audit report.

The Companies Act 2006 makes it an offence for a company's officer knowingly or recklessly to make a statement in any form to an auditor which:

- Conveys or purports to convey any information or explanation required by the auditor and
- Is misleading, false or deceptive in a material particular

2 Regulation of auditors

Requirements for the **eligibility**, **registration** and **training** of auditors are extremely important as they are designed to maintain standards in the auditing profession.

2.1 National level

The accounting and auditing profession varies in structure from country to country. In some countries accountants and auditors are subject to strict legislative regulation, while in others the profession is allowed to regulate itself. We cannot look at every country, but some of the examples below will show you the divergence of structure and we can make some general points.

2.1.1 United Kingdom

In the UK there are a number of different accountancy, or accountancy-related, institutes and associations, such as the Association of Chartered Certified Accountants (ACCA), the Institute of Chartered Accountants in England and Wales (ICAEW) and the Institute of Chartered Accountants of Scotland (ICAS). All these bodies vary from each other but they are all characterised by various attributes:

- Stringent entrance requirements (examinations and practical experience)
- Strict code of ethics
- Technical updating of members

2.1.2 France

In France, the accounting profession is split into two distinct organisations:

- Accountants (Ordre des Experts Comptables et des Comptables Agréés)
- Auditors (Compagnie Nationale des Commissaires aux Comptes)

Most members of the auditors' organisation are also members of the more important accountants' organisation. Examinations, work experience and articles are similar to those of the UK accountancy bodies. The profession's main influence is through the issue of non-mandatory opinions and recommendations of accounting principles relevant to the implementation of the National Plan.

2.1.3 Germany

The main professional body in Germany is the Institute of Certified Public Accountants (Institut der Wirtschafstprüfer). Members of this institute carry out all the statutory audits, and are required to have very high educational and experience qualifications. The Institute issues a form of auditing standard but this is tied very closely to legislation. As well as auditing, members are mainly involved in tax and business management, with no obvious significant role in establishing financial accounting principles and practices. There is no independent accounting standard-setting body.

2.1.4 USA

In America, accountants are members of the American Institute of Certified Public Accountants (AICPA), a private sector body. Although the Securities and Exchange Commission in the USA can prescribe accounting standards for listed companies, it relies on the Financial Accounting Standards Board (FASB), an independent body, to set such standards. In turn, FASB keeps in close contact with the AICPA, which issues guidance on US standards and which is closely involved in their development.

2.1.5 General points

It can be seen from the above paragraphs that the accounting and auditing profession in most Western Countries is regulated by legislation to some extent. In the UK and the USA the profession effectively regulates itself, ie regulation is devolved from statute to the private bodies involved in the accountancy profession. In many European countries, statutory control by governments is much more direct.

2.2 EC member states

Persons carrying out audits in EC member states must have the permission of the relevant authorities. In the UK the relevant authorities are **Recognised Supervisory Bodies** (RSBs). As well as giving authority, RSBs in the UK supervise and monitor auditors. In other countries however supervising and monitoring is carried out by a state body or by the national government.

The Companies Act 2006 defines an RSB as a body established in the UK which maintains and enforces rules as to the

- Eligibility of persons for appointment as a statutory auditor
- Conduct of statutory audit work

The following bodies are all RSBs:

- ACCA
- ICAEW
- ICAS
- ICAI (Institute of Chartered Accountants in Ireland)
- AAPA (Association of Authorised Public Accountants)

Professional qualifications, which will be prerequisites for membership of an RSB, are offered by **Recognised Qualifying Bodies** (RQBs) approved by the government. RQBs include ACCA, ICAEW and ICAS amongst others.

2.3 International level

Regulations governing auditors will, in most countries, be most important at the national level. International regulation, however, can play a major part by:

(a) Setting **minimum standards** and **requirements** for auditors
(b) Providing **guidance** for those countries without a **well-developed national regulatory framework**
(c) Aiding **intra-country recognition** of professional accountancy qualifications

2.3.1 International Federation of Accountants (IFAC)

IFAC, based in New York, is a non-profit, non-governmental, non-political international organisation of accountancy bodies.

IFAC came into being in the 1970s as a result of proposals put forward and eventually approved by the International Congress of Accountants. IFAC's mission is:

'The development and enhancement of the profession to enable it to provide services of consistently high quality in the public interest'.

IFAC co-operates with member bodies, regional organisations of accountancy bodies and other world organisations. Through such co-operation, IFAC initiates, co-ordinates and guides efforts to achieve international technical, ethical and educational pronouncements for the accountancy profession.

Any accountancy body may join IFAC if it is recognised by law or general consensus within its own country as a substantial national organisation of good standing within the accountancy profession. Members of IFAC automatically become members of the International Accounting Standards Committee Foundation, which is an independent not-for-profit, private sector organisation which sets international financial reporting standards through its standard-setting body, the International Accounting Standards Board.

2.4 Regulation, monitoring and supervision

Each country's regulation of external audits will differ. Most regimes do have certain common elements, which we examine in detail below. Briefly these are as follows.

(a) **Education and work experience**: the IFAC has issued guidance on this.
(b) **Eligibility**: there may well be statutory rules determining who can act as auditors. Membership of an appropriate body is likely to be one criteria.

(c)   **Supervision and monitoring**: these activities came under particular scrutiny in a number of countries during the 1990s. Questions were asked about why auditors have failed to identify impending corporate failures, and whether therefore they were being regulated strongly enough. The supervision regime has come under particular scrutiny in countries where regulation and supervision is by the auditors' own professional body (self-regulation). Suggestions have been made in these countries that supervision ought to be by external government agencies.

2.5 Education, examinations and experience

IFAC issued the Statement of Policy of Council *Recognition of Professional Accountancy Qualifications* primarily to tackle the problems of intra-country recognition of qualifications. It sets minimum standards for accountancy qualifications. It looks at three main areas.

2.5.1 Education

The theoretical knowledge to be contained in the body of knowledge of accountants should include at least the following subjects.

Compulsory knowledge	<ul><li>Analysis and critical assessment of financial statements</li><li>Audit</li><li>Consolidated accounts</li><li>Cost and management accounting</li><li>General accounting</li><li>Internal control systems</li><li>Legal and professional requirements relating to audit/accountancy</li><li>Standards relating to financial statements including the IFRS for SMEs</li></ul>
Knowledge to be included where relevant	<ul><li>Basic principles of the financial management of undertakings</li><li>Business, general and financial economics</li><li>Civil and commercial law</li><li>Information technology and systems</li><li>Law of insolvency and similar procedures</li><li>Mathematics and statistics</li><li>Provision of financial services, advice, etc</li><li>Professional conduct and ethics</li><li>Social security and law of employment</li><li>Tax law</li></ul>

Accountants should have covered these subjects in a breadth and depth sufficient to enable them to perform their duties to the expected standard.

2.5.2 Examinations

Accountants should demonstrate that they have passed an examination of professional competence. This examination must assess not only the necessary level of **theoretical** knowledge but also the ability to apply that knowledge competently in a **practical** situation. Objective evaluation of professional examinations is a key requirement.

2.5.3 Experience

It is crucial to any professional to have not only a sound theoretical knowledge but also to be able to apply that knowledge competently in the world of work.

It is suggested that, prior to qualification, an individual should have completed a *minimum* of two years approved and properly supervised practical experience primarily in the area of audit and accountancy and in a suitable professional environment.

2.6 Eligibility

Eligibility to act as an auditor is likely to arise from membership of some kind of regulatory body.

Bodies of this type will offer qualifications and set up rules to ensure compliance with any statutory requirements related to auditors. In this way national governments will control who may act as an auditor to limited liability companies, or to any other body requiring a statutory audit.

In some countries, regulation is devolved to professional accountancy bodies by the statutory authorities. On the other hand, the regulatory body could be a direct extension of national government.

The regulatory body should have rules to ensure that those eligible for appointment as a company auditor are either:

- **Individuals** holding an **appropriate qualification** or
- **Firms controlled** by **qualified persons**

Regulatory bodies should also have procedures to maintain the competence of members. The regulatory body's rules should:

- Ensure that only **fit and proper** persons are appointed as company auditors
- Ensure that company audit work is conducted **properly** and with **professional integrity**
- Include rules as to the **technical standards** of company audit work (eg following International Standards on Auditing)
- Ensure that **eligible persons** maintain an appropriate level of **competence**
- Ensure that all firms eligible under its rules have arrangements to prevent:
  - Individuals not holding an **appropriate qualification**
  - Persons who are **not members** of the firm from being able to exert influence over an audit which would be likely to affect the independence or integrity of the audit

The regulatory body's rules should provide for adequate monitoring and enforcement of compliance with its rules and should include provisions relating to:

- **Admission** and **expulsion** of members
- **Investigation of complaints** against members
- **Compulsory professional indemnity insurance**

Up-to-date lists of approved auditors and their names and addresses should be maintained by the regulatory body. This register of auditors should be made available to the public.

Membership of a regulatory body is the main prerequisite for eligibility as an auditor. Some countries allow a 'firm' to be appointed as a company auditor. A firm may be either a body corporate (such as a company) or a partnership.

A person should be **ineligible** for appointment as a company auditor if he or she is:

- An **officer or employee** of the company
- A **partner or employee** of such a person
- A **partnership** in which such a person is a partner

There may be further rules about connections between the company or its officers and the auditor, depending on local statutory rules.

2.7 Supervisory and monitoring roles

Some kind of supervision and monitoring regime should be implemented by the regulatory body. This should inspect auditors on a regular basis.

The frequency of inspection will depend on the number of partners, number of offices and number of listed company audits (these factors may also be reflected in the size of annual registration fees payable by approved audit firms).

The following features should be apparent in each practice visited by the monitoring regulatory body.

(a)   A **properly structured audit approach**, suitable for the range of clients served and work undertaken by the practice.

(b)   **Carefully instituted quality control procedures**, revised and updated constantly, to which the practice as a whole is committed. This will include:

- Staff recruitment
- Staff training
- Continuing professional development
- Frequent quality control review

(c)   Commitment to **ethical guidelines**, with an emphasis on independence issues

(d)   An emphasis on **technical excellence**

(e)   Adherence to the **'fit and proper' criteria** by checking personnel records and references

(f)   Use of internal and, if necessary, external **peer reviews**, consultations etc

(g)   **Appropriate fee** charging per audit assignment

3 International Standards on Auditing

International Standards on Auditing are set by the **International Auditing and Assurance Standards Board**.

3.1 Rules governing audits

We discussed in unit 1 the various stakeholders in a company, and the various people who might read a company's accounts. Consider also that some of these readers will not just be reading a single company's accounts, but will also be looking at the accounts of a large number of companies, and making comparisons between them.

Readers want **assurance** when making comparisons that the **reliability** of the accounts **does not vary from company to company**. This assurance will be obtained not just from knowing that each set of accounts has been audited, but knowing that this has been done to **common standards**.

Hence there is a need for audits to be **regulated** so that auditors follow the same standards. As we see in this unit, auditors have to follow rules issued by a variety of bodies. Some obligations are imposed by governments in law, or statute. Some obligations are imposed by the professional bodies to which auditors are required to belong, such as the ACCA.

International Standards on Auditing (ISAs) are produced by the **International Auditing and Assurance Standards Board (IAASB)**, a technical standing committee of IFAC, which also issues standards relating to review, other assurance, quality control and related services. An explanation of the workings of the IAASB, the authority of ISAs and so on are laid out in the *Preface to the International Standards on Quality Control, Auditing, Review, Other Assurance and Related Services*, and we will look at this below.

IAASB Pronouncements	
International Standards on Auditing (ISAs)	To be applied in the audit of historical financial information
International Standards on Review Engagements (ISREs)	To be applied in the review of historical financial information
International Standards on Assurance Engagements (ISAEs)	To be applied in assurance engagements dealing with subject matters other than historical financial information
International Standards on Related Services (ISRSs)	To be applied to compilation engagements, engagements to apply agreed upon procedures and other related services engagements as specified by the IAASB

IAASB Pronouncements	
International Standards on Quality Control (ISQCs)	To be applied for all services falling under the IAASB's engagement standards (ISAs, ISREs, ISAEs, ISRSs)
International Auditing Practice Statements (IAPSs)	Provide interpretive guidance and practical assistance to professional accountants in implementing ISAs and to promote good practice

3.2 Preface

The preface restates the mission of IFAC as set out in its constitution: 'The development and enhancement of an accountancy profession with harmonised standards able to provide services of consistently high quality in the public interest'.

In working toward this mission, the Council of IFAC established the International Auditing Practices Committee, precursor to IAASB, to develop and issue, on behalf of the Council, standards and statements on auditing and related services. Such standards and statements improve the degree of uniformity of auditing practices and related services throughout the world.

Within each country, local regulations govern, to a greater or lesser degree, the practices followed in the auditing of financial or other information. Such regulations may be either of a statutory nature, or in the form of statements issued by the regulatory or professional bodies in the countries concerned. For example, in the UK, the Auditing Practices Board (APB) sets ISAs, and the Companies Act 2006 provides legislative regulations.

National standards on auditing and related services published in many countries differ in form and content. The IAASB takes account of such documents and differences and, in the light of such knowledge, issues ISAs which are intended for international acceptance.

3.2.1 The authority attached to ISAs

The preface also lays out the authority attached to ISAs in general:

Authority of International Standards on Auditing

International Standards on Auditing (ISAs) are to be applied in the audit of historical financial information.

The IAASB's Standards contain basic principles and essential procedures (identified in bold type black lettering) together with related guidance in the form of explanatory and other material, including appendices. The basic principles and essential procedures are to be understood and applied in the context of the explanatory and other material that provide guidance for their application. It is therefore necessary to consider the whole text of a standard to understand and apply the basic principles and essential procedures.

In exceptional circumstances, an auditor may judge it necessary to depart from an ISA in order to more effectively achieve the objective of an audit. When such a situation arises, the auditor should be prepared to justify the departure.

Any **limitation** of the applicability of a specific ISA is made very clear in the standard.

ISAs do **not** override the local regulations referred to above governing the audit of financial or other information in a particular country.

(a)   To the extent that ISAs **conform** with local regulations on a particular subject, the audit of financial or other information in that country in accordance with local regulations will automatically comply with the ISA regarding that subject.

(b)   In the event that the local regulations **differ from**, or conflict with, ISAs on a particular subject, member bodies should comply with the obligations of members set forth in the IFAC Constitution as regards these ISAs (ie **encourage changes** in local regulations to comply with ISAs).

3.2.2 Working procedures of the IAASB

A rigorous due process is followed by the IAASB to ensure that the views of all those affected by its guidance are taken into account. The following diagram summarises the process followed in the development of IAASB standards.

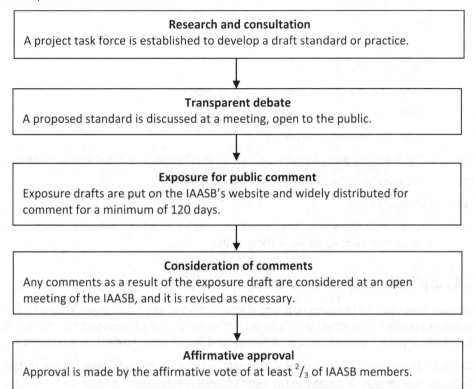

Research and consultation
A project task force is established to develop a draft standard or practice.

Transparent debate
A proposed standard is discussed at a meeting, open to the public.

Exposure for public comment
Exposure drafts are put on the IAASB's website and widely distributed for comment for a minimum of 120 days.

Consideration of comments
Any comments as a result of the exposure draft are considered at an open meeting of the IAASB, and it is revised as necessary.

Affirmative approval
Approval is made by the affirmative vote of at least $^2/_3$ of IAASB members.

3.3 Current ISAs

The following table sets out those ISAs.

No	Title
200	Objective and general principles governing an audit of financial statements
210	Terms of audit engagements
230	(Redrafted) Audit documentation
240	(Redrafted) The auditor's responsibilities relating to fraud in an audit of financial statements
250	(Redrafted) Consideration of laws and regulations in an audit of financial statements
260	(Revised and Redrafted) Communication with those charged with governance
300	(Redrafted) Planning an audit of financial statements
315	(Redrafted) Identifying and assessing the risks of material misstatement through understanding the entity and its environment
320	Audit materiality
330	The auditor's responses to assessed risks
402	Audit considerations relating to entities using service organisations
500	Audit evidence
501	Audit evidence – additional considerations for specific items
505	External confirmations
510	(Redrafted) Audit engagements – opening balances

No	Title
520	Analytical procedures
530	Audit sampling and other means of testing
540	(Revised and Redrafted) Auditing accounting estimates, including fair value estimates and related disclosures
560	(Redrafted) Subsequent events
570	(Redrafted) Going concern
580	(Revised and Redrafted) Written representations
610	Considering the work of internal auditing
620	Using the work of an expert
700	The independent auditor's report on a complete set of general purpose financial statements
701	Modifications to the independent auditor's report
710	Comparatives
720	(Redrafted) The auditor's responsibility in relation to other information in documents containing audited financial statements

3.4 Application of ISAs to smaller entities

Although ISAs apply to the audit of financial information of any entity regardless of its size, small businesses possess a combination of characteristics which make it necessary for the auditors to adapt their audit approach to the circumstances surrounding the small business engagement.

IAPS 1005 *The special considerations in the audit of small entities* was issued in March 1999 and discusses how various ISAs apply to the audit of small enterprises.

3.5 The IAASB Clarity project

This section highlights an important issue regarding ISAs issued by the IAASB, known as the **Clarity project**.

In 2004, the IAASB began a comprehensive programme to **enhance the clarity** of its ISAs by setting an **overall objective** for each ISA and improving the **overall readability and understandability** through structural and drafting improvements.

At the end of 2008, the IAASB had finalised all its clarified ISAs, and auditors all over the world now have access to 36 newly updated and clarified ISAs and a clarified ISQC.

The improvements arising from the Clarity project can be summarised below:

- Identifying the auditor's **overall objectives** when conducting an audit
- **Setting an objective** in each ISA and establishing the auditor's obligation in relation to that objective
- **Clarifying the obligations** imposed on auditors by the requirements of ISAs and the language used to communicate these requirements
- **Eliminating** any possible **ambiguity** about the auditor's requirements
- Improving the **overall readability and understandability** of the ISAs through structural and drafting improvements

Unit Roundup

- Many companies are required to have an audit by law, but some small companies are exempt. The outcome of the audit is the **audit report**, which sets out the auditor's **opinion** on the financial statements.

- The law gives auditors both rights and duties. This allows auditors to have sufficient power to carry out an independent and effective audit.

- Requirements for the **eligibility**, **registration** and **training** of auditors are extremely important as they are designed to maintain standards in the auditing profession.

- **International Standards on Auditing** are set by the **International Auditing and Assurance Standards Board**.

Quick Quiz

1 What makes a person ineligible for appointment as a company auditor?

2 A person does not have to satisfy membership criteria to become a member of an RSB.

   True ☐

   False ☐

3 The ACCA has its own monitoring unit which inspects registered auditors on a regular basis.

   True ☐

   False ☐

4 What is the function of IFAC?

1   An officer or employee of the company
    A partner or employee of such a person
    A partnership in which such a person is a partner

2   False. All RSBs have stringent membership requirements.

3   True

4   The function of IFAC is to initiate, co-ordinate and guide efforts to achieve international technical, ethical and educational pronouncements for the accountancy profession.

Now try the question below

Audit implications   18 mins

The purpose of an audit is for the auditor to express an opinion on the financial statements.

The audit opinion may also **imply** certain things are true. What are these additional factors which are implied by the audit report?   **(10 marks)**

Answer

Audit implications

In the UK, such implications include the following:

- Adequate accounting records have been kept.
- Returns adequate for the audit have been received from branches not visited.
- The accounts agree with the accounting records and returns.
- All information and explanations have been received that the auditor believes are necessary for the purposes of the audit.
- Details of directors' emoluments and other benefits have been correctly disclosed in the financial statements.
- Particulars of **loans** and **other transactions** in favour of **directors** and others have been correctly in the financial statements.

Specimen Paper

INSTITUTE OF FINANCIAL ACCOUNTANTS

NEW SYLLABUS 2010: SPECIMEN PAPER

P1. Financial Accounting and IFRS for SMEs

Instructions to candidates

1. Time allowed is 3 hours and 10 minutes, which includes 10 minutes reading time.

2. This is a closed book examination.

3. Use of a silent, non-programmable calculator, which is NOT part of a mobile phone or any other device capable of communication, is allowed.

4. A formulae sheet, present value and annuity tables are printed at the end of the questions.

5. Put your candidate number on the top of each answer page.

6. Start each new question on a new page.

7. Include any workings.

Answer the following questions:

Part A: all THREE questions

Part B: answer TWO questions

Part C: answer ONE question

Part A - Answer all questions

All calculations must be made to the nearest $'000

Question 1

(a) In each of the scenarios below, the reporting entity concerned is required to report under the IFRS for SMEs.

A publishing company has a new book department that sells its books to retailers on a 'sale or return basis. An invoice for the books was sent to a customer on 15 December 2010 when the books are despatched to the retailer. These books can be returned to the company within three months of receipt for a full refund. At 31 December 2010 it is impossible to estimate the number of books that will be returned.

Required

Describe the required accounting treatment of the transaction at the company's year-end on 31 December 2010. **(3 marks)**

(b) On 30 September 2010 a company sells plant for $240,000 of which $180,000 is for the equipment and the additional $60,000 is a service agreement for the next 2 years.

Required

Describe the accounting treatment for the above transaction at the company's year-end on 31 December 2010. **(3 marks)**

(c) A company has made an offer to its customers that if within a six-month period ending 31 March 2011 they purchase goods to the value of $50,000 or more, they will receive a retrospective discount of 2.5%. At 31 December 2010, the supplier's year-end, one customer had bought goods amounting to $40,000 between 1 October 2009 to 31 December 2010.

Required

Calculate the entries that should appear in the company's statement of comprehensive income for the year ended 31 December 2010. **(4 marks)**

(Total = 10 marks)

Question 2

Harrison Co's statement of financial position at 31 December 2009 included the following information in the note for property, plant and equipment:

	Cost	Accumulated depreciation
	$	$
Freehold property	6,000	2,500
Plant and machinery	3,500	1,650

The following events occurred during 2010:

(i) On 1 January the company revalued its existing freehold property to its current market value of $7 million. Additional freehold property was purchased during 2010 costing $500,000.

(ii) During 2010 the company scrapped plant and machinery, which originally cost $1,750,000 and had a carrying value at 31 December 2009 of $500,000. Additional plant and machinery costing $1,800,000 was purchased during the year.

(iii) Depreciation of freehold property is 2% per annum on the straight-line basis with no residual value Depreciation rate for plant and machinery was 10% per annum with no residual value. The company charges a full year's depreciation in year of purchases or valuation and none in the year of sale.

Required

Prepare a reconciliation of the carrying amount of property, plant and equipment for the year ended 31 December 2010 in accordance with Section 17 of the IFRS for SMEs. **(10 marks)**

Question 3

The following items have been brought to your attention prior to the preparation of the financial statements of Russell Co, an organisation manufacturing packaging equipment and member of a group of companies for the year to 31 March 2010.

(a)   A customer is claiming damages against the company for injuries sustained whilst on company premises. As the company failed to display a warning notice you are advised that it is likely to be found negligent and that it is probable that the company will have to pay damages in the region of $80,000 (an estimate based on professional opinion). **(3 marks)**

(b)   A customer is suing the company for damages of $50,000, claiming that a fault in a product sold by the company caused him personal injury resulting in him losing his job. Legal advice taken by the company indicates that, as company products are manufactured according to accepted standards and are thoroughly tested before being passed fit for sale, the claim is unlikely to be successful. **(3 marks)**

(c)   The company bought goods on 1 November 2009 costing $600,000 from a fellow group company. Payment for the goods was made on 23 February 2010.

If the transaction had been at arm's length the goods would have cost $700,000 and had the normal credit terms of 30 days. **(2 marks)**

(d)   Trade receivables of Russell Co includes a loan to a customer. It has been discovered the company is owned by the wife of Russell Co's Finance Director **(2 marks)**

Required

Describe how each of the above cases will be disclosed in the financial statements of Russell Co according to the IFRS for SMEs. **(Total = 10 marks)**

Section B – Answer all questions

Question 4

Having just produced Yorkshire's statement of financial position at 31 December 2010 and statement of comprehensive income for the year ended 31 December 2010 you now need to produce the statement of cash flows from the following information.

The statement of comprehensive income for the year ended 31 December 2010, and the statements of financial position at 31 December 2010 and 2009:

Statement of comprehensive income for the year ended 31 December 2010

	$,000
Revenue	720
Cost of sales	(140)
Gross profit	580
Administrative expenses	(160)
Operating profit	420
Finance costs (net)	(28)
Profit before tax	392
Income tax expense	(124)
Profit/Total comprehensive income for the year	268

Statements of financial positions

	2010	2009
	$'000	$'000
Non-current assets	1,278	1,336
Current assets	24	20
Inventories	76	58
Trade and other receivables	48	56
Bank	148	134
	1,426	1,470
Equity		
Share capital $1 shares	396	364
Retained earnings	686	490
	1,082	854
Non-current liabilities		
Debentures	200	500
Current liabilities		
Trade payables	12	6
Tax	102	86
Interest owing	30	24
	144	116
	1,426	1,470

The following information is also available with respect to the year in question:

(i)   Non-current assets with a net book value of $30,000 were disposed resulting in a loss of $18,000.

(ii)   The depreciation charge was $118,000.

(iii)   Dividends paid amounted to $72,000

Required

(a)   Prepare a statement of cash flows as per section 7 of the IFRS for SMEs using the indirect method for the year ended 31 December 2010.   **(14 marks)**

(b)   Describe four financial indicators that can be identified from the statement of cash flow you
       have produced.   **(4 marks)**

(c)   If your company wished to produce its cash flow statement using the direct method describe
       the information you would be required to produce.   **(2 marks)**

                                                                                  (Total 20 marks)

Question 5

The management of TransLondon is considering whether to acquire the next two lorries for cash at a
cost of $60,000 or by means of a finance lease with the following terms:

(i)   Eight lease payments of $11,000 paid annually in advance on the 1 January starting on 1 January
       2010

(ii)   the rate implicit in the lease is 12.6%

Required

(a)   Show the amounts to be included in the statement of financial position at 31 December 2010
       and statement of comprehensive income for the year ended 31 December 2010 for the finance
       lease.   **(12 marks)**

(b)   What are the accounting treatment, if

       (i)   the lorries are purchased for cash; or
       (ii)   the lorries purchased using a long-term loan

                                                                                        (5 marks)

(c)   Explain three of the reasons why Trans London might decide to use a lease rather than buying
       the lorries outright.   **(3 marks)**

                                                                                  (Total = 20 marks)

Section C

Question 6

On 1 October 2009 Head Co acquired 2 million ordinary shares in Subsidiary Co costing $7.5 million. The summarised financial statements for the company are as follows:

Statements of comprehensive income for the year ended 30 June 2010

	Head $'000	Subsidiary $'000
Revenue	24,000	18,000
Cost of sales	(14,500)	(12,000)
Gross profit	9,500	6,000
Administrative expenses	(4,250)	2,800
Profit before interest and tax	5,250	3,200
Finance costs	(360)	(600)
Profit before tax	4,890	2,600
Income tax expense	(1,450)	(800)
Profit for the period	3,440	1,800

Statements of financial position at 30 June 2010

	Head $'000	Subsidiary $'000
Non-current assets		
Property, plant and equipment	16,000	14,000
Investments	10,000	–
	26,000	14,000
Current assets		
Inventory	2,000	1,100
Receivables	1,500	600
Bank	500	400
	4,000	2,100
Total assets	30,000	16,100
Equity and liabilities		
Ordinary $1 shares	3,250	2,500
Retained earnings	18,000	5,000
	21,250	7,500
Non-current liabilities		
10% loan notes	–	6,000
9% loan notes	4,000	–
Current liabilities		
Payables	4,750	2,600
Total equity and liabilities	30,000	16,100

The following information is available:

(i)   The fair value of Subsidiary's assets at date of acquisition were equal to their book value except for its plant which had a fair value of $1,200,000 in excess of it book value. The plant has not been adjusted to its fair value. Subsidiary depreciates its plant at 20% per annum on a straight-line basis, which is to be charged to cost of sales.

(ii) The goodwill is to be amortised over 10 years.

(iii) Since the acquisition, Head sold goods originally costing $2.5 million to Subsidiary at a price of $4 million. Subsidiary still had one third of these goods in stock at 30 June 2010.

(iv) Revenue and profits are assumed to accrue evenly throughout the period.

(v)   No dividends were paid during the period.

(vi) The non-controlling interest is to be valued at its proportional share of the fair value of Subsidiary's net assets.

Required

Prepare a consolidated statement of comprehensive income for the year ended 30 June 2010 and a statement of financial position at that date. **(30 marks)**

Specimen Paper
Answers

SPECIMEN PAPER 2010 - SUGGESTED ANSWERS

P1. Financial Accounting and IFRS for SMEs

Note:

- This does not represent a complete worked set of answers but is provided to show what is sought within questions and how marks may be allocated.

- The format asked for in the question is not necessarily provided in the answers below, however, it is expected that candidates should provide answers in the format asked for to achieve the marks indicated.

Section A

Question 1

(a) Section 23 of the IFRS for SMEs revenue should only be recognised when it is probable that the **economic benefits associated with the transaction** will flow to the entity. At present there is **uncertainty** about the sales which can only be known when a sale is made or the three months period has passed so items will be treated as consignment stock. **This will result in revenue recognition being at a later date than the invoice date.**

1 mark for each of the above points underlined to maximum of 3 marks

(b) $60,000 to be spread over the period of 2 years from 30 September 2010

Revenue – sale	$180,000	**(1 mark)**
Maintenance – 3/24 × 60,000	$7,500	**(2 mark)**
Deferred income	$52,500	**(1 mark)**

(c) Company C will need to pro rata the sales as follows:

Sales = 40,000 × 6/3 = $80,000 which is more that the $50,000.	**(2 marks)**
Company C should therefore accrued the discount of $40,000 × 2.5% = $1,000	**(2 marks)**

Question 2

Harrison Co

Note reconciling opening and closing property, plant and equipment

	Freehold property $'000	Plant & machinery $'000	Total $'000	Marks
Cost/valuation				
At 1 January 2010	6,000	3,500	9,500	2
Revaluation	1,000		1,000	2
Additions	500	1,800	2,300	2
Disposals		(1,750)	(1750)	1
At 31 December 2010	7,500	3,550	11,050	1
Depreciation				
At 1 January 2010	2,500	1,650	4,150	2
Revaluation	(2,500)		(2,500)	2
Disposals (1,750 – 500)		(1,250)	(1,250)	1
Charge for year 7500 × 2%	150		505	
3,550 × 10%		355		2
	150	755	905	1
Net book value at 1 January 2010	3,500	1,850	5,350	2
Net book value at 31 December 2010	7,350	2,795	10,145	2

Total 20 marks/ 2 = 10 marks

Question 3

(a)   Failure to display a **warning notice would create an obligating event**, and since it is probable, in the **opinion of an expert, that there will be a transfer of economic benefits**, the company should **make a provision for $80,000**.

3 marks per underlined comments

(b)   The claim is based on a **past event**, but the **transfer of economic benefit (payment) will only arise if a court confirms the obligation**. In this case it is not probable that the court will confirm the obligation and therefore no provision should be made. If it is considered that **confirmation of any obligation is remote the company could just ignore the claim and not even disclose by way of a note**.

3 marks per underlined comments

(c)   As it is a **related part transaction as the companies are under common control and the transaction was not at arm's length** the purchases should be **increased from $600,000 to $700,000**.

2 marks per underlined point

(d)   Trade receivables of company include a loan to a **customer, which it has been discovered is a company owned by the wife of the Finance Director**.

This is a related party transaction as the wife of the Finance Director is a **close family member of a key management personnel of company**.

2 marks per underlined points

Section B

Question 4

Yorkshire
Statement of cash flows for the year ended 31 December 2010

	$'000	$000	Marks
Cash flows from operating activities			
Profit before tax	392		1
Adjustments for:			
Depreciation	118		1
Loss on sale of non-current asset	18		1
Finance costs	28		1
	556		
Increase in inventories (24 -20)	(4)		1
Increase in trade and other receivables (76 – 58)	(18)		1
Increase in trade payables	6		1
	540		
Finance costs (working 3)	(22)		3
Tax paid (working 2)	(108)		3
Net cash from operating activities		410	1
Cash flows from investing activities			
Purchase of non-current assets (working 1)	(90)		4
Proceeds from sale of non-current assets (30 – 18)	12		2
Net cash used in investing activities		(78)	1
Cash flow from financing activities			
Proceeds from issue of share capital (396-364)	32		1
Repayment of debentures	(300)		1
Dividends paid	(72)		1
Net cash from financing activities		(34)	1
Net decrease in cash and cash equivalents		(8)	
Cash and cash equivalents at beginning of the period		56	1
Cash and cash equivalents at end of the period		48	1
			28

26/2 = 14 marks

Working 1

Non-current assets

Balance b/d	1,336	Sold	30
Difference = Purchases	90	Depreciation	118
		Balance c/d	1,278
	1,426		1,426

Working 2

Taxation

Difference = tax paid	108	Balance b/d	86
Balance c/d	102	Charge for year	124
	210		210

Working 3

Finance costs

Difference = paid	22	Balance b/d	24
Balance c/d	30	Charge for year	28
	52		52

(b)   Four events identified by the above statement of cash flows

        1– Operating activities are generating a net cash inflow
        2 – There has been an overall net decrease in cash and cash equivalents during the year
        3 – Debentures amounting to $300,000 have been repaid during the year.
        4 – Non-current assets amounting to $90,0000 have been purchased during the year.

        Credit will be given for other appropriate points

                                                1 mark per point to maximum of 4

(c)   Direct method

        1 - Major classes of gross cash receipts
        2 - Major classes of gross cash payments

                                                1 mark per point

Question 5

(a)

Year ending	Amount at start of year	Lease payment	Sub-total	Finance charge at 12.6%	Amount owed at end of year	Marks
	$	$	$	$	$	
2010	60,000	(11,000)	49,000	6,174	55,174	3
2011	55,174	(11,000)	44,174	5,560	49,734	
						3

Non-current assets	$60,000	1
Plant under finance leases	$60,000	1
Depreciation (60,000/8)	$7,500	1
Current liabilities		
Current obligations under finance leases	$11,000	1
Non-current liabilities		
Non-current obligations under finance leases	$44,174	1
Income statement		
Depreciation on plant held under finance leases	$7,500	1
Finance charges on finance leases	$6,174	1

                                                (Total = 12 marks)

(b)   Non-current asset same in both cases as above.   **(1 mark)**

        (i)   Bought for cash: would have reduced bank balance and current assets   **(2 marks)**
        (ii)   Bought using a loan: liabilities would have increased   **(2 marks)**

(c)   •   Easier to obtain a lease rather than a loan
        •   Lease is often cheaper than a loan
        •   Can provide flexibility especially when technology is being replaced
        •   Makes cash flows more even rather than having a large initial payment

                                                1 mark per valid point

Section C

Question 6

Consolidated statement of comprehensive income for year ended 30 June 2010

	H	9/12 S	Adj	CIS	Marks
	$'000	$'000	$'000	$,000	
Revenue	24,000	13,500	(2,000)	35,500	1
Cost of sales	(14,500)	(9,000)	1,620	(21,880)	2
Gross profit	9,500	4,500	(380)	13,620	
Admin expenses	(4,250)	(2,100)	(162)	(6,512)	1
Operating profit	5,250	2,400	(542)	7,108	
Finance costs	(360)	(450)		(810)	1
Profit before tax	4,890	1,950	(542)	6,298	
Income tax expense	(1,450)	(600)		(2,050)	1
Profit for the period	3,440	1,350	(542)	4,248	
Profit attributable to:					
Owners of the parent				3,644	1
Non-controlling interest				604	1
					8

Consolidated statement of financial position at 30 June 2010

	H	S	Adj	CBS	Marks
Non-current assets					
Goodwill			1458	1458	1
Property, plant & equipment	16,000	14,000	1200	31020	2
			(180)		
Investments	10000		(7500)	2500	1
	26,000	14,000	(5,022)	34,978	
Current assets					
Inventories	2000	1100	(200)	2900	1
Receivables	1500	600		2,100	1
Bank	500	400		900	1
	4,000	2,100	(200)	5,900	
Total assets	30,000	16,100	(5,222)	40,878	
Ordinary shares	3250	2500	(2000)	3250	1
			(500)		
Retained earnings	18,000	5,000	(3,650)	18,574	1
			(270)		
			(162)		
			(144)		
			(200)		
NCI			1704	1,704	1
				23,528	
				6000	1
Non-current liabilities					
10% notes		6,000		4000	
9% Notes	4,000				1
Current liabilities	4,750	2,600		7,350	1
	30,000	16,100	(5,222)	40,878	13

Workings

				Marks
1.	*Group structure*			
	H owns 2/2.5 million shares in S = 80%			1
	Owned for 9 months of the year			
2.	Post acquisition reserves of S = 1800 × 9/12 = 1,350			1
	Pre acquisition reserves = 5,000 – 1,350 = 3,650			1

3. *Goodwill*

Consideration			7,500	
Fair value of net assets at date Of acquisition				1
Ordinary share capital	2,500			
Post acq reserves	3,650			
Fair value adj	1,200			
80% 0f net assets	7,350	5,880		4
Goodwill		1,620		
Impairment 1620 × 10% = 162				1
Balance sheet value = 1620 – 162 = 1458				1

4. *Non-controlling interest*   4

20% of net assets (7,500) =		1,500
FV adj (20% × 1,200 – 180 (working 5))		204
		1,704

5. *Fair value depreciation*   4
Plant increased by $1.2 million
Depreciation charge is1.2/5 = $240
Charge in consolidated account = 240 × 9/12 = 180

6. *Non-controlling interest*   4

Profit before interest and tax	3,200	
Depreciation re FV adjustment	(180)	
NCI = 20% ×	3,020	= 604

7. *Inventories – provision for unrealised profit*   4
Sales = $2 million – needs to be eliminated
COS = $1.4 million
Profit $0.6 million × 1/3 = $200
Reduce sales and cost of sales by $2 million
Inventory to be reduced by £200,000 and cost of sales increased

8. *Retained earnings*

			Marks
H	18,000		1
S post acq (1,350 × 80%)	1,080		2
Impairment	(162)		1
FV adj dep (180 × 80%)	(144)		2
PUP	(200)		1
	18,574		
			33

Mathematical tables

MATHEMATICAL TABLES

Present value table

Present value of $1 = (1+r)^{-n}$ where r = discount rate, n = number of periods until payment

This table shows the present value of $1 per annum, receivable or payable at the end of *n* years.

Periods					Discount rates (r)					
(n)	1%	2%	3%	4%	5%	6%	7%	8%	9%	10%
1	0.990	0.980	0.971	0.962	0.952	0.943	0.935	0.926	0.917	0.909
2	0.980	0.961	0.943	0.925	0.907	0.890	0.873	0.857	0.842	0.826
3	0.971	0.942	0.915	0.889	0.864	0.840	0.816	0.794	0.772	0.751
4	0.961	0.924	0.888	0.855	0.823	0.792	0.763	0.735	0.708	0.683
5	0.951	0.906	0.863	0.822	0.784	0.747	0.713	0.681	0.650	0.621
6	0.942	0.888	0.837	0.790	0.746	0.705	0.666	0.630	0.596	0.564
7	0.933	0.871	0.813	0.760	0.711	0.665	0.623	0.583	0.547	0.513
8	0.923	0.853	0.789	0.731	0.677	0.627	0.582	0.540	0.502	0.467
9	0.914	0.837	0.766	0.703	0.645	0.592	0.544	0.500	0.460	0.424
10	0.905	0.820	0.744	0.676	0.614	0.558	0.508	0.463	0.422	0.386
11	0.896	0.804	0.722	0.650	0.585	0.527	0.475	0.429	0.388	0.350
12	0.887	0.788	0.701	0.625	0.557	0.497	0.444	0.397	0.356	0.319
13	0.879	0.773	0.681	0.601	0.530	0.469	0.415	0.368	0.326	0.290
14	0.870	0.758	0.661	0.577	0.505	0.442	0.388	0.340	0.299	0.263
15	0.861	0.743	0.642	0.555	0.481	0.417	0.362	0.315	0.275	0.239

	11%	12%	13%	14%	15%	16%	17%	18%	19%	20%
1	0.901	0.893	0.885	0.877	0.870	0.862	0.855	0.847	0.840	0.833
2	0.812	0.797	0.783	0.769	0.756	0.743	0.731	0.718	0.706	0.694
3	0.731	0.712	0.693	0.675	0.658	0.641	0.624	0.609	0.593	0.579
4	0.659	0.636	0.613	0.592	0.572	0.552	0.534	0.516	0.499	0.482
5	0.593	0.567	0.543	0.519	0.497	0.476	0.456	0.437	0.419	0.402
6	0.535	0.507	0.480	0.456	0.432	0.410	0.390	0.370	0.352	0.335
7	0.482	0.452	0.425	0.400	0.376	0.354	0.333	0.314	0.296	0.279
8	0.434	0.404	0.376	0.351	0.327	0.305	0.285	0.266	0.249	0.233
9	0.391	0.361	0.333	0.308	0.284	0.263	0.243	0.225	0.209	0.194
10	0.352	0.322	0.295	0.270	0.247	0.227	0.208	0.191	0.176	0.162
11	0.317	0.287	0.261	0.237	0.215	0.195	0.178	0.162	0.148	0.135
12	0.286	0.257	0.231	0.208	0.187	0.168	0.152	0.137	0.124	0.112
13	0.258	0.229	0.204	0.182	0.163	0.145	0.130	0.116	0.104	0.093
14	0.232	0.205	0.181	0.160	0.141	0.125	0.111	0.099	0.088	0.078
15	0.209	0.183	0.160	0.140	0.123	0.108	0.095	0.084	0.074	0.065

Annuity table

Present value of an annuity of 1 ie $\dfrac{1-(1+r)^{-n}}{r}$ where r = discount rate, n = number of periods

Periods					Discount rates (r)					
(n)	1%	2%	3%	4%	5%	6%	7%	8%	9%	10%
1	0.990	0.980	0.971	0.962	0.952	0.943	0.935	0.926	0.917	0.909
2	1.970	1.942	1.913	1.886	1.859	1.833	1.808	1.783	1.759	1.736
3	2.941	2.884	2.829	2.775	2.723	2.673	2.624	2.577	2.531	2.487
4	3.902	3.808	3.717	3.630	3.546	3.465	3.387	3.312	3.240	3.170
5	4.853	4.713	4.580	4.452	4.329	4.212	4.100	3.993	3.890	3.791
6	5.795	5.601	5.417	5.242	5.076	4.917	4.767	4.623	4.486	4.355
7	6.728	6.472	6.230	6.002	5.786	5.582	5.389	5.206	5.033	4.868
8	7.652	7.325	7.020	6.733	6.463	6.210	5.971	5.747	5.535	5.335
9	8.566	8.162	7.786	7.435	7.108	6.802	6.515	6.247	5.995	5.759
10	9.471	8.983	8.530	8.111	7.722	7.360	7.024	6.710	6.418	6.145
11	10.37	9.787	9.253	8.760	8.306	7.887	7.499	7.139	6.805	6.495
12	11.26	10.58	9.954	9.385	8.863	8.384	7.943	7.536	7.161	6.814
13	12.13	11.35	10.63	9.986	9.394	8.853	8.358	7.904	7.487	7.103
14	13.00	12.11	11.30	10.56	9.899	9.295	8.745	8.244	7.786	7.367
15	13.87	12.85	11.94	11.12	10.38	9.712	9.108	8.559	8.061	7.606

	11%	12%	13%	14%	15%	16%	17%	18%	19%	20%
1	0.901	0.893	0.885	0.877	0.870	0.862	0.855	0.847	0.840	0.833
2	1.713	1.690	1.668	1.647	1.626	1.605	1.585	1.566	1.547	1.528
3	2.444	2.402	2.361	2.322	2.283	2.246	2.210	2.174	2.140	2.106
4	3.102	3.037	2.974	2.914	2.855	2.798	2.743	2.690	2.639	2.589
5	3.696	3.605	3.517	3.433	3.352	3.274	3.199	3.127	3.058	2.991
6	4.231	4.111	3.998	3.889	3.784	3.685	3.589	3.498	3.410	3.326
7	4.712	4.564	4.423	4.288	4.160	4.039	3.922	3.812	3.706	3.605
8	5.146	4.968	4.799	4.639	4.487	4.344	4.207	4.078	3.954	3.837
9	5.537	5.328	5.132	4.946	4.772	4.607	4.451	4.303	4.163	4.031
10	5.889	5.650	5.426	5.216	5.019	4.833	4.659	4.494	4.339	4.192
11	6.207	5.938	5.687	5.453	5.234	5.029	4.836	4.656	4.486	4.327
12	6.492	6.194	5.918	5.660	5.421	5.197	4.988	4.793	4.611	4.439
13	6.750	6.424	6.122	5.842	5.583	5.342	5.118	4.910	4.715	4.533
14	6.982	6.628	6.302	6.002	5.724	5.468	5.229	5.008	4.802	4.611
15	7.191	6.811	6.462	6.142	5.847	5.575	5.324	5.092	4.876	4.675

Index